MORE ADVANCE PRAISE FOR ASH CARTER'S
INSIDE THE FIVE-SIDED BOX

"Ash Carter undertakes to describe what it is like to run the largest enterprise in the world, the U.S. Department of Defense, and he tells his story in a clear and compelling manner. No one should consider taking on any job in the Pentagon, or trying to deal with big national security issues, without reading this book."

   —William J. Perry, Secretary of Defense (1994–1997) and author of
     My Journey at the Nuclear Brink

"As Secretary of Defense, Ash Carter was both an ideal public servant and also a model any manager can learn from. Read this book and you will see why the Department of Defense awarded him its highest civilian medal five times."

   —Reid Hoffman, cofounder of LinkedIn and coauthor of *Blitzscaling*

"For those who served with Ash Carter in the Pentagon, he is a trusted comrade and beloved icon. With his brilliant narrative of how the five-sided behemoth actually functions, the former Defense Secretary is now a deft guide and thoughtful interpreter of what may be the most complex bureaucracy in history."

   —Stan McChrystal, General (Retired), U.S. Army

"*Inside the Five-Sided Box* offers a fascinating insight into the inner workings of the Pentagon and yet another demonstration of the sharp strategic mind and outstanding sense of leadership Ash Carter displayed."

   —Jean-Yves Le Drian, French Minister for Europe and Foreign Affairs

"At a time when too few understand the critical role of the Department of Defense, Secretary Carter's book bridges this divide with intelligence, insight, and character. An engaging read that illuminates what the public needs to understand to support the military we deserve."

   —Jennifer Pahlka, founder and executive director of Code for America

INSIDE THE FIVE-SIDED BOX

Lessons from a Lifetime of
Leadership in the Pentagon

ASH CARTER

DUTTON

DUTTON

An imprint of Penguin Random House LLC
penguinrandomhouse.com

LIBRARY OF CONGRESS CATALOGING-IN-PUBLICATION DATA

Names: Carter, Ashton B., author.

Title: Inside the five-sided box: lessons from a lifetime of leadership in the Pentagon / Ash Carter.

Description: New York, New York: Dutton, [2019]

Identifiers: LCCN 2018060527 | ISBN 9781524743918 (hardcover) | ISBN 9781524743932 (ebook)

Subjects: LCSH: Carter, Ashton B. | United States. Department of Defense. | United States—Military policy—Decision making. | Pentagon (Va.) | United States. Department of Defense—History. | United States. Department of Defense—Procurement. | United States. Department of Defense—Officials and employees—Biography. | Cabinet officers—United States—Biography.

Classification: LCC UA23 .C2746 2019 | DDC 355.6092 [B]—dc23

LC record available at https://lccn.loc.gov/2018060527

Excerpts from *Preventive Defense: A New Security System for America* by Ashton B. Carter and William J. Perry (Brookings Institution Press, 1999). Used by permission of Brookings Institution Press.

Excerpt from "The Pentagon Must Think Outside of Its Five-Sided Box" by Ashton B. Carter, published in *The National Interest*, December 11, 2016. Used by permission of *The National Interest*.

Excerpt from "No Exceptions: The Decision to Open All Military Positions to Women" by Ash Carter, a report published by the Belfer Center for Science and International Affairs, December 2018. Excerpt from "Shaping Disruptive Technological Change for Public Good" by Ash Carter, a lecture given at the Aspen Strategy Group, August 2018. Excerpt from "Reflections on American Grand Strategy in Asia" by Ash Carter, a report published by the Belfer Center for Science and International Affairs, October 2018. Excerpt from "A Lasting Defeat: The Campaign to Destroy ISIS," by Ash Carter, a report published by the Belfer Center for Science and International Affairs, October 2017. Excerpts from Ash Carter's autobiography, published in *Harvard Kennedy School Magazine*, 2006. Used by permission of the Belfer Center for Science and International Affairs, Harvard Kennedy School.

These selections have been adapted for their appearance in this book.

To the troops,
and to the civilians and defense workers who support them,
who make it possible for Americans and others around the world
to live their lives, dream their dreams, and raise their children in safety

CONTENTS

PART FOUR

THE BIG PICTURE: DEFENSE STRATEGY IN A TIME OF TRANSITION

PART FIVE

PEOPLE MATTER MOST

WELCOME TO MY WORLD

A t eight a.m. on Wednesday, February 18, 2015, I sat down for the first time at the desk once used by General John "Black Jack" Pershing, the man who built the American army that won the First World War, in the office of the Secretary of Defense of the United States. On the desk sat a telephone with programmed lines connected to the office of President Barack Obama as well as to other leaders who are among the most powerful people on Earth, including the Secretary of State and the chairman of the Joint Chiefs of Staff. Located on the second floor of the eastern side of the outermost E ring of the fabled Pentagon building in Washington, D.C., the office commands a view of the Potomac River and the stately Jefferson Memorial on the opposite bank. Beyond that, though hidden from sight, are the National Mall, the U.S. Capitol, and the White House, where the men and women of the U.S. Congress and the presidential administration spend most of their days—many of them people with whom I'd be working closely in my new role as America's twenty-fifth Secretary of Defense.

From Jack Pershing's desk, I would be shaping and overseeing the efforts of some twenty-six thousand people within the vast Pentagon building itself—long the world's largest office building, housing military and civilian personnel engaged in projects and programs ranging from war planning to logistics, intelligence analysis to acquisitions management, and human resources to cybersecurity.

But the network of people and teams that the SecDef is responsible for extends far beyond the walls of that five-sided building. It includes people in and out of uniform engaged in an amazing array of missions in hundreds of unlikely places. They're stationed at over 800 bases in 80 countries and at hundreds of forward-operating bases and combat outposts (at the peak of the war in Afghanistan, there were more than 250 such outposts in that country alone).

At their core, they are warriors. But they also include physicists, chemists, and computer scientists sponsored by the Defense Advanced Research Projects Agency (DARPA), the legendary research arm that spawned the Internet and invented the first drones, working on scientific breakthroughs with military applications that the rest of the world may not hear about until decades from today.

They include Special Forces with iron warrior skills as well as profound knowledge of local customs who are training militaries from the mountain enclaves of Afghanistan to the villages of Africa to keep the peace, uphold the law, and provide humanitarian aid within their borders. They include data experts charged with launching, monitoring, and downloading data from scores of satellites that circle the planet, gathering information of incredible value to geophysicists, climatologists, oceanographers, and, of course, military targeters and planners. They include soldier-statesmen with decades of knowledge and experience in fields ranging from international diplomacy to military science, educating the next generation in classrooms at West Point, Annapolis, and a host of other educational institutions.

And that's not all. The list also includes thousands of doctors and nurses who operate one of the world's largest systems of hospitals and clinics, providing unmatched care to those who serve our nation, as well as hundreds of the world's shrewdest cyber-warriors, engaged day and night in keyboard defending against shadowy hackers from around the world—Russia, China, North Korea, and right here in the United States. It includes shipbuilders, aircraft designers, chipmakers, troop trainers, and other private-sector workers in a defense industry that employs as many people as the Department of Defense (DOD) itself does.

So vast is the DOD and so multifarious are its missions that it dwarfs most institutions on Earth. The DOD owns and maintains more than thirty million acres of real estate, an area larger than the state of

Pennsylvania. Older Army and Air Force bases are located in an American geography that mostly traces the grim lines of the Indian wars of the 1880s, while the Navy boasts plum waterfront properties on the Atlantic, Pacific, and Gulf coasts. In recent decades, the pattern of military real estate development has shifted south, following the seniority of powerful congressional supporters and benefiting from the advantages offered by warm climates for year-round training.

The DOD also employs more men and women than Amazon, McDonald's, FedEx, Target, and General Electric—combined. It conducts more research and development than Apple, Google, and Microsoft—again, combined. And it manages more than half the U.S. federal budget, excluding entitlements and interest on the national debt—a budget of more than $700 billion, a sum larger than the GDP of Sweden. Above all, it helps protect the peace and freedom of billions of people on every continent, leads the worldwide fight against terrorism, and provides support to countless humanitarian efforts around the world—all courtesy of the American people.

Although that Wednesday morning was the first time I'd spent the day sitting at Pershing's desk, it was far from the first time I'd been in the secretary's office. On my first day as SecDef, I probably understood more about the scope of the job I was assuming than most of my predecessors and as much as previous longtime hands George C. Marshall and my friend William J. Perry did. This was not because of any special brilliance on my part, but simply because I'd spent thirty years of my life getting preparation for this assignment, working in and around the Pentagon at almost every level of its vast bureaucracy—unlike most of my predecessors, who had lots of valuable experience, though not within the Pentagon itself. Over the decades, I'd come to learn a lot about the complex and enormously consequential work of the Defense Department—how it calls upon the talents of a remarkable array of men and women and impacts the lives of countless people around the world.

After serving in a series of DOD positions dating back to 1981 in the Reagan administration, I'd held the number three job in the Pentagon, sometimes described as "acquisition czar." Later I filled the number two job, as chief operating officer of the DOD. So when I was asked to be

SecDef, I was pretty well prepared on day one. I knew what I wanted to accomplish, and I felt as ready as one can be to handle whatever curve-balls history might throw me. That's a good thing, because the Defense Department I was asked to lead faced—and faces—a daunting array of varied, complicated challenges around the world.

From that day, my life as SecDef was a whirlwind. A typical month included a wild assortment of activities: travels around the globe to meet with military leaders, ministers of defense, and heads of state from countries on every continent, including longtime allies of the United States and potential adversaries; speeches before audiences of diplomats, historians, scholars, and journalists to explain the threats and challenges facing our country and the strategies and policies we're pursuing to address them; visits to factories, laboratories, workshops, and university campuses where the high-tech weapons systems of today are being constructed, and those of tomorrow are being imagined; top-secret meetings in the Oval Office and the White House Situation Room with the president and other members of the National Security Council to debate and approve plans for military operations in far-flung corners of the world; and, most important, visits with the troops in every imaginable setting and circumstance—sailors and jet pilots on aircraft carriers in the South China Sea, Army and Marine Corps units in historic stateside camps preparing for deployment overseas, soldiers and officers in dusty, dangerous camps in Iraq and Afghanistan, and wounded warriors laboring with loved ones and therapists to take the first, painful steps to recovery.

All these activities, and a lot more besides, are part of the routine work of a SecDef, and all are part of the big picture I hope to paint in this book.

You may wonder whether the whole story of the Pentagon can be told without revealing classified information. It's true that a SecDef handles a great mass of documents tagged with various levels of official secrecy. But in almost every case, they are classified not because they contain dramatic revelations about defense policy or history but because they mention details about the technical characteristics of weapons or war plans. These details would be uninteresting to anyone but an expert, working either at the Pentagon itself or for a potential enemy. A small handful of exotic weapons and sensitive operations are "fact of" classified, meaning that their very existence is secret, but in truth these are of marginal importance in the big picture of American defense. So I can explain almost everything you're likely to want to know about the DOD without revealing any top-secret information.

Mysteries about the department are another matter. To most outsiders, the Pentagon is a giant black box, important and fascinating but largely unknown. Even those who've served in the military or worked for the department don't know how it all works, because it is too vast and complicated. My unusual background makes me one of the few people equipped to describe and interpret it all, because I've seen it all—and that's what I have tried to do in this book.

How can any one person hope to encompass the complexities of a gigantic global enterprise like the DOD—let alone ensure that all its operations are serving to defend the American people and promote the common good with efficiency, integrity, and honor? How is the Pentagon striving to adapt to a rapidly evolving world, in which extraordinary changes in technology, demographics, politics, and strategic alignments are posing unexpected challenges to policy makers and military leaders? And what do American citizens need to understand about this huge and powerful organization that acts in their name, helping to shape the future not just of our nation but of life on Earth?

This book offers my answers to those questions.

PART 1

A USER'S GUIDE TO THE MILITARY-INDUSTRIAL COMPLEX

CHAPTER 1

HOW NOT TO WASTE $700 BILLION

The Secretary of Defense is in charge of the largest and most complex organization in the entire world. He is responsible for preventing and waging war, for leading the largest workforce in the country, and for directing the nation's largest research and development enterprise. DOD also spends more money than any other entity in the American economy, on average a staggering $700 billion every single year. This is seven times the size of New York City's budget, twenty-five times the size of Apple's operating expenses, and a larger budget than that of all but eight countries. The $700 billion defense budget is equal to that of all the other federal government agencies combined. (Together, DOD and the other federal agencies make up about 30 percent of the total federal budget; the rest goes to Social Security, Medicare, and Medicaid, the social safety net, and interest on the federal debt.)

What kind of spending needs can possibly justify a budget of this size? What is all this money spent for? Is it spent well or wasted? How much is enough? How should we decide between spending to protect the country today versus investing in defense preeminence in the future? An essential job of the Secretary of Defense is to ensure that these questions are answered and that all this money is spent wisely and efficiently.

Among secretaries of defense, I had an almost unique vantage point on these matters: I had seen the Pentagon not only from "up on the bridge," where policy is made, but also from "down in the engine room," where all the gears turn and the money is spent. Beginning in 1980, I held a series of DOD jobs, including the number three and number two jobs, before becoming SecDef in 2015. The number two is deputy secretary, the chief operating officer of the Pentagon, who puts the budget together and runs the department. The number three is the undersecretary for acquisition, technology, and logistics, or the "acquisition czar," as the press likes to say. The undersecretary oversees the buying of the ships, airplanes, tanks, and satellites, as well as a dizzying array of other goods and services. His office is responsible for purchasing jet fuel and heads of lettuce, building combat outposts in war zones, mowing the lawns on parade fields, and researching concepts for top-secret weapons.*

I understand why defense spending is a perennial and easy target for politicians, the news media, and interest groups from the political left, right, and center. For decades, the United States has spent far more on its military than any potential adversary. In recent years, its defense budget has exceeded that of the next seven largest military powers in the world combined. Taxpayers have a right to know why such enormous sums are necessary, particularly in a world where money for health care, education, research and development, civil infrastructure, social safety-net programs, and other vital purposes is often hard to come by. And the frequent requests for increased defense spending that citizens encounter during congressional hearings or budget debates only heighten the skepticism that many people feel.

What's more, whenever huge amounts of money are spent for any purpose, it's exceedingly difficult to ensure that every dollar is spent wisely. That's especially true when the activities being funded are as varied, complex, and specialized as those being managed by DOD. Throw in the intense political pressures surrounding every Pentagon spending program—starting with 535 members of Congress, each with an interest in promoting the maintenance of military bases and private contractors in his or her home district—and you have a scenario in which at least isolated instances of wasteful, excessive, and sometimes even corrupt spending are almost inevitable.

---

* In this sentence and in a few other places in this book, I use "he," "his," and other masculine pronouns to refer to hypothetical or unspecified DOD officials or troops. This is purely for simplicity and to avoid the awkwardness of "he or she" and similar constructions; no disrespect is intended to the many dedicated women who serve.

The result, over time, is a series of horror stories about profligate Pentagon spending that have lodged themselves in the national consciousness—$640 toilet seats, $435 hammers, and payoff scandals like the case of Randall "Duke" Cunningham. (A congressman from California and a member of the Defense Appropriations Subcommittee, Cunningham was accused of taking lavish gifts from contractors in exchange for help in landing lucrative Pentagon deals. In 2005, he pleaded guilty to numerous charges and spent seven years in federal prison.) Few citizens know the details behind these iconic cases, although they help sustain a vague yet almost universal impression that the Pentagon budget is hopelessly out of control and that a high percentage of the money spent is utterly wasted.

But how representative are these horror stories? And what can be done to prevent them from happening again?

Where Your $700 Billion Really Goes

It's important to put Pentagon spending in perspective, since numbers without context mean little. According to the Congressional Budget Office, the defense budget for 2016 represented about 3.1 percent of U.S. gross domestic product (GDP)—a sizable sum, no doubt. But it's actually a modest amount compared with many previous defense budgets.

During the Reagan defense buildup of the 1980s, defense spending exceeded 6 percent of GDP, about double today's figure. After the collapse of the Soviet Union, it fell dramatically. (You can win bets by challenging people to answer the trivia question "Which Secretary of Defense presided over the largest sustained drop in military spending?" The surprising answer: the well-known hawk Dick Cheney, who served as SecDef under the first President Bush. Dick just happened to be in office when the Berlin Wall fell and support for Cold War military spending plummeted.) Defense spending rose again in the wake of the 9/11 terror attacks. The most recent high point came in 2011, when the combined effects of the war in Afghanistan and a lingering recession boosted the share of GDP dedicated to defense spending to 4.5 percent.

Turn back the clock a bit further, and all these sums are dwarfed by historical spending on defense. At the height of the Cold War, the United States regularly spent close to 9 percent of GDP on defense. And the highest figure in history, unsurprisingly, came during the all-out effort of World War II, when the military gobbled up fully 41 percent of GDP.

These historical data offer some important lessons. First, it's false to assume—as many Americans do—that the military budget is an irrational juggernaut driven mainly by raw political factors, such as the power of Pentagon bureaucrats and greedy defense contractors. I sometimes hear cynics remark, "Everyone knows a government budget never shrinks—only grows!" The seesaw history of defense spending shows that this is a myth. Defense spending rises and falls in response to changing circumstances, as of course it should.

Second, while shifting political currents have an effect on military spending, it's a fallacy to assume that higher Pentagon budgets are driven by hawks (historically mostly Republicans), while cuts in those budgets are pushed by doves (mostly Democrats)—though, to be sure, those tendencies have generally characterized the two parties in recent decades. A complex array of factors beyond ideology is actually involved. I've already pointed out that the biggest drop in defense spending occurred under Republican leadership, during the era of the post-Soviet "peace dividend." Here's another counterintuitive fact you can use to win bar bets: Every federal budget proposed by the Obama administration but one called for *higher* levels of Pentagon spending than Republicans in Congress ultimately approved. Those Republican members were not so much defense doves as deficit hawks. Only later did the political charge emerge that the liberal Obama "decimated" our military by slashing budgets in the face of protests from conservatives. The real cause of military budget cuts was concern over the deficit, and the major cause of budget turbulence detrimental to DOD was bipartisan gridlock. Both of these gripped Washington after the economic downturn of 2008.

Perhaps the most important lesson to be drawn from this quick historical survey of defense budgets has to do with the unequaled spike in military spending during the 1940s. That spike was driven not by politics but by the appalling lack of preparedness the United States faced as a result of its demobilization and withdrawal from the world following World War I. In the 1920s and 1930s, Americans decided they didn't want to support a significant military establishment, and they got away with it—for a time. But the bill came due when the Axis powers launched their effort to rule the world, crushing most of our allies and soon threatening our own freedom. The United States was forced to respond by converting civilian industry to military production, rationing goods at home, and turning millions of citizens into newly minted troops. Years of warfare and millions of casualties were also part of the price we paid.

With the Axis defeated, most Americans vowed to never repeat the mistake we'd made between the world wars. Rather than demobilizing and withdrawing behind our borders, we accepted a new role as the world's leading peacekeepers. The decades since 1945 have not been without conflict. But it's no accident that, in all that time, no would-be world conqueror has dared to launch a global war in pursuit of his ambitions.

Bob Gates, a good friend of mine and one of my finest predecessors as Secretary of Defense, has occasionally garnered applause during speeches with the line "Our defense experts have *never* successfully predicted where our next war would be fought." In support of this point, Bob cites such unforeseen conflicts as the U.S. invasion of Grenada in 1983. His point is that much of our defense spending, while it helps to build a generally strong future force, can't be justified by any specific future scenario. It's a valid point, but one that can easily be misunderstood. It's true that, for decades, the United States invested hundreds of billions of dollars on weapons systems and troop deployments designed to forestall wars that never took place—such as a nuclear exchange with the USSR, a battle to liberate Western Europe from the communists, a defense of Taiwan against an invasion by mainland China, and a defense of South Korea against a North Korean assault. But does that reflect a failure of prediction and therefore a waste of resources? Just the opposite is true. The fact that we foresaw the possibility of such conflicts and invested in the resources to prevent them represents a success of historic proportions.

Wars that never happen don't get written about by historians or analyzed by pundits. But these nonevents mean the survival of freedom for huge swaths of humanity and millions of lives saved. Money spent to produce those results was scarcely wasted. In fact, that's exactly the reason we spent most of our defense dollars during the postwar years.

The American role in deterring potential enemies around the world means that the U.S. defense establishment has a completely different mission than the military of any other nation does. Because we need to be prepared to intervene rapidly in locations around the globe, we must maintain forces that are far larger, better equipped, and more widely dispersed than those of other countries with no such responsibilities. This helps to explain why, for example, we find it necessary to maintain eleven aircraft carrier strike groups while no other nation has more than one.

Yes, maintaining armed forces of this size and quality is expensive. Three to 4 percent of GDP is a big investment in our nation's security. But if we tried to cut that figure drastically, as some have suggested, we might find ourselves, in time, in a battle for survival against a major global adversary like China or Russia—a battle whose demands would make today's defense budget appear pitifully small.

It's also important to understand the specific items that make up our $700 billion defense budget.

First, let's note that some defense-related spending is *not* included in the DOD budget. The biggest such chunk is more than $100 billion spent on benefits and services for the nearly ten million veterans and family members who are eligible, which is reflected in the budget of the Department of Veterans Affairs. Other non-DOD budget items include atomic energy defense activities managed by the Department of Energy and the national security activities of such agencies as the Coast Guard and the Federal Bureau of Investigation.

A big slice of the DOD budget itself goes to paying America's all-volunteer military force. In fiscal year 2016, just under $140 billion was spent on direct personnel costs, with billions more spent on related costs such as family housing. These figures alone help to explain much of the discrepancy between the U.S. military budget and the budgets of other countries, whether allies or potential adversaries of ours. We pay the troops well, and in return we recruit many of the highest-caliber people in the nation. By contrast, most other countries rely on draftees whom they pay relatively poorly. As a result, their talent pool is far less deep than ours is—a huge advantage to the United States in times of conflict.

However, a large chunk of the Pentagon budget—more than half the total—is spent on buying goods and services from outside suppliers. The Defense Department itself does not build a single rifle, tank, or airplane. Instead, those and thousands of other necessities, from boots, blankets, and computers to the meals ready to eat (MREs) devoured by troops stationed around the world, are purchased through contracts parceled out to the vast network of corporations that make up the fabled "military-industrial complex." There are about ten million such separate contracts awarded every year. More than ten thousand "contracting officers," trained and authorized by law to spend the taxpayer's money, sign these contracts. The number of Americans employed by defense contractors exceeds the nearly three million uniformed military and civilian personnel of the Defense Department. This makes DOD the largest employer in the economy by far. Managing these contracts is therefore the key to spending the taxpayers' defense dollars wisely.

Unfortunately, when this much money is at stake, safeguarding every dollar is a Herculean task. As a result, financial scandals have bedeviled defense spending throughout our history, from profiteering during the Revolution and the Civil War to the provision of tainted meat in World War I rations and the infamous $640 toilet seat during the Reagan administration, when I had my first Pentagon job. Each scandal brings disrepute to the whole enterprise, and for good reason.

It's easy to decry "bureaucracy" and "red tape"—or to darkly condemn the Pentagon and the entire military-industrial complex as a vast "swamp" in need of draining. It's quite another to take on the tough, detail-oriented job of actually making the inevitable complexity of government spending *work*.

But is the problem of wasteful defense spending insoluble? Having been immersed in the details of Pentagon spending programs for decades, and having grappled with the challenge personally during my tenure as the Pentagon's acquisition czar, I will answer, "Absolutely not."

Fixing a Fiasco: The Joint Strike Fighter Saga

The story of the Joint Strike Fighter (JSF) illustrates both the scope and complexity of the challenges involved in managing a huge, complicated weapons program and some of the specific, concrete steps that can be taken to cut those challenges down to size.

When I became the acquisition czar in early 2009, JSF was to be the next fighter-bomber aircraft for all three services that flew them—the Air Force, the Navy, and the Marines—hence "Joint," although with some unavoidable variations. For example, the Navy needed the plane to have a stiff spine so that it could be catapulted off an aircraft carrier; the Marines needed a big fan in the fuselage to slow the jet's descent when landing on a small naval vessel; and the Air Force wanted a cannon to give fire support to troops on the ground. These variations didn't transform the JSF from a one-plane project into a three-plane project, but rather something in between—about two planes' worth of content, if you like.

It was also supposed to be a "fifth generation" aircraft with ultra-advanced technologies better than anything that had come before: stealthier; connected by a secure Internet to everything else in the air, in space, and on the ground to make each JSF super-smart and super-aware; and capable of delivering a variety of weapons that were also smart. All this advanced technology made sense: the days when speed or altitude or dogfighting ability was the key ingredient in the effectiveness of tactical aircraft were long behind us.

The services planned to buy 2,443 JSFs, making it the largest acquisition program in the Defense Department. In addition, foreign militaries, including our closest allies, planned to buy well over 1,000 of the aircraft themselves. JSF would, quite simply, corner the worldwide tactical fighter market. So a lot was at stake in this program.

But when I became undersecretary, JSF was in deep trouble. It was costing twice as much to design and develop as planned, projected manufacturing costs had also doubled, and the schedule was slipping every year. To the press, to Congress, to my bosses at that time, to the president—and to me—this was ridiculous.

One issue I recognized immediately was the program management. JSF was run by a single joint Air Force–Navy–Marine program office, with Lockheed Martin the prime contractor. (Other companies had subsidiary roles; for example, Northrop Grumman and BAE Systems were making parts of the airframes, and Pratt & Whitney were building the engines.) But when I started asking for data from the program office, the briefing charts I got back all had Lockheed Martin's logo on them. How much government supervision was this thing really getting?

I called the program manager, a Marine Corps major general, to my office. He gave a pretty upbeat summary of the program, which puzzled me, since it was way over cost and behind schedule. I asked to see the contract. It specified that the Defense Department would pay the costs incurred by the contractors in doing the development work, then tack on an "award fee" of up to 15 percent, which would provide the contractors' profit. I was startled when the general informed me that he had awarded about 85 percent of the maximum allowable award fee every single quarter since he had become the program manager. When I asked why, he explained, "I like working with the Lockheed Martin executive, and he told me that if he doesn't get at least eighty-five percent of the award fee, he'll be fired."

I was stunned. Both the contractor and the program manager had an incentive to pay a handsome profit even if the program was a mess—which it was. I decided on the spot to fire the program manager.

Digging deeper into the history of the JSF, I discovered that my predecessors, going way back to the 1990s, had decided that it was important to protect this *joint* project from interference by the entrenched air establishments of the services: the Air Force at Wright-Patterson Air Force Base, in Ohio, and the Navy-Marine Naval Air Systems Command ("Navair") at Patuxent River Naval Air Station, in Maryland. This had a certain logic: history shows that interservice rivalries can complicate, slow, and sometimes derail acquisition programs. But over time, treating the JSF project as a "hothouse flower" insulated from outside critiques meant our best tactical airplane experts had no opportunity to weigh in on its problems. This lack of input had damaged the program rather than protecting it.

I therefore decided to name a new program manager from Navair—a superstar, if possible. I got one. Vice Admiral Dave Venlet had just stepped down as commander of Navair and was planning a Florida retirement with his wife, Bunny. But I asked him to change his plans, knowing that his enormous stature among airplane builders and on Capitol Hill would make a huge difference to the JSF program. After conferring with Bunny, he agreed to pull his retirement papers.

With new management in place, I turned to the cost and schedule issues. We arranged a Sunday-morning meeting that brought together several key executives from Lockheed Martin, including Robert Stevens, the company's CEO, along with the Pentagon officials most involved in the project. Each side was asked to present its analysis of the current state of the JSF program and a plan for the future. The Lockheed Martin presentation not only failed to alleviate my concerns; it heightened them and made me really angry on behalf of American taxpayers. I got the strong sense that the company officials were basically unconcerned about the delays and cost overruns, feeling that their profits were assured no matter what happened.

At one point in the meeting, after we'd made it abundantly clear that the grossly inflated price for the JSF jets was unacceptable, CEO Bob Stevens casually said to me, "Well, if you tell me how much money you have, I'll tell you how many planes you can buy."

I was taken aback. Rather than negotiating a fair price with us, Stevens was behaving as if his company were entitled to all the money the taxpayers could afford. And although he obviously had a per-plane price in mind, he didn't care to divulge it openly, nor would he agree to a fixed-price contract holding him to it. I found this cavalier attitude offensive. With deeper disrepute, the JSF program would go down the political drain, and we wouldn't be able to buy any of these needed aircraft.

With all this in mind, I let his question hang in the air unanswered for a moment. Then I replied, "How about none?" With that, I walked out of the room. "None" was a reasonable prediction in the political climate surrounding this out-of-control program.

I gave the Lockheed Martin people a little time to think about what had just happened. When our conversation resumed, they realized that we were serious about cleaning up the problems rather than merely papering over them. Parceling out responsibility for the huge existing mess was an unavoidable part of the discussion. We decided that we couldn't ascribe all the program's problems to the contractor, since some of the deficiencies clearly were on the side of the government. Nonetheless, we levied a hefty chunk of the cost overrun—$614 million—against Lockheed Martin's award fee, which was eminently fair.

We then made a series of important changes to ensure that the program's future would not resemble its past. These included taking the complex Marine Corps version of the plane off the critical path for completion, so its unique design challenges wouldn't hold up the simpler Air Force and Navy versions. We also reduced what's called *concurrency*—a common practice in which production begins while development is incomplete. This inevitably resulted in some early aircraft having to be rebuilt to correct design flaws discovered in later testing. To control costs, we slowed the ramp-up of initial production, disappointing the contractors who would be doing the work.

The most critical issue went to the heart of the planned production contracts, which would have obligated DOD to pay the full costs, not a fixed price. I therefore determined to change the contract type to a fixed price based on our best estimate of the cost. To be fair, we agreed to share the remaining cost uncertainty. If the program cost more than estimated, we would split the overrun up to a limit of 20 percent; after that, all the overrun would fall on the contractors. If the program cost less than we estimated, the contractor would get to keep half the savings. This contract type had the right profit incentive built in. A crack DOD team, led by Dave Venlet and Shay Assad, the acting deputy undersecretary for acquisition and technology, managed the negotiations and made sure these principles were built into the final agreement.

Properly incentivizing productivity in the defense industry is the most important tool in defense management. Decades of experience show that harnessing the power of American private industry for defense is better than trying to build up-to-date technological systems within the government. The Soviet Union tried that, and it didn't work out very well. So our defense contractors need to run as private businesses—which means that the Pentagon must make it attractive for such businesses to bid on government work.

That's not as easy as it sounds. Many companies simply won't bid on government projects, in part because of the ever-increasing complexity of government procurement rules. In other cases, companies don't believe that defense projects have sufficient profit potential to make them worthwhile. Defense work needs to be reasonably profitable, or Wall Street won't support the stock of defense-oriented businesses, which are mostly public companies listed on the New York Stock Exchange.

Still another problem for defense industry firms is the competition for the brightest young technology experts, who find start-up companies in fields like artificial intelligence, biotech, and social media more attractive. The result has been a progressive aging of the science and engineering workforce of the defense industry. Many companies have engineer workforces whose average age is approaching fifty. This has seriously weakened the defense industry's research and development capabilities.

For all these reasons, in recent years the number of companies serving the defense market has been dwindling. Under the circumstances, it's imperative for acquisition executives and the senior defense leadership to make sure that defense work is attractive enough that good companies are willing to do it, but not so lucrative that it becomes an embarrassment to and drain on the taxpayer. Profit must be used as an incentive to obtain what the warfighter and taxpayer need—superior systems at a price the nation can afford.

This means tying profit to performance. In low-rate initial production, a fixed price with sharing of overruns and underruns, as with JSF, accomplishes this. When developing systems with highly predictable costs—for example, an aerial refueling tanker derived from commercial airliners, as discussed below—it is also reasonable for DOD to demand a fixed price in the contract. But in the development phase of new and technologically complex systems like JSF, no one really knows what a successful design will cost. So to be fair and to get contractors to bid, DOD needs to agree to reimburse costs as they are incurred and add profit to that. This reasonable, indeed ineluctable, logic should dictate DOD's contracting approach in such cases.

All the changes I instituted triggered the full lobbying energies of Lockheed Martin, and I began to receive unusually detailed letters from Capitol Hill questioning my judgment—mostly from members of Congress with JSF jobs in their districts. I stuck to my guns, strongly backed by President Obama, DOD Secretary Gates, and the influential Senator John McCain (R-AZ). Their support made it easier for me to insist on the adjustments that ultimately turned the JSF program around.

Today, the Joint Strike Fighter—now known as the F-35—is being built and fielded by the U.S. military and bought by the militaries of our most important international allies and partners. Within a few years, production costs for the F-35 first leveled off and then began to decline. These improvements are expected to continue as production rates increase and the assembly line and supply chain are wrung out. Frank Kendall, my successor as undersecretary, has led an effort to reduce ownership costs of the aircraft, which, in the decades to come, will actually end up representing the bulk of the expense associated with the F-35.

I'm still not satisfied. I would like to see prices continue to decline, ongoing maintenance costs to be sharply controlled, and international orders to increase. But the crisis is behind us.

It's worth noting that the F-35 will almost surely be the *last* generation of tactical fighters ever developed, as changes in the nature of battlefield technology are expected to make such aircraft increasingly vulnerable in the decades to come. Whatever replaces the tactical fighter in warfare is likely to be even more advanced and complex, representing an equally daunting acquisition and management challenge.

Striking a Fair Deal: How to Get the Contracting Process Right

If JSF was the poster child for out-of-control defense program management when I became acquisition czar, the Air Force's aerial refueling tanker replacement program was the poster child for botched contract competitions.

The tankers were basically commercial-design planes in which the seats were removed and replaced with bladders filled with jet fuel. When another military aircraft needed fuel, it would pull up behind the tanker in flight, and the tanker would either stick out a proboscislike probe from its tail or a drogue dangling from its wing and pump fuel into the nose of the receiving plane while both tanker and receiver flew together in a supertight formation. (Film footage of this delicate and awesome feat, which I had seen performed many times over the years from both tankers and receivers, serves as the opening sequence of Stanley Kubrick's mordant Cold War comedy *Dr. Strangelove*.) Tankers extend the range of any military plane and thereby enhance the global reach of American military power.

The contract to build a new fleet of tankers to replace our old models, dating back to the 1950s, would be the largest contract in the history of defense. It involved a single order of 179 airplanes worth more than $30 billion, with the winner having the best shot at building an additional 350.

Unfortunately, by the time I became acquisition czar in 2009, three efforts to issue a contract for the tanker had been made, each ending in a fiasco. Eight years of effort had yielded nothing but reams of paperwork and countless hours expended in costly arguments among Pentagon officials, contractors, and lawyers. On one occasion, a Pentagon official had negotiated a sweetheart sole-source deal with Boeing while simultaneously pursuing employment with the company. In the ensuing scandal, unearthed by Senator McCain, both the acquisition official and the Boeing CFO received prison sentences. Thanks to episodes like this, the tanker program had become a byword in the press and Congress for politicization and corruption in contracting.

I was determined to break this pattern once and for all. The project was important in itself. But just as important was reclaiming the good reputation of the government acquisition process.

Defense contracts are supposed to be awarded in "free, fair, and open competition." This principle offers two clear benefits. First, it means that the government will get the benefits of competition when it buys things from private companies, ensuring that the taxpayers get the best value for their dollars. Second, it is supposed to insulate the contract award from politics: competition is open to any qualified bidder, no matter what state or congressional district they are from.

Of course, the principle of free competition hadn't sufficed to eliminate the specter of politicization and unfairness. Protesting contract awards had become increasingly common among Washington lawyers, who saw it as a potentially lucrative business. To be clear, only about 2.5 percent of Pentagon contract awards are protested, and only about 2 percent of the protests are actually upheld by courts. But the existence of such protests serves to pressure the acquisition workforce and gives members of Congress whose districts have lost desirable contracts an ax to grind. As undersecretary, I wanted to make our contracting process so letter-perfect that no protest would even be plausible.

We knew that Boeing and Airbus, the world's two biggest aircraft makers, would compete for the tanker contract. DOD regarded both Boeing and Airbus as suitable to make U.S. Air Force tankers. Though Boeing is headquartered in the United States and Airbus in Europe, both have global supply chains. Airbus, in particular, promised to do final assembly of the tankers in Alabama, then home to two powerful senators: Richard Shelby and Jeff Sessions, both members of important committees with responsibility for oversight of defense matters.

We knew the competition between the two giant companies would be intense. To ensure its fairness and efficiency, we had to do two things right: we had to spell out the terms of the competition as precisely and clearly as possible, and we had to shelter the process from political interference. In summer 2009, I buckled down to work on both tasks.

One of the huge problems with the previous attempts to award the contract was that too much room had been left for subjectivity in the design and pricing process—room for favoritism and politics to fill in. So I spent several months working on the tanker request for proposal (RFP). I spent hours and hours with the program office team at Wright-Patterson Air Force Base, near Dayton, where all the major Air Force airplane-acquisition programs are housed.

The team we had working on the tanker program included some of the best professionals in the department. The program manager within the Air Force was Major General Chris Bogdan, one of the service's best technologists, whom I would later put in charge of F-35 because of the successful job he did on the tanker. I got priceless help from Deputy

Secretary of Defense Bill Lynn and Air Force Secretary Mike Donley, both longtime Pentagon insiders and former staffers on Capitol Hill. We had long sessions in which they would troubleshoot drafts of the RFP, looking for logical or political weak points.

General Raymond E. Johns Jr. was head of the Air Force's air transportation command and was therefore the closest thing to a single "customer" for the tanker. I put Ray in charge of deciding which tanker features should be listed as must-haves, which as extras.

In long, very technical meetings, we boiled down what DOD would need in the coming decades to 372 basic features and spelled them all out. This was laborious and made my head hurt. But because this would be the biggest contract award in history, each detail was in fact worth a lot. Competing vendors would have to offer airplanes that had all 372 features. We knew that both the Boeing 767 and the Airbus A330, on which the competitors were basing their entries, could be adapted to have all of them. Bids that met the 372 basic specifications would be compared on price. This would be the most important determinant of who won.

By November 2009, the RFP was ready—and I considered it bulletproof. It was impossible to argue that the RFP favored either Boeing or Airbus. It was "right down the middle," as I put it. Through our painstaking work, the subjectivity was wrung from the tanker competition, and with it the room for corruption and politics.

An unprecedented briefing was arranged for members of both the Senate and the House, many of whom had a rooting interest based on which companies had operations located in their districts. With help from Lynn and Donley, I reviewed charts showing the content of the RFP—in effect, the algorithm for picking the winner of the biggest defense competition in history. We explained how and why adjustments to the math used in judging the price quotes were needed to account for the strengths of each bidder. For example, Airbus's 330 was bigger and carried more fuel—an advantage, since it could refuel more aircraft in one sortie. But Boeing's smaller 767 was more fuel-efficient and so would cost less to fly—an advantage to Boeing. Bid prices would be precisely adjusted to reflect these differences.

By the end of the briefing, no one in Congress could dispute the fairness of our process.

I drew three main lessons from this experience. The first is the importance of doing the painstaking work of deciding what the Pentagon needs and what it should pay in advance. The second is the importance of having DOD experts who know the product inside and out and can craft an incontestable RFP. The third is the value of transparency. Having reviewed the algorithm built into the RFP with both vendors, members of Congress, and even the press, there would be no mystery or room for debate surrounding the tanker contract program. The winner and loser would be clear—fair and square.

Now phase two of the process began. I turned the judging over to a professional source-selection board. We chose a dream team of our best acquisition professionals from around the DOD. Then I locked the board away at Wright-Patterson Air Force Base, keeping its membership a closely guarded secret. Otherwise the press and even interested parties might try to pressure them. I have kept that promise of confidentiality to this day.

But the drama wasn't over. Circuslike publicity surrounded the tanker competition. Commuters riding the Washington subway saw ads from Boeing and Airbus touting their versions of the tanker. Full-page ads were run in newspapers, and commuters around the country heard radio ads during rush hour. While all this was going on, I learned one morning of a mistake that could have cost the whole ballgame.

The preliminary bids came into Wright-Patt. There they would get a first look from the dream team to see if the bids were fully compliant with the RFP. If not, the vendors would have a chance to correct them. Providing such feedback to the vendors and asking for a revised proposal was standard practice.

But what happened next was far from standard. The mail clerk stuffing the envelopes giving feedback put Airbus's bid information into the envelope meant for Boeing and vice versa. Divulgence of bid information would be ample grounds for the General Accounting Office or a court to scuttle the entire competition.

We went into overdrive to correct the error before it could do any damage. Because the swapped envelopes had already been delivered to their destinations, it was too late to recall them. We informed both bidders and asked them to lock down both mailings and the personnel who had handled them. Both complied promptly, since neither wanted the whole apple cart upset, either. We also sent the DOD's best cyber-experts from the National Security Agency (NSA) to check computer logs to see who had viewed the disks containing the bid information. They confirmed that only clerical staff had viewed the documents. Those staff members gave sworn affidavits that their higher-ups had not seen the data, and then they were temporarily removed from the tanker project.

The competition hadn't been compromised. We had dodged one bullet.

Then came the Ukrainians. At the last minute, an attorney representing the Antonov Company indicated that it would like to be a third bidder. Antonov had built the largest airlifters for the Soviet military during the Cold War. This development posed an absurd but real problem. Given the history of the tanker project, we had to be squeaky clean in all respects; free and open competition had to mean free and open. So we had to let the Ukrainians bid. This meant delaying the whole process for a few weeks until we could get them briefed on the RFP and they could submit a bid. Making the whole thing even odder was the fact that the communications with Antonov were transacted through a couple of lawyers the Ukrainians had hired.

At last, the day to submit the final bids arrived. They were all supposed to be delivered to a particular office building at Wright-Patt by noon. One inflexible rule that courts have upheld is that late bids are disqualified—period.

The Boeing and Airbus bids arrived before noon. But there was no sign of the Antonov bid.

A few minutes before noon, a taxi driver from Dayton arrived at the gate to the base. Security was so tight that the driver was not allowed to enter, despite the fact that he had a note saying he was bringing a bid on the tanker project and giving the building number to which he had been instructed to deliver it. This poor taxi driver had only been in the United States a few months and couldn't fathom the importance of his mission—which raises the question why the Ukrainians entrusted their bid to such an uncertain delivery channel. Eventually the guards at the gate contacted the program office, and clearance was given for the delivery. The driver found the building and delivered the Antonov bid—which consisted of a single paper copy contained in a Whitman's Sampler chocolates box!

By this time, it was after noon. Thanks to the strict rule about timeliness, the sketchy bid could be disqualified without tainting the whole competition. (Antonov later protested its disqualification, but the protest was rejected.) Another bullet had been dodged.

As the day approached to name the winner, the media frenzy surrounding the announcement intensified. In response, we tightened the secrecy around the source selection board further. The day before we announced the award, not even Secretary Gates knew who had won. (He had asked me not to tell him so that he could honestly tell inquiring members of Congress and White House staff that he didn't know.) Shortly before five p.m. eastern standard time, after the stock market had closed, we made the big announcement.

The winner was Boeing—and as it turned out, it wasn't close. I therefore had no doubt that any legal protest that Airbus might have wanted to file would have been meritless. Still, the company executives would have been within their rights to take that step. I believe it is to the lasting credit of Airbus and its two leaders on the tanker project—Sean O'Keefe and Ralph Crosby—that they did not contest the award. On the Tuesday following the announcement, Sean called me to say that Airbus would abide by the award. It was a moment of quiet triumph for the Pentagon acquisition process and for our valuable, long-term relationship with the defense industry.

The tanker project was finally under way.

Years later, as Secretary of Defense, I toured the cabin of the fourth KC-46 aerial refueling tanker to be built. It had a grand total of fifty-five miles on it, having been flown down from the assembly facility in Everett, Washington, to Boeing Field near Seattle-Tacoma Airport. But there were numerous problems with the early jets, and they were not fully certified till later, and at a cost higher than Boeing had estimated. However, under the fixed-price contract we had insisted upon, that was Boeing's problem, not DOD's or the taxpayers'. And given the size of the contract, the project is still very good business for Boeing.

Eventually, more KC-46s will be produced, and the Air Force is preparing to use them to replace the existing fleet of 415 older tankers, guaranteeing the global reach of our fighting forces for decades to come. For me, each plane is a monument to the power of fair, efficient contracting to buy security for the American people without wasting taxpayer dollars.

Real Reform Versus the Fad du Jour

As the JSF and tanker stories illustrate, the problems of contract management are complicated, but they're not insurmountable. Unfortunately, pressures from well-intentioned but sometimes misguided defense experts, consultants, and members of Congress often drive the Pentagon's processes in the wrong direction. As a result, most of the periodic paroxysms of "acquisition reform" that sweep through government have been amateurish and counterproductive. I know, because I've had a front-row seat for several of them.

The very first acquisition effort I worked on was an exception to the rule. I helped implement the recommendations of the Packard Commission, which were generally thoughtful and effective. Dave Packard, famous for founding Hewlett-Packard Corporation in his garage, was a predecessor of mine as deputy secretary of defense, and someone whom I met on several occasions during my thirties. He was called in after the $640 toilet seat scandal to chair a commission charged with improving the administration of DOD, including acquisitions. The 1986 report issued by the Packard Commission made some sensible and fundamental recommendations that are now in the acquisition law, including the existence of the job I went on to hold—acquisition czar.

Unfortunately, other efforts to reform the acquisition process have not been so useful. When Dick Cheney became secretary in 1989, he unwillingly inherited the results of a fad for making acquisition contracts fixed price no matter what their nature, a preposterous mandate given the speculative nature of some futuristic projects. One celebrated case involved the A-12 Navy stealth bomber. No accurate price could possibly have been put on this project in advance. Sure enough, the contract could not be executed as signed. It had to be canceled entirely, causing the whole project to be terminated. Decades of lawsuits ensued.

Later, an opposite fad became popular. Cost-reimbursable contracts became the norm, as in the original JSF contract and the early, failed attempts to award a tanker contract. Even on projects where a reasonably accurate price easily could have been determined and adhered to, the government instead agreed to pay whatever costs were incurred by the contractor. Because companies had no incentive to control costs, cost overruns went wild.

Still another fad in the decade preceding me was the practice of taking basic management of programs away from DOD program managers, technologists, and flight test centers and handing it over to contractors, under the rubrics of "total system program responsibility" or the "lead systems integrator" role. The idea was that the government supposedly could not hire senior managers to run these programs as skillfully as the contractors could.

This theory had a grain of truth in it. Executives for private contractors are generally higher-paid than their government counterparts, which makes it easier for those companies to attract top-flight executives. And beginning in the 1990s, the armed services had stopped training and promoting officers for their acquisition skills to the degree they'd done during the Cold War, when buying weaponry to deter the Soviet Union was a central preoccupation of the military. But the fact is that DOD workers have tremendous dedication to their mission, and many have decades of valuable experience that some private contractors lack.

Most important, putting the contractor and not the warfighter or the government official in the driver's seat leads to an inevitable conflict of incentives—with predictable results. The Army's Future Combat Systems project to build new armored vehicles, new radios, a secure mobile Internet, and other important and interdependent systems was awarded to Boeing in 2003 on this let-the-contractor-do-it basis. Years and billions of dollars later, it had virtually nothing to show for the time and money spent—no vehicles, no secure Internet, not even the right kind of radios (for the war in Iraq, we bought them from RadioShack). In my first summer as acquisition czar, I canceled Future Combat Systems on behalf of an angry Bob Gates.

The reason fads tend to capture the fancy of would-be reformers is that they promise a shortcut to reducing costs, improving efficiency, eliminating corruption, and guaranteeing fairness—all by simply writing some new mandate or procedure into the rule book. In reality, however, there are no shortcuts. The key to acquisition improvement can be found where it has always been: in rigorous attention to fundamentals and the sound judgment of DOD experts with intelligence and integrity.

Bang for the Taxpayers' Buck: The Better Buying Power Program

When I took over the acquisition job, I resolved to avoid fads and emphasize a return to fundamentals to obtain greater efficiency and productivity in defense spending. I called this initiative Better Buying Power (BBP), a phrase that seemed to me to sum up our goal. I created BBP in my first year as acquisition czar, and it continued—and continued to develop—under my able successor, Frank Kendall. I tried to avoid buzz phrases like "acquisition reform" and "changing culture" that suggested pendulum swings, and focused instead on acquisition fundamentals. The acquisition guidance I gave to the department under BBP described the logic of the fundamentals and reinforced the importance of using them, training our workforce in them, and then backing up the workforce when they made hard decisions based on fundamentals. After a summer-long department-wide effort to draft the new guidance, I issued it to the department's ten thousand acquisition officers in September 2010.

A key fundamental was to target affordability as a requirement for a successful program, alongside more familiar requirements like technological success and wartime prowess. Far too many programs begun in the decade before had simply not fit into even the much larger defense budget of 2010. In summer 2009, we were forced to cancel many of them.

Programs that got the ax included the Future Combat Systems project I mentioned earlier, the infamous presidential helicopter, a wildly expensive bomber, weather and communications satellites, a huge laser mounted in the fuselage of a 747, and a redundant engine for JSF (a politically inspired addition by Congress, intended to give General Electric an equal share to the incumbent Pratt & Whitney). We needed some of these capabilities, but we would have to start over on versions that made affordability a goal. Those starting a program would thenceforth need to have an analysis, approved by the acquisition czar, that showed it would fit into a reasonably sized future defense budget. This sounds pretty basic, but in fact its formal implementation was new.

Of course, just using "affordability" as a mantra isn't enough. A practical method for estimating the likely costs of a new defense system was an essential prerequisite. The Office of the Secretary of Defense did have a systems analysis shop, where I had my own first Pentagon job in 1981. One job of those talented people is to estimate the costs of a given new system using historical data on past programs, updated using current prices for material and labor, as well as information about the costs of new technologies. This is fine for internal budgeting, but it won't work for contracting. It makes no allowance for changing circumstances, essential design adjustments, and, above all, contractor incentives. It just lays a pile of money on the table.

Under Better Buying Power, I stressed to program managers who were writing RFPs and negotiating contracts that they should push all involved to produce defense systems for the lowest possible price. This meant understanding not just what a program *will* cost based on past practices, but also what it *should* cost with the affordability goal in mind. "Should-cost" estimates are done by taking the system apart and asking for data from the contractor, from the market (for pieces that are sold commercially, as most are), and from experts on emerging technologies, and then considering changes in the plan or the contract negotiation when the math doesn't meet the affordability target. Should-cost analysis requires program managers with total mastery of their projects, good business skills, and the ability to assess trade-offs in design. I promised that if a defense agency saved money this way, it could "keep" most of the money for its other priorities. This gave each agency an incentive to put should-cost into practice.

One early example of should-cost in action was the replacement for the Ohio-class nuclear missile submarines, which dated back to the era of my first Pentagon job in the early 1980s. By 2020, we'll need to begin replacing Ohio-class subs, despite heroic efforts to extend their lives. In 2010, I began working on a should-cost analysis for the Ohio replacement program with Shay Assad, the acting deputy undersecretary for acquisition and technology, and Sean Stackley, the Navy acquisition czar. Both were black belts in their profession.

The features of the first design would have busted the Navy budget wide open. The reasons for this gold-plated design were understandable. It had been more than three decades since the first Ohio-class sub was designed. In the intervening years, the incredibly skilled people in DOD and the industry who did this work had been working on ways to improve and enhance every part of the submarine. When it came time to plan the next generation, they all pitched in their best ideas. The result was a great submarine design—but not one the country could afford. The initial will-cost estimate was around $7 billion for each sub after the lead one. Since at least twelve subs would be needed in total to keep enough at sea or ready to go to sea (with a few at a time in maintenance) for nuclear deterrence, it was clear that the cost would simply have to be trimmed. We set ourselves the ambitious goal of $5 billion per boat.

The team examined every parameter of the design, deleting features that were not absolutely needed and reducing the size of whatever could be shrunk. Every bit of interior space saved meant a smaller hull, which meant a smaller nuclear power plant—and a significant cost reduction. These kinds of informed design trade-offs require real experts. Fortunately, the Navy had them. Applying should-cost to projects throughout the armed services will necessitate a renewed effort to recruit and retain skilled acquisition professionals.

More efficient acquisition practices also require a real partnership with industry.

Defense industry employees and executives are patriotic and

mission-devoted, and many are themselves military veterans. But business is business, and if they are to succeed in labor markets and stock markets, they need to mind their bottom lines. The taxpayer shares an interest in their viability.

At the same time, the Pentagon is the customer on behalf of the American people. So we need to make sure the defense companies' financial interests are aligned with the warfighters' and the taxpayers' interests in performance and cost. We accomplish this mainly by making sure that the contracts we sign contain appropriate incentives for the specific type of project.

The fixed-price-plus-profit contract approach used in the JSF and tanker programs illustrates some of the issues involved in fine-tuning contract incentives. In my Better Buying Power guidance, I told acquisition officials to err toward fixed price wherever reasonable, including about a fifty-fifty sharing of overruns and underruns up to an overrun limit of 20 percent. Writing the price into the contract keeps both parties to the business transaction working in the same direction—against ballooning costs. But I explicitly cautioned against dogmatism in this and other matters. If the RFP asks for something speculative that neither DOD nor any contractor can fully spell out in advance, let alone put a price on, then the contract should be cost-reimbursable. Otherwise a contractor either won't bid or will dumb down the product into something his company can assume financial responsibility for. That's not a way to get the world's most advanced weapons.

Contracts and procedures are important. But by far the most powerful instrument in the Pentagon's acquisition toolbox is competition. A contractor that fears losing Pentagon business to a rival is a better bidder and negotiating partner. Head-to-head competitions like the Boeing-Airbus faceoff over the airborne tanker result in great savings for the taxpayer—an estimated $3 billion in the tanker case. My BBP guidance therefore stressed to the acquisition workforce the importance of harnessing the competitive juices of industry for value to the taxpayer and warfighter.

But head-to-head competition is not always possible in the defense market. There are only a few shipyards in the country; only two make submarines, and only one makes nuclear aircraft carriers. We don't need and can't afford more. In these cases, we must find another way to harness the power of the competitive urge.

One strategy to achieve this is a contract that puts savings right into the contractor's pocket as well as the taxpayers' pocket, as with the fifty-fifty sharing of JSF. In effect, this makes the contractor compete with himself for profit. Another strategy is asymmetric competition—for example, making the beginning of a new program compete for budget dollars with the tail end of the program it replaces. An example is the idea of buying more of the aging Boeing F-18 jets for the Navy to use on aircraft carriers, rather than opting for the more modern, stealth-equipped, and more costly Lockheed Martin JSF. Apparently the then President-elect Trump was advised to do this by Dennis Muilenburg, the CEO of Boeing, in an understandable attempt to create more business for his company by appealing to Trump's self-image as a shrewd dealmaker. However, weighing the true risks and benefits of such a trade-off is a complex task that shouldn't be decided based simply on cost.

An asymmetric strategy of a different kind is to take two entirely different weapons that do the same military mission and have them compete against each other for the same slice of the budget—for example, an Army rocket system versus an Air Force smart bomb.

So, a variety of different competitive strategies are possible. But one way or another, as I said in the Better Buying Program guidance, every program manager should be able to explain to me a competitive strategy of some sort for his program.

One thing that struck me forcefully as I settled into the job of acquisition czar in early 2009 was that half of the $400 billion per year of the defense budget that went into contracts to the defense industry was not for planes, ships, tanks, radios, satellites, or any physical goods at all, but rather for services. These span an enormous range, from mowing the lawns at bases to conducting scientific R&D, and from feeding soldiers in the field to fixing airplanes.

Despite the huge sums spent on acquisition of services, the lore on acquisition reform almost totally ignores services. So, too, I discovered, did the curriculum of our major training courses for the acquisition workforce. DOD's tradecraft in buying services is not nearly as developed as it is for weapons systems, with its decades of ups and downs, debate, and reform efforts.

Some of the keys to buying services are the same as those for buying goods—for example, specifying the requirements in an RFP. But they often have special twists that contract officers need to be aware of—for example, the tendency to specify a certain number of "butts in seats" rather than precisely defining the work to be done. (When hiring a contractor to mow the lawn, you simply specify how often it needs to be mowed, not how many people will be in the crew.) As with buying weapons, competition is important in buying services. But the qualifications of service contractors are intangible, and buyers often find it difficult to state them in an RFP.

Making all these challenges more difficult for me as acquisition czar was the fact that many of the DOD leaders who have to buy services are not acquisition professionals at all. They are base commanders who want their lawns mowed or their dining halls staffed, trainers who want ranges and runways maintained, and, above all, wartime commanders who need supplies shipped and troops fed in the field. These leaders need some minimal acquisition training, and they need help from contracting professionals when making major decisions, like the huge logistics contracts for the wars in Iraq and Afghanistan.

To improve our husbandry of the $200 billion of taxpayers' money spent every year on services, my Better Buying Power guidance directed the Army, Navy, Marines, and Air Force to appoint a senior officer charged with overseeing the acquisition of services. The difference these officers made was felt immediately. Ironically, one positive sign was the fact that I began receiving complaints from members of Congress as the services began re-competing and tightening cost controls.

One day, I took a call from a congressman who had been persistently unpleasant and personal in criticizing the new Air Force services acquisition chief, a highly qualified general named Wendy M. Masiello. He was upset because she'd been making life harder for his favorite military contractor. When the congressman asked me what I planned to do to rein in the general, I replied, "The general is doing exactly what I've asked her to do—and what the taxpayers deserve."

As the call ended, I told one of my staff members, "Make sure Wendy doesn't get bullied anymore." I didn't realize that the line to the congress-man's office was still open.

Minutes later, an indignant fax came into the office from the congress-man, who had heard my remark. I called him back immediately. "I'm sorry you heard my remark," I said, "but I'm not sorry I said it."

The congressman must have respected my directness, because from that day forward, he used a more polite tone in lobbying on behalf of his business constituents. What's more, the story got around the department, spreading the message, "Secretary Carter stands up for his people." That helped strengthen the determination of our acquisition officers to do the right thing, regardless of political pressures.

In October 2016, six years after I issued the first Better Buying Power guidance, Frank Kendall assembled data on the results. These showed that the patient, back-to-fundamentals approach to acquisition reform made a significant difference in even the largest and most complex pro-grams. The cost growth in both development and production of such pro-grams was sharply curtailed since 2010. Moreover, the cost controls did not occur at the expense of industry profit; the data show that profit mar-gins for all the major defense contractors remained the same from 2010 to 2016—proof that we can rein in costs without endangering the economic viability of our defense industrial base.

Better Buying Power offers lessons about how government programs can be made more efficient in the future. And the payoffs, though easy to overlook, are huge and important. There's a direct link between faster, smarter acquisition policies and on-the-ground accomplishments—from bloodless deterrence of aggression by potential adversaries like Russia and China to battlefield victories against ISIS in Iraq.

CHAPTER 2

WORKING AT WAR SPEED

In every war, American troops have to contend with one or more characteristic enemy weapons: for example, the Japanese Zero fighter planes and the German Panzer tanks in World War II, or the Soviet-made AK-47 assault rifles used by the Viet Cong. One characteristic—and deadly—weapon of the twenty-first-century wars in the Middle East has been the improvised explosive device (IED).

The IED is crude—a kind of homemade bomb that insurgents often place under or alongside roads or trails to target troops when they're most vulnerable—but it is easy to construct using readily available commercial materials, such as fertilizer. It is also difficult to detect and easily disguised in the surrounding terrain, such as in trash heaps or even animal carcasses. Long before the wars in Afghanistan and Iraq, IEDs had been the weapon of choice for guerrillas and terrorists from Northern Ireland to Chechnya, and their use in asymmetric warfare had been extensively studied. But by the early 2000s, the widespread availability of new technologies, such as wireless transmitters, electronic triggers, and longer-lasting batteries for detonators, had rapidly increased their efficiency and potency. Within months of the start of hostilities in Afghanistan and Iraq, IEDs were causing some 60 percent of U.S. troop casualties.

In April 2009, when President Obama named me to serve under my old friend Bob Gates as undersecretary for acquisition, technology, and logistics—the acquisition czar—I inherited a system that had not been designed to respond nimbly to a quickly evolving threat. As Gates told me, "The troops are at war, but the Pentagon is not." With thousands of

U.S. troops being killed and injured by IEDs, my job would be to push that system to respond.

The Pentagon, I found, was still following its usual cumbersome peacetime procedures. The office of the acquisition czar included no one with a specific assignment to keep track of the needs associated with our ongoing wars. There were people working on planes and ships and tanks, people who did logistics, and people in charge of buying frozen ground beef and having it loaded aboard warships before they sailed from port—but no one was focused on the changing needs of the troops in the Middle East.

There were (and are) also acquisition executives for each of the armed services—the Army, the Navy, and the Air Force. (The Marines are part of the Department of the Navy, and do their acquisitions through that branch.) They respond to the secretaries of each of these branches and are appointed by the acquisition czar in tandem with the secretaries. Furthermore, none of their major acquisition programs can be approved without the undersecretary's sign-off. So their work is closely linked with that of the acquisition czar. But I found they were all focused heavily on major long-term projects—the planes, ships, and tanks of the future—rather than immediate, short-term needs affecting troops on the ground today.

What's more, each branch had its own idiosyncratic interests and preferences in regard to acquisitions, often based on historical and cultural factors. For example, the Marines are obsessed with amphibious vehicles, because amphibious landings are the one type of operation they excel at beyond all others. Right now, with the Marines operating amphibious vehicles that date back to the 1960s, they are desperately eager to develop new models—despite the fact that most strategists seriously question whether any future war will ever require us to storm a beach again.

Then there is the Air Force, which has steadily resisted the pressure to develop and implement drone-based warfare, despite its usefulness in specific types of combat—particularly the sort of counterinsurgency and anti-terrorism work we are doing in Iraq and Afghanistan. One reason for the reluctance of the Air Force to embrace drones is that drones have no pilots aboard, but rather are operated by joystick-wielding computer geeks based in the States. If you want to build a career in the Air Force, you do it by flying combat aircraft, just like the heroic airborne warriors of the past—so drones are simply not of interest.

Cultural challenges like these contribute to the clumsiness of our military's acquisition system. But the core problem for the troops in Afghanistan and Iraq was the fact that those who made the major decisions didn't see it in their job description to be involved in supporting the real wars of today, but instead to be buying only the sexy, complex, advanced systems for possible wars of tomorrow. For example, I learned that none of my predecessors as acquisition czar had ever traveled to Afghanistan or Iraq in their official capacity.

As a result of these organizational obstacles, the Pentagon had done too little to respond to the IED threat. Systems to thwart the explosive devices—for example, sensors that detect IEDs in the ground and electronic jammers that prevent their detonation—were not being provided in anything close to the necessary numbers. Neither was gear designed to protect U.S. troops from the devices.

Make no mistake, the people at the Pentagon were not indifferent to the dangers posed by IEDs to the troops. Any employee of the department, uniformed or civilian, would have been horrified by the idea that their failure to act had resulted in American deaths. But most people who work in the vast and sprawling defense system are understandably wrapped up in its day-to-day affairs. The urgency of fighting wars gets lost in the bureaucratic scrum.

I set about rewiring the system to force it to respond to the immediate needs of the troops—in particular the IED threat. One early problem we worked on was the need for gear that could protect the private parts of our soldiers from the devastating impact of an IED. Too many service members were losing their genitals along with their legs, and commanders reported that many of the men and women they led were haunted by the fear of such injuries—understandably so.

We found that the British were providing special undergarments—so-called ballistic underwear—to their own troops. The designs ranged from extra-thick conventional underwear made of tough fabrics that would resist relatively small fragments to garments that incorporated armored plates resembling the old jockstrap cups that most men who have played sports will recall. I had my staff devise a plan to procure and distribute such underwear to all the troops deploying to Afghanistan. We mandated the provision of male and female versions of the garments offering varying levels of protection (at the option of the troops themselves) and that each person being deployed get multiple pairs so that they could be laundered.

A bureaucratic hurdle immediately blocked our path. We discovered that the only manufacturer of ballistic underwear was a British company. Unfortunately, well-intentioned "buy American" rules imposed by Congress made it cumbersome for us to purchase foreign goods. This catch-22 rule was obviously idiotic, but before we could act, we had to jump through a number of legal hoops to obtain an exemption from the rule—a typical example of the nonsense built into our procurement system, regardless of the urgency of wartime.

Once we secured the exemption, we were able to make ballistic underwear a part of the regular kit every soldier took to the Middle East. The result was a roughly 32 percent drop from 2010 to 2011 in the number of catastrophic genital injuries to U.S. soldiers who encountered IEDs.

It's impossible to overstate the difference this made to the men and women involved. During one of my visits to injured troops at the Walter Reed National Military Medical Center in Bethesda, Maryland, I met the father of one soldier who'd had both legs amputated above the knee— the result of an IED attack. Thankfully he'd been wearing his ballistic underwear at the time. His dad gave me a hug and said, "My son will always have to use prosthetics to walk, but at least I still have a chance of being a grandfather." Scores of other military families shared similar experiences.

Later, the DOD team that had led the ballistic-underwear program proudly presented me with a framed pair, the crotch emblazoned with the signatures of all the team members. Those in charge of decorating my office would never allow me to hang this unusual memento on my office wall. When I subsequently became Secretary of Defense, I displayed it in the storeroom behind my office.

Of course, ballistic underwear was only a partial solution to the IED threat. With too many U.S. troops continuing to suffer catastrophic injuries and deaths as a result of powerful IEDs, our commanders in the field demanded more help. Many urged the creation of armored trucks to protect the troops from IEDs—mine-resistant, ambush-protected vehicles, which are referred to as MRAPs. These trucks feature a heavily armored protective shell suspended some distance above the ground, which gives the blast some space to weaken. They're also equipped with a V-shaped hull rather than a flat hull, which partly deflects the blast to the sides rather than having it fully absorbed by the vehicle itself.

MRAPs had been built and shipped to U.S. forces in Iraq as early as summer 2006. But these MRAPs were wholly inadequate for use in Afghanistan. Their so-called leaf-spring suspensions worked well on the relatively flat terrain of Iraq, but when crossing rivers or navigating ravines in craggy, mountainous Afghanistan, these vehicles would roll over, pinning and crushing the troops inside.

The mainstream acquisition system responded too slowly. The perception of the Army acquisition bureaucracy, supported by the chief of staff of the Army and the secretary of the Army, was that new MRAPs could not be designed, funded, and built before the war in Afghanistan ended—which meant nothing could be done.

To tackle the problem, SecDef Gates decided to create a task force to accelerate the development and fielding of MRAPs for Afghanistan. But when I came on board in 2009, I discovered that the program was still lagging. Strong personal intervention by top leaders was required.

I developed a friendly yet combative relationship with Robert F. Hale, the comptroller of DOD. Bob was a very able financial manager who played a vital role in the department. But his insistence on crossing every *t* before approving a single dollar of spending, no matter how urgent the need, left many of his colleagues frustrated. We used to joke that the comptroller's office must have a sign bearing the slogan "I'm not happy till you're not happy."

After my umpteenth respectful clash with Bob over freeing up funding for the MRAPs program, I finally complained to our boss Bob Gates. The secretary hadn't realized that the comptroller's office had become one of the roadblocks to fixing the problem. He listened carefully to my litany of complaints and told me, "I'll see what I can do."

I don't know exactly what kind of lightning bolt Gates flung from his post at the top of the organizational mountain, but it worked. The very next day, Bob Hale was at my office, asking, "What can I do to help with the MRAPs project?" Within a few days, the money we needed began to flow, and from then on, Hale and I were pulling on our oars together rather than working at cross-purposes.

As a result of these efforts, we were finally able to address the IED challenge. We arranged for the design and fabrication of a new kind of MRAP with an independent suspension, which we dubbed the MRAP all-terrain vehicle (MATV). Thousands were rapidly built and shipped to Charleston, South Carolina, where they were equipped with radios, communications gear, and a number of secret devices. Then they were loaded onto C-17 transport aircraft and flown directly into Afghanistan, where troops would undergo several days of training in using them. Finally, the MATVs found their way to the remote outposts of the country, where they immediately began saving lives.

The accelerated design, fabrication, and deployment process led to a few interesting twists and turns in the story. For example, testing with dummies revealed the need for upgrades and improvements to our original MATV design. We found that underbelly IED attacks produced a large number of compression fractures. The floor to which the seat was bolted would quickly accelerate upward, compressing the spine of a soldier and killing or paralyzing him. We responded by suspending the seats on harnesses from the ceiling rather than bolting them to the floor. The hull bows in response to a blast underneath, and the roof gets less of a jolt than the floor.

As the program continued, deploying the MATVs to Afghanistan as quickly as possible posed its own problems. I wanted to ship as many as one thousand vehicles a month. And while the commanders were eager to get them, they pushed back against this pace, saying they had space to store only five hundred or so at a time. Why? Because there was no concrete produced in Afghanistan, which made it impossible to pave enough land for the large parking facilities needed. We ended up trucking in supplies of concrete all the way from Pakistan so that larger parking fields could be built. The rate at which MATVs could arrive in Afghanistan ultimately increased to more than one thousand per month.

I also discovered that my order to ship all the vehicles immediately to theater had been taken literally and to an extreme—not an uncommon occurrence in the Pentagon. This had the unintended consequence of leaving no MATVs at all in the United States, which meant that troops couldn't practice using the vehicles in our combat training ranges or at the home stations where they prepared for deployment. I adjusted the orders to make sure that a few vehicles were kept in the United States for training.

Combat experience showed the need for further design improvements in the vehicles. For example, some troops shielded from an IED blast were nonetheless found dead in their harnessed seats when the vehicle was opened. Autopsies showed they had bled to death. It turned out that the shock wave from the explosion had propelled their legs toward the ceiling, snapping their femurs, which, in turn, penetrated their femoral arteries. We had to quickly retrofit all the vehicles with foam floors to absorb some of the blast.

Still another example of a design adjustment that we needed to make on the fly arose when we were planning the surge in Afghanistan. I got a call one day from General David Petraeus, then the commander of coalition forces in Afghanistan. "We're having a problem with visibility," Dave told me. "It's causing real troubles for the troops. Can you look into this urgently?"

The very next day, I got on a helicopter to the Aberdeen Proving Ground in Maryland, our principal vehicle R&D facility. I drove around the testing range in the MATV model that Dave had mentioned, and I saw the problem he'd described. One of the ways we'd modified the MRAP for the rough terrain of Afghanistan had been to lower the vehicle's center of gravity, making it more stable and less prone to tipping. But to make this possible, we'd had to reduce the size of the windows, which are made of extremely heavy ballistic glass—thicker and heavier, in fact, than the steel used in the truck's side panels. Once we figured out the problem, we could see how to fix it: We simply lowered the windows by a few inches, which gave the troops the additional visibility they needed. This design change was implemented immediately.

Dave was so appreciative of our quick response that he has retold this story many times. "That's the kind of rapid acquisition, the rapid processes, the decision making that has to take place," he said in one interview. "We didn't convene a committee, we didn't have large meetings—we didn't have to do all those other things. Some of these issues you can see are pretty straightforward and you don't need to go through a lengthy process to direct changes."

Despite the various adjustments we had to make to the MRAP program, we were able to ramp it up exceptionally quickly. In just sixteen months, we built and fielded more than eight thousand MATVs for Afghanistan. It was the biggest, fastest industrial defense procurement program since World War II.

It's hard to overstate the importance of this program. Casualty rates among soldiers riding in MATVs were about 75 percent lower than those in the Humvees they replaced.

How Flawed Strategic Thinking Impacts the Acquisition Process

The acquisition hurdles we had to overcome to protect the troops from IEDs didn't arise in a vacuum. They existed because, at the outset of the wars in Iraq and Afghanistan, the top leadership at the Pentagon was operating within a strategic framework that was deficient in several significant ways.

One problem was that, in the early years of this century, the Pentagon was prepared almost exclusively for traditional military-versus-military conflict, of the kind our country's forces have fought throughout U.S. history. That meant our strategic thinking became outmoded within a few weeks of our invasion of Iraq. When Saddam Hussein's army collapsed, the conflict didn't end. Instead, an array of new enemies emerged, consisting of terrorists and insurgents rather than regular troops. Less prepared to fight a foe without uniforms, command centers, or traditional organizational structures, the U.S. military initially failed to realize that it needed entirely new strategies, technologies, and methods to meet the new strategic threat.

In the years that followed, to its credit, the Pentagon successfully executed a major shift in its thinking, moving from a focus on traditional great-power rivalries to a new focus on stateless players with minimal infrastructure, no fixed territorial centers, and ever-changing strategic and tactical approaches. In fact, we ultimately *overshifted*, falling into the opposite trap of neglecting the continuing threats from traditional big-power adversaries like Russia and China. Our defense establishment is now working to remedy that mistake. This pattern of pendulum swings leading to overcorrections—and, ultimately, the need to swing back to achieve a better strategic balance—is a common problem at the Pentagon, as it is in many other organizations that grapple with continually shifting challenges. Hence the familiar warning against the mistake of "fighting the last war," which applies not just to military strategists but also in business, politics, and many other competitive endeavors.

The second big strategic mistake we made was believing that the new wars we'd embarked on in Afghanistan and Iraq would be over in a matter of months. Since it normally takes years to develop new military capabilities, the Pentagon assumed there'd be no point in launching any new weapons programs designed specifically for Afghanistan or Iraq. As Secretary of Defense Don Rumsfeld famously remarked, "You go to war with the army you have, not the army you might want or wish to have at a later time." Unfortunately, this approach tacitly foreclosed the possibility of making any changes to the tools provided to our forces. That proved to be disastrous when unforeseen developments on the battlefield, like the emergence of roadside IEDs, demonstrated the inadequacy of the existing equipment and the views inherited from wars of the past.

Important historical factors help to explain this attitude.

For decades, the Pentagon's thinking was dominated by the Cold War, in which our potential enemy was a lumbering giant called the Soviet Union. It was a formidable and fearsome adversary, constantly seeking to improve and expand the weaponry and other resources arrayed against us. But its approach to military development tended to be systemic, steady, and predictable rather than strikingly innovative and creative. So our massive acquisition and logistic systems, built on the assumption that the next great war would involve the use of large armored formations and nuclear weapons to defend our allies in Western Europe against invading armies from the USSR, reasonably adopted a slow-and-steady approach. Pentagon planners operated on ten- and twenty-year timelines. They focused on designing and building fleets of missiles, submarines, and aircraft that would be more advanced than the Soviet models, as well as on very-long-range futuristic research by centers like the Defense Advanced Research Projects Agency (DARPA).

The Vietnam conflict offered a major challenge to that philosophy. Suddenly we found ourselves embroiled in a battle against guerrilla insurgents in an unfamiliar cultural, political, and physical environment. The U.S. military entered the war using tactics and forces designed for the Cold War and only gradually developed the very different approaches demanded by Southeast Asia, including the reliance on Special Forces, the creation of a network of sensors along the Ho Chi Minh Trail, and the use of heliborne assaults to seize terrain and engage opposing forces behind enemy lines.

After the Vietnam War ended, our focus changed again. During the decade and a half from 1975 to 1989, the Russian threat returned to center stage. Under President Reagan, the Pentagon focused on outcompeting the USSR in building big, technically advanced weapons systems, convinced that there was no way the creaking Soviet economy could keep up with our dynamic capitalist system. The fall of the Soviet empire in 1989 proved that assumption was correct.

What followed was a period of drift. The 1990s were a decade when defense spending fell sharply (thanks to the "peace dividend" made possible by the end of the Cold War) and Pentagon strategists struggled to define a new mission for which our still-massive military should prepare. The nominal focus of investment that emerged was the so-called two-war strategy: the idea that the United States should be prepared for two major "regional contingencies," one in Northeast Asia and one in Southwest

Asia. We developed plans to defeat potential aggression by Iraq under Saddam Hussein and by North Korea under Kim Il-sung and, later, Kim Jong-il; and even when we didn't explicitly identify them, everyone knew who they were. Taking on both simultaneously would be a quantitative challenge but not a qualitative one. During this period, there was no real pressure in any part of the political spectrum to increase the defense budget, except for the usual local constituent and contractor lobbying and military supporter organizations arguing for steady salary increases for the troops. Under the circumstances, the Pentagon's system for developing weaponry and equipping the troops continued to lumber on in a style not far removed from the old, slow-moving fashion we'd become accustomed to during the Cold War.

Factor in the procedural impediments that always slow military acquisitions—including the time-consuming process for choosing a system, the complex contract-writing process, and a two-year budget that requires advance congressional approval for every dollar spent—and you can see why the United States was initially caught flat-footed by the fast-changing challenges of the post-9/11 wars. When the terror attacks of 2001 hit, the Pentagon was a bit like a successful corporate giant confronted by a nimble start-up armed with a disruptive new technology. In this case, the "start-up" consisted of cells of fighters scattered around the globe, with no central organizing authority and without access to state-of-the-art weaponry, but with a shared hatred of the United States and a willingness to improvise viciously destructive attacks on military and civilian targets alike, using any methods and materials they could get their hands on.

America's military had to learn to be responsive and agile—and to learn it fast. After all, our adversaries had no intention of slowing down their own innovating to make things easier for us. We had to figure out how to fight back without letting our bureaucracy slow us down. When devising crucial and urgent acquisition projects, rather than trying to set precise requirements, specifications, and quantities in advance, we had to move quickly on the basis of minimal information. As I like to say, we had to learn how to "acquire, *then* require." The ways we scrambled and improvised to address the IED threat illustrate the shift.

Meeting Urgent Needs: Building a System to Bust the Bureaucracy

As acquisition czar, I was determined to do more than simply solve the IED problem. I wanted to try to fix the problems posed by our cumbersome acquisition system more generally. So I also energized and expanded the existing system for identifying and acting on urgent wartime requests in the future.

The system was built around documents that describe Joint Urgent Operational Needs (JUONs). A JUON is drafted by a commander following a simple formal process, describing at least notionally a new piece of equipment, weaponry, defensive gear, or any other resource that the troops need. The JUONs system had been created in 2004, but it had been allowed to languish, often unused, in the years since then.

The word *Joint* in the JUONs acronym refers to requests originating with the joint commander in a combat zone, such as Iraq or Afghanistan. Commanders in the field know from firsthand experience what kinds of equipment their troops need. But they don't manage the machinery that produces the equipment, which is based back home in the United States. And because the need is *urgent*—the *U* in JUONs—I made it my business to ensure that items requested via this system would be provided as quickly as possible, with a minimum of red tape.

Making the JUONs system fast and responsive didn't happen automatically. We had to devote time and energy to working on it. Sometimes I had to help the commanders in the field in crafting their JUONs. They were understandably preoccupied with the daily challenges of fighting a war, and they lacked the technical expertise required to fill in the form with precision. After a while, the commanders got into the habit of calling me to say, "I need some kind of gadget that can solve the following problem—let me tell you about it." And together we would figure out how to define what the troops required.

Piece by piece, we found ways to make the JUONs system work faster and better. Here's a simple example.

One morning, General Stanley McChrystal, commander of the

International Security Assistance Force for Afghanistan, was participating as usual in the weekly secure-video teleconference that the Secretary of Defense would hold with senior commanders overseas. I sat in on all those meetings for many years, including the period when I was acquisition czar. In this particular meeting, Stan was discussing with Bob Gates some of the challenges he was having with visually identifying and targeting enemy resources—cars filled with insurgent fighters, for instance.

"Don't you have drones equipped with video cameras to hunt down those folks?" Bob asked.

"We do," Stan agreed. "But nowhere near enough. I'd say that the drones we've got are only about fifteen percent of what we need to give us the persistent video coverage we want."

Bob Gates turned to me with a "sounds like you need to do something about that" look on his face—understandably, because as the acquisition czar, I had to come up with a solution to this sort of problem. But this was the kind of urgent challenge that the Pentagon's traditional acquisition machinery was ill-equipped to handle. Among other problems, drones are complicated and time-consuming to design and build, and they require dedicated, specially trained crews to monitor and control them. We could quickly supply Stan with a few more drones and the training needed to run them—but seven times as many? No way.

So I went back to my office and got in touch with Stan's intelligence chief. He happened to be Michael Flynn, the general who would, years later, become a controversial figure in the early months of the Trump administration. But at that time, Flynn was a skilled and effective intelligence officer, and I knew that he could help me figure out more precisely what Stan and his people needed in the way of video-surveillance help.

Sure enough, a long talk with Flynn helped me realize that solving most of the missing intelligence problem wouldn't require drones at all. Drones are particularly well designed to track the movement of vehicles on a road. There's really only one big road in Afghanistan—the Ring Road, known as Route 1—and sometimes we need to fly drones along Route 1 to see, for example, whether terrorists are implanting IEDs there. But as we delved into the details, I realized that a lot of drones were then being used to circle a fixed location, such as a U.S. base or a village.

This is the kind of assignment where the flexible mobility of a drone isn't really demanded.

We came up with a simple solution: balloons equipped with video cameras. Known as aerostats, these 115-foot-long, blimp-shaped balloons don't need pilots working in command centers back in California, the way military drones do. Instead, they are monitored by contract workers on the ground in Afghanistan. They fill up the aerostat with helium, connect it to a big concrete block so it won't blow away, and let the aerostat rise a few thousand feet into the air. Since the pressure of the helium inside the balloon is just a little greater than that of the air outside, the bullets some insurgents fired at it would cause only very slow leaks, to little effect. The bullet holes could be patched whenever the aerostat was winched down for periodic maintenance.

Controlling the cameras on the balloons was also simple. The contractors sit in a van nearby and keep an eye on the video feed, which is also transmitted to a military command post in the same vicinity. The commanders there can ask the contractors to direct the camera as needed: "We've got a patrol going out to the west, so look in that direction," or "Check out this part of the local market—we suspect it's being infiltrated," or "Show us the house on the next corner—we think some people are building IEDs in it."

With Mike Flynn's help, I figured out that what Stan's people needed were aerostats—much cheaper and easier to provide than drones. We wrote up a JUON form to spell out the need.

Now I had to get the JUONs system cranking. A few months earlier, we'd created a team of Pentagon leaders with the authority to push JUONs through the system. We called it the Warfighter Senior Integration Group (SIG). I chaired it with the director of operations for the joint staff, and our meetings included everybody who mattered in the whole department, from top generals to senior staffers—some fifty people in all.

We held the SIG meeting every Thursday morning at seven a.m., a time chosen specifically to be convenient for our commanders in Iraq and Afghanistan. Others in government tended to hold meetings with our warfighters during the afternoon hours in Washington, D.C.—which might be three or four in the morning for Stan McChrystal, David

Petraeus, or Joseph F. Dunford Jr. in theater. If you're the president of the United States, you can get away with that. But I had no intention of putting our poor warriors through the same ordeal. So seven a.m. for us was a more respectful time, as far as I was concerned, though it made some in the Pentagon grumpy.

Each meeting focused on a series of JUONs that were waiting to be addressed. On a given Thursday, in addition to talking about aerostats, we might work out the details around providing dogs specially trained to sniff out IEDs, constructing forward-operating bases and combat outposts, providing ballistic underwear to protect warriors' private parts, and even getting an adequate number of porta-potties shipped to where they were needed.

As you can see, some of the challenges tackled by the SIG group involved technical innovations, while others were about buying things off the rack—but doing it quickly. And we were spending enormous amounts of money, which created its own political and organizational challenges. For example, in Afghanistan, the amount of money the Pentagon spent in 2010 was equal to the Afghan national GDP. We were building the Afghan army—paying their salaries, building their bases and training facilities, and even buying the chicken and bread they served in their dining halls. That kind of spending has to be managed intelligently. To help boost the local economy, we purchased as much as we could locally. But not everything we needed was available that way—for example, we found we had to turn to Europe to buy enough lettuce to feed salads to the troops. Because there were no cement factories in Afghanistan, we were having supplies of cement shipped in from Pakistan when we needed to build protective Jersey barriers or pour an airport runway. In other cases, we created local facilities to meet our needs. We built bottling facilities around Iraq and Afghanistan to provide safe drinking water for the troops, as well as generating plants to produce a reliable supply of electrical power.

All this spending adds up to a gargantuan effort, and managing it efficiently hadn't been receiving any centralized priority. So all of it went into the SIG meetings. The goal: to create a system that could move as fast as events on the ground demanded.

We brought the need for camera-equipped balloons to the SIG, marking it as a super-urgent challenge on which American lives depended.

The officers in charge of budgeting, ordering, and shipping equipment were instructed to make it a top priority. Within days, dozens of aerostats were on their way to Afghanistan. Later, we even built a helium factory in Kandahar to fill the balloons. To this day, they are floating over the bases where U.S. soldiers and their local allies have worked, spotting bad guys and helping our forces thwart their deadly operations.

The SIG continues to operate even now, and I have many fond memories of the team I assembled when it was first created. Jay Paxton, the joint staff officer in charge of operations, was my co-chair. Jay was a great guy, and he and his wife, Debbie, became close friends with my wife, Stephanie, and me. We shared many days of austerity in Afghanistan in the time before good dining facilities and air-conditioned quarters were built. Jay liked to share wisdom from a library of aphorisms that he attributed to an apocryphal "gunny [or gunnery] sergeant." Thus, "The gunny says that, in the Marine Corps, you never get what you expect, but you always get what you inspect"—a reminder to check your supplies before going out in the field.

Others who traveled with us included my military assistant Sam Said (and later Ron Lewis); Tom Dee, who made sure each of the armed services was pulling its weight; Dick Ginman, who handled the contractors; Army officers Pete Chiarelli and Tony Ierardi; and logistics expert Alan Estevez. Early in one trip to Iraq and Afghanistan, Alan lost his bag, and there was no chance it would catch up with us as we hopped from place to place by plane and helicopter. Alan showed remarkable good humor as he survived the trip using spare items of clothing and toiletries scrounged from the rest of us.

The SIG had two informal mottos: "Nothing is too small" and "We work for you." The message was that here, at least, was one Pentagon team for whom the needs of the troops would always be job one.

Equipment That Only Nature Can Produce

Not every urgent need that the troops experience can be solved simply by designing equipment or building factories. When warfighters in Afghanistan demanded military working dogs in unprecedented numbers, I

found myself becoming an expert in the procurement of a unique resource that can be produced only using methods designed by Mother
Nature herself.

I learned from dog breeders and the Pentagon buyers who worked
with them that different kinds of military tasks are handled best by various breeds of dogs. For example, there are attack dogs that accompany
guard forces and will fiercely engage with threatening individuals when
commanded to do so by their handlers. We use many of these in Afghanistan, where they support the Air Force security teams assigned to
protecting our airbases.

Then there are sniffer dogs that are trained to find dangerous objects
concealed in packages or hidden in someone's clothes, much like the
beagles that perform these tasks in U.S. airports. Sniffer dogs are divided into two categories: leashed and unleashed. The leashed type are
good within confined spaces and are comfortable having many people
around, but complicated environments may confuse them. The unleashed sniffers are particularly prized among the troops in Afghanistan.
They can be let loose by their handlers to walk trails ahead of a patrol,
sniffing for explosives that feature the telltale smell of fertilizer. When
they find a bomb, they alert their handlers by sitting or pawing the
ground, and an explosive ordnance demolition team is called in to eliminate the hazard.

Over time, we've also developed technological tools to protect the
troops against explosives—for example, vehicles outfitted with chains attached to huge wheels mounted in front of a tractor. The chains flail the
ground in front of the vehicle, harmlessly detonating any IEDs triggered
by pressure plates. This is actually an old design that dates back to the
world wars. Of course, it doesn't work with IEDs that are triggered by
command wires or cell phone signals.

In any case, dogs remain the champions among bomb detectors.
Their remarkable ability to identify even faint odors has been honed
through evolution over thousands of generations, and experts at DARPA
tell me it will be a long time before any high-tech sensor can match it.

Just as important, military dogs are beloved by the troops, and especially by the soldiers designated as their handlers. Lonely troops who are

thousands of miles from home find the friendly presence of these canine allies immensely comforting.

This means that acquiring enough dogs to supply the needs of our overseas forces is a high-priority challenge, and one that's not easy to meet. Because there are only so many mama dogs to begin with, the only way to add large numbers of dogs quickly is to employ global sourcing. This we did, scouring the world's kennels for suitable breeds. The breeders themselves do most of the training, preparing the dogs to perform up to standards and specifications that we set for them.

Maintaining the supply is complicated by the fact that military dogs, like soldiers, can suffer from post-traumatic stress (PTS). A dog that has been exposed to gunshots, explosions, and other forms of violent combat often shows symptoms such as irritability, fearfulness, and unwillingness to work. Dogs suffering from PTS usually need to be relieved of duty, which means a painful separation from their loving handlers. Some have to be euthanized, while others are shipped to kennels back in the United States for possible adoption. In a few cases, they are able to be reunited with the soldiers they befriended. When this happens, it's a satisfying end to a story of mutual dedication and service.

Getting It There: Logistics for the Worst Place on Earth

Acquiring stuff for troops at war isn't the only enormous challenge that Pentagon managers face. Getting the stuff to them can be almost as difficult.

Spin a globe, and you'll find no place more forbidding than Afghanistan when it comes to waging war. Afghanistan is landlocked and surrounded by countries with which the United States has difficult relations at best—Iran, Pakistan, Uzbekistan, Tajikistan, and Turkmenistan. The terrain is forbidding, with the craggy Himalayas to the north and vast deserts in the south, where the temperature routinely rises to 120 degrees Fahrenheit. The only highway to speak of is the Ring Road, which starts from the capital of Kabul and proceeds down to Kandahar, up west to Herat, and on around to Kunduz in the north. It's partly unpaved, barely maintained, and crowded with pedestrians, animals, and broken-down vehicles, providing an endless opportunity for raids on U.S. convoys and implantation of roadside bombs. Many other roads are twisting, single-lane mud trails that are even more difficult to travel.

This is the environment in which the surge announced by President Obama in 2010 had to be implemented. The job fell to the DOD's logistics community, which proudly calls itself Log Nation, and which I headed as part of my job as acquisition czar. Log Nation was asked to construct over 250 new forward-operating bases and combat outposts in locations throughout the country, some atop formerly empty hilltops, some replacing Soviet bases from the disastrous war of the 1970s and 1980s. Log Nation also had to administer the enormous contracts that gave huge global defense contractors like DynCorp the tasks of transporting materials, overseeing base construction, and building security barriers, as well as providing safe food, buying and delivering fuel, running facilities ranging from dining halls and exercise rooms to movie theaters, and carrying out a host of other titanic logistical feats.

As you can imagine, the work undertaken by Log Nation was incredibly complicated. All of it was compounded by the sheer difficulty of getting anything into Afghanistan in the first place.

It was necessary to go to the expense of flying into the country all weapons, ammunition, troops, and sensitive military supplies like communications and intelligence sensors. Everything else had to come in by ground, via a limited number of so-called ground lines of communication (GLOC). Each of the many brigade combat teams that rotated into and out of Afghanistan every year would bring in their own equipment— armored vehicles, weapons, radios, and so on. A needless expense? Not really. Troops love their own equipment and fight much better when using the same equipment they've trained on. So we took it all in and took it all out with every change of rotation.

The southern GLOC through Pakistan, which originated in the port of Karachi, was by far the easiest. Leased vessels carrying military cargo would dock there, and the containers would be loaded aboard what we called "jingle trucks," the South Asian vehicles painted in colorful psychedelic patterns. In Pakistan, most of the trucking was controlled by the military, like much of the rest of the economy. From Karachi, these trucks would make their way through one of the fabled gates of Afghanistan—either Torkham Gate through the Khyber Pass or Chaman Gate en route to Kandahar.

They ended up in the vicinity of a major U.S. base—at Kandahar, for example—where they would be parked for twenty-four to forty-eight hours in large "soak yards" outside the base perimeter. This gave us an opportunity to examine the trucks and make sure they were free of explosives. It also helped to discourage the thousands of potential suicide bombers—most would give up and simply walk away after a few hours of waiting had passed. Finally, we'd let the trucks inside the base. There the containers would be unloaded, stacked, and used for storage or even as housing for workers brought in from third countries like Bangladesh.

It took me a couple of years to discover the somewhat dismaying fact that shipping companies like Maersk were charging us a rental fee for their containers during all the months when they sat idle in our camps. Understandably, Maersk was reluctant to send its own people to pick up the empty containers, and I was strongly opposed to spending taxpayers' money to ship them back to the United States. Eventually we solved the problem by negotiating a drastically reduced rental rate. These are the kinds of small but important details a logistics chief must pay attention to.

We soon decided we needed an alternative to the southern GLOC, which was dependent on the consent and cooperation of the Pakistani government. A western route through Iran was out of the question. So the enterprising Log Nation created a northern distribution route (NDS) that began in the Baltics, and then went through Russia and central Asia. Of course, this required the consent of Russia and the central Asian countries. Generally, they permitted the route to operate, but they imposed restrictions on the kinds of cargo that could get through, meaning nothing that was conspicuously military, at least from the outside.

The NDS entered Afghanistan through the third of the country's fabled gates, Hairatan, north of Mazar-i-Sharif. The route deeper into Afghanistan then passed through the notorious Salang Tunnel, which was long, poorly maintained, and approached by narrow, curving roads—a dangerous nightmare in poor weather. Still, it was an essential alternative to the southern GLOC and therefore critical to the war effort.

Log Nation had still other complications to deal with. Many of our forward-operating bases and combat outposts were built, in whole or in part, on former Soviet minefields, which meant the ground had to be swept to establish a safe perimeter for operations—a highly dangerous task. Nor did the threats end there. In most places, the perimeter barriers were cyclone fences, which were vulnerable to terrorist breakthroughs. A truck filled with high explosives could crash through the fence and be detonated before the drivers were gunned down by U.S. security forces. This possibility required constant vigilance. Eventually, we built large earthen barriers that reduced the problem.

Another danger was posed by the contractor workforce on the U.S. and coalition bases. General Stanley McChrystal had mandated that we try to use Afghan contract laborers in preference to the third-country nationals from places like India, Turkey, Pakistan, and Eastern Europe who often supported our logistics efforts. This made good sense, but it added complications: these local workers all had to be carefully screened each day when they came to work and departed. At the giant airbase in Bagram, north of Kabul, for example, the thousands of workers who entered through the main gate were made to walk "the long mile" where they were constantly surveilled, one at a time, and subjected to body searches far more intrusive than anything you've ever experienced at a U.S. airport.

The effectiveness of these measures meant that most suicide bombings took place just outside rather than within coalition bases, though occasionally an Afghan national would elude the safeguards and pull off an attack. Shortly before my last trip to Afghanistan as SecDef, an Afghan national who worked at a machining facility at Bagram Airbase managed to smuggle in tiny amounts of explosives every day for months, despite the Americans' routine searches. Eventually, he assembled a passable suicide harness and walked down the busy main avenue of the base, looking for a cluster of troops he could kill. Fortunately, he came to believe he was being followed, which forced him to detonate in a sparsely populated spot. He still killed a number of people, including five Americans.

When I visited that exact spot a few days later, my wife, Stephanie, was with me. It was sobering to meet with the soldiers and civilian workers whose lives had been shattered so suddenly. They appreciated my presence, but they valued Steph's even more. Later, during the farewell ceremony when I left office in January 2017, Joe Dunford shared part of a letter written by the unit commander after our visit. He wrote, "Much as I treasure the engagement I had with Secretary Carter, it pales in comparison to the hug I received from Mrs. Carter. . . . When Stephanie walked toward me with open arms, I forgot I was in Afghanistan, far away from the people I love. I forgot about being a commander for one minute, and I felt like a person again." The comment highlights what is special about Stephanie. It also shows the incredible stress the troops must endure every day of their deployment in a war zone like Afghanistan.

In the world of business, companies like Walmart and Amazon are famous and highly respected for the efficiency and skill with which they manage complicated logistics challenges. They do fine work, but I'd venture to say that the problems they must tackle pale alongside the dangers and complexities that the U.S. military must address in places like Afghanistan. It's another point worth pondering for those who wonder why the DOD must spend so much money equipping the troops. It's less about waste and more about the incredible difficulty of meeting complex human needs in some of the most remote and threatening regions of the planet.

Tools for the Wars That Might Be

As acquisition czar, I became acutely aware of the fact that our strategic thinking about specific global threats was not evolving as rapidly as those threats themselves. Building on everything we learned from energizing and accelerating the JUONs process, it became clear that we also needed something brand-new—a system that would identify emerging needs not for the wars that *are*, but for the wars that *might be* in the near future.

The challenges faced by the U.S. Navy in the Persian Gulf offer an example. Just as the IED challenge changed constantly in Afghanistan, the antiship cruise missile threat changes continually in the Gulf. At the Pentagon, we tend to take the long-range view about strategic problems, as illustrated by massive projects like the Joint Strike Fighter I described in the last chapter. Some challenges absolutely demand that sort of big-picture approach. But if your mode of thinking is too consistently JSF-like, you may end up building solutions for ten years in the future while failing to keep up with the short-term competitive challenges—which could mean ships of ours being sunk by cruise missiles in the Persian Gulf six months from now. Imagine if a war broke out tomorrow in a given theater. What would the local commander lack that he should have? What sorts of steps would we wish we had taken today?

To address these requirements for the future wars that might be, we came up with the idea of documents defining Joint Emergent Operational Needs (JEONs). These were designed to fill in the gap between immediate projects, designated by JUONs, and the major programs designed for needs that might exist ten or twenty years down the road, which traditional acquisition projects like the Joint Strike Fighter program are intended to meet.

To turn the idea of JEONs from a theory into a reality, I began working with the commanders in various theaters. For example, I visited with Admiral Robert F. Willard, commander of the U.S. Pacific Command (PACOM). PACOM was responsible for the rapidly evolving threat posed by China, which had long been neglected by our big strategic thinkers in the Pentagon. The Chinese challenge was changing very fast, and PACOM was falling behind.

So I started to work with Admiral Willard and his staff, saying, "Imagine that we go to war against China next month. What do you need? What's missing? What would we all regret not having done? What could make the difference between victory and defeat?" These questions became the basis of a series of fascinating conversations—some in person, some via teleconference. More important, they also helped launch what would soon be known as the Asia-Pacific Rebalance.

One of the concrete solutions to potential future problems that emerged from this discussion is the digital-radio frequency memory (DRFM) jammer.

Jammers are designed to thwart radar. Suppose I am sending an airplane into hostile territory. A radar system operated by the enemy will send out a pulse toward my airplane, and then an echo signal bounces off the airplane back to the radar receiver. The radar receiver detects that return signal and recognizes it as having the same characteristics as the outgoing pulse. By measuring how long it took to go round-trip and other features of the pulse, it can tell how far away the airplane is, how quickly it is traveling, and so on.

To thwart radar systems, jammers were invented. Most jammers just "scream" loudly—that is, they emit a powerful pulse that "shouts down" the radar returns, which are faint. Usually the jammer is located on another airplane in the vicinity whose purpose is to confuse the enemy radar—for example, the Navy Growlers, which carry big jammers. They're designed to escort our aircraft fleets into battle and to help them escape early detection by the enemy.

Of course, radar engineers have responded by finding ways to filter out the loud noise created by jammers and to make each pulse emitted different from the last. In response, the jammers have had to get smarter. The ultimate smart jammer would be one that receives the radar pulse and very quickly generates a fake signal, seemingly identical to the real one, but that seems to locate the airplane somewhere else. And that's what the DRFM does. It's basically an electronic chip that performs the necessary calculations to generate the deceptive jamming signal and does so at incredible speed.

The DRFM chip was actually invented here in the United States around the year 2000, but it wasn't initially designed for military use. Instead, it was used for various purposes in cell phones, Wi-Fi networks, and other civilian applications. The Chinese then bought it and deployed it in their planes.

Admiral Willard and I realized that, in a war-that-might-be against China, our lack of DRFM chips could have serious implications. The fact that the Chinese had actually leapfrogged ahead of the United States using our own technology was a potentially devastating self-inflicted wound. The twin causes were American complacency and the Pentagon's failure to remain up-to-date with the latest digital technology—a topic I'll explore in more detail in a later chapter.

The DRFM gap was exactly the kind of emerging need for which the JEONs system was devised. One of the first JEONs we generated was a request to move quickly to outfit U.S. planes and ships with DRFM jammers while also preparing our own radar equipment to deal with such jammers. In this way, we readied our forces for a possible conflict with an adversary already using the same equipment.

The JEONs process that I devised is still being used in the Pentagon. It's an innovation that will make a significant difference in American preparedness for the wars of the future and in our ability to protect the lives and well-being of the troops.

CHAPTER 3

A SCIENTIST IN THE PENTAGON

The crucial factors that determine whether defense spending is done right or wrong are numerous and complex, but in the end, they boil down to one thing: employing a system for making and implementing decisions that are driven by *facts*—scientific and technological data, an honest assessment of the strategic challenges our nation faces around the world, and the real-world dangers the troops grapple with every day. When leaders in the Defense Department make decisions that are firmly grounded in these facts—and then implement those decisions with consistency and integrity—they rarely go far wrong. When, instead, they make decisions driven by political expediency, pressures from interest groups or lobbyists, or flawed interpretations of reality shaped by ideology or wishful thinking, they run the risk of making errors that will compromise American security and cost lives.

I am a scientist by inclination and training—which means that a policy of using hard facts as the basis for action is deeply ingrained in me. What's more, my first experiences in government were centered squarely on the challenge of applying sound scientific analysis to major defense decisions that were, inevitably, caught up in political controversies. As a result, I was exposed early and often to one of the central challenges faced by any government policy maker: figuring out how to make solidly fact-based decisions in an atmosphere of intense, emotional, often vitriolic political debate—and how to win enough support for those decisions so that they can be effectively carried out for the good of the country.

In this sense, my entire public career, dating back four decades, was a training ground for the work I did in the Defense Department during 2009–2017. From the moment I got the first call to serve our country in 1980, I've been practicing the art of being a scientist in the government, attempting to bring the virtues of fact-based decision-making to a world where facts don't always get the attention they deserve—while also learning something about politics and the world.

The Politics of Technology: The MX Missile Basing Dilemma

I describe myself as a scientist at heart. But the physical sciences aren't the only subject I might have devoted myself to. When I somewhat unexpectedly won admission to Yale University, I was an intensely serious student—what would probably today be called a "grind." I was conscious of how lucky I was and contemptuous of the "preppies" who wasted their time and tuition money by partying. I ended up pursuing two entirely different majors: physics and medieval history. It was a right brain, left brain thing. There was no relationship between them in my mind except that both fascinated me.

I liked dusty archives, learning to decipher manuscripts in medieval script, and learning all the languages necessary to read the primary and secondary historical literature, especially Latin. I wrote a senior thesis on the use of Latin by contemporary monastic writers to describe the vibrant world of twelfth-century Flanders in which they lived. I enjoyed English legal history and the foundations of the common law as established in the eleventh through thirteenth centuries. I also did a lot of work on the hagiography of Saint Denis, patron saint of the French monarchy during its formative period in the ninth century.

Physics was entirely different: clean and modern, logical and mathematical. (Back then, we physicists noted that people who weren't smart enough for physics ended up as computer scientists.) I was lucky enough to be asked by a professor to assist him on an experiment in elementary particle physics at the then-new Fermilab outside Chicago, home of the world's largest particle accelerator. I would fly back and forth from New Haven, Connecticut, to Chicago, feeling very serious and very important.

We were involved in the search for the quark, a subatomic particle then only theorized. I eventually wrote my senior thesis, which was later published, on the "charmed quark."

As far as course choice was concerned, I had no interest in between the extremes of medieval history (history, language, philosophy) on the one hand, and science (physics, chemistry, biology, mathematics) on the other. I have taken exactly zero social science courses in my entire life. My arrogant view at the time was that life would eventually teach me political science, sociology, psychology, and economics, but it would never teach me linear algebra or Latin. It seemed best to get my tuition's worth from the other topics and get my social science for free!

The end of college brought the usual crisis of what to do next. I was rescued by being awarded a Rhodes scholarship that entitled me to free study at Oxford University. Many Rhodes scholars pursue a second bachelor's degree or a master's degree at Oxford, but I was still a man in a hurry. I decided I would use the free funding to get my doctorate in theoretical physics. Oxford did not have enough money to have world-class experimental facilities in elementary particle physics, but it had a great theoretical physics department. All you need for theoretical physics is a pencil and paper and the ability to sit for hours of intense concentration with a page of equations in front of you.

I worked on the theory of quantum chromodynamics, the quantum field theory then postulated to explain the behavior of nuclear reactions and the structure of the subatomic zoo of particles. Unfortunately, it was a mathematical theory so complex that its equations could not be solved. I found a way to solve its equations in certain special circumstances, thus allowing it to be tested against experiments.

Oxford was a very lively intellectual community. The expatriate Americans would spend long hours debating the topics of the day. Much of my otherwise lacking social science training occurred by osmosis in the pubs with Rhodes friends.

I had no doubt, however, that I wanted a career of thinking and publishing in academia, then meaning theoretical physics. I therefore went back to the United States to start to climb the academic ladder in physics, beginning in the usual way, with a postdoctoral appointment. I wrote several papers. The one of which I am proudest dealt with "time-reversal invariance," the proposition that the world could run backward according to the same laws by which it runs forward. While this may seem like a bizarre concept, such a symmetry in nature would actually be a fundamental property of our universe, which, I posited, would be disproved by the discovery of a particular type of reaction involving a particle called a B meson. In recent years, this precise phenomenon has, in fact, been detected—which is a big reason that my paper is rather famous and is still frequently cited.

I was happily building an academic career in theoretical physics, working as a research associate at Rockefeller University, when a serendipitous opportunity opened up an entirely new vista for me. The year was 1979. The Cold War was ratcheting up to a new peak of tension as the nuclear arsenals of the world's two superpowers attained new levels of destructive power.

My field of physics dated back to the wartime Manhattan Project, and many of the senior figures in my field had long worked on military technology—not just its development, but also its control. Having participated in developing the nuclear weapons that had helped win World War II and maintain the peace during the Cold War, they were also conscious of the dangers such weapons posed. They felt they had a moral obligation to apply their knowledge to helping protect the world against those dangers. And one of the lessons they taught the younger generation was that we had inherited this same obligation. So I was flattered, but not surprised, when a couple of senior figures in the field urged me to take a one-year leave of absence from theoretical physics to tackle some practical work related to nuclear weapons. They were Richard Garwin and Sidney Drell.

Dick Garwin was a famous physicist and senior fellow at IBM. He was a favorite protégé of both Enrico Fermi and Hans Bethe, two leading lights of the Manhattan Project, for the very good reason that he, too, was a superb physicist. Dick had basically designed the first thermonuclear explosion. It took place in a test on an island in the Pacific. It was not really a bomb, but more like a room-size facility, because the materials that were fused were in liquid form, filling a huge tank. The solid form that makes up the thermonuclear stages of modern bombs are made of solid materials that are more compact and can therefore be shaped into a bomb. However, Dick's experiment showed that an H-bomb was possible.

Sid Drell was the director of the Stanford Linear Accelerator Center, one of the major elementary particle laboratories in the world. One of his many contributions to America's defense technology—highly classified at the time he made it—was his work in helping to create the first digital spy satellite. Before that, satellites used to contain traditional cameras that used film. They would periodically drop canisters of film that would descend to Earth through the atmosphere, slowed by a parachute, to be retrieved by a Navy plane equipped with a giant hook. Then the film would be sent to CIA headquarters for development and analysis.

This process was digitized with Sid's help in the late 1970s. The KH-11 satellite had the very first charge-coupled device (CCD), a technology still widely used in digital imaging; the cell phone in your pocket contains a CCD-like device. This enabled spy satellites to take digital images and beam them down. It's a powerful tool not just for military applications but also for all kinds of scientific uses; the Hubble telescope, which has provided astronomers with unprecedented views of space, is basically a spy satellite pointed upward rather than toward Earth. Sid worked on this program. He had also served as the external examiner for my Oxford doctoral thesis.

As you can see, Dick and Sid were two remarkable figures. Now they recruited me to join a team of scientists being assembled at the Congressional Office of Technology Assessment, whose job was to analyze all the various ways that the MX intercontinental ballistic missile (ICBM) could be protected from a nuclear first strike from the Soviet Union.

The "MX" stood for "missile experimental," but by 1979 it was far from experimental. It was a huge missile that could carry ten warheads with great accuracy to the Soviet Union. Under the doctrine of mutual assured destruction, which held that nuclear deterrence required weapons systems on both sides with the unquestioned power to devastate the enemy, the role of the MX missile was to offset the giant Soviet SS30 missile.

Of course, mutual assured destruction meant that offensive nuclear weapons should be designed to withstand a first strike with the ability to retaliate powerfully against the opponent. If that first-strike survival capability is absent or uncertain, the possessors of those weapons will feel that they have no choice but to strike first when tensions escalate—and the other side, knowing this, will conclude that they are forced to strike first. That is a dangerously unstable situation that makes nuclear war far more likely.

So achieving survivability was an essential criterion for the successful deployment of the MX missile. But the problem was that no one could figure out how to do this. Given the fact that the Soviet Union had thousands of warheads it could use to target the MX missiles—and that Soviet missiles had become increasingly accurate over time—how could the survival of the MX missiles be guaranteed? A fierce debate erupted among defense experts. Some forty different schemes were proposed, involving methods for hiding the missiles, moving them around, or trying to deceive the Soviets about their locations so as to complicate the challenge of targeting them. None of the options appeared particularly attractive.

By 1979, Jimmy Carter's Defense Department had concluded that the best idea was to hide 200 MX missiles in 4,600 silos—essentially, holes in the ground—in the Great Basin area of Nevada and Utah. The missiles would periodically be shifted from one set of locations to another, thereby making it impossible for the Soviets to guess which silos contained real missiles and which contained harmless dummies. And targeting all 4,600 silos would have created a daunting challenge.

Unfortunately, this "racetrack" concept also held enormous complications for U.S. planners. It would have been the largest public works project in history, requiring the construction of 4,600 underground shelters connected by an elaborate system of roadways for transporting the constantly moving missiles by truck. As soon as the Carter administration announced the plan, intense criticism erupted.

The uproar was particularly great in the areas of the country most directly affected. Some local leaders favored it, noting the thousands of jobs it would have created for engineers and construction workers, and those who would feed and house them. But many others were opposed. At community meetings in Beaver County, Utah, the manager of a local cattle operation expressed skepticism over claims by the Air Force that grazing herds would be unaffected by the new missile sites. "We'll lose half of Beaver County to MX," he declared. Environmental groups and businesspeople dependent on travel and tourism echoed his concerns. The governors of Nevada and Utah both expressed concerns over environmental damage.

Congress ordered a scientific audit of the options. Garwin and Drell recruited me for "just one year" to participate in that study. In May 1980, the assignment became official, in the form of a formal "letter of request" sent to the Office of Technology Assessment by Morris "Mo" Udall and Ted Stevens, the chair and vice chair of the OTA's board.

In response to this letter, our team set to work on our study. We were given access to all the classified information we needed. Our task was to examine the various MX basing alternatives—and I mean every alternative. In addition to the racetrack approach, we considered the possibility of putting MX missiles onto almost everything that could possibly move under, on, or above the surface of the earth. At one point, we even studied the idea of putting the 200,000-pound MX missiles on balloons and having them fly continuously over the United States so that the Soviets would not be able to track them. Had they been built, these 14-million-cubic-foot airships would have been the largest blimps since the Graf Zeppelin! Today, with the Cold War a thing of the past, it is hard to believe that such notions were once taken seriously.

By 1981, Ronald Reagan had assumed the presidency. He and his defense secretary, Caspar Weinberger, were certainly not wedded to the racetrack concept; in fact, Reagan himself called it an unworkable "Rube Goldberg scheme." Nevada Senator Paul Laxalt, a key Reagan ally, also came out against the racetrack plan. And another devastating blow came in June 1981, when the powerful Mormon Church issued a statement opposing it. It read in part, "Our fathers came to this western area to establish a base from which to carry the gospel of peace to the peoples of the earth. It is ironic, and a denial of the very essence of that gospel, that in this same general area there should be constructed a mammoth weapons system potentially capable of destroying much of civilization." By this point, the racetrack plan was virtually dead.

Around the same time, our study group issued its report. It took the form of a book titled *MX Missile Basing*, published by the Office of Technology Assessment. (It became a famous work, at least in the technical circles where such books are read, and is available to this day to anyone willing to do a bit of a search.) We found that the racetrack system would probably *not* guarantee the survivability of the MX missiles unless absolute secrecy about the missiles' locations was maintained. We also found that some other proposed basing modes, including the use of small submarines or aircraft, might be able to achieve survivability if specific technological qualifications were met—but that it would likely take a number of years before this could be achieved. In short, we concluded that there was no perfect solution to the MX basing dilemma, but that one or more approaches might eventually produce acceptable results.

In the end, the MX missile did not become the mainstay of national defense that its developers had once hoped. In 1983, President Reagan announced that the MX missile—now renamed the Peacekeeper—would be put into service in existing silos designed for the older Minuteman missiles, a vulnerable temporary solution until a survivable one was developed. Fifty Peacekeepers ended up being deployed. During the same period, the U.S. and USSR were involved in negotiations on the Strategic Arms Reduction Treaty (START II), under which ICBMs were allowed to carry only a single warhead. As the Minuteman fleet could carry a smaller number of warheads for far less money, and the Peacekeeper was proving highly unreliable in field tests, the United States agreed to remove the Peacekeeper from its nuclear force as part of this treaty. Although START II was not ratified by the United States, the Peacekeeper missiles were removed anyway, with the last one going out of service on September 19, 2005.

The MX basing project was a significant one for my career. I'd had the good fortune to work on what was then a very hot issue with a very talented team of scientists, a collaboration from which I learned a lot. I began to develop a bit of a reputation in scientific defense circles, including among legends I got to know, such as Hans Bethe and Edward Teller.

The MX missile saga infused me with a deep fascination with the problems of international security—an interest that was entirely new to me. I had not previously been interested much in public affairs; I hadn't studied them or participated in student politics at Yale or Oxford. But the seriousness of the Cold War's dangers could not be ignored. I decided I had to change careers. I also flattered myself into believing that the two poles of my training—physics and history—might come together in the quest to manage the dangers of the Cold War.

Into the Maelstrom: The War over Star Wars

Believing I might have something unique to contribute, I decided I should go to the place where America's Cold War efforts were run: the Pentagon. I joined the systems analysis department in the Office of the Secretary of Defense, the fabled shop where Bob McNamara's "whiz kids" were once employed. I was hired as a "science advisor" under a so-called schedule B-9 appointment, a federal job category created after the Soviet launch of the Sputnik satellite as a way of making it easier for the government to hire technology experts for high-priority programs. My job covered strategic nuclear forces, strategic defenses including missile defenses, space and intelligence systems, command-and-control systems, and nuclear weapons. I could easily understand these technologies and some of the policy issues that arose.

For the first time, I had an office in the fabled Pentagon building. Its layout is quite simple: five concentric pentagonal rings, labeled from E on the outside to A on the inside. The face of the E ring on the river side, overlooking the Potomac, has a beautiful view of the skyline of downtown Washington and is coveted real estate. The Secretary of Defense and his principal subordinates are housed on the third floor. Just down the hallway hang portraits of all the secretaries of defense—the twenty-four who preceded me, and now mine, the twenty-fifth. (One of the few laws passed by Congress the year I retired forbade the use of taxpayer money for oil paintings of former cabinet secretaries. So Stephanie commissioned Mark Adams, a friend of ours who's a fine portrait painter, to do mine, and my successor, Jim Mattis, honored me with a gracious ceremony in the Pentagon auditorium on the day it was officially installed.)

As with so much in the DOD, tradition and protocol dictate many details of the layout of the Pentagon. Because it's the oldest service, the Army gets a nice piece of real estate right down the hall from the SecDef's office. Then comes the Navy, founded after the Army. The Air Force came along too late, I suppose, to get third-floor real estate, but it did get the fourth-floor E ring on the river side, which puts it right above the SecDef's office—not a bad deal. On the second floor, immediately below the secretary's office, are the chairman of the Joint Chiefs and the Joint Staff.

Over the years, I got to know every corner of the Pentagon. I can tell you where the Army's command-and-control office is, where secret bombers are designed, and where the National Military Command Center is. I soon learned how long it would take a visitor to reach my office from a starting point anywhere else in the vast building. When I was undersecretary, I would sometimes work with a senior Army acquisition executive whose office was on the opposite side of the Pentagon from mine. Every time he showed up in my office, he was panting and covered in sweat. My staff was genuinely concerned that he might one day arrive and collapse with a heart attack.

I'm fortunate enough to remember the "old Pentagon," which had a lot more character than today's version. When I first worked there, it still had the smell of old paint and stale cigarette smoke it must have had since World War II (smoking was still permitted in my earliest days there). In those days before email, messages were delivered by hordes of couriers pushing carts filled with packages labeled "confidential," "secret," and "top secret." A remnant of the huge stenographic pool that had helped fill the building during the war were the wondrously sized bathrooms. Those old men's rooms boasted fifteen stalls down one long wall and fifteen urinals down the other, with eight sinks for washing up. All this was done away with when the Pentagon was renovated after 9/11. Now the men's rooms have two stalls and two urinals each, and the women's rooms are not much different.

Also after 9/11, the building was secured. During my first job there, I'd leave the door to my office open all day (and Ruth, the secretary, would hang a wreath on it at Christmastime). In summer, I could fling the window open and hear the birds chirping outside. Today the doors all have coded locks and electromagnetic shielding to make them impervious to electronic surveillance, and the windows are blast-resistant and bulletproof, since an amazing number of enterprising citizens take rifle shots at the building from the nearby highways.

Still, some vestiges of the old Pentagon remain. Much of the furniture still dates from World War II: big leather chairs with brass tacks on them, which are hot, sticky, and uncomfortable. There's a picture of me in my office as SecDef that you can compare with a similar shot of Bob McNamara from half a century earlier. We're sitting behind the same desk (Jack Pershing's) with the same big bank of secure phones on the carved table behind us, and the lamps and pictures and everything else are in exactly the same places.

I have to admit that I love the Pentagon, warts and all. During my years there, I enjoyed getting a little exercise by strolling the miles of corridors and greeting some of the thousands of employees, many of whom I'd gotten to know. And the building has just the right balance of proximity to—and necessary distance from—the fervid political scrum of downtown Washington.

By contrast, I never understood how anybody could stand to work in the White House. It's a rabbit warren, crowded and close. There's nowhere to stretch your legs except the parking lot outside the West Wing—unless you're the president, who has his own lawn to walk on. Honestly, I don't know what I would have done if I did work there.

In any case, I enjoyed my first Pentagon job and actually liked working at what we denizens all called "ground zero"—a bit of black humor that captured the spirit of the time. However, I was pretty far down in the bureaucracy, and in time I began to feel stifled by it. I began to wonder whether there was any way I could combine my first career, academics, with my second, international security affairs. The Massachusetts Institute of Technology and Harvard were two places where that seemed possible, and I ended up spending time at both. After a two-year stint at MIT (1982–1984), I moved to Harvard's John F. Kennedy School of Government in 1984, where I would remain for the next nine years. Harvard provided me with a great opportunity to think and write about technology and world affairs, to teach students to do things better than their parents' generation had, and, on occasion, to illuminate and influence policy.

One such occasion arose during my time at MIT, when I became embroiled in a technological debate that would prove to be more significant and even more contentious than the MX missile issue. This was the battle over President Reagan's Strategic Defense Initiative, often referred to as Star Wars—the idea of using space-based weapons such as lasers, particle beams, or other exotic technologies to shoot down attacking missiles.

Reagan had been a fan of missile defense dating back to the 1960s, when support for other types of missile defense had become a staple of a certain largely, but not exclusively, Republican part of the defense establishment. Now, as president, he had developed an enthusiasm for the Star Wars concept because of his admirable repugnance for nuclear weapons— an attitude he has shared with many American presidents.

Reagan's desire to develop a foolproof defense against nuclear weapons and so render them useless was completely understandable. Unfortunately, no one had yet figured out how to do this. Missile defense had been studied for many years by the defense community, including by me. Billions had been spent on it. It had proved to be one of the most difficult military missions of all, and thus far none of the systems devised were capable of blunting the effects of a nuclear onslaught.

Nonetheless, Reagan was a true believer in the potential of Star Wars to protect America from the Soviet Union's nuclear weapons—then numbered in the tens of thousands, and multiplying rapidly. Because I'd developed significant expertise regarding missile defense, I was asked to conduct a study of the Stars Wars concept for the Congressional Office of Technology Assessment, this time commuting from Cambridge, Massachusetts.

I agreed to do it, and I embarked on a research project that lasted about a year, spending much of my time back in Washington, in the Pentagon, or at various defense laboratories and contractors in the Washington area or around the country. I studied the range of possible technologies for space-based missile defense: chemical lasers, excimer lasers, X-ray lasers, free-electron lasers, and nonlaser Star Wars approaches like neutral-particle beams fired from big battle stations in space.

I found that while missile defenses might serve some specialized purposes, such as defending American missiles, there was no reasonable prospect of using Star Wars to defend the country or its population as a whole. There were several reasons for this.

First, none of the laser or other technologies had reached the point of maturity and power that would enable them to shoot down ascending missiles from the Soviet Union, nor were they anywhere close to achieving such power. I couldn't predict whether or when such maturity would be achieved, but it would certainly take a long time. It has not happened to this day, almost forty years later.

Second, I pointed out that even lasers with adequate power would not constitute a foolproof defense. For one thing, the lasers would have to be positioned in space over the Soviet Union as a nuclear war began. This meant the Soviets would dedicate energy and resources to attacking the satellite battle stations containing the lasers, which would be extremely vulnerable. After all, space has no terrain, and satellites can scarcely be outfitted with armoring or shielding of any significance. Once the orbiting laser stations had been destroyed or disabled, the Soviets would be free to attack the United States with impunity.

Finally, even if these difficulties could be overcome, the cost would represent another enormous obstacle. Since satellites must orbit the earth to avoid falling to the planet's surface, only the satellites in the orbital arc directly over the Soviet Union at the moment of an attack would be able to participate in the defense. This meant that we'd have to build a whole ring of satellites to be sure of having one or two in the right position at the right time. What's more, every time the Soviet Union added missiles, we would have to add entire rings of additional satellites to make sure there were enough to shoot down all the missiles. In a cost-based competition, they could ultimately exhaust us.

So for both technological and systemic reasons, the Star Wars missile defense scheme was pure fantasy.

I set to work writing up these conclusions in a fairly sober and straightforward fashion. Within the scientific and technological community, there was substantial consensus that my analysis was correct. But on March 23, 1983, as I was preparing the final version of my report, President Reagan went out and dramatically announced his full commitment to Star Wars. In a live broadcast from the Oval Office, Reagan asked:

> What if free people could live secure in the knowledge that their security did not rest upon the threat of instant U.S. retaliation to deter a Soviet attack, that we could intercept and destroy strategic ballistic missiles before they reached our own soil or that of our allies?
>
> I know this is a formidable, technical task, one that may not be accomplished before the end of this century. Yet, current technology has attained a level of sophistication where it's reasonable for us to begin this effort. It will take years, probably decades of effort on many fronts. There will be failures and setbacks, just as there will be successes and breakthroughs. And as we proceed, we must remain constant in preserving the nuclear deterrent and maintaining a solid capability for flexible response. But isn't it worth every investment necessary to free the world from the threat of nuclear war? We know it is.

Reagan went on to declare, "I call upon the scientific community in our country, those who gave us nuclear weapons, to turn their great talents now to the cause of mankind and world peace, to give us the means of rendering these nuclear weapons impotent and obsolete."

Reagan's full-throated embrace of Star Wars meant that I was on course for a head-to-head collision with the president of the United States. For a young and little-known physicist still in the early stages of a career in and around government, this was a dismaying prospect. I discovered that being embroiled in intense political controversy is a good way of getting one's name and work known quickly—for better and for worse.

My report, titled *Directed Energy Missile Defense in Space*, was officially released on April 24, 1984. Its key sentence, frequently quoted in news coverage, described the prospects for success of a system of space-based missile defense as "so remote that it should not serve as the basis of public expectation or national policy."

Among critics of Star Wars, of course, the report made me something of a darling. But being the first observer with the audacity to publicly declare that the emperor had no clothes did not make me popular with the White House or with the allies and supporters of President Reagan, including leaders at Caspar Weinberger's Pentagon. They naturally wanted to defend the president's favorite military initiative. But because I had myself been a member of the Defense Department team shortly before, they couldn't say that I didn't know what I was talking about or that my information about Star Wars was inaccurate. So they did what members of a political tribe always do when confronted with an unwelcome message that is difficult to refute: they set about attacking the messenger.

Officials at the Pentagon and the White House began to criticize me in the press. This was my first full-on exposure to the rough edges of public life. Since I was the sole author of the study (not a member of a team, as in the MX basing project), I was completely exposed. And I was bewildered by the onslaught. I was absolutely confident in my scientific analysis, and I knew that the scientific community overwhelmingly agreed with it—so I couldn't understand why there could be public controversy about it. I didn't then understand that when a president says something, however wild, plenty of people will echo and support it, and treat dissent as something close to treason.

The defenders of Star Wars tried two specific paths of attack. The first was to accuse me of having divulged classified information—or at least to strongly imply that this was the case. For example, the conservative columnists Rowland Evans and Robert Novak described my report as the work of an "M.I.T. professor" who had been given "carte blanche to prowl the most secret nuclear labs" in an effort "to bring down the Star Wars program." This was preposterous, since the Army had reviewed my draft report and made the redactions needed to produce an unclassified report. This meant that no legal case could be made against me, but the smears in the press still rankled.

The more serious attack was an effort to undermine me and the quality of my scientific analysis. Weinberger's Pentagon wrote a lengthy and detailed chapter-by-chapter rebuttal of my study. They sent it to Congress and demanded that my analysis be withdrawn on the grounds that it was technically flawed, citing their own rebuttal as evidence. That would have truly left me high and dry.

But I wrote my own rebuttal to the Pentagon's attack, which turned out to be easy, because almost every point in it was stupid. Still the verbal assaults on me continued. The whole experience made me exceedingly nervous. I was afraid that my career in physics and in defense circles was destroyed before it had even started.

In the midst of all this, I received a phone call one night that I will always remember.

The call was from Michael May, a scientist I knew, a former director of Lawrence Livermore National Laboratory, the second bomb-design laboratory (after Los Alamos) founded by Edward Teller. The Livermore lab was dominated by technical cheerleaders for Star Wars, which made the message this scientist delivered to me both unexpected and enormously welcome.

"We both know that your report on Star Wars is supported by just about everybody in the scientific community," May said. "I just want to let you know that I'm thinking about you, because I know how tough things must be for you right now. Hang in there, Ash."

It was just a phone call, but receiving it at that difficult moment did wonders for my morale.

Then the leaders in Congress took an important step. They commissioned a review of my work, naming a three-person panel of distinguished experts to study the controversy and advise the Congressional Office of Technology Assessment. The panel was led by Professor Charles H. Townes, one of the inventors of the laser, who was also a close friend and big supporter of Ronald Reagan's.

A second member was Bill Perry, who had been the weapons czar in the Pentagon during the Carter administration and was most well known for beginning the stealth aircraft programs. He would later become Bill Clinton's deputy secretary of defense and Secretary of Defense, thus being the first person to occupy each of the top three positions in the Pentagon (a distinction I would later share with him). At the time, I didn't know Bill Perry well, but he later became a mentor of mine as well as a close friend.

The third member of the panel was General Glenn Kent (Retired), who was one of the brilliant leaders of the scientific cadre at Air Force Systems Command during its heyday in the Cold War. Thus, the panel included representation from the scientific and military communities as well as from both political parties. The members were provided with my original report, the Pentagon's response, and my rebuttal, together with whatever classified information they required or requested to carry out the review.

Their review was swift and decisive. John H. Gibbons, director of the Congressional Office of Technology Assessment, summarized its key findings succinctly in a letter addressed to a Pentagon official who had demanded that my report be "withdrawn"—meaning repudiated:

> On the basis of the responses I have received from these reviewers [i.e., Townes, Perry, and Kent], I have concluded that:
>
> 1. There are no technical errors or flawed assumptions that would seriously mislead either a lay or a technical reader.
> 2. The Background Paper [my report] neither describes nor misrepresents the goals of the SDI as such. It lists a number of possible goals for strategic defense, and correctly comments that some of these would be more difficult to attain than others.
> 3. While disagreements about details, analytical approaches, or the chances for success are inevitable in a complex subject where so much research remains to be done, the paper is a lucid, useful and generally reliable introduction to its subject.
>
> Therefore, I do not believe it appropriate to withdraw the paper.

As soon as this review was issued, the Pentagon fell silent, and the issue was effectively dropped completely overnight. The Defense Department and the Reagan administration ultimately began speaking publicly about much more modest goals for missile defense, tacitly acknowledging that the grandiose dream of rendering nuclear weapons ineffective had never been based in reality.

Even more than the MX basing debate, the Star Wars controversy brought home to me some of the most difficult realities of technological decision-making in a political environment. The whole experience left me with a vivid sense of how superficial and even dishonest the "analysis" behind important public policies can be. My background was in the abstract world of physics, where the disinterested pursuit of truth for its own sake is taken for granted—at least as an ideal. The world of technology (specifically defense technology), where scientific findings are applied to practical problems, is much messier. As soon as I weighed in with my negative assessment of Star Wars, an entire team of opinion shapers, representing the political arms of one of the two dominant political parties in Washington, swung into action against me, with no apparent concern for the scientific merits of my argument. Their opposition appeared to be driven chiefly by the desire to secure a political victory for their team rather than by an informed concern for the future of their country. The fact that investing in space-based laser defense would have been a vast waste of money that might even contribute to a dangerous destabilization of the global nuclear balance didn't deter them from marshaling their specious arguments against me. The only thing that mattered was winning the political battle.

For me as a scientist, it was disheartening to observe the gulf between the disinterested dedication to truth that I'd been trained to believe in and the single-minded quest for political victory that dominated Washington.

On the other hand, the end of the Star Wars story was reassuring. When the select panel of experts whose impartiality and expertise were unimpeachable weighed in, both sides of the controversy accepted their verdict. And I soon found myself befriended by a number of members of the defense establishment from both parties.

James Schlesinger, who served as SecDef and CIA director under Presidents Nixon and Ford as well as Secretary of Energy under President Carter, invited me to join him as a member of the board of the MITRE Corporation, a nonprofit research firm that does work for the federal government. MITRE built the Integrated Air Defense System beginning in the 1950s, and then helped design the radar planes that played a big role in Operation Desert Storm (the first Gulf War, 1990–1991), advanced communications systems and satellites, and much more.

I was by far the youngest member on this distinguished board, which included Brent Scowcroft, Bill Perry, John Deutch, and other famous names. We went on field visits to military facilities around the United States, a real eye-opener for me and an opportunity to get to know these great figures. Jim did a lot for me: he'd spotted me, sensed my potential, and taken a liking to me. I've tried to do the same thing by paying forward to the next generation myself.

I'll never forget how, the night after I was confirmed as assistant secretary, this great national leader drove out to my little brick rental house in Arlington, Virginia, to congratulate me. I was at the dinner table with our kids, then two and five years old, when in strode big Jim to shake my hand. What a boost that was for me

Years later, in 2014, I got a call from one of Jim's devoted daughters. She told me that he was in Johns Hopkins Hospital—not for the first time—and suggested that I call him to cheer him up. I said, "Of course," but then boarded an airplane to Europe for a three-day trip, thinking I could call Jim when I got back. He died while I was in Europe. It's a moment I can never get back. I've learned that when people important to you become old and sick, every minute with them matters. It still breaks my heart that Jim didn't get to see me as SecDef.

Another member of the defense establishment who befriended me at this time was Brent Scowcroft, national security advisor to President Ford and to President George H. W. Bush. Scowcroft instituted the system, still in use, of a hierarchy of deliberative meetings with the National Security Council (NSC) chaired by the president and the cabinet members, and cascading to the deputy secretaries, then to assistant secretaries in interagency working groups, and so forth on down. This hierarchical arrangement is very important to the efficient workings of White Houses, which are typically run by close political associates of the president who often lack policy experience. It still exists in Trump's White House, though it's not clear that he pays any attention to it. Brent was an infinitely patient listener and an inclusive convener, as demonstrated by his ability to keep Bush's senior national security team—a collection of strong egos—in close alignment.

Back in the 1980s, Brent invited me to join the Aspen Strategy Group, where senior figures in national security assemble every summer. I got to know leaders in defense, foreign policy, and business from both parties (including my friend and later boss, Bob Gates) in a setting where we could have open, off-the-record conversations, then spend afternoons and evenings hiking and taking meals together. Like the National Security Council itself, it's a symbol of civility and bipartisanship, two qualities in short supply today. Brent is now living in northern Virginia and is currently too ill to take visitors, though I keep making the offer.

A third close connection of mine that dates to this period is with Bill Perry. As I'll describe later, Bill and I served together in the Clinton administration. Later, Bill invited me to be a partner in an investment firm he founded called Global Technology Partners. I didn't like being an investment banker and was only moderately successful, but in my five years in the job I was able to set aside enough money to buy a house in Maine and finance the educations of my two kids.

When Bill sought an academic appointment at Stanford University and needed an established academic leader (as I was by then) to vouch for his worthiness to join the guild, I was able to return the favor. I had a senior position at Harvard at the time, and we eventually established a partnership between our two universities known as the Preventive Defense Project. This enabled us to work together almost every day on a wide variety of projects around the world. Bill and I became so close that, when I got remarried, Bill stood in for my father, who had passed away. Bill and I still speak about once a week.

The opportunity to launch lifelong friendships like these made the painful moments of the Star Wars controversy more than worthwhile. I'd had my first brush with some of the worst aspects of political infighting—but also an inspiring taste of vindication for the truth, with the support of good people from both sides of the aisle.

Master of Cold War Strategy: Working for Paul Nitze

In the mid-1980s, while at Harvard, I was approached by the legendary Paul Nitze, who was aware of my knowledge and independence in the Star Wars matter. Originally an investment banker, Nitze was part of the old generation of Wall Street leaders who joined the World War II effort on the financial and economic side, even as the scientific giants of Harvard University, MIT, Columbia University, and others had led the war effort on the technological front. He served as a Pentagon official through World War II and well into the Truman administration. In 1950, he was the principal author of NSC-68, a secret memo urging a huge military buildup as part of the effort to deter aggression by the Soviet Union, which came to be one of the pillars of America's Cold War strategy. Later, during the Eisenhower administration, he served as president of the Foreign Service Educational Foundation while concurrently serving as an associate at the Washington Center of Foreign Policy Research and the School of Advanced International Studies (SAIS) at Johns Hopkins University.

Nitze was a staunch anti-communist. He consistently argued against major arms control agreements, especially during the Carter administration. He favored the dramatic buildup of U.S. nuclear forces that we associate with the Reagan administration but that, in fact, had begun during the Carter administration. Reagan then appointed Paul Nitze to be his senior representative for arms control negotiations with the Soviet Union.

In that role, one of the key issues Nitze had to grapple with was the charge by the Soviet Union, supported by many U.S. arms control experts, that Reagan's Strategic Defense Initiative would constitute a violation of the 1972 Antiballistic Missile (ABM) Treaty, which effectively placed limits on the development of missile defenses. His goal was to try to keep open the arms control door while also creating some room for scientists to pursue the Strategic Defense Initiative. This meant defining the line between research, which the ABM Treaty allowed, and development, which was forbidden. Nitze asked me to join his team as a part-time advisor, to help him discern where this line should be drawn.

Thus began a second phase of commuting to Washington, where I would stay in a small hotel across the street from the State Department while researching the issues that Nitze was concerned about. His office was on the fabled seventh floor, right around the corner from Secretary of State George Shultz, and he arranged for me to have a small working space in his suite. I found that Nitze was a fascinating man who lived up to his legendary reputation. He was impeccably polite, polished, extremely smart, and very open to information, with which I began to ply him.

I also used to travel for briefings to Nitze's summer home in Northeast Harbor, Maine, where he summered near Caspar Weinberger and Zbigniew Brzezinski, who had been Carter's national security advisor. During our meetings there, Nitze would serve lunch, which invariably consisted of a few leaves of lettuce with olive oil dressing, a bowl of clear broth with three or four grilled scallops floating in it, and a glass of iced tea with a sprig of mint. This was probably a healthy repast for a slender man in his eighties, but nowhere near enough for a young man in his twenties. The first time I went, I was starving by the time he dropped me off late in the day at Bar Harbor airport. On future trips, I learned my lesson: When I got to Boston's Logan airport to change planes, I would buy a hamburger and stick it in my briefcase alongside the top-secret documents. (I had what's called a courier pass, which authorized me to have and transport classified materials.) After Nitze dropped me off at the airport in the afternoon, I would open the briefcase and eat my second lunch.

Nitze also sent me on a couple of foreign missions. Once I traveled to Berlin—still divided by the famous wall—where I went through the legendary Checkpoint Charlie, trailed everywhere by intelligence officials of the East German Stasi, to meet with Soviet leaders.

Another time, I went to Moscow to investigate a Soviet satellite under construction that the super-hawkish Defense Intelligence Agency said might have been a prototype for a space-based laser weapon. The

Russians claimed that it was a scientific satellite designed to study Phobos, one of the moons of Mars. I traveled there accompanied by Brent Scowcroft and Edward C. Meyer (known as "Shy"), the former chief of staff of the Army. My mission was to inspect the satellite and offer my scientific judgment as to its real purpose.

Late one dark winter afternoon, I went out to one of the facilities of the Soviet space program just outside Moscow, was gowned and masked, and led into a clean room where the Phobos probe satellite sat. It matched the description of our intelligence reporting on the outside, but I needed to examine its technical characteristics.

Roald Sagdeev, the director of the Soviet space program, and his assistants were very helpful in going through the technical details of the satellite with me. It had a laser that was quite bright but gave out only billionth-of-a-second pulses—suitable for ionizing some molecules from the surface of Phobos for research purposes, but not strong enough to burn a hole in anything. I concluded that the satellite was harmless as a weapons system, which I was able to go back and report to Nitze.

Sagdeev himself proved to be a wonderful, jovial, very intelligent man. Later that decade, in the Gorbachev era, he and a few other scientists from the Russian Academy of Sciences became key interlocutors of the West in matters of arms control as well as key responders to their own Chernobyl reactor accident. I became good friends with Roald over the years. Ultimately, he immigrated to the United States, became a professor at the University of Maryland, and married Susan Eisenhower, the granddaughter of Dwight Eisenhower. Susan was also a friend of mine and an expert Sovietologist.

Looking back on this episode in my career, I find it a fascinating slice of life from a time when America's defense establishment—like much of Washington—was a far more collegial and bipartisan place than it is today. Coming from the world of theoretical physics, I wasn't originally associated with either the Democratic or Republican parties, still less with either doctrinaire liberalism or conservatism. However, because I'd authored a report that had seriously—and effectively—challenged the conceptual underpinnings of a project embraced by a Republican president, by the mid-1980s I'd been labeled in some eyes as a member of the Democratic camp.

Yet despite all this, Paul Nitze—a dyed-in-the-wool Republican often regarded as a classic Cold War hawk—had no hesitation about seeking my advice on scientific and technical issues about which he knew I was an expert. Nor did others working in the Pentagon during the Reagan administration challenge my presence at Nitze's side, warn against my malign influence, or try to "purge" me and my views.

Instead, the general assumptions were that real expertise is valuable and important; that people of good faith who disagree on some issues can work together productively on others; and that the national interests of the United States would, of course, take precedence over any purely partisan or ideological conflicts that might arise among individuals.

From the vantage point of 2019, those times seem almost idyllic.

Solving the Loose-Nukes Dilemma: The Nunn-Lugar Program

In 1991, with the unraveling of Stalin's empire, we were seeing something unprecedented: the disintegration of a nuclear power. Those worried about the danger of nuclear weapons had heretofore been concerned either with a nuclear exchange—deliberate or resulting from miscalculation during a superpower crisis—or with the spread of nuclear weapons to other governments. From these two traditional concerns had sprung, respectively, arms control agreements like the Strategic Arms Limitation Talks (SALT) and the Strategic Arms Reduction Treaties (START), and the Nuclear Nonproliferation Treaty and a system of export controls on nuclear technology. Some farsighted Americans, beginning in the Eisenhower administration, had also worried about a loss of control of nuclear weapons to a few madmen or a crazy general, as portrayed in the movie *Dr. Strangelove.* From this third concern had sprung a system of codes and locks on U.S. (and, we later learned, Soviet) nuclear weapons to prevent their unauthorized or accidental use.

No one in the atomic age had yet had to face the prospect of an entire continent strewn with nuclear weapons undergoing a convulsive social and political revolution. But that's what was happening in the summer of 1991. At hundreds of locations over the vast area from the West German border to Vladivostok, the makings of some 150,000 Hiroshimas—supplies of highly enriched uranium and plutonium, along with fully assembled bombs of all types—had been deployed by the Soviet state.

My Harvard colleagues and I wrote a detailed study of this unprecedented problem and what to do about it called *Soviet Nuclear Fission: Control of the Nuclear Arsenal in a Disintegrating Soviet Union.* The recommendation we made at the end of that volume was that the U.S. government should create a program offering cooperation and assistance to the fragments of the Soviet Union to make sure the Soviet nuclear legacy was not abused. Our study laid out such a program in detail. We said it should cover weapons and fissile materials, factories and technology, military and scientific personnel—in short, the entire Soviet nuclear establishment.

The administration of George H. W. Bush did not embrace the idea. Some leaders in the State Department and the National Security Council could see its importance, but the Defense Department, then led by Dick Cheney, Paul Wolfowitz, Scooter Libby, and Steve Hadley, was cool to the idea. I remember Don Atwood, Cheney's deputy secretary of defense, responding to our proposal with the remark, "Guys, we just spent fifty years trying to make these people go broke. Why ever would we help them now?"

The more farsighted branch of the U.S. government on this issue turned out to be Congress. Senators Sam Nunn (D-GA) and Richard Lugar (R-IN) had long been concerned with defense matters, including the nuclear threat. They also knew how to overcome the partisan barriers that so often limit the impact of Congress.

The matchmakers who brought the ideas of the Harvard study together with the authority and skill of Nunn and Lugar were Bill Perry and David Hamburg, president of the Carnegie Corporation of New York.

On November 19, 1991, Hamburg invited me and Bill Perry, along with our colleague John Steinbruner of the Brookings Institution, to a meeting in Senator Nunn's office. Dick Lugar participated as well. I briefed the senators on the Harvard study, and we were pleased to learn that Senators Nunn and Lugar and their staff members Robert Bell, Ken Myers, and Richard Combs had been working on a similar scheme for joint action to control the "loose nukes" from the breakup of the USSR.

It was one of those rare, serendipitous moments when the right people come together at the right time to make history happen. When our formal meeting ended, I stayed behind with Bell, Myers, and Combs to begin drafting what would become known as the Nunn-Lugar legislation.

Two days later, Nunn and Lugar convened a bipartisan group of senators at a working breakfast, and they asked me to brief them on my plan. Nunn and Lugar then asked their colleagues to support legislation that would authorize the Pentagon to initiate U.S.-funded assistance to stem the loose-nukes problem. The senators in attendance responded favorably. Not all their support was motivated strictly by the problem at hand; some was obtained through horse trading of the kind that most citizens have come to regard as unseemly, but which has played a crucial role in greasing the wheels of democracy for generations. (I'll never reveal the details of the negotiation session, having enjoyed the rare privilege of witnessing it in return for a vow of secrecy.)

On November 28, 1991, just nine days after the legislation had been drafted in Lugar's office, the Nunn-Lugar amendment to the annual defense bill passed the Senate by a vote of 86 to 8. Les Aspin gathered the necessary support in the House of Representatives, and the legislation passed the House shortly thereafter on a voice vote.

In March 1992, after the legislation had gone into effect, I joined Senators Nunn, Lugar, John Warner (R-VA), and Jeff Bingaman (D-NM), as well as David Hamburg and staffers Bell, Myers, and Combs, on a trip to examine the problem firsthand. By then, we were visiting not the Soviet Union but the newly independent states of Russia and Ukraine. Leaders in the new states were eager to learn more about the program and to meet the two senators whose names were quickly becoming known throughout the "nuclear archipelago" of the former USSR.

This was a memorable trip. Communism had already begun to crumble, and Moscow was filled with small street markets selling goods at amazing prices. John Warner proved himself an inveterate shopper, taking every moment between important meetings with Kremlin leaders to browse the stalls. I soon learned why. It turned out that this man who'd once been married to Elizabeth Taylor was currently dating the TV journalist Barbara Walters, and he was buying little keepsakes to present to her when he returned home. Later, when our plane stopped to refuel in Shannon, Ireland, John insisted that we all catch a bus to a favorite Irish pub he knew where he treated us to a Guinness and some salmon and oatcakes. I developed a soft spot for John Warner that remains to this day.

Ten months later, Bill Clinton became president, and it was on his watch that the principal successes of Nunn-Lugar were achieved—the denuclearization of Ukraine, Kazakhstan, and Belarus, and the stabilizing of the Russian military and military-industrial-nuclear complex during a high-risk period of drastic downsizing and political turmoil. Bill Perry and I both took Pentagon jobs in the Clinton administration—Perry as deputy secretary of defense and then Secretary of Defense, and me as assistant secretary of defense with specific responsibility for the Nunn-Lugar program.

But implementing the Nunn-Lugar vision was easier said than done. The staff structure I inherited, which would be responsible for spearheading implementation, had a branch that targeted the Soviet Union and another that had negotiated arms control agreements with the Soviet Union. But no one had ever *assisted* our Russian adversaries, which meant that a whole new organization had to be set up for Nunn-Lugar.

The key officials in the new organization were Gloria Duffy, Susan Koch, Laura Holgate, and the policy chief for the region, Elizabeth Sherwood. They set about crafting a set of objectives and identifying facilities and officials in the new countries that could serve as our working partners. They made scores of visits to the former Soviet Union, frequently to remote sites under very difficult conditions. They all happened to be women, which startled the disbelieving generals in Moscow, Kiev, Minsk, and Almaty. It took a while for them to realize that these capable women really did carry the authority of the Secretary of Defense.

Crafting objectives for Nunn-Lugar that we could share with our partners in the former Soviet Union necessitated some lengthy negotiations. The Russians were suspicious about the real objectives of their American interlocutors, and they were reluctant to expose closely guarded military secrets to their former archenemies. They were also intent on receiving not just help in dismantling weapons but also social assistance for their people—understandably so, since the shutdown of a large portion of the Russian nuclear arsenal would put thousands of soldiers, scientists, engineers, and support personnel out of work.

This created another set of complications. We insisted that the assistance we would provide had to be delivered "in kind" rather than in cash, which we feared might disappear amid the shrinking economies and growing crime in what were, after all, countries in profound social revolution. Onerous audits and inspections were required by the Pentagon legal office. Pentagon lawyers were terrified at the prospect that some of the taxpayers' money might be misspent; one of them warned me, "If any of this cash goes astray, we're all going to spend the rest of our lives testifying about it."

As a result of these restrictions, the Pentagon's ponderous acquisition bureaucracy now had to carry out multimillion-dollar engineering projects in places like Pervomaysk, Ukraine; Engels, Russia; and Semipalatinsk, Kazakhstan—places where U.S. industry had never before done business.

Congress sometimes also made implementation difficult. The original Nunn-Lugar legislation did not actually appropriate money from the U.S. Treasury; it only authorized the SecDef to take money from other Pentagon programs and "reprogram" it to Nunn-Lugar. One can easily imagine the lack of enthusiasm for the Nunn-Lugar program within the Pentagon bureaucracy when it required reallocating funds from other projects. Therefore, the first budget DOD submitted after we took office in 1993 contained a dedicated appropriation for Nunn-Lugar.

However, now that real money was being requested to fund Nunn-Lugar, the ambivalence of many members of Congress became apparent. Some found the very notion of providing assistance to the former Soviet enemy unfathomable. Others balked at paying for the social programs that were essential to getting the job done—for example, housing for officers whose bases were being closed and defense-conversion assistance for weapons factories. Others clung to the idea that the Pentagon's job was simply to fight and that its money should be spent only on tanks, planes, and ships. And a few others seemed to assume that, with the Cold War now over, the nuclear dangers of that era would simply disappear by themselves—an impression heightened by the lack of media attention to the loose-nukes danger.

We argued that Nunn-Lugar was "defense by other means." Its contribution to U.S. security was at least as great as that of any other program in the defense budget. What's more, the Department of Defense was the correct agency to manage the program because we had the expertise to dismantle weapons and to work with our counterparts in the former Soviet countries.

In the end, we secured the funding needed, and the Nunn-Lugar program moved into high gear.

The technical challenges were enormous. Nuclear command and control is not a purely technical system. It is a *human* system, which means it cannot be immune to the social change around it. Every commander and unit in possession of any nuclear weapons—and the Soviet Union had fabricated hundreds of thousands of them—could get physical custody of the weapons, in most cases could detonate them, and in virtually all cases could take them apart and sell the fissile material to a terrorist or proliferator.

This meant that we needed the cooperation of literally thousands of people to carry out Nunn-Lugar properly. All these far-flung weapons would need to be collected at central locations and put in secure facilities where they could not fall victim to what was essentially a looming civil war across the continent. Further complications included the tons of highly enriched uranium and weapons-grade plutonium the Soviets had accumulated over the years; the industrial facilities and sophisticated laboratories in which these materials had been made; and the ballistic missiles, bombers, submarines, and other delivery vehicles scattered throughout the region.

The results of the program were better than I'd dared to hope. All nuclear weapons were eliminated from the non-Russian successor states to the Soviet Union, averting what would have been the biggest and most dangerous burst of proliferation in the history of the atomic age. Thousands of nuclear weapons targeting the U.S. were dismantled, along with hundreds of bombers, missiles, submarines and submarine missile launchers, and other delivery systems. Hundreds of tons of fissile materials have been secured in safer conditions, and thousands of former weapons scientists are now employed in peaceful projects. And even today, the Cooperative Threat Reduction Program—the successor to Nunn-Lugar, now housed in the State Department—continues to support projects to secure weapons of mass destruction (including biological and chemical weapons), working with partner nations in the former Soviet Union and elsewhere.

None of these successes would have been possible without the inspired support of Bill Perry and of President Clinton, who never failed to push the issue of nuclear safety when meeting with Boris Yeltsin. At two Clinton-Yeltsin summits I attended—one in the Kremlin and one in Hyde Park, New York—Clinton bypassed his advisors, who were focused on the political management of the North Atlantic Treaty Organization (NATO) enlargement, to raise issues of Nunn-Lugar implementation with an ailing and unpredictable Yeltsin. Vice President Al Gore, working with his counterpart, the Russian Prime Minister Viktor Chernomyrdin, showed the same steady attention to the issue of nuclear safety.

The peaceful disintegration of an empire that commanded half the world for half a century was a major achievement for humankind, and historians in ages to come will note the disasters that might have been which were averted through Nunn-Lugar. The clarity of vision and thoroughness of follow-through of the Nunn-Lugar program during the Clinton years shines brightly as an example of the U.S. government, executive and legislative branches alike, serving this nation's and the world's deepest security interests. It is an achievement of President Clinton's that does not receive the credit it deserves.

My work on the MX missile basing debate, the Star Wars controversy, and the Nunn-Lugar program exposed me to some of the political crosscurrents that inevitably impact national policies. It became clear to me that, at times, private interests as well as ideological forces can shape and even distort debates that ought to be focused on factual issues and the long-term welfare of the American people. Yet I came away from these experiences strengthened, not weakened, in my resolve to contribute my knowledge and expertise to public policy in scientific matters. In my career since then, I haven't hesitated to make the tough calls about defense-technology matters, regardless of political pressures. I've had to stand up to pressures from members of Congress, powerful lobbyists, and corporate CEOs, and sometimes from the administrations I've served—up to and including the president. It's not easy to do.

But the truth matters—and in most cases, in the long run, the truth wins out. At least, that has generally been the case in my public career until now. In times of extreme partisan polarization, those in leadership roles may feel tempted to skew their judgments according to what is ideologically correct or politically expedient. It may work for a while—but plans made without due regard for fact generally backfire, reflecting the way reality ultimately takes revenge on those who try to ignore it. That's why we can't afford to lose our faith in truth as our essential compass.

PART 2

MANY HANDS ON THE TILLER

CHAPTER 4

THE WHITE HOUSE IS ON THE LINE: SERVING THE PRESIDENT WHILE SERVING THE NATION

On the morning of Monday, November 24, 2014, my cell phone rang. The glowing letters on the screen announced, "No Caller ID." Most people might assume a salesperson offering carpet-cleaning services or a vacation timeshare was on the line. But for me, as a veteran of the upper levels of life in Washington, D.C., it meant only one thing: the White House was calling.

Of course I took the call. It was Denis McDonough, President Obama's trusted chief of staff. "Hi, Ash," Denis said. "I'm calling about Chuck. He's decided that he's not going to run through the tape at Defense. The president would like to talk to you about taking his place."

Denis's shorthand needed no translation. After twelve years as a Republican senator from Nebraska, Chuck Hagel had been asked by President Obama to replace Leon Panetta as Secretary of Defense. That had been less than two years earlier. Everyone in D.C. had heard that Chuck's tenure at the Pentagon was a bit rocky. Now Chuck had decided to call it quits rather than hang on to the end of the president's second term two years hence—and, unbeknownst to me, my name had surfaced as a likely replacement.

I had conflicting thoughts and reactions. "Denis, this is a surprise," I replied. "And quite an honor. But you know, it's awfully sunny out here in Palo Alto! At this moment, I'm glancing out my window at a cyclist in shorts zipping down the bike path past my back porch. I'm just a short walk from my new office at Stanford. And Stephanie loves it here, too."

The truth is that I had very mixed feelings about the possibility of rejoining the Obama team. There were two years left in the administration. It wouldn't be enough time to finish everything I would want to do at Defense, but it would be enough time to get it all started. That was the appealing part. And I was genuinely honored at the thought of assuming the top job at the department I'd served, in varying capacities, for more than thirty years.

Still, I wondered about the circumstances. Why exactly was Chuck leaving? Did it reflect significant dysfunction in the Obama White House or, more broadly, a toxic environment in Washington? How much would I or any replacement really be able to accomplish?

I gently probed Denis on the background of Chuck's decision, but Denis was vague, saying only that Chuck had been struggling at Defense "for some time." Denis wasn't one to trade in gossip.

I moved on to a second question. "You know I'm not looking for a job," I said. "Is this a serious request? Does it come directly from the president?"

"I wouldn't have called you otherwise," Denis responded. "The president is serious about you. And he wants a face-to-face, not a phone call."

I agreed to fly back east. Two days later, I was ushered into the Oval Office for ninety minutes of conversation alone with President Barack Obama.

The president said he wanted a Secretary of Defense who could help him "at the table," meaning in the White House Situation Room, where the world's most urgent challenges are addressed. When I pressed him on whether he was really looking for a secretary with strategic opinions of his own, he seemed a little offended. "It's like asking me if I still beat my wife!" he replied. (I later came to learn that this was a favorite expression of Obama's when asked a question he felt should answer itself or was otherwise inappropriate.) "Yes, that's exactly what I want," he insisted.

On the flight east, I'd written a list of four issues I wanted to raise with the president: the Middle East, especially the advance of ISIS; the war in Afghanistan; China and the "rebalance" to the Asia-Pacific region, which I regarded as the central strategic issue of the era; and the defense budget, which had been held hostage by partisan gridlock since I'd joined the

Obama administration for a previous stint back in 2009. I wanted to make sure our thinking was aligned on these crucial matters.

When the president asked me whether I had any questions, I named my four big concerns. But before we had a chance to discuss them, the White House scheduler poked her head into the office. "I'm sorry to interrupt, Mr. President," she said, "but it's time for you to go out to the East Lawn to pardon the Thanksgiving turkey."

I asked to take the weekend to confer with Stephanie. The president and I shook hands and agreed to have a follow-up call on Monday.

When I got to my gate at Dulles, Denis called. "The president said your meeting went well," Denis told me. In the months to come, I would realize that this was standard operating procedure for the Obama White House. Late every afternoon, Obama and Denis would meet to download the day before the president went upstairs to be with his family. When I needed to hear about the president's thinking, I would likely hear it from Denis after one of these sessions. Having received this brief bit of feedback, I boarded the plane back to California.

I spent the weekend discussing the job with Stephanie and with a small handful of trusted advisors, especially my longtime mentor Bill Perry and my good friend Bob Gates, two former secretaries of defense. Bob stressed that the president should understand that I had "moved on with my life" and was happy with what I was doing. I decided that, if the president offered me the job on Monday, I would accept it—but that if he seemed to be deliberating among a group of candidates, I would pull out. Neither my interests nor those of the nation would be well served by my becoming SecDef if it turned out that I was the president's second or third choice for the position.

On Monday evening, I was attending a dinner with technology leaders in downtown San Francisco. As time passed and it grew late back on the East Coast, I began to think the call from the White House might not come. Then, around eight p.m.—eleven p.m. in Washington—my cell phone rang.

It was President Obama. He picked up our conversation from Wednesday without missing a beat. "Let me give you my thoughts about the four issues you raised," he said. We spent several minutes reviewing his ideas and his chief concerns about each topic. I was impressed by his responsiveness and by the clarity of his thinking, and, as we talked, I could see that there was no unbridgeable divide between us in any of these areas.

When the president asked me, "Will you take the job?" I replied that I would be honored.

I hurriedly sent Stephanie a text: "It is done."

I didn't realize how ambiguous the message was. Stephanie immediately texted me back: "What does THAT mean?"

"I accepted the job," I replied.

I returned to my dinner, and Steph called Bill Perry with the news. We both knew that without his example and support, I would never have had this opportunity.

By the way, accepting a job offered by the president is *not* a no-brainer—contrary to what you often hear ("If the president offers you a job, you have no choice but to accept"). The truth is that your duty, as a prospective government official, is to serve your country and to serve the president. To do the former, you must stay true to your values, and to do the latter, you must have a reasonable expectation of a good working relationship with the president. Obama's gracious readiness to discuss the four issues I'd raised with him laid to rest any doubts I might have had on either score. I could see that I stood a reasonable chance of being listened to, and there seemed little likelihood of any fundamental clash of values between me and the president, which meant I'd be able to carry out the administration's policies with all my energies and with a clear conscience.

By contrast, I couldn't accept a job offer from someone like President Trump. By no means do I disagree with all his policies. But there would be major differences between us on important issues like Russia, the Middle East, and the importance of alliances. More important, I couldn't support decisions about defense made on sudden impulse. Nor could I disrespect the institution of the DOD by agreeing to hold a grand military parade whose sole purpose would be to stroke the presidential ego. (At this writing, it appears the parade is not going to happen.) Above all, I could not support an administration characterized by repeated acts of offensive behavior like those I would fire an officer for committing—racist remarks, hateful and divisive speech, casual references to sexual assault and adultery, and so on.

In some circumstances, the best way to serve your country is to say no to a presidential appointment. I'm glad that's a choice I've never had to make.

The day after accepting Obama's offer, I began the arduous task of filling out the security clearance forms, financial disclosure documents, and other paperwork required for a government job. I'd done this task multiple times since 1981, but Uncle Sam always insisted I start from scratch every time, including listing the same references who could vouch for me from childhood to the present day. (I assume that the lady who'd lived across the street from me when I was a tyke always said "Ash was such a nice boy" every time the investigative agent returned.)

Thankfully, I had help with all these details from Anita Breckenridge, the president's amazingly efficient deputy chief of staff and longtime confidante, as well as from Bill Perry's capable assistant at Stanford, Deborah Gordon, and two former assistants of mine, Gretchen Bartlett and Julie Park. We spent two days wrangling the forms. Then I flew back to Washington for a secret meeting with the White House counsel's office to confirm that there was nothing compromising they needed to know about me. During such interviews, I'm always tempted to emulate the witty William F. Buckley. According to an old story—perhaps apocryphal—when a colleague was being vetted for a job in the Nixon White House, Buckley was asked, "Do you think there is anything about this man that might embarrass the president?" In his best pseudo-British accent, Buckley replied, "I should think the opposite is more likely!" However, the friendly but humorless demeanor of the lawyers across the table from me made it clear that this was no time to crack wise.

The next day the president nominated me publicly as Secretary of Defense in the Roosevelt Room at the White House. Vice President Biden attended—he and his wife, Jill, are old friends of mine and Stephanie's, and his presence was important to us. Also on hand were Denis, Susan Rice, and other members of the White House staff, along with my friends Steve Hadley, Liz Sherwood-Randall, and Senator Carl Levin (D-MI). Especially meaningful to me was the attendance of Brent

Scowcroft, one of my most admired mentors. My immediate predecessor as SecDef, Chuck Hagel, was traveling overseas. I'd spoken to him by phone that morning. Chuck had a deserved reputation for being a bit of a hothead, but he had always been courteous to me, and even in this moment, which must have been difficult for him, he was gracious. "Thanks for calling, Ash," he said. "But this is your day. Enjoy it."

President Obama was generous in his remarks about me that morning:

> Today, I'm pleased to announce my nominee to be our next Secretary of Defense, Mr. Ash Carter.
>
> Now, with a record of service that has spanned more than 30 years—as a public servant, as an advisor, as a scholar—Ash is rightly regarded as one of our nation's foremost national security leaders. As a top member of our Pentagon team for the first five years of my presidency, including his two years as deputy secretary, he was at the table in the Situation Room; he was by my side navigating complex security challenges that we were confronting. I relied on his expertise, and I relied on his judgment. I think it's fair to say that, Ash, in your one-year attempt at retirement from public service, you've failed miserably. (Laughter.) But I am deeply grateful that you're willing to go back at it.

He went on to describe a few of the highlights of my previous career in defense, and to outline a number of key challenges I would be facing in my new role as SecDef. In my response, I thanked President Obama, offered a nod to my distinguished mentors and predecessors, and promised to keep faith with the men and women of "the greatest fighting force the world has ever known." I gave a version of the three commitments I would subsequently include in virtually all my speeches as SecDef—to protect and support the troops; to provide the president with candid advice and with "excellence in execution" of his decisions; and to be a Secretary of Defense for the future as well as the present.

Then, the ceremony concluded, I went down to a private West Wing office and phoned a few key members of Congress, such as Senator John

McCain, whose support I needed both for my confirmation and to succeed as SecDef.

There was one difficult bump on the road to my confirmation by the Senate. When being considered by President Obama, I'd alerted him to the fact that I'd been told I needed to have a major operation to correct a spinal irregularity that I'd had since birth. I'd scheduled the procedure shortly before Christmas, not realizing a call from the White House would be coming. "Go ahead," Obama had told me. "We'll do whatever we need to do to make it work out."

So on December 8, 2014, just a few days after the president announced my nomination, I went under the knife for the nine-hour procedure. When I woke up, the superstar surgeon who had done the procedure told me that he'd found it necessary to do an even more extensive procedure than planned. I was too groggy to take it all in, but I was glad the job had been taken care of once and for all.

Little did I know what I was in for. After a ten-day hospital stay, I went home and used the holidays to recuperate physically and prepare for my confirmation hearings in January. I spent days studying briefing books provided by the Pentagon to bring me up-to-date on new developments in the year since I'd been away from the department. Then I made appointments for one-on-one meetings with the many senators—more than fifty in all—who'd asked to see me. With a long incision and a host of staples down my back, it was impossible for me to remain seated upright for very long. Thankfully, Vice President Biden thoughtfully made his Capitol office available as my informal headquarters and resting place between meetings. A few minutes flat on my back on the sofa in his office, reviewing my conversation with one senator before moving on to the next, made it possible for me to survive those long, grueling days—all without using any pain medication, which might have dulled my mental faculties.

Then the day for my confirmation hearing arrived. Senator John McCain, whose history as a torture victim in Vietnam had left him deeply sympathetic to anyone suffering from chronic pain, had promised to quietly arrange a break midway through the hearing so that I could stretch out for a few restorative minutes. Unfortunately, McCain was unexpectedly called away, leaving the hearing in the hands of his colleague Carl Levin. Mid-morning, as my back was becoming painful, Senator Levin glanced at a note passed to him by McCain's chief of staff, Chris Brose.

"I understand Mr. Carter has recently had back surgery," Levin announced into the microphone. "So we'll take a break now and give him a chance to rest his back."

I couldn't allow this to stand in the record. Why start my tenure as SecDef by raising questions about my stamina? "I appreciate the indulgence, Senator," I quickly interjected. "But I'm fine. Let's continue."

I gritted my teeth and went on answering questions for another few agonizing hours. Somehow my responses passed muster.

I was on my way to the job of a lifetime—a seat in the president's cabinet, as a member of the most powerful leadership team in the world. I'd begun the latest phase of my education in what it's like to juggle the immense responsibilities of running the DOD while directly serving a president who faces the intense political pressures of today's hyper-partisan Washington.

Forging a Staff

As I settled in to the job of SecDef, I needed to quickly surround myself with a smart, experienced staff. I had one big advantage going for me: having served on the Obama transition team back in 2008, I'd had plenty of opportunities to assess and recruit talent.

An early star find was Air Force Lieutenant Colonel Sami Said. Back in 2008, he'd been assigned to assist me as I worked out of a Pentagon cubbyhole, held meetings around the Pentagon and Washington, and assembled papers for President-elect Obama on assigned topics like intelligence, acquisitions, and space. I labored dutifully to produce papers, which were then shipped out to the real transition hub in Chicago, where they were, as far as I could tell, totally ignored. Sami Said was a huge help to me—whip smart, and one of those people who grasp what you need immediately and often anticipate what your next question will be before you say a word.

When I was later confirmed as undersecretary, I asked Said to be my senior military assistant and to help me put together the office. At the time, the office of the undersecretary, located in one of the top suites in the Pentagon's E ring, was a complete shambles, with wires hanging out of the overheads and all the desks empty. The contractor manning the phones would answer by giving his own name rather than identifying it as the office of the number three official at the Department of Defense. Sami helped me straighten it all out.

As undersecretary, I kept my eye out for other good people. Said brought up some of the contract personnel who assisted the civilian workforce down in the bowels of the acquisition office. I watched them work the phones and process the paperwork for me, and one person in particular caught my eye. This was Julie Park, a preternaturally gifted organizer. Ultimately, I helped Park become a full-time civilian employee at the department and brought her into my front office, both as deputy and as SecDef. I ultimately made her the director of protocol for the entire DOD. Julie has since founded her own business but continues to work for me part-time.

For the civilian chief of staff and deputy chief of staff of the office, I chose Wendy Anderson, a former congressional staffer well connected in Washington. To assist her, I brought in young Jonathan Lachman, a student of mine years back at Harvard. Both were green at acquisition, but like fine racehorses, they repaid my bets on them with interest. Years later when I became deputy secretary, Julie, Wendy, and Jonathan all came with me. Sami, by then, had had to rotate back into the Air Force and, sadly, wasn't available.

With this staff-building experience under my belt, I was able to tackle the same task as SecDef with confidence.

I inherited Bob Work in the number two job of deputy secretary. Bob was a simply spectacular deputy, and I know what it means to say that, having occupied the job myself. Shortly after my confirmation, I called Bob into my office and told him I had no intention of replacing him. "Bob, I've had your job," I continued. "I know how to do your job. Now I don't have your job. I have this job, so I'm not going to do your job. I need you to do it. I know you'll do it well, and you know I'll know if you don't. Come to me for help when you need it, but I'm going to count on you to run the building while I am paying more attention in this role to the world outside."

Bob readily agreed, and our partnership worked perfectly.

A sensitive job at DOD is that of the director of legislative affairs. I'd been deeply impressed with Steve Hedger, the director of the same office at the White House, who'd helped with my confirmation. I respectfully "stole" Hedger from the Obama team to make him part of my own. Steve knew all the key people on Capitol Hill and could maintain relationships of trust with them while remembering that his first job was to represent the interests of DOD—a rare combination of traits among legislative affairs people.

I also was fortunate enough to inherit a number of talented people within DOD. One was Marcel Lettre. He and I had worked together at Harvard back in 2000. He entered government service after 9/11, serving with Denis McDonough on the staff of Senator Tom Daschle and then on that of Senator Harry Reid. Later, my predecessor, Chuck Hagel, made him undersecretary of defense for intelligence, a role in which I was happy to retain him.

Then there were a couple of people who got away. Jonathan Lachman stayed with me through my tenure as deputy secretary, but then was poached away to become head of national security budgeting for the Office of Management and Budget, a hugely powerful job from which I couldn't possibly lure him.

Michèle Flournoy is an old friend who had served as undersecretary for policy when I was undersecretary for acquisition, technology, and logistics. In that role, she had been the highest-ranking woman in the history of DOD. I would have liked to keep her on, but she had moved on by the time I became SecDef. Fortunately, her place had been taken by Jim Miller, another old friend and an enormously capable person.

Another teammate I wish I could have kept was Jeh Johnson, a New York lawyer who'd been one of my colleagues in the Pentagon cubbyholes the Obama transition team worked in. He'd developed a stellar reputation as general counsel of the Air Force in the Clinton administration, and after the transition he became general counsel of the DOD. He was so effective and politically savvy that he'd worked on a number of sensitive special assignments for SecDef Bob Gates, including overseeing the end of the "Don't ask, don't tell" policy that had excluded openly gay service members. When I was deputy secretary, Johnson and I had traveled to the Guantánamo detention center together to study the situation there. I'd have loved to keep him on as general counsel, but before I became SecDef, he'd been elevated to a cabinet post of his own, as Secretary of Homeland Security. I later awarded him the DOD's highest civilian award in recognition of his wonderful cooperation with us on many sensitive security matters.

Remaining to be filled were the jobs of my senior military aide and my chief of staff. For the former post, I selected General Ron Lewis, a gifted leader who was a spectacular aide and confidant. The disappointing, even tragic story that later unfolded I will detail in a later chapter.

But when it came to choosing a chief of staff, I got very lucky. I had known Eric Rosenbach for years. He'd spent time at Harvard, where I'd known him well, and he'd worked on the Hill, including for Senator Chuck Hagel. Above all, he'd been an effective assistant secretary of defense for global security and homeland defense, a very big job. He's one of the few people who really understand cyber-warfare. He'd also dealt effectively with space, missile defense, responses to disasters like hurricanes, and a whole welter of highly sensitive issues.

Eric is mature, has great people skills, and over the years has truly been my right-hand man and alter ego. He was in on virtually every event, decision, and initiative recounted in these pages. Years later, when I was finished being secretary and went to Harvard to take over as the director of the Belfer Center, one of the terms in my negotiation was that Eric be brought up to Cambridge to be codirector with me.

Rounding out the front office team were Ylber Bajraktari on operational and policy matters, Beth Foster on personnel, Sasha Baker on technology and budgets, and Katherine Carroll on sensitive legal and policy issues.

I also must mention a team of people who were not technically part of my staff but to whom I owe an enormous debt. These were the personal security officers (PSOs) who protected me and Steph—Army military police with superb training. The SecDef lives in a fishbowl, constantly observed and photographed, and is a target for the radicalized and the disgruntled wherever he goes. The PSOs followed me everywhere, especially when I was traveling in war zones, and did everything possible to guarantee my safety. They also paid discreet attention to small but essential things like finding a safe men's room for me to stop at in the middle of a long day.

The PSOs drove me around in heavily armored cars, kept my schedule a closely guarded secret, and enabled me to stay in constant communication with Washington under the most difficult circumstances. For example, when I was staying in a hotel in a foreign capital, the PSOs would occupy a suite nearby. If I needed to speak with the president, I'd visit their apartment and take part in a teleconference with him. I had to wear headphones to block out the ear-splitting squawking noise being produced by special speakers in the room, designed to prevent any bugs planted in the room from picking up our conversation. Somehow putting up with that infernal racket was another part of the PSOs' thankless duties.

In return for the utter professionalism the PSOs displayed, Steph and I tried to extend to them all the courtesies we could. For example, we would never surprise them with our departure from our guarded residence, but would always text them with an advance heads-up: "Taking a walk in 15," or "Trip to pharmacy at 11:30." That was the least we could do for these dedicated pros, who over time became good friends to both of us.

With a great staff in place, I was ready to hit the ground running as SecDef. One of the most important job requirements would be getting to know as much as possible about the working style and the decision-making practices of my new boss, President Barack Obama.

Presidents I've Known

Barack Obama was the fifth president I served in one way or another, but just the second whom I can say that I got to know well.

Ronald Reagan was the president whose administration I offended with my honest appraisal of the technical merits of the Star Wars missile defense system, which was a favorite project of his. My dissent led to my being pilloried in parts of his inner circle. Nonetheless, I got to serve his administration as an advisor on nuclear weapons and related issues, thanks to the personnel policies of Caspar Weinberger's Pentagon, which was willing to hire a scientist with no political ties at all, and to the openness of officials like Paul Nitze, who appreciated my expertise and my readiness to offer candid advice untainted by ideology.

I served the administration of Reagan's successor, George H. W. Bush, through my membership in such influential government groups as the Defense Science Board and the Panel on National Security of the President's Council of Advisors on Science and Technology. My acquaintance with the first President Bush was deeper than with President Reagan, though not intimate. I respected him as a highly experienced foreign policy and defense expert, personally familiar with many of the world's most important leaders, and grounded in the post–World War II international order forged over decades by a distinguished array of statesmen from both major political parties. The deft management of the complications related to the breakup of the Soviet Union by President Bush and his team is one of the foremost examples of the phenomenon I mentioned earlier in this book— the potential disaster that doesn't happen, which therefore tends to be unrecognized and underappreciated by the general public and even by many historians.

President Bush's successor, Bill Clinton, was the first president I worked with rather closely—and that was an experience I'll never forget. I found him to be a wonderful person to work for—smart verging on brilliant, deeply knowledgeable, and highly energetic. Even more impressive, although I was "just" an assistant secretary of defense at the time, he knew who I was, paid close attention to my ideas and insights, and made me feel as though the things I worked on really mattered. (Of course, I'm not the only person to have had a similar experience with Bill Clinton. His ability to engage closely with people at every level has been remarked upon by countless people over the years and is a crucial part of his unsurpassed gifts as a natural-born politician.)

Here's a small but telling example: I was part of the delegation accompanying Clinton on a trip to Russia, climaxing in an important meeting with Boris Yeltsin in the Kremlin. My main objective on this trip, as I'd told the president, was to try to ensure that the discussions between the two leaders would include the war on Bosnia, with a special focus on getting Yeltsin to agree not to send troops into the region independently. But this, of course, was just one of the topics that Clinton and Yeltsin would be dealing with during their summit.

On the big day, a group of us attended the ceremony in a vast room where President Yeltsin welcomed us to the Kremlin. The formalities over, Clinton and Yeltsin disappeared behind a set of tall, white doors for a private discussion of the crucial issues our nations faced together. The rest of us waited outside, chatting. The group included Leon Panetta, then Clinton's chief of staff and later Clinton's SecDef.

After half an hour or so, the doors opened, and the two leaders emerged, smiling for the photographers. The next thing I knew, Clinton had broken away from the group and headed directly for me. He draped an arm around my shoulders—I'm a big man, but Clinton is an inch or two taller—and leaned down to say in my ear, "Ash, I'm so sorry, but I just couldn't get it."

As it happened, Yeltsin later did agree to hold back on sending Russian troops alone into Bosnia. But I'll always remember the time when the president of the United States felt that I, a junior member of his administration, was entitled to an apology and an explanation for his failure to win a concession I'd ask him to seek. Classic Bill Clinton. Treating people this way won him a huge amount of devoted work from appreciative members of his team.

Another time, I was summoned unexpectedly to the Oval Office—"The president wants to speak with you" was the message. I arrived to find President Clinton on the phone with Leonid Kuchma, the president of Ukraine, a country I'd recently visited as part of my work in implementing the Nunn-Lugar program to eliminate or safeguard the nuclear weapons of the old USSR. Kuchma had previously been general director of Yuzhmash, the Ukrainian aerospace company that had built the missiles we'd been dismantling under Nunn-Lugar.

I knew right away what the call was about. I'd been managing a small but festering conflict with Ukraine over one detail of the program. The

Ukrainian nukes included a number of intercontinental ballistic missiles known as SS-19s, fueled with a liquid propellant known as unsymmetrical dimethylhydrazine (UDMH), but dubbed "heptyl" by Russian engineers. We'd been telling our Ukrainian partners to discard the valueless heptyl by simply burning it. But they were mired in the old Soviet mindset and assumed that everything that cost money was worth money. So they were insisting that we fund them to store the heptyl.

I was surprised and dismayed to see that the Ukrainians had now escalated this argument all the way to the White House. Clinton looked puzzled as he listened to Kuchma. His responses were noncommittal, including promises that "the matter will get my personal attention" and so on. Finally, the president hung up the phone, turned to me, and said, "Do me a favor, Ash—make sure he never calls me about heptyl again!"

I did. We made sure the heptyl got stored in aluminum tanks in Ukraine, and we did it without paying their government a dime for the privilege.

I didn't work in the Pentagon during the administration of President George W. Bush, though I did continue to serve as a member of the Defense Science Board and the Panel on National Security of the President's Council of Advisors on Science and Technology. (My sponsor for these positions, SecDef Donald Rumsfeld, actually had to get the president's political advisor Karl Rove to okay me.) I was also asked by Condoleezza Rice to join the International Advisory Board to the Secretary of State, chaired by Jim Schlesinger, and I was part of this group from 2004 to 2009. These are further illustrations of the degree to which national security and defense remained largely bipartisan matters until relatively recently.

By 2009, I'd had almost three decades of professional experience under presidents from both parties. Now, as a member of Barack Obama's cabinet, I would have the opportunity to serve directly as one of the president's most powerful deputies and top advisors. Over time, I got to know President Obama fairly well, and I found him to be an amazingly capable and complex, many-sided man with a personality very different from that of President Clinton.

As I think most people realize, Barack Obama is very smart. He is also intensely detail-oriented and focused. As I quickly discovered, the way he recalled the four questions I'd raised during our initial conversation about becoming SecDef and responded to them in our second call without skipping a beat was typical Obama: he pays attention, remembers what people say, and responds with quickness and clarity. In those respects, he resembles Bill Clinton. And like Bill Clinton, he is capable of engaging in conversation on a remarkably wide array of topics with knowledge, intelligence, and subtlety—an important trait for a president in our complicated, multifaceted world.

On the other hand, Obama is quite a bit younger than Clinton—born in 1961, fully fifteen years after Clinton. He is also seven years younger than I am, which in itself is not a significant difference. But I had gotten into national security in a serious way as early as 1980, when the Cold War was still underway. This meant that I sometimes had firsthand acquaintance with an issue, a personality, or a series of events that was unavoidably a matter of secondhand knowledge for Obama.

To his credit, President Obama recognized the limits of his personal knowledge. At moments when I thought it would be useful to offer him background understanding that he might not naturally possess, he listened with respect and interest, and generally made good use of what he heard. He invariably knew more about a topic than one might expect a president to know. He is a quick learner, and during his time in office he made no disastrous miscalculations like those experienced by most of his predecessors.

But Obama did sometimes exhibit a bit of the overconfidence, even arrogance, that can come from being both very smart and comparatively young. As an example, I'd point to his publicly expressed disdain for what he called "the Washington playbook"—the supposed set of unwritten guidelines for U.S. foreign policy dictated by "the establishment" and often parroted by mainstream pundits in the media and elsewhere. Obama would sometimes even appear to take mischievous pleasure in ignoring the playbook and choosing an unconventional policy path—as if tweaking the expectations of the establishment is a worthwhile goal in itself. He did this in 2013 when he decided not to enforce the "red line" his administration had previously drawn against the use of chemical weapons by the Assad regime in Syria. Obama may have been right in choosing not to launch a military strike when such weapons were used by Assad. But explaining away the downside of not enforcing the red line as an artifact of some conventional playbook was too dismissive, and therefore left the impression that red lines in general were meaningless.

There's no doubt that "conventional wisdom" can become hidebound, outdated, and inflexible, and that it needs to be shaken up periodically through probing analysis and fresh thinking. But my experience suggests that, in most cases, conventional wisdom does in fact contain a healthy helping of wisdom—which means it's risky to discard it without having a very good reason to do so. In my view, President Obama, or at least those who spoke for him, was at risk of going too far in assuming that conventional wisdom is generally wrong.

I hasten to add that there is no comparison on this score between President Obama and his successor in office, who, as I write (in early 2019), seems to delight in trashing conventional wisdom and decades' worth of hard-earned international norms for no better reason than sheer ego or perhaps whimsy. If President Obama, in my judgment, tilted a bit too far away from respect for systems, processes, and norms, President Trump has tilted so far that the country's protective warning lights should be flashing.

During my two years as President Obama's Secretary of Defense, I came to recognize his intuitive understanding of the gap between policy making and policy execution, and we shared an appreciation for the importance of minute attention to detail in planning military operations. Ironically, I think President Obama could have done a better job in one of the areas of leadership in which his reputation is generally highest: communication with the public, specifically in regard to issues of national security.

Candidate Obama had railed against what he viewed as President George W. Bush's oversimplification of security issues, focusing especially on the Iraq invasion—falsely justified, poorly implemented, and damaging to our national interest. Obama promised a renewed focus on the importance of nuance and detail in foreign policy. Coupled with Obama's personal and intellectual style—careful and acute, but also lean and parsimonious—this reaction shaped Obama's style of speaking about national security strategy. Like a pointillist painter, he disdained broad brushstrokes and often refused to connect the dots, even when they were crying out for connection.

A popular joke in Washington foreign policy circles used to be that "Obama's foreign policy is better than it sounds." There was a lot of truth in that joke. Historians are likely to conclude that the Obama administration deserved more credit for its strategic accomplishments than it received. It's not an uncommon pattern. As I've noted, in foreign policy as in other fields, disasters that are averted through foresighted planning usually get ignored, until history is written years later.

Like all people—including presidents—Barack Obama has both strengths and weaknesses. Fortunately for the country (and for me as a member of his team), Obama's strengths greatly outweigh his weaknesses. In addition to his sharp, subtle mind—which I've already mentioned, and for which I think he generally receives due credit, even from his critics—Obama also has a number of gifts that make him an exceptional leader.

One is the fact that his thinking is not only smart but *orderly*: Obama doesn't forget or overlook important details, he examines issues in a logical and comprehensive way, and he addresses problems in a methodical fashion so that loose ends are rarely left dangling. These may sound like mundane matters, but anyone with much experience in a large organization can tell you that leaders with these vital habits are unfortunately rare.

Another invaluable trait of Obama's is that, in meetings, he is decisive and communicates his intentions clearly. I never left a meeting of the National Security Council or a one-on-one session with the president without knowing precisely how he'd chosen to resolve an issue and exactly what he expected me to do about it. Again, these are behaviors that can go unappreciated until you join an organization where they are lacking—as they often are.

I also credit Obama for a remarkable degree of openness and respect for varied opinions. While he and I shared most fundamental principles and policy preferences, there were numerous times when I recommended a specific strategy or approach that he did not favor. In virtually every instance, he gave me a fair chance of presenting my case and listened thoughtfully to my arguments. Sometimes I won him over. Other times, I did not—and then he always did me the courtesy of explaining why he'd chosen a different course. The sense that the president regarded me as a valued colleague whose thoughts and experience he respected made it that much easier for me to be an enthusiastic member of his team, even when I had to carry out a policy that wouldn't have been my first choice.

Above all, President Obama did not play games. I never saw him pit one staffer against another, criticize anyone behind their back, say one thing while thinking another, or fudge the truth to make himself look good. With Obama, I always knew where I stood. And I always knew that, whether I won or lost a particular policy battle, he and I always had the same goal at heart—to serve the American people as best we could.

When it comes to presidential leadership, it doesn't get much better than that.

How Not to Be Micromanaged

The choice to send young American men and women into harm's way was something that President Obama always took very seriously. That may be one of the reasons that all three of his previous secretaries of defense complained publicly about having their battlefield decisions "micromanaged" by President Obama.

Actually, this was nothing new. I'd heard this same complaint from every one of the eleven secretaries I worked for in my thirty-five previous years in the DOD. It's a complaint that feeds one of the widespread misperceptions of the DOD—that the U.S. military would have no problems if only the politicians would "get out of the way" and let the generals do what they want. (People have been saying this since at least Vietnam, and probably longer than that.) This simplistic notion reflects the unfortunate culture gap between the military and civilian sides of our country; and by exalting one side and denigrating the other, it also contributes to widening that gap.

I understand why my predecessors complained about "backseat drivers" in the White House. No one wants to be micromanaged. But many of the most crucial decisions made in the DOD need to be vetted by the White House, since the president is ultimately responsible for them and for their success or failure. This managerial process makes friction, conflict, and occasional resentment all but inevitable.

However, I was not micromanaged. The main reason for this was the way in which I handled relations with the White House.

An incident early in my tenure helped guide my approach. One Friday night, I got a call from Susan Rice, the president's national security advisor. "You just sent over a CONOP for the president to sign," she began. She was referring to a "concept of operation," a detailed plan for a military operation of a gravity that required the president's approval. "It's Friday, Ash, and if he needs to look at it over the weekend, he will. But I wonder why CONOPs always seem to come over late on Friday. Is that about the need for a decision, or about the bureaucracy? In the past, it made him feel as though his Secretary of Defense just sends him whatever the people below him request, making him do all the scrubbing. This is why he doesn't trust your stuff."

A light bulb lit up for me. From that moment forward, I insisted on setting the highest possible standards of thoroughness and detail in every plan my team members developed. I believed that making sure that any ideas we presented to the president were letter-perfect would be the best way to win his trust, and thereby to greatly reduce instances in which my decisions were second-guessed, delayed, or overruled.

Thus, in 2015, when Chairman of the Joint Chiefs Joe Dunford and I concluded that we needed to create an Expeditionary Targeting Force (ETF) to conduct high-risk raids against ISIS, we laid the groundwork for its authorization by the president very carefully.

The ETF would be designed to capture or kill leaders deep in ISIS-occupied territory, which at that time included large swaths of eastern Syria and western Iraq. Unlike air strikes, ETF raids by U.S. Special Forces (typically accompanied by Iraqi forces) would aim not just to eliminate an ISIS leader but also to capture his cohorts and seize his cell phone, notebooks, and computers. Thus, the ETF would feed a virtuous circle: a raid would yield more intelligence to guide more raids, which could in turn guide yet more raids—or air strikes, ground operations, disruptions of ISIS financing, and other crippling moves.

I was intimately familiar with capture/kill operations of this kind. The United States had conducted them in Iraq and Afghanistan when I came into the Pentagon for my second tour of duty in 2009; they were perfected when Generals Stan McChrystal and Dave Petraeus were commanding and I was working on their equipment and logistics as undersecretary. But they hadn't been used in Iraq since the withdrawal of most U.S. forces in 2011. To begin them again, I needed the president's permission.

Getting Obama's approval would be no slam-dunk. Lots of things can go wrong with raids like these: bad intelligence, bad weather, equipment breakdowns, and more. There were many questions of a nontactical nature to answer, such as which key leaders on Capitol Hill or in foreign governments needed to be informed beforehand, what to do if someone screwed up, and what to do with people we captured. And because these raids entailed putting U.S. forces at risk, we knew that the president would surely be demanding about getting the right answers—as would I. Accordingly, Joe Dunford and I, along with our commanders on the ground, worked hard to scrub the concept.

All the while, we kept it out of the press to avoid complicating the decision for the president. In our first conversation about my becoming SecDef, President Obama had offered me one warning: "If you have something to tell me, come and see me. I don't want to read about it in the newspaper. Don't jam me."

I knew exactly what he meant. Unauthorized leaks are often used by administration officials to force the president's hand by mobilizing public opposition or support for a proposed policy before a decision is ripe. Presidents resent getting boxed in like that—and rightly so. That's one of the little-understood reasons why controlling leaks becomes such an obsession for so many administrations. To avoid this, Joe and I enforced strict secrecy about the plans as our team developed them.

Joe and I set about seeking an opportunity to conduct a capture/kill operation that would demonstrate what an ETF could do. When we found the right target and the details were set, we presented the CONOP in one of our weekly Oval Office meetings. Seeing that we'd done our homework thoroughly, President Obama gave us the go-ahead.

In May 2015, the Army's Delta Force raided a house in northern Syria used by Abu Sayyaf, a close crony of the ISIS leader Abu Bakr al-Baghdadi and a member of the supposed cabinet of the so-called ISIS state. Abu Sayyaf was killed in the raid, and his wife and a few others at the site were captured along with numerous documents and electronic devices—while all the raiders got back safely. In short, the raid was a spectacular success. It was a brilliant model for the kind of operation we hoped the ETF could conduct.

Obama authorized us to create the ETF and seek opportunities to use it, stipulating that we needed to come back to him to describe the CONOP before launching a raid. We proceeded on that basis for a few months. However, once Obama got used to the capability and gained confidence in it—and when he could see that Joe and I were scrubbing the CONOPs thoroughly—I asked him to delegate decision authority to me. Only if I thought an operation was particularly tricky would I come to him in advance.

The president agreed. We were over the hump of micromanagement.

The story illustrates one of my strongly held beliefs about leadership: that sweating the details on crucial operations is part of the job of a leader. I personally worked over CONOPs, usually multiple times, until they met the standard I thought a president would reasonably demand. It's striking how the issue of micromanagement seems to disappear when leaders do their jobs at the granular level needed to guarantee quality.

Team Obama: We Have to Stop Meeting like This

Much more frustrating for me than micromanagement was "microstrategy," the term I used with my staff when characterizing many White House meetings. These meetings were of various types and flavors, with varying degrees of usefulness to me and, I suspect, to other participants.

Principals Committee meetings (PCs) were chaired by National

Security Advisor Susan Rice and included me, the chairman of the Joint Chiefs of Staff (first Marty Dempsey, later Joe Dunford), Secretary of State John Kerry, Director of National Intelligence Jim Clapper, CIA Director John Brennan, and UN Ambassador Samantha Power, plus any other cabinet members and senior officials relevant to a particular issue (for example, the treasury secretary, the attorney general, or the FBI director). Many lower-level team members would also be present, seated quietly in chairs against the wall while the principals themselves sat around a central table.

Susan was an excellent chair, very bright, highly organized, and deliberate. She'd served as assistant secretary of state for African affairs under Madeleine Albright and later as UN ambassador, and in her role as national security advisor (NSA) she'd learned fast and grown on the job. We'd known each other for about twenty years, spending time together in Colorado every summer as participants in the Aspen Strategy Group.

As national security advisor, she had a somewhat different approach to defense matters from that of her predecessor, Tom Donilon. Tom was a good friend of mine and an exceptional public servant, but I felt that his career had given him a visceral distrust of the DOD; he viewed it as a kind of dark star across the Potomac that needed to be reined in by the State Department and the White House. Susan took a more congenial approach to my department. She was also a good strategic thinker, able to wrap her mind around big subjects like Russia and China. We didn't always arrive at the same judgments, but at least we were having the right conversations.

Despite Rice's strengths, the PCs she ran had serious problems from my point of view. Most of them ended up focusing principally on military matters—an appropriate subject for an interagency meeting, to be sure. But when important strategic issues beyond the purely military are never addressed, neither the cabinet members nor the president himself is well served. The result was a bunch of people with mixed levels of knowledge and experience tossing around ideas for military strategy, a practice I began to refer to as "playing with little tin soldiers"—not a very good use of our time.

Furthermore, while DOD was required to prepare and present

CONOPs about military actions we were planning, other departments were never asked to make comparable presentations. That actually would have been a useful exercise—for example, to ask the State Department to craft a diplomatic CONOP to accompany the conduct of freedom of navigation operations in the South China Sea. But these were never asked for and never provided. As a result, when we conducted such operations, the ultra-prepared Chinese diplomats and propagandists ran circles around our ambassadors in Asia, giving misinformation to the press and, on several occasions, to influential former U.S. officials.

Another problem was with the documents prepared for PCs. Rather than being organized around broad strategic issues, they were usually focused on a list of specific decisions the staff wanted to extract from the president, or a set of "deliverables" for an upcoming head-of-state meeting. The closest they came to presenting strategic alternatives was to offer two straw men bracketing an insipid rendition of the status quo.

Making matters worse, these papers were long, poorly written, and generally arrived either late the night before a meeting or early the next morning. No SecDef could possibly be expected to read and reflect on a paper on that timetable. And partly as a result of the poor preparation, the meetings themselves tended to rapidly descend from strategy into detail—frequently lawyerly minutiae that should have been settled in advance of the meeting.

Early in my tenure, I complained to Susan about all this. She snapped, "Policy making is the most important part of your job."

I retorted, "No, it's not. I have to lead millions of men and women, and to manage half of the federal government. That's just as important. And certainly more important than reading papers written by your team."

For a moment, Susan was taken aback. Then she laughed and said, "I see your point!"

Unfortunately, nothing changed in the way PCs were run. But this kind of exchange illustrates why at least I had a very good relationship with Susan Rice. We could have a sharp exchange, yelling at each other into the phone, then quickly patch things up.

The meetings of the National Security Council had papers that were just as bad as those for the PCs. But the meetings themselves were much more strategic, centered on major issues that President Obama was grappling with. Obama generally welcomed frank discussion, and I tried to play a part in stimulating such discussion—for example, by volunteering to offer my observations and opinions first once the issue had been placed on the table. The president told me privately that he appreciated my doing this. I'd suspected he would, based on an exchange in our first meeting before he named me SecDef. "I know something about how frustrating it can be to run an organization," I told him. "You sit at the end of a long table, and after an hour you close the meeting and walk out muttering to yourself, 'Do I have to think of every solution myself?'" The president laughed and nodded in rueful empathy, and I promised myself that if I became secretary, I would pitch in during meetings rather than holding back. Joe Dunford did the same, both in meetings with the president and at my own meetings at the Pentagon.

Like the PCs, the NSC meetings were populated with both high-ranking officials and subordinate staffers, all sitting against the walls and taking notes. These would become the basis of a cascade of "back briefs" in the various agencies, where people down through the layers of bureaucracy were eager to hear the latest policy scoop. I always wondered about how my words and those of others around the table would end up being distorted and misunderstood through multiple levels of retelling. Those note-takers were also the sources of many a leak to the news media as well as plenty of the gossip that endlessly circulates around Washington.

Thoughts like these were certainly on the president's mind as well. At several of the meetings I attended, he drew uneasy laughter by sardonically remarking, "You folks are sure taking a lot of notes for your memoirs." To set his mind at ease in my own case, at the first NSC meeting I attended, I conspicuously closed the notepad before me and folded my hands atop it, a practice I followed at later meetings as well. This wasn't solely a courtesy to the president: I find it easier to concentrate on a conversation when I'm not trying to write at the same time. Luckily for me, Joe Dunford proved to have a steel-trap memory for what transpired at our meetings, and I could rely on him afterward to remind me of Obama's exact words if my own recollections faltered.

Most valuable to me were my private meetings with the president in the Oval Office. I got to set the agendas for these meetings. Sometimes I brought along a story or an anecdote I thought the president would find useful. Other times we just focused on the one-page list of four or five topics that I worked hard to cull in advance with Joe and my staff.

The meetings ran between forty-five and ninety minutes, and, though theoretically held weekly, they actually happened two or three times a month because of scheduling difficulties. And they weren't literally private: I always took Marty or Joe with me if they were in town, and Susan was almost always there, and sometimes the vice president. White House Chief of Staff Denis McDonough didn't attend these meetings, though I wish he had, not only because of his good judgment and his closeness to the president, but also because many of the issues I needed to talk to the president about were broader than national security policy, involving topics like the budget, military activities in space (a special interest of Obama's), cyber-defense, congressional affairs, and so on.

There's a useful manager's adage I try to follow: "Give praise in public but criticism in private." President Obama seemed to follow this rule, and on the rare occasions when he became annoyed with me, I was glad he did.

Once, for example, I'd begun to take steps to reorganize a part of the DOD, figuring I had authority to do it on my own. This was the move to elevate the cyber-command unit, charged with protecting the nation from online attacks, to the status of a full-fledged combat command, and to partially separate it from the National Security Agency (I'll explain in more detail later). In our next one-on-one meeting, I explained to the president what I was doing in the presence of our staff members. After the meeting ended, the president said innocently, "Ash, can you stay behind a minute?" as others filtered out of the Oval Office. He closed the door and told me this was a matter I should have referred to him. "It's not your decision, Ash," he admonished me. "It's not even close!"

Obama was right—I should have consulted with him before making this decision. I hadn't meant to end-run the president. I was just in a hurry to get things done, as usual. I made a mental note never to make the same mistake again—and I never did.

Defense and State: A Crucial, Tricky Partnership

In any administration, the relationship between a Secretary of Defense and a Secretary of State is an important one. I have seen it range from very antagonistic to very cooperative. In the Carter years, Harold Brown at Defense tangled with Cyrus Vance at State; the same happened under Reagan, with Cap Weinberger at Defense and George Shultz at State. My friend and predecessor Bill Perry made it a point to get along with his cabinet teammates Warren Christopher and, later, Madeleine Albright.

When there is friction between the departments, it sometimes bubbles up from below. The SecDef often has to deal with complaints from staff about the difficulties of working with their counterparts at State. I made such complaints myself when I was assistant secretary to Bill Perry. The tension at lower levels is natural enough. Every single thing the United States does in a foreign country must be approved by the ambassador to that country, who, of course, is a State Department employee. That includes everything from arms sales and troop deployment to any visit to a country by an official of the Defense Department, uniformed or civilian. This is a cherished power of ambassadors around the world, and they don't hesitate to use it.

Of course, DOD employees tend to resent having to pass every plan by a State Department counterpart. But in the great majority of cases, the input provided by ambassadors is highly constructive, sometimes including a warning of unintended consequences that helps to forestall an ill-conceived DOD plan. For this reason, a wise SecDef will strive to set a cooperative tone. That's what Bill Perry did when I was assistant secretary. He made it very clear that he would never carry my quarrels forward to Warren Christopher, and that I would need to work things out myself.

Taking a cue from Bill, I began having weekly brown-bag lunches with other assistant secretaries around town, including officials in both the White House and the State Department. I also made a point of taking them on trips with me when I had a military airplane at my disposal. The result was excellent interagency teamwork on issues ranging from relations with the former Soviet Union to nuclear nonproliferation.

When I became SecDef, I was determined to set the same tone with John Kerry's State Department. I'd known John and his wife, Teresa, for many years and had worked with him on defense-related issues when he was a senator. He'd even asked me to advise and travel with him at several points during his presidential campaign of 2004, and I'd done so, bending my general rule not to participate in partisan politics. (That failed campaign led to a comment that I often heard John make during his years as Secretary of State. When asked, "How does it feel to have the job you've always wanted?" he would reply, "I wanted to be president." I always had the feeling that hearing John say this so often made President Obama a little uncomfortable.)

John and I got along fine, and in general I was strongly supportive of his work at State. But as a practical matter, our orbits overlapped less than one might imagine. John's big preoccupations were the Paris Climate Accord, the Trans-Pacific Partnership, the Iran nuclear deal, international human rights, and the Syrian civil war. The DOD's day-to-day involvement in these matters was not nearly as intense as John's. Moreover, John's near-complete absorption with these important matters meant that he was able to give only cursory attention to the things that mattered most to me: China, Russia, North Korea, Iran's nonnuclear machinations, Afghanistan, and, above all, the need to destroy ISIS. So in general, John worked in his lanes while I worked in mine. His diplomatic achievements were titanic.

John's involvement in the Syrian civil war was one area in which we saw things differently. Neither I nor any of my predecessors as SecDef had advocated involving the U.S. military in the Syrian civil war. Had we chosen to interpose American might, we could have deposed Bashar al-Assad, but Iraq had just reminded all of us—and particularly President Obama—about the difficulties of governing places you have conquered. Still, John Kerry desperately wanted some military card he could play at the diplomatic table. The problem was that there were no good ways to produce that card without getting embroiled in an all-out war. Similarly, he long cherished forlorn hopes of somehow working with the Russians to bring about an end to the Syrian conflict. In both cases, I pushed back against what I saw as Kerry's misguided ideas, and in both cases Obama followed my advice.

John and I also had very different working styles. I tended to be deliberate and methodical, two tendencies driven in part by my personality and in part by the burden of managing a vast, complex bureaucracy with enormous day-to-day responsibilities. As Secretary of State, running a much leaner operation, John retained something of the style of a senator, alighting briefly on many issues and never dwelling long on any one. In addition, John was an enthusiastic phone talker, while I found face-to-face meetings and written missives more effective.

These differences in temperament and working style led to some minor friction. In my early weeks as SecDef, John would call me at any hour about an issue that happened to drift across his desk—often about a topic of only peripheral interest to me, and rarely at a time that was convenient for me. These calls generally didn't lead to much, and over time they tapered off.

When you're helping to run an institution as vital to the safety and well-being of the world as the U.S. government, you have a responsibility not to let personal idiosyncrasies get in the way of smart, efficient management. John Kerry and I found ways to accommodate each other's differing styles, and our departments ending up working productively together. And despite all that has happened since then, I believe that John's legacy of diplomatic accomplishments will live on.

Telling the President What He Needs to Hear

As I'll explain in a later chapter, the members of the Joint Chiefs of Staff, though they serve as leaders of the five branches of America's military, are *not* officially in the chain of command—the hierarchy that connects the president of the United States, through the Secretary of Defense, down to individual troops on the ground. There's good reason for this. If the joint chiefs—including the chairman of the Joint Chiefs of Staff— were part of the chain of command, their advice could not be truly independent of those higher and lower in the chain. And the independence of that advice is crucial to its value to the president. That's part of what I had in mind when I pledged in the Roosevelt Room to provide the president with "my most candid strategic advice" and to ensure he received "equally candid military advice."

While the principle is quite clear, its practice is more complicated. It must be clear to the president that the SecDef is prepared to give him access to professional military advice even if it is contrary to the views of the secretary himself. This can be hazardous, since if the bureaucracy, the press, and Congress get wind of such rifts, they will play havoc with them to the detriment of the president and his administration. Nevertheless, the two-part system prescribed in the law, which includes both a civilian-led chain of command and access to professional military advice, will not work if both parts of the system are not real.

My own belief in this system was put to the test soon after I became secretary. A proposed military operation in the Middle East came up for discussion at an NSC meeting, and I found it necessary to disagree with both the chairman of the Joint Chiefs and the regional commander. I told then-chairman Marty Dempsey, Vice Chairman James "Sandy" Winnefeld Jr., and the commander of U.S. Central Command (CENTCOM) Lloyd Austin in advance that I had a different view and intended to give it to the president. They appreciated my honesty, and we all prepared to deal with the potential awkwardness of the meeting. Marty was traveling, so Sandy would represent him.

When the crucial issue came up, I volunteered to speak first. After telling President Obama my view, I invited Sandy to speak. "Mr. President," Sandy began, "the chairman, I, and General Austin disagree with the secretary." The reaction from everyone made it clear that this sort of open disagreement wasn't something that had happened often. Utter silence descended on the room. Susan stared at me, her look sending the message "I hope you know what you're doing." Obama himself, looking nonplussed, asked a few questions, then pronounced his verdict as to which course of action we would follow.

It's an example of how in stride this moment was taken that I can't now recall whether the president followed my advice or Marty's.

Demonstrating early in my tenure as SecDef that neither I nor our military leaders were afraid to expose a disagreement among us was worth a lot. I believe it disarmed those who might try to use dissent among the principals as an argument against the president and his policy. And it's an approach that serves the president as intended by the Constitution and the law.

The Art of Advising

An effective SecDef must be someone who has devoted time and energy to understanding and then practicing the art of being an effective advisor. It's a skill that is not as common as one might assume.

The presidents I've worked for have all valued candid advice, even when it contradicts their own views. The only proviso is that the advisor must provide loyal implementation of policy when his own recommendations are overruled. That happened to me many times while I was serving in the Clinton and Obama administrations, including during my tenure as SecDef. I see no difficulty in serving loyally despite policy differences, as long as those differences are not too numerous and too great. That's why I asked President Obama about his views on those four key issues before I accepted his offer to become SecDef. If he and I had been far apart on these points, it would have been hard for me to provide him with the kind of service he needed and wanted.

I found that being a truly helpful advisor to a president involves three elements. First, in any given situation, it's essential to understand what the president's intent truly is. A wise advisor tries to get inside the boss's head to understand what his thought process is. That's the only way that you can engage him to get him to the place you think he needs to be. If I thought the president's goal was wrong, I at least began by acknowledging it, thereby showing that I had listened to and understood his reasoning. Only then did I try to offer an argument in favor of a different goal. Policy decisions are hard enough without injecting negative attitudes into the discussion.

Second, it's important to distinguish the president's intent from any specific idea he has for realizing that intent. Making this distinction creates the opportunity for you to offer an alternative approach that still respects his underlying intent. Thus, I found that President Obama usually responded favorably to a suggestion prefaced with the words "Another way to get where you want to go would be . . ." This formulation acknowledged that the president was trying to go in a certain direction and made it clear that I respected his intent, even though I recommended a different way of reaching it.

Third, it's crucial to offer the president whole solutions rather than partial ones. Joe Dunford is an example of a leader who did this when advising me. I felt that he always "put himself in my shoes"—he tried to address all the different dimensions of a problem that I, as SecDef, had to address, from the military and the political to the economic and the logistical. Many less-skilled advisors provide advice that reflects their narrow perspective and so solves only a portion of the problem—like a single piece of a vast jigsaw puzzle. The best advisors are those who help the boss solve the entire puzzle, or at least attempt to provide enough pieces to bring the whole solution within reach. That's what I always tried to do for President Obama.

Politics and Policy: The Guantánamo Dilemma

It's inevitable that presidential decision-making will often be affected by political considerations—indeed, it's highly desirable, since "politics" is simply a way of describing the relationship between public opinion and government policy in a democratic society. But managing the relationship between politics and policy with wisdom and integrity isn't easy, as anyone who has participated in decision-making at the highest level can attest.

One of the most contentious and dramatic issues of both the Bush and the Obama presidencies was the military-run detention facility at Guantánamo Bay Naval Station in Cuba. Obama's 2008 platform had included a pledge to "close Gitmo," and many of his supporters and his friends in the liberal press put pressure on him to keep that promise after he was elected. The zealots for this cause included members of the White House staff. Obama shared their beliefs to the extent that Susan told me that one of the main reasons my predecessor, Chuck Hagel, had left the Pentagon was that he hadn't done enough to help Obama achieve that goal.

My own views about Gitmo were pretty clear. In the aftermath of 9/11, it was necessary to find someplace to detain terrorists captured on the battlefield. The Guantánamo facility was a reasonable choice. But by the time I became SecDef, I believed that, on balance, it was desirable for the United States to wind down Gitmo. There were several reasons for my view.

One was the difficulty of applying a basic system of justice to those held prisoner there. This was not like a traditional prisoner-of-war situation where the uniform gives everything away. In the effort to seize major terrorist leaders, some innocent bystanders and minor flunkies had been caught up. In countries like Afghanistan, it wasn't even possible to check many people's identities, because—as we found out when it came time to recruit and train a new Afghan army—most young Afghans did not know the date or even the year of their birth, nor have anything but a single name (overwhelmingly "Mohammad"). Inevitably, not everyone held at Guantánamo deserved to be there.

From the moment it opened, Guantánamo had become an embarrassment, one that reflected poorly on the DOD, harming the reputation of an institution that held itself to the highest standards. Early in its existence, the open cages of Camp X-Ray had sparked international outrage. I had visited as deputy secretary of defense, and I knew that conditions had come a long way from those early days. The facilities now had individual cells as well as common rooms with an opportunity for detainees to interact with one another, prepare meals together, and so forth. The improved conditions were in part the result of relentless scrutiny by a group from the New York City Bar that had championed the detainees and encouraged them to contest their conditions.

So conditions at Gitmo were no longer abusive. But my visit there showed me that they were still extremely unpleasant—and not only for detainees. It is, to be blunt, lousy duty for the soldiers, sailors, doctors, and nurses assigned to the camp. During off-hours, there is nothing to do and nowhere to go except the postage-stamp-size naval facility itself. Worse, the work itself can be deeply degrading, especially when detainees do things like throw feces or splash urine on our personnel. I really didn't like the idea of people from my department working in those conditions.

What's more, running the detention facility was expensive. Some of the facilities, including the dining hall used by our own guards, were shabby with age and badly in need of renovation, but appropriating the necessary money was not popular in Congress. Both those who wanted to close Gitmo and those opposed to "coddling" detainees routinely blocked spending to keep up the facilities, even when the U.S. guard force would benefit.

For all these reasons, I favored closing Gitmo. But the precise language that I used in talking about it with Obama as well as with members of Congress and the general public was "I'm in favor of closing Gitmo safely." The word "safely" made all the difference.

Some of the detainees could be moved out of Gitmo, and the safe way to do that was called "transfer." That meant remanding them to the care and responsibility of another government, which would guarantee they wouldn't return to the terrorist battlefield, advocate for terrorism, or participate in recruiting terrorists. The government watchdogs would observe and restrict their movements to ensure these guarantees were met.

Under the law, the responsibility for ensuring that these conditions were in place before recommending a detainee for transfer rested with the Secretary of Defense. The law also stipulated that I needed to seek the inputs of the Secretary of State, the director of national intelligence, the director of the CIA, the Secretary of Homeland Security, the director of the FBI, and the chairman of the Joint Chiefs of Staff. The rules for transfers were tough—appropriately so.

The other side of the coin was the reality that some detainees at Gitmo would never meet my definition of "safe." This meant that it was not possible to literally close Gitmo unless an alternate detention facility could be found for these worst cases. Thus, my own approach to the Gitmo dilemma was to review individual cases for transfer when possible while also trying to find somewhere to put those detainees who would never be eligible for transfer.

This approach made common sense. I had an easy time explaining it to Congress and the press, and even the yahoos on both sides of the issue found it impossible to refute any of the logic. For example, early in 2016, I appeared on a TV show from Davos, Switzerland, where I was asked, in effect, whether the Obama administration was seeking to set loose a bunch of terrorists eager to return to the battlefield against America.

"In my judgment," I retorted, "there are some detainees that can't safely be released. And that's why we're not going to let them go." The response took all the steam out of the implied accusation. It cut through the for-or-against dichotomy, which assumed two polar positions, neither of which made sense.

Encounters like this showed that my stance was sustainable and politically safe for me and for the president. However, I still had the ideologues in the White House to contend with. They were constantly leaking stories to the press, especially the *New York Times*, making the claim that "the Pentagon is trying to stop Obama from closing Gitmo, but the White House is determined to plow on." What these people didn't realize was that these stories actually strengthened my hand. They made me look like the one who was sensible and cautious, taking seriously our obligation to keep the American people safe. Unfortunately, they were hardly helpful to the president himself.

I usually found the antics of the ideologues amusing, but one time they went too far.

We were sitting around the Situation Room waiting to begin a Principals Committee meeting when one of these White House staff munchkins walked around the table putting a single sheet of paper at each place, including mine. I glanced at the paper. It was a "proposed timetable" that would force the Secretary of Defense to make a final decision on a proposed transfer of a Gitmo detainee within a fixed number of days. The paper had received no discussion or editing from any of the key decision-makers.

This tactic of springing a document on people without warning or vetting—known as "table dropping"—had always been offensive to me. It violates all the rules of good process and fair treatment. I picked up the paper, crumpled it into a ball, and threw it at the White House staffer who had given it to me, saying, "Don't table-drop shit."

That story—minus the expletive—ended up in the *New York Times* a few days later, and subsequently in a colorful *New Yorker* article. I was okay with that. In fact, from my point of view, almost everybody won in this foolish episode. The White House staff had demonstrated its zeal for the cause of closing Gitmo, the *New York Times* showed off its insider access, and I was reinforced as the guy who was proceeding soberly and conservatively. The only loser was Obama himself, who appeared to have lost control of his own administration. He deserved better.

The remaining question was what to do with those who couldn't be safely transferred, whose number I estimated at around forty. Where else could we put them other than Gitmo? I began to tackle this thorny question with the able help of my deputy secretary, Bob Work.

One option was to put them in an existing federal prison. Such prisons have a good track record at keeping dangerous people—rapists, mass murderers—safely incarcerated. But the Justice Department was not enthusiastic about this possibility and raised lots of legal objections to it.

Another alternative more under my control would be to put them in a military detention facility like the ones at Fort Leavenworth, Kansas, or Charleston, South Carolina. It would require some additional construction, special training for the detention force, and protection from assault from the outside—by teams of jihadis, for example. But this idea was squelched by the same impulse that often prevents the building of sewage treatment plants, airports, and nursing homes—the "not in my backyard," or NIMBY, syndrome. People in the Leavenworth and Charleston areas were worked into a lather about the danger of having terrorist detainees in their midst.

As a result, influential senators like Lindsey Graham of South Carolina and Pat Roberts of Kansas, who might otherwise have supported the plan, came out against it. In fact, Pat called me up one day to say, "I just had a press conference with the Kansas press and told them that I will never, ever, ever allow you to use Leavenworth for Gitmo detainees." If I tried to force the plan through, he would "fight to the death," and so on.

When pressed to offer a different solution, Roberts (and others like him) would simply declare that Gitmo should not be closed. Instead, we should "throw away the key" and let the remaining highly dangerous detainees end their lives there. In practice, that's what may end up happening. Most of the detainees are now quite old, and their numbers will decline naturally in the years to come.

I was happy to have been able to come up with an approach to the Gitmo dilemma that largely defused the politics of the issue, though it did not resolve it once and for all. Most important, I insulated President Obama against opponents from both ends of the political spectrum, freeing him to apply his time, energy, and political capital on other challenges.

The Gitmo story is a vivid illustration of why an effective SecDef needs to be politically astute—not to "play politics" with issues of national defense, but precisely the opposite: to protect the department and the entire administration from political pressures that might otherwise force decisions that would be harmful to the nation.

Wag the Dog: Waging War for the Sake of Votes?

In today's cynical atmosphere, I'm often asked whether, as SecDef, I was ever pressured to launch a military attack for purely political reasons. In fact, it seems that many people today *assume* that the "wag the dog" scenario, involving a president starting a war simply to attract votes and distract from political problems at home, is a common reality.

The truth is that it's just not so. In my thirty-five years in and around the DOD, I never witnessed a military action being initiated purely for political purposes.

The closest thing I've seen to a wag-the-dog war is the kind of small-scale military attacks—often derided as "pinpricks"—that presidents choose to launch as a way of demonstrating moral principle or issuing a warning to an adversary without making a major, risky commitment of U.S. troops. These half-measure assaults are actually pretty common. Examples include President Clinton's cruise missile strikes on bin Laden's camps in Afghanistan in response to al-Qaeda's attacks against U.S. embassies and President Trump's cruise missile strikes on Syrian facilities associated with chemical weapons' use early in his administration.

Somewhat similar was Obama's half-hearted support for the Syrian opposition, which I believe was adopted in part to stave off calls by Congress and others to unwisely wage a full-scale invasion to topple the tyrannical regime of Bashar al-Assad. What all these half-measure efforts have in common is that they "send a message" on behalf of the United States—which is, in effect, a form of political action, whether domestic, or foreign, or both.

This isn't the only way that politics impinges on decisions regarding military action. In fact, one of my jobs as SecDef was to help the president figure out how to do what was necessary to protect the country in a way that was, at minimum, politically sustainable, and, at best, politically advantageous.

Here's an example: When I decided that we would need to progressively increase both the number of U.S. troops in Afghanistan and their authority to conduct operations, I didn't hesitate to say so to President Obama. But at the same time, I was well aware that he had run for office in 2008 in part on a pledge to "end two wars." So I knew I needed to prepare carefully to make the idea of a troop increase as politically palatable for him as possible.

Doing this required two steps on my part. First, I gave him as much advance warning as possible so he could have time to wrap his political mind around the choreography of making and then announcing the decision. Since the campaign plan laid out each future move, the process could begin weeks in advance and gave the White House staff plenty of time to challenge my recommendation, prepare their own arguments for the president, and work with my own staff to reach a shared understanding of what needed to be done.

Second, when I was ready to make a formal proposal to the president, I shared the details with only Joe Dunford and a small handful of key commanders and staff members to minimize the probability of leaks. This would help the president represent the decision as his own, letting him reap whatever political benefits it could offer even as he was forced to accept the political costs it carried.

In a similar way, I worked hard to minimize the fallout for the president whenever I was forced to recommend an action that I knew would be politically difficult for him. I believe President Obama recognized and appreciated these efforts.

On the other hand, it's sometimes necessary to deliberately and carefully insulate the DOD from politics.

During the kaleidoscopic presidential election campaign of 2016, which involved, at various times, more than twenty candidates from both parties, I wanted to do my best to make sure that politics stopped at the water's edge—and at the Pentagon walls. So I was ready with my response the very first time in the election cycle that members of my Pentagon leadership team were asked a politically loaded question.

It happened on February 25, 2016, when Joe Dunford and I testified at a hearing concerning the defense budget before the House Appropriations Committee. During the question-and-answer period, Betty McCollum (D-MN) cited some statements in defense of torture and the killing of the families of Islamic terrorists made by a person she described as "a leading candidate for president." Of course, she was quoting some inflammatory remarks recently made by then-candidate Donald Trump. Representative McCollum then asked, "General Dunford, do you support allowing U.S. troops or the intelligence community to use torture to exact information from suspected terrorists?"

I quickly intervened. "Congresswoman," I said, "before the chairman answers your question, I really need to say something, and the question is a fair question. I want to say something about the framing of it that I believe in very strongly, however. Which is, this is an election year. We will have a new president. I recognize that. I feel very strongly that our department needs to stand apart from the electoral season. So I respectfully decline to answer any questions that arise from the political debate going on. I just don't think that is appropriate. And I want General Dunford especially, even more so than me, not to be involved in political debates."

A bit of back-and-forth ensued, in which the representative acknowledged the importance of my point, and the underlying question about torture was separated from any current political debate. Joe then stated that he agreed with the congresswoman that torture was not the kind of American value that U.S. troops should represent.

I had to repeat my little lecture on the importance of separating politics and defense on two later occasions before the members of Congress finally got the idea that I wasn't going to go down that road. They then stopped trying to get me or the members of my leadership team to respond to questions framed in political terms.

To serve a president well, a Secretary of Defense had better be politically savvy—because politics isn't just the air they breathe in Washington; it's also the means by which the people convey their needs, values, and preferences to those they choose to serve. But to serve the nation well, a Secretary of Defense also needs to know when to draw the line against politics and how to insulate the department against the partisan games that could easily distract us from our mission. It takes experience and a modicum of wisdom to understand the difference—as well as the readiness, when necessary, to put the mission ahead of one's own career.

CHAPTER 5

A BOARD OF DIRECTORS WITH 535 MEMBERS: THE ARTS OF DEALING WITH CONGRESS

In recent years, "gridlock in Congress" has come to be a constant complaint among political pundits, in the news media, and even among many in Congress itself. The complaint has become so familiar that many citizens may regard it as simply a fact of life. Few realize how new it is—and what serious consequences real gridlock in Congress can produce.

I caught a glimpse of that reality in 2013 when partisan warfare in Congress became so intense that most of the federal government actually had to shut down. The result was a disgrace to our nation: a period when vital needs went unmet, when crucial services were not provided, and when millions of citizens were needlessly subjected to confusion and anxiety, all because of a political battle of wills that served no purpose except to gratify the ambitions of a relatively small group of ideologues and those who finance campaigns.

The Constitution stipulates that Congress holds absolute control over the power of the purse. It's a powerful prerogative to which the members have understandably clung over the centuries. Presidential administrations, which tend to get the bulk of the blame in the media and in political campaigns for "runaway spending" and budget deficits, actually take a backseat to Congress in this regard. Each year, the Office of Management and Budget, headed by a presidential appointee, proposes a spending plan that specifies levels of funding for each government department. But every dollar spent by the Department of Defense and by every other government agency must somehow, sometime, get approved by a congressional vote.

Unfortunately, the clarity of the constitutional mandate has become muddied over time, thanks to the failure of Congress to live up to its responsibility.

By October 1, Congress is supposed to pass a budget for the fiscal year that begins on that date. This requires an *appropriations* bill, which permits the actual spending of government funds for particular purposes, and which must originate in the House. By contrast, an *authorization* bill is just a bunch of regulations with no meaning in terms of dollars; it simply allows the creation or continuation of a particular office, agency, or activity of the government without providing any funding. An authorization bill may originate in either the House or the Senate. So the passage of an appropriations bill—actually a collection of twelve or thirteen such bills, covering the entire federal government—is the crucial fiscal event. Without an appropriations bill, the government can't legally spend a dime, except for certain forms of spending that are officially defined as "emergencies" and a number of activities that are funded by long-term or mandatory appropriations.

In fact, a government employee who permits spending without the support of an appropriations bill could theoretically be indicted, convicted, and jailed under the provisions of the Antideficiency Act, which dates back to 1870. (No one has ever actually been convicted of violating the Antideficiency Act, although government employees have often suffered administrative penalties for doing so. When I was acquisition czar, everyone who worked for me was fearful of inadvertently running afoul of the Antideficiency Act.)

The problem is that Congress has gotten into the habit of routinely failing to pass the essential appropriations bills. Instead, it passes a mostly meaningless authorization bill. Many members then publicly crow about passing a "defense bill," knowing that most citizens don't know the difference. This kind of political gamesmanship makes me furious.

But then it gets even worse. When Congress can't agree on an appropriations bill, it passes what is called a *continuing resolution* (CR) to enable the government to remain in operation. A CR lets the government spend the same amount of money, for precisely the same purposes, as it spent the previous year. It doesn't let any government department increase, decrease, or change the budget in any way. The only exceptions are specific changes inserted into the CR by members of Congress, mostly in response to political demands of the moment.

As you can imagine, operating under a CR severely limits the ability of the Pentagon (and all other government departments) to carry out its missions effectively. Taken literally, a CR means that, for example, the Navy is required this year to build the same ships it built last year—an absurd idea. It also means that any new program that Congress may have mandated through an authorization bill simply can't be put into effect. Neither can any improvements, expansions, eliminations, or reforms of existing programs.

Furthermore, since CRs typically extend funding for just a few months at a time, they make it hazardous for government agencies to enter into long-term contracts for any services they must purchase, from maintenance of military bases to overseas logistics. As every manager knows, short-term contracts are always more expensive than long-term ones. So the uncertainty and turbulence caused by the lack of proper budgeting processes create inefficiency and waste taxpayer dollars. It's a highly ironic outcome, since the legislators who refuse to pass appropriations bills often claim to be motivated by a desire to reduce wasteful spending.

For all these reasons, I've always hated continuing resolutions—as practically everyone who works in government does. But I had to learn to deal with them in each of my Pentagon jobs. Thankfully, defense budgets generally don't change entirely from one year to the next, so operating under a continuing resolution is not impossible. But it's far from ideal. And over time, the problem kept getting worse. During the eight years of the Obama administration, Congress never managed to pass a budget by the end of the fiscal year.

In a worst-case scenario, Congress can't even manage to pass a CR. That's when a partial government shutdown kicks in. I saw the impact this can have in 2013, when I was serving as deputy secretary of defense under SecDef Leon Panetta.

As usual, Congress had been unable to pass an appropriations bill for the 2014 fiscal year, which began on October 1, 2013. So far, so bad. But the Republican-led House proceeded to transform a minor problem into a major one by instead producing a series of CRs that removed funding for the Patient Protection and Affordable Care Act—that is, Obamacare. The Democratic-led Senate predictably refused to let their signature legislative victory be destroyed through this budgetary maneuver. The two parties played chicken over the people's government. The result was an impasse that prevented agreement on any CR at all. So when the morning of Tuesday, October 1, arrived, the federal government was officially without funding.

The effects throughout the government were immediate and painful. Fortunately, some of the most urgent forms of spending, including veterans' benefits and Social Security payments, receive long-term funding and so were not halted. But other valuable services were shut down. The closure of some highly symbolic operations, such as the national parks, was widely covered in the news media as a marker of how seriously political dysfunction was affecting our national self-image.

My biggest concern, of course, was the impact on military operations and readiness. The DOD activities that were affected were wide ranging. We had to stop paying some of the department's thousands of civilian employees as well as some military personnel, who had to work without salaries, wondering when they'd get their next paychecks. At the last possible moment prior to the shutdown, Congress had passed a bill called the Pay Our Military Act, which provided salary payments for troops considered to be on active duty and for civilian workers directly supporting them. But the law was written in haste, meaning the guidance it provided was ambiguous and confusing. It didn't cover everyone in the department, and significant non-salary payments, such as housing allowances for families of deployed soldiers, were also uncovered, causing meaningful hardship to many thousands of military families.

Hundreds of training programs and military operations deemed nonessential under the Antideficiency Act were canceled. Some entire operations in other departments, such as the U.S. Merchant Marine Academy, were shut down altogether. The DOD military academies were variously affected; many classes and activities that relied on civilian employees were canceled. And payments to civilian companies with

Pentagon contracts were halted, affecting millions of workers. During the week following the October 1 shutdown, a number of businesses announced plans for employee furloughs, including five thousand workers at United Technologies and three thousand at Lockheed Martin. Weapons production was severely curtailed, as were research and development projects, testing programs, and other activities affecting our defense capabilities.

Scrambling to deal with these mushrooming problems was bad enough. As the budget deadline neared, I and other Pentagon personnel had to devote hundreds of hours to studying the legislative and regulatory requirements under the law, making contingency plans for dealing with them without severely damaging the country's long-term preparedness, and then implementing those plans—practically a full-time job in itself. All of this represented a major waste of time, money, and other resources. But most distressing to me were some specific program shutdowns that directly affected the troops and their families.

I was particularly galled by the fact that the emergency-only spending rules under the Antideficiency Act prevented the payment of death benefits to families of fallen troops. These benefits, which many Americans know little about, include an insurance payment of around $100,000, burial expenses, a twelve-month housing allowance, and some other modest payments. Not much, but the least we can do for those who have given their all. The funds are typically disbursed within about three days.

A few days after the shutdown started, news stories began to appear about the added suffering being inflicted on the families of soldiers killed in action. The *New York Times* reported on the deaths of Sergeant Patrick C. Hawkins, Private First Class Cody J. Patterson, Sergeant Joseph M. Peters, and First Lieutenant Jennifer M. Moreno, all killed by explosives in Kandahar Province, Afghanistan. Their bodies, the paper said, "will arrive at Dover Air Force Base in Delaware on Wednesday. . . . But if their families want to meet the plane, they will have to pay their own way to Delaware."

This was totally unacceptable to me. So I called Ken Fisher and asked for his help. Ken is a member of a New York–based family that is prominent in real estate development and management. The late Zachary Fisher and his wife, Elizabeth, had been dedicated to military and veterans' causes. In 1990, they founded the Fisher House Foundation to build "comfort homes" where families of wounded warriors can stay near military hospitals on bases while their loved ones are being treated. More than seventy of these Fisher Houses are currently in operation. Ken and other members of the family have carried on this legacy.

I told Ken, "I need millions of dollars, fast." And I explained the cause, which he immediately grasped and embraced. Within twenty-four hours, Ken called me back to say he'd raised $13 million—more than enough to provide advance payments to cover the needs of the bereaved military families.

It's noteworthy that when I first called Ken for help with this emergency, the DOD's general counsel was sitting by my side, shaking his head disapprovingly. He'd warned me that seeking private funds for government purposes isn't normally legal. I decided to ignore the advice. I told Ken, "I dare anyone to haul me into court for providing death benefits to the families of fallen heroes."

Thankfully, the government shutdown ended fairly soon. Late in the evening of October 16, Congress passed the Continuing Appropriations Act of 2014, and President Obama signed it shortly after midnight. Federal funds began to flow again, and we didn't have to depend on Ken's charitable moneys to meet the needs of the families of fallen heroes. But I'll always be grateful to him and to his network of patriotic donors for their response to my request—and angry at Congress for making it necessary.

Why Not "Run the Government like a Business"?

When they hear stories like this, most citizens get upset—and rightly so. But in reaction, some become believers in the popular notion that many of our nation's problems could be solved if only we ran government "more like a business." This notion underlies a lot of the political posturing in

Washington, from demands for a balanced budget (supposed to be more "businesslike") to the theory of the "CEO president" overseeing cabinet members who run their departments like divisions of a giant corporation. The dream of the ultra-efficient CEO president probably influenced the outcome of the 2016 election, since candidate Donald Trump had built an image as the ultimate business executive through his reality-television show *The Apprentice*. (Actual New York businesspeople have said the opposite was true.)

There's no doubt that government leaders can learn from the play-book of successful business leaders. Like any big company, the government spends huge sums of money; makes major capital investments in land, equipment, and technology; manages large numbers of employees; and is required to provide excellent service to a demanding base of "customers"—in this case, the American people. The Defense Department, in particular, also mirrors the world of business in that it must compete aggressively against powerful rivals—enemies and potential enemies from around the world. Recognizing these commonalities, smart public servants know there is wisdom to be gleaned from the practices of the best corporate managers. That's why insights from business have helped inspire some aspects of successful government-reform movements throughout history, including the Better Buying Power program that I implemented at the Pentagon.

In most ways, however, running a government agency like the Defense Department is very different from managing a business, no matter how big or powerful. A vast number of stakeholders powerfully impact the work of the Pentagon, from others in government to opinion shapers in the media, our international allies, and, of course, the American people themselves. Businesses, too, and especially public companies, have multiple stakeholders. But they have nowhere near the same requirements for transparency and public accountability. Moreover, some of the stakeholders to whom the Pentagon must respond are unusually demanding. I don't think the average corporate board of directors writes a list of 3,500 guidelines for the CEO to follow every year. But that's a fair description of what Congress does. The annual defense authorization bill, as I've noted, doesn't actually provide any money for the department but spells out a mind-numbing list of detailed regulations, including some as trivial as a requirement that the department submit a report on a species of bird known to nest at a naval base. Every year, the act is used by members of Congress as a vehicle for every pet cause and project simply because everyone knows it *must* get passed. And afterward, members from both parties preen themselves in public over this accomplishment, which they hail as an example of "rising above gridlock" and "supporting the troops"—all a complete fiction.

In reality, the NDAA is a purely regulatory bill that imposes a preposterous level of micromanagement that no self-respecting business executive would ever tolerate. In my last year as SecDef, Congress passed an NDAA including 3,500 pages of regulations I had to follow—but not a single budget appropriation bill! It's a problem much more real and troublesome than the supposed micromanagement imposed by the White House, which I largely avoided through the approach I described in Chapter 4.

Furthermore, the Defense Department is unlike virtually any business in that it has little or no choice about the tasks it undertakes. Most companies freely choose the products or services they offer and the customers to whom they cater. Those in charge of corporate strategy try to pick target markets that play to their business's strengths, and they work hard to maintain their focus on those strengths. By contrast, DOD does not have the luxury of choosing the missions it must undertake.

Nor does the DOD get graded on a quarter-by-quarter basis, the way Wall Street tends to measure the effectiveness of corporate CEOs. The SecDef is given command of an organization that has been in existence for over 240 years, and, if worthy of the job, he makes decisions based on the knowledge that it will continue to operate for centuries to come. So planning with a long time horizon is essential. Strategic threats can evolve over decades, and it's not unusual for the Pentagon to oversee investments that take 20 years or more to come to fruition. (I described the challenges of managing such long-term projects in Chapter 1.) On the other hand, changes in presidential administrations, which occur every 4 or 8 years, often lead to whipsaw shifts in policy, especially when the other party takes over. Corporations don't generally have to deal with the problem of being taken over by a group that is ideologically hostile to everything the previous administration had planned—but federal departments do.

It's true, then, that running the Pentagon requires the organizational, strategic, and financial acumen that it takes to guide a giant global corporation. But the job *also* involves subtle and complex demands that are far more difficult than those of business, which is why calls to "run the government like a company" are naive and simplistic. These demands are particularly galling when they come from politicians and pundits with no business experience themselves.

Cabinet members and others charged with getting things done in government have no choice but to find ways to make an often-dysfunctional system more responsive. Much of the challenge originates with Congress, a collection of 535 individuals who each have their own agenda, pet peeves, and favorite projects, and constituents who need to be mollified and, one hopes, impressed.

The Roles of Congress

Article I of the U.S. Constitution describes the structure, functions, and powers of Congress. Many of the rules that govern the activities of the federal government today can be traced to specific language in this article. For example, the annual struggle to pass appropriations bills, and the threat of shutting down the government when Congress fails to do so, is based on the wording of Section 9, Clause 7, which begins "No Money shall be drawn from the Treasury, but in Consequence of Appropriations made by Law." Congress is granted the power to authorize activities on behalf of the national defense by a series of clauses in Section 8, including Clause 12, which gives Congress the power "to raise and support Armies, but no Appropriation of Money to that Use shall be for a longer Term than two Years"; Clause 13, "to provide and maintain a Navy"; and Clause 14, "to make Rules for the Government and Regulation of the land and naval Forces."

In practical terms, however, Congress has three main functions that apply to DOD. One is to provide oversight of the executive branch—part of the American system of division of powers and of checks and balances that is at the heart of our democratic governance. This function is not explicitly mandated anywhere in the Constitution. But it's strongly implied in the broad authority described in the final clause of Article I, Section 8: "To make all Laws which shall be necessary and proper for carrying into Execution the foregoing Powers, and all other Powers vested by this Constitution in the Government of the United States, or in any Department or Officer thereof."

It's hard to see how Congress could decide which laws are "necessary and proper" for the government to carry out its powers without monitoring what the executive branch is doing, how programs are being administered, and how well national problems and needs are being addressed. For this reason, Congress has, in fact, exercised oversight responsibilities since the earliest years of the republic, and many laws and congressional rules have reinforced, structured, and codified this activity. Anyone who runs a federal agency—especially one as large and consequential as DOD—must be prepared to work with members of Congress as they exercise their right to oversee executive actions.

The second congressional function that affects DOD—and the most absolute as defined in the Constitution—is the power of the budget. I've already shown some of the challenges this power can create when it's not exercised responsibly.

The third and final responsibility of Congress that's closely related to the work of DOD is the power "to declare War," as stated in Clause 11 of Article I, Section 8. Note that, in practice, the power to declare war has become separate and different from the power "to authorize the use of military force." The relationship between these two powers has been a source of dispute between the executive and legislative branches on and off throughout our history, and especially in the decades since the Tonkin Gulf incident of 1964 led to the congressional authorization that was ultimately used to justify the decade-long war in Vietnam.

As SecDef, I had to manage within the constraints involved in each of these three congressional prerogatives. I have no problems with any of them, either philosophically or in practical terms, so long as they're applied reasonably. That is sometimes the case, but less often today than it was in the past.

Congress as Watchdog: Running the Oversight Gauntlet

In carrying out its oversight function, Congress acts as a watchdog on behalf of the American people. As SecDef, I had my work overseen by four congressional committees: the Senate Defense Appropriations Subcommittee, the Senate Armed Services Committee, the House Appropriations Subcommittee, and the House Armed Services Committee. I had no problem with being summoned to Capitol Hill under appropriate circumstances to give testimony, to provide expert advice from my subordinates regarding possible legislation, and to answer questions myself about defense policies and activities. I was also comfortable with having members of my staff and other departmental leaders, such as the chiefs of staff of the five branches of the armed services, called before the committees—again, under appropriate circumstances.

Occasionally, however, the calls from Congress did *not* fit the "appropriate circumstances" limitation. Sometimes we got requests that were unreasonable or even downright insulting. A committee might ask me to appear while specifying that Joe Dunford, the chairman of the Joint Chiefs of Staff, should *not* attend—or it might call for Joe to appear while specifically excluding me. Invitations like these were often motivated by a desire to sow or exploit apparent differences of opinion among members of the Pentagon leadership team, which I didn't appreciate and refused to countenance. In other cases, I was invited to appear jointly with some official from outside DOD, which might put me in the position of commenting on policies or activities that were none of my business. And in still other cases, I was summoned on very short notice, asked to appear on a date when I wasn't available, or called to testify about some unreasonably trivial matter.

When these sorts of inappropriate requests arrived, I would ask my legislative affairs director to handle them. A good one—and, in Steve Hedger, I had a good one—knows how to fend these off without needlessly burning any bridges.

As for the substance of the congressional oversight process, it rarely leads to the kinds of spectacular exposures of wrongdoing or dramatic political clashes that we associate with episodes like the Army-McCarthy hearings, the Watergate investigation, or the Benghazi hearings. Most often, the ideas and information that surface during congressional hearings are used to inform the writing of laws. Sometimes the results help to make the operations of government more fair, effective, efficient, and responsive to the needs of citizens. In other cases, just the opposite happens.

Unfortunately, in the majority of instances that I experienced during my years in the DOD, the new provisions written into law by members of Congress eager to change the actions and policies of the Pentagon have done more harm than good. The authorization bills related to the DOD that are passed every year reflect the often-amateurish ideas of legislators and their staffers, who sometimes know very little about how the Defense Department actually works. They write regulations, rules, and restrictions based on ideological agendas, requests from donors or constituents, or ideas cooked up by journalists, think-tank experts, or consultants. As a result, Title 10 of the U.S. Code grows by several thousand pages every year. This just makes an already tough managerial job even tougher.

Periodically, members of Congress decide to put their weight behind a program of "reform" for the Pentagon. While this is unquestionably a legitimate expression of their oversight power—and reform is certainly needed in many quarters of DOD—the results of the reforms mandated by Congress have been uneven at best. Shortly before I became acquisition czar, the Weapon Systems Acquisition Reform Act of 2009 was passed. Largely penned by the deeply knowledgeable Senators Carl Levin and John McCain, the act created three new suboffices within my office to emphasize three functions that they believed were not being given adequate attention: cost assessment and program evaluation, developmental testing and evaluation, and systems engineering. I agreed on the merits and said so in my confirmation hearing. (It would have been hazardous to my confirmation to do otherwise!) However, I also believed that these functions could and should be performed by the people already there, and that adding three new boxes to the Pentagon organization chart would just add to the bureaucratic bloat for which we were already rightly criticized.

After confirmation, I duly set up the offices. They quickly began to build themselves into new fiefdoms, asserting their law-given authority to demand that program managers win their consent before any program could be brought to me for approval. In effect, this represented a set of additional "flaming hoops" to the gauntlet that a program manager had to jump through—judging programs rather than helping them succeed. The offices were staffed mostly by people who were much older than the program managers. I didn't consider the sight of a young colonel perspiring in front of a panel of stern, elderly experts in a conference room to be an enhancement of the acquisition process.

Somewhat comically, a few years later, after I'd departed that job, the same congressional committees that had mandated the creation of the new departments concluded that the office of the acquisition czar had now become too large! It would have been logical for them to ask the professionals in the Pentagon the best ways to trim and simplify. Instead, acting on the naive advice of think-tank experts, Congress took away some boxes their staff members thought could be eliminated.

In addition, since they felt that the office as a whole had become bloated, they split it down the middle—one half for acquisition and maintenance of weapons systems, one half for research and technology. So their solution to the problem of an office that they themselves had excessively expanded was to turn it into *two* offices. This was particularly absurd because every enterprise in the history of innovation has struggled to bridge the gap between research and product development—so deliberately separating the two functions was exactly the opposite of what we needed.

This is the way too much congressional oversight of the Pentagon operates—not in the form of thoughtful, well-managed support for a hardworking and knowledgeable management team, but rather as a series of pendulum swings from one well-intentioned but extreme fad to the next. Most of these "improvements" are sprung on the department with no consultation or input from real experts.

Even seemingly simple changes to the way the Pentagon operates—for example, budget cuts or increases—often lead to unintended consequences that complicate our work rather than improve it. The complex, arcane rules controlling government programs mean that significant changes to specific activities—shutting down a weapons project, for instance—often take years to implement. In the short run, Pentagon managers are forced to scramble to try to implement the changes that members of Congress have ordered. As a result, budget adjustments mandated by Congress generally end up forcing cuts or increases in all the wrong places—and still more headaches for the DOD personnel who are required to live with the consequences.

Congress would do better to invest its time and energy in passing appropriations bills in a timely manner rather than dreaming up more regulations and half-baked "reforms." In addition, a defense budget that is reasonably stable from one year to the next, facilitating intelligent long-range planning, would be a godsend—and would save the taxpayers countless billions of dollars. And when regulations and department structure need changing, some back-and-forth with the experts and with those who must implement change would also be helpful.

Testifying Before Congress: A Survival Guide

As you can see, I have some strong feelings about the shortcomings of Congress, especially in recent years. But dealing with Congress is an unavoidable part of the job for anyone in a leadership role at DOD—and that includes providing testimony at hearings on the Hill.

I have testified before Congress many times, and over the years I've developed a good idea of the tradecraft involved in doing it right. I've appeared before innumerable committees focused on potential congressional actions or legislation. Even more daunting, I've had to survive Senate hearings in order to be personally confirmed to a Pentagon post no fewer than four times—to serve as assistant secretary, undersecretary, deputy secretary, and SecDef. This is like being a Roman gladiator thrown into the lions' den four times and surviving. The fact that I managed to do this was no accident. I worked at it.

My son is an expert on cybersecurity. In January 2018, he was asked to appear before the Subcommittee on Emerging Threats and Capabilities of the House Armed Services Committee. The topic would be China's pursuit of emerging and rapidly developing technologies, a subject he has been studying closely. Seeking advice on how to handle his first congressional hearing, he turned to the expert he knew best—his dad. The suggestions I provided will illustrate some of the fine points of maintaining positive and cordial relations with Congress—in other words, keeping the lions at bay.

Here's the advice I shared with my son.

Many young people are taught to give speeches or talks; college students today often learn to create PowerPoint presentations. These are all one-way media in which the speaker controls the agenda. A congressional hearing is quite different. Others, through their questions, eventually control the agenda. (In this sense, a hearing resembles a press conference or a town council meeting.) Your goal as a witness in a hearing is to seize and retain control as fully as possible right from the very beginning.

The first step is to compose a written statement. You won't be presenting this statement orally, but it will be entered in the Congressional Record, which captures the official history of legislative deliberations. (Its existence is actually mandated by the Constitution, Article I, Section 5, Clause 3: "Each House shall keep a Journal of its Proceedings, and from time to time publish the same.") The members of Congress won't read your written statement, but their staff members will, and they'll use it as the basis of the members' opening statements and the first few questions they'll ask. It will also be reviewed and used after the hearing by expert analysts and by those few members of the press still willing and able to dig into subjects in any depth. So it needs to be good—clear, precise, and accurate.

Submit your written statement twenty-four hours before the hearing. If it's late, the congressional staff members won't be able to adequately prepare their bosses; they'll be annoyed at you and they may take it out on you through hostile questioning. But don't talk about it or leak it to the press beforehand, or the members will feel as if you were trying to put them at a disadvantage through your maneuvering—another way of inviting combative exchanges.

The substance of your written statement will depend, of course, on the topic you've been invited to discuss. But it should begin with an expression of thanks, in the form of "Thank you, Chairman X and Ranking Member Y, for inviting me to testify at this hearing today." (The ranking member is the senior committee member from the party that is in the minority in the chamber.)

Then you should go on to subtly praise the members for having some interest in your topic among all the other things they have to worry about. For example, you might say why it is so important for people like you to help them out: "It's vital that the leaders of Congress should be fully informed about the trends that are helping to shape the future of our nation, including the issues of A, B, and C that we are here to consider today."

Then introduce yourself briefly, assuming you are not yet a well-known figure like the SecDef. Two or three sentences will be plenty. It's likely that the members will have only a vague sense of who you are, based on a brief explanation from a staff member, so it's helpful to establish why you are an expert who is worth listening to. Of course, you should do so in a way that is straightforward and factual, not self-aggrandizing or "puffy."

Having concluded these preliminaries, you can now explain in writing the main concepts and information that you want to deliver to Congress. The written statement can be lengthy—when testifying about a complex matter, such as an annual budget proposal, I might provide a statement running 7,500 words or longer. But make sure it can be easily scanned so that staffs that are pressed for time can quickly get the gist of what you have to say. Inserting subheads that break your statement down into sections and summarize the sequence of ideas can be very helpful.

You almost certainly have an argument that you are trying to make—a policy approach that you want to convince Congress to adopt. Make sure that argument comes through clearly and explicitly. But don't simply state your own position; in your written statement, try to anticipate every likely objection and counterargument to your own, and give a reasonable answer to each one. This won't guarantee that you will win the debate, but it is good discipline for you. It also reduces the chance for needless misunderstandings and makes it harder for members of Congress or outside critics to claim you ignored one complication or another.

Next, compose the oral statement—the presentation you will actually deliver when you're called upon. This must be much, much shorter than the written statement—no more than two pages of single-spaced text, or about a thousand words. Keep the same preliminaries as in the written statement—the expression of thanks, the statement about the importance of the topic, and the brief description of your credentials. Then offer a very crisp summary of your written statement. Avoid listing facts, statistics, or ideas. Instead, tell a story that illustrates your central theme. People understand and remember stories much better than facts, no matter how important.

More challenging, be prepared to improvise to a degree on the day of the hearing. By the time you're called to speak, the chairman and the ranking member will have already made their opening statements. It's polite and highly effective to acknowledge something they said. If at all possible, agree with them. Even if you think that their approach to the topic is wrongheaded, you can agree with their recognition of the importance of the issue while suggesting that you will offer a different perspective on it.

Similarly, make an effort to respond to other witnesses who may have appeared before you. If you've heard statements you consider inaccurate or ill-considered, rebut them in a polite, respectful manner and without personalizing the disagreement. If you've heard statements you agree with, say so and thereby remove that issue from the debate.

Your oral statement will be followed by questions from the members— and here is where your preparation will really be tested.

At least a week before your scheduled testimony, begin thinking about all the questions that a curious and intelligent individual might ask about your topic, and especially about the policy position you support. Also try to anticipate the questions that might be asked by someone who is *not* particularly well-informed, as well as someone eager to demolish your argument. Force yourself to consider uncomfortable questions that you may face—about the weaknesses in your presentation, the facts you've ignored or omitted, the reasonable objections that opponents have embraced. Write out answers you can use if confronted—and do your best to make them concise, fact-based, and respectful but forceful.

Doing all this writing in the solitude of your office is important—but even more important is practicing to perform orally in front of a live audience. I recommend getting some friendly colleagues to pepper you with questions for an hour or so—the same kind of "murder board" that I did scrupulously before every hearing, even after I'd had years of experience. Not only does this give you the chance to hear, and think about, a number of surprising and challenging questions you wouldn't anticipate on your own, but also it lets you brainstorm and debate possible responses with a team of sympathetic supporters. I always conducted murder boards with my staff. I would invite Joe Dunford to participate so he could benefit from the same back-and-forth debate, and to give the two of us the chance to recognize any places where our views might be construed as conflicting. The murder boards also helped me determine whether I really knew what I was talking about. More than once I sharpened my position on an issue or even changed it after a murder board showed me I'd gotten it wrong.

Finally, get a piece of white cardboard (my favorite writing surface) and write down all the key facts and phrases you may want to cite during your testimony. (I am able to print neatly and rather small, which helps.) The process of creating this tool will help solidify the items in your memory, and having it in front of you on the table as you testify will greatly enhance your confidence. You'll know that when a question makes you draw a blank—a common occurrence—you can just glance down to recover the words or numbers you need.

So that's the process I used to prepare for congressional testimony, and it's the one I recommend to anyone else in the same position.

It may seem slightly odd that the Secretary of Defense, ostensibly one of the most powerful people in the world, should need to go through such training to prepare for questioning from his colleagues in government.

But we've all seen how being unprepared for a curveball from an influential representative or senator can get a cabinet officer in trouble, generating a needless controversy that might take weeks to defuse. I preferred to invest my time, thought, and energy beforehand and so prevent such controversies from ever arising.

I may not have transformed the lions of Congress into tame beasts, but at least I managed to escape repeatedly with my skin intact.

Congress as Purse Keeper: The Annual Budget Maze

Having discussed the role of Congress as watchdog, let's consider its other constitutionally mandated responsibilities, beginning with control of the budget.

As I've noted, the Constitution stipulates that the Congress holds absolute control over the power of the purse. So I knew that whenever I sent over a defense budget to Congress, I was merely making a proposal. The legislative branch would have the final say.

As SecDef, I was reasonably comfortable with this reality. I knew that Congress would never pass a budget without making changes, many of them for reasons I considered inane or excessively political. I found this annoying and considered it an implied insult to the professional judgment of those in DOD who had drafted the proposed budget in the first place. However, the reality was that the congressional tinkerings usually only amounted to about 10 percent of the budget. Sometimes that 10 percent included items that the president or I considered high priorities—but at least the 90 percent went unscathed. I could live with that.

Much more troublesome to me was the routine failure of Congress to pass a timely appropriations bill, forcing the country to cope with repeated last-minute showdowns over passing a CR to keep the government running—and even the occasional government shutdown, like the one we lived through in 2013.

Sadly, this wasn't the only budget-related pathology I had to deal with as SecDef. Another was the debt ceiling, a legislative control on spending that actually dates back to the Second Liberty Bond Act of 1917, which was passed to authorize funding for World War I. The law requires Congress to periodically raise the debt ceiling to allow the Treasury to continue to incur the debt needed to fund government—for example, by issuing bonds. Because the new debt is needed simply to pay for spending that Congress has already authorized—and because it's widely understood that a default by the United States on its financial obligations would have a devastating impact on the world economy—the idea of failing to raise the debt ceiling is fundamentally ludicrous. Still, the periodic need to officially raise the limit has been used increasingly as an excuse for partisan and ideological grandstanding, as well as for additional bouts of nail-biting over the possibility of another government shutdown.

Complicating this pathology further was the Budget Control Act of 2011, intended to cap deficit spending. This law put a ceiling on the defense budget, so we could not ask for additional funding. It also provided that, if no budget was passed by the end of the fiscal year, so-called sequestrations would kick in—across-the-board budget cuts with just a few specified exceptions, including salaries for members of the military. In March 2013, the sequestrations hit, forcing significant spending cuts in various defense programs, particularly operations and maintenance activities aimed at enhancing the training and readiness of combat troops during their "at home" periods between overseas deployments.

Another piece of the Rube Goldberg budgetary machinery is the system for funding so-called overseas contingency operations (OCO). This process, which relies on a special supplemental appropriations bill and is separate from the usual appropriations process, has been an important part of Pentagon funding since just after 9/11. Originally created to finance the wars in Iraq and Afghanistan, OCO funding is now contained in one or more bills passed every year, in amounts that have sometimes exceeded $100 billion. Nominally, this is considered "emergency spending," but as these wars in the Middle East have continued for many years, OCO funding has in effect become part of the normal budget-request process. Nonetheless, according to a dictum by the Congressional Budget Office, OCO funding is *not* subject to the caps created by the Budget Control Act.

Obama and his team came into office feeling that the Bush administration had abused OCO. They had some reasons for this belief. The Bush defense team had used OCO moneys to pay for things like contracts to build jet fighters, reasoning that the planes were needed to replace older aircraft that had been worn out during the Iraq and Afghanistan wars. It's doubtful that projects like these really qualified as "emergency spending." Gambits like this help explain why OCO funding is sometimes referred to as a "slush fund" for the Pentagon.

However, I was always a big supporter of OCO funding and other similar forms of supplemental spending. They provide a degree of flexibility that's essential to the smooth running of Pentagon operations. For example, when a major hurricane strikes the United States, the DOD is called upon to spend billions to support the relief efforts. But such hurricanes occur only, on average, once every two or three years—which means it would be wasteful to budget for them annually. Supplemental funding lets us request the money only when it's needed.

OCO also insulates the funding of troops in wartime—truly essential spending—from the budgetary shenanigans that congressional gridlock has increasingly produced. And because it is not capped by the straitjacket of the Budget Control Act, it is "free money" in deficit terms. Why not accept it?

Over the years, I argued in defense of OCO against a series of White House budget directors who opposed it almost as a matter of theological purity. I thought of them all as good people who happened to have an unfortunate bee in their bonnet about this issue. And since President Obama himself never raised it with me, I felt no need to back down. In the end, I always got the OCO funding we needed.

Many citizens wonder about the extent to which the Pentagon spending process is inherently political. Congress, which controls the purse strings, is an eminently political body. The former use of so-called earmarks, which let members of Congress channel specific amounts of money included in appropriations bills to particular projects—usually in their home districts—was a pretty low-cost system that served as a safety valve for the political pressures elected officials naturally face. I understand that the elimination of earmarks beginning in 2011 has actually increased the partisan gridlock over bigger issues. The compromises needed to effect these small transactions tended to serve as a lubricant for dealmaking on larger matters.

As the Pentagon's chief acquisition executive, I had duties separate from the political fray in Congress. My constituents were the warfighters and the taxpayers. Thus, I always tried to protect the system and the members of my team from political interference. This is why we worked hard to frame the criteria for acquisition decisions clearly, and then allowed an expert source-selection committee to pick the winning contractor. This process minimized the scope of subjective factors and errors in acquisition decision-making and execution, which could become an avenue for politicization.

Sometimes members of Congress would visit me to make a pitch on behalf of a company located in their districts, regarding this as simply a form of "constituent service." Some of them honestly didn't realize that the acquisition czar didn't make all the contracting decisions personally. Perhaps in the cities and states they hailed from, politics controlled the contracts drawn up for building bridges, schools, and hospitals.

My answer was always the same: "Your candidate will get a fair shake, and nothing more." This allowed them to report back to their constituents that they'd made the case on their behalf. On the rare occasions when they tried to go further—for example, by pressuring or intimidating a member of my Pentagon team—I pushed back forcefully. The acquisition cadre really appreciated having me stick up for them when they were doing the right thing.

Congress as Warmakers: The Power to Declare War

The Constitution is very clear about vesting the power to declare war solely in Congress. But that document was drafted and adopted in a very different time—an era when armed conflict embroiling the nation within hours or even minutes was impossible. There was no need to envision a system that would allow the United States and its military to respond almost instantaneously to an attack by an adversary. There was no such phenomenon as global terrorism, in which non-state actors with lethal weapons might launch a deadly, warlike assault on large numbers of American citizens at any time. Nor did the United States have a network of overseas partnerships and commitments—political, economic, and military—that might call upon the nation to respond to aggression in far-away lands.

Over the past two centuries, all these circumstances have become real. This is why none of the armed conflicts the United States has been engaged in during recent decades have involved a formal declaration of war, passed by Congress. That's how it has to be. There is no way that the president and the SecDef can do the job they need to do to protect the United States in today's world while waiting for a timely declaration of war. Remember, this is a Congress that can't even pass a defense budget.

Nonetheless, it wouldn't be politically tenable or appropriate to exclude the legislative branch altogether from the serious choices that revolve around the making of war. The power of the purse is one way that Congress can exercise its authority in regard to warmaking. In addition, I believe that the constitutional powers of Congress properly extend to conflicts that are both large in scale and lasting in duration. Thus, when the president on his own authority wages war in response to an external threat, the importance of having Congress authorize or approve the president's actions grows larger as the duration and cost of the conflict grow and as the risks to the nation and to American interests increase.

During my time as SecDef, this issue came into play in connection with two acts authorizing the use of military force that were passed after 9/11: one for the war on terror, focused on al-Qaeda in Afghanistan; and another for the war in Iraq, focused on Saddam Hussein. These two acts ended up being used to justify a wide range of military actions in a variety of settings. In fact, according to a May 2016 memo issued by the Congressional Research Service, the 2001 Authorization for the Use of Military Force (AUMF) related to terrorism had been cited thirty-seven times in connection with actions in fourteen countries and on the high seas. The direct connections to the needs associated with the original AUMF had become increasingly tenuous. Nevertheless, according to lawyers from the Department of Justice, the 2001 AUMF on al-Qaeda justified fifteen years of action against Islamist extremist groups, most of which claimed connections to Osama bin Laden's group. In particular, the ongoing campaign to defeat ISIS fell comfortably within the scope of the 2001 AUMF.

However, in 2015, some members of the Senate, led by Tim Kaine (D-VA), proposed a new authorization for the use of military force. President Obama supported the concept, and members of the administration worked with Congress to craft the language of the bill. I was asked to testify regarding this bill before the Senate Foreign Relations Committee. In effect, my testimony stated that I didn't believe I needed a new law formally authorizing our campaign against ISIS (and similar or related actions). However, I had no problem with Congress passing such a law, provided it met two criteria.

First, the law should not limit the campaign in any way that I might reasonably have to extend it. However, if the campaign grew and expanded in a major way, it would be within the power of Congress to require a new authorization bill. For example, if the fight against ISIS ended up requiring large-scale, sustained ground combat, I would anticipate and support Congress wanting to authorize that. By definition, such circumstances would provide the time needed for an appropriate debate.

The second criterion was that the process by which the law was passed and the law itself should be unambiguously supportive of what I was actually asking the troops to do. I would not support a bill that might appear to question the mission of men and women who were risking their lives for the country.

Subject to those stipulations—both of which I felt were adequately met by the language of the bill that Congress was then considering—I had no objections to the passage of a new authorization bill.

In the end, by spring 2015, congressional leaders decided to scuttle the new AUMF, having concluded they simply didn't have sufficient support to pass the bill. In effect, this meant that Congress was tacitly accepting the fact that President Obama and the DOD were sufficiently empowered by the 2001 AUMF to carry out the ongoing mission to defeat ISIS. That's an assessment with which I concur—as do the majority of constitutional scholars.

History tells us that the tug-of-war between Congress and the executive branch over war powers (as well as other prerogatives) is likely to go on forever. I think that's what the founders intended. It's healthy for government officials to be subject to scrutiny and pushback from others with their own independent sources of authority. Operating within this system of checks and balances can be frustrating at times. It certainly isn't designed to maximize speed and efficiency. But it's the best way we've yet discovered to rein in the excesses and errors that inevitably seem to occur when any set of decision-makers becomes intoxicated with its own power.

CHAPTER 6

COMMUNICATING WITH THE PRESS AND THE PUBLIC

On the morning of January 12, 2016, I was attending a long-planned meeting at the State Department. John Kerry and I were hosting a visit by two of our overseas counterparts, the foreign minister and the defense minister of the Philippines. No major issues were on the table; the meeting was a routine but important relationship-building exercise, like many of those I attended.

Then, quite suddenly, all hell broke loose.

The cell phone in my pocket began buzzing. Almost simultaneously, so did the phones in the pockets of John Kerry and the various team members who were in the room with us, including Joe Dunford, the chairman of the Joint Chiefs of Staff, and Peter Cook, the Pentagon's top press liaison. It was obvious that something urgent was happening. We excused ourselves to take the calls.

All of us were getting the same confusing but alarming message: The U.S. Navy had lost contact with two boatloads of sailors in the Persian Gulf. When last heard from, they'd been close to Farsi Island, not far from the border of Iranian territorial waters. No one knew what this meant. Was it a mere communications breakdown? Were the sailors dead or alive? Had they been taken prisoner by the Iranian government, or perhaps by a group of extremists or terrorists?

Whatever the facts, this had all the makings of a major international crisis.

With apologies to our friends from the Philippines, we cut the meeting short and leaped into action. I told Joe Dunford, "Joe, go back to the

Pentagon and monitor the situation from there. Don't let anybody hurt our guys. But don't start a fight without checking with me first." In a few moments, Dunford was on his way. Soon thereafter, I heard from him that Lloyd Austin, then commander of CENTCOM, which oversees the U.S. military presence in the Middle East, had already sent jets scrambling over Iranian territory. It was a show of strength designed to send a powerful message to a potentially hostile government with a history of taking American hostages. A search-and-rescue mission had also been launched. It still wasn't clear exactly what had happened.

Meanwhile, John Kerry was on the phone. Just six months earlier, he'd completed the negotiations for the complex and controversial deal that halted Iran's program to develop nuclear weapons. That meant he still had the phone number of his Iranian counterpart, foreign minister Mohammad Javad Zarif, programmed into his cell. Within five minutes he had Zarif on the line—the first of several conversations they would have inside an hour.

The picture of what was happening gradually began to emerge. The two small U.S. boats, on their way from Kuwait to Bahrain, had evidently strayed into Iranian territorial waters—whether due to mechanical malfunction or navigational error was unclear. Two Iranian vessels had spotted the boats and boarded them. The ten American crew members—nine men and one woman—had been taken prisoner.

Kerry was very clear in his conversations with Zarif. "This incident can easily become a crisis with grave results for your country," he warned him. "Our people must not be harmed, and they must be released swiftly. If you do this, we can prevent this situation from escalating into something very dangerous."

Zarif understood the message, and he assured Kerry that the Americans were being "treated well." But at first, he was unable to promise that they would be promptly freed. Agonizing minutes passed while we waited to hear whether Zarif could persuade the other leaders of the Iranian government to avoid ratcheting up the tensions.

While matters hung in the balance, Peter Cook, heading back to his press office at the Pentagon, heard something that made his heart leap into his throat. In the hallway, he encountered a breathless Lolita "Lita"

Baldor, a veteran AP reporter who'd been covering the defense beat for years. "Peter," she said, "can you confirm that Navy sailors have been taken prisoner in Iran?"

Cook's brain started racing. The news about the incident was supposed to be tightly under wraps. Someone within the government must have leaked it—an all-too-frequent event that causes many a headache for DOD leadership. But this leak was far more dangerous than most. Once the story hit the airwaves and the Internet, passions on all sides could be inflamed. Hard-liners in Iran could denounce "American treachery" and demand that the sailors be held and perhaps tried for their "crimes." Hard-liners in the United States, many of them still unhappy over the nuclear deal, could demand immediate military action against Iran. In this scenario, the lives of the sailors could become pawns in an international showdown—the last thing we wanted.

All this could be the price that the United States, and the world, might have to pay for the news scoop that Lita Baldor was, for the moment, sitting on.

Cook asked Baldor to step into his office. He quickly outlined the seriousness of the situation, which Baldor immediately grasped. Cook then called Baldor's editors at AP and repeated the same message to them: Releasing this story prematurely could endanger the lives of the U.S. sailors. It could also needlessly escalate tensions with Iran and perhaps, if worse came to worst, provoke a war.

"If you hold on running anything for the moment," Cook offered the AP team, "you can be the first to report the full story, including what we hope and believe will be a confirmation that the sailors are safe and will be released."

Cook's plea carried credibility. Before joining my department, he'd been the chief Washington correspondent for Bloomberg Television. The free-press instincts of a seasoned reporter were deeply ingrained in him. Reporters knew that the only reasons Cook would try to delay or even quash a truthful news story were to protect the security of military operations and to avoid endangering the lives of American service members.

Baldor and her editors knew that the risks must be very real for Peter Cook to be asking them to delay publication. But keeping an important story from the American people also went against their values as journalists. They would have to be convinced that Cook's concerns were irrefutable. The three-way telephone conversation among Cook and the AP team became increasingly intense.

Cook was still negotiating with AP by telephone half an hour later, when Zarif finally called back. He'd obtained a firm commitment from the Iranian government to release the sailors. They'd recognized that the incursion by the American boats had been inadvertent, not an act of aggression or espionage, and they understood the kind of retribution they'd face if they dared to turn the event into a military confrontation.

We all breathed a sigh of relief. I was able to call Joe Dunford with the positive news and a "Stand down" order to the troops on alert. At the same time, Peter Cook shared the news with AP. Lita Baldor had her scoop, and the danger of an explosive international conflict was averted.

This story offers a vivid illustration of the complicated relationship between the news media and the DOD. On the one hand, an informed public is essential to democracy. The American people need to know what the U.S. military is doing on their behalf, and as SecDef, I recognized and respected my obligation to keep them fully informed. On the other hand, a truly "transparent" government can't carry out all its jobs effectively—including such essential jobs as keeping the peace and protecting the lives of Americans.

A delicate balancing act among important, sometimes conflicting values is demanded. That's one of the reasons I dedicated a significant amount of my energy as SecDef to thinking about relations between the Pentagon and the press, and to managing them responsibly.

Communication Matters

For more than a decade and a half since September 11, 2001, U.S. forces have been involved in nearly constant war. Informing the public about what the troops are doing and why is critical to maintaining citizen support for their efforts. In a democracy, the people deserve to know what is being done in their name. The troops themselves, as well as their families and friends, need to understand the purpose of their mission and the reasons they are being asked to sacrifice. And leaders and citizens from around the world—whether they are from countries allied with the United States or from countries that may be potential adversaries of ours—need to understand what we are doing on the world stage and why. If we don't explain our purposes, members of the media, pundits, and opinion-shapers will claim to explain them for us, not always with clarity, accuracy, or honesty.

For all these reasons, it's essential for the Pentagon to run a press operation that is professional, disciplined, and as open as possible, balancing the need for public information with the need for security around ongoing operations. In a very real sense, in a democracy like the United States, the citizens are just as involved in shaping the management of the Pentagon as those more obvious wielders of power, the White House and Congress. And most communication with the citizens takes place through the news media—the reporters, editors, broadcasters, producers, and commentators on TV, the radio, and the Internet, and in newspapers and magazines, who inform, educate, and occasionally confuse and mislead the American public about the purposes and workings of national defense.

As SecDef, I spent a lot of my time and energy handling the press. I never sought deferential treatment from the press, nor did I use selective leaks or glad-handing in an effort to generate adulatory puff pieces from friends in the media (as some in government do). But I did want the media to report our actions carefully and accurately, and with due respect for the gravity of our mission, the complexity of the decision we faced, and the dedication of the troops.

The process began with assembling a team of communications professionals to represent the department. As SecDef, I wanted a respected professional journalist rather than a defense official to speak for me, and a civilian rather than a military officer. My model was the press office my predecessor Bill Perry had set up, led by the former *Wall Street Journal* reporter Ken Bacon. That meant moving aside Admiral John Kirby, whom Chuck Hagel had used as a spokesperson for the department.

(After retiring from the Navy, Kirby became spokesperson for John Kerry's State Department.)

Peter Cook turned out to be an excellent choice as my assistant for public affairs. Peter surrounded himself with a team of superb people, including Gordon Trowbridge, who'd been a reporter for twenty years before becoming a speechwriter for Senator Carl Levin; Jeremy Martin, a thirty-year Army veteran; and Carl Woog, one of the most creative communicators in Washington. They were bolstered by Navy Captain Jeff Davis, who oversaw a team of Pentagon press officers responsible for fielding an endless number of media inquiries from around the world every day. Although Peter himself was not an expert on defense matters when he took the job, he quickly developed the expertise on a wide array of detailed issues that an effective press spokesperson must have. And I made sure that Peter was in the room for all of my most important deliberations, so he could speak authoritatively on my behalf—a fact that the press knew and appreciated.

It's also important for the media to hear from commanders on the ground. They're the ones whose words are authentic and therefore trusted by the public and the troops themselves. Military leaders in Baghdad and Kabul were particularly important voices; they could give front-line facts about deployments, operations, victories, and setbacks—as well as occasional mistakes, as when an air strike caused unintended civilian casualties. Being honest about what we'd done right and wrong was critical to maintaining American credibility both at home and abroad—and especially among the families of the troops, who were never far from my mind. The commanders were the ones best positioned to provide such candor.

Surprisingly, however, most senior officers are a bit hesitant about speaking to the press. For some, it's simple modesty or shyness. Others may have been burned by having their words twisted in a news report, leaving them reluctant to talk to reporters again. I felt that it was important for the commanders to become comfortable as public spokespeople. I asked Peter to help them. He and his team worked with the commanders, coaching them on how to plan their talks to the media, how to anticipate and prepare for challenging questions, how to talk about setbacks without seeming defensive, and how to correct an ill-informed or hostile reporter while remaining professional and respectful. The commanders appreciated Peter's help. Many praised him for helping them develop confident public voices—and never muzzling them.

As for me, others can evaluate my performance as a spokesperson for the department. My main goal was to communicate honestly, clearly, and professionally about the work of the department—work that I knew was some of the most important being done by anyone in the world, and that therefore deserved to be explained with seriousness and integrity.

When preparing for a press appearance, I generally composed my own material. As an experienced writer of books and articles, I was picky about language and word choice. When a major announcement was in the offing, I would often devote most of a weekend to composing a first draft, since it was impossible to fit the job into a busy workweek. Then I'd send the draft to my speechwriting team and others on my staff. After they'd had a chance to study it, we'd all get together and critique it, a process a little like the murder boards I'd engage in before a congressional hearing. This would help me to anticipate likely questions, as well as fine-tune the structure, tone, and choice of words used in my statement.

I came to respect the power of *repetition* to ensure that a message is heard, understood, and believed. I worked hard to define key concepts in a few words that were precise and memorable, and then to use those phrases on every possible occasion. Thus, I consistently referred to America's troops as "the finest fighting force the world has ever known"— a description that was both completely accurate and deeply appreciated by the troops themselves. As the campaign against ISIS intensified, I sought a phrase that would describe our goal with the perfect blend of clarity and strength. Eschewing less-forthright verbs like "degrade," I ended up saying that we sought "defeat" for ISIS. I added the modifier "lasting" to further suggest a strategy of enabling our allies in the region to maintain peace and security after we'd left. The result was "a lasting defeat," a phrase I used countless times in speeches, interviews, congressional hearings, and troop talks. I knew it had been successful when I heard our generals, press officers, and even President Obama himself talking about the goal of "a lasting defeat."

My insistence on using such catchphrases made my speeches a little predictable for members of the press who traveled with me and heard me speak repeatedly; in fact, I understand that some of them enlivened the task of listening to my speeches by playing "Ash Carter Bingo," earning points every time they heard me use one of my favorite lines. I didn't mind. My goal wasn't to entertain, but to ensure that the right message got hammered home. Repetition was a key tool in my arsenal—especially important in today's flabby information sphere.

My straightforward style of speech wasn't very flashy and didn't attract a lot of media coverage. Reporters who chose to profile me sometimes described me as a "technocrat," perhaps reacting to my scientific training as well as to my approach to decision-making, which I tried to base strictly on facts and data. I sought to be precise and deliberate, and to express myself in a tone that was sober and thoughtful.

It didn't bother me to have a relatively low profile among the most powerful leaders in Washington. I was less concerned about communicating with the D.C. elite than I was about keeping in touch with the troops and their families. They were the ones bearing the brunt of the mission, and they were the ones who needed to hear from me—to know that the SecDef was thinking about them, that he understood the challenges they faced, that he had thought long and hard about every sacrifice he asked them for, and that he deeply respected and appreciated what they do for our country.

A Changing Media Landscape

For government officials, our reliance on the news media as the primary channel we use in communicating with the public has become particularly complicated. The vast majority of newspeople want to be ethical, honest, and responsible in the ways they inform and educate the citizens. But in an era when the media are under ever-growing economic, professional, and political pressures, maintaining consistently high standards of integrity is increasingly difficult for them.

As SecDef, I found that the journalists we had to deal with split pretty clearly into two groups: the really good and the pretty bad. The best professionals in the Pentagon press corps were led by Bob Burns of the Associated Press and included reporters from news outlets such as Reuters, *Stars and Stripes* (the official newspaper of the military), the major newspapers, and journalists from some of the television news networks. They had been on the job long enough to know much of the relevant history of the department, were deeply knowledgeable about defense matters, and cared about the people and issues they were covering.

They also had lots of sources both inside and outside the department, as well as high ethical standards when it came to reporting potential failures or misdeeds. That meant we knew it was impossible to conceal anything significant from them—and so we almost never tried. I sometimes wished they didn't have the stories they had, but I quickly learned that being candid about problems generally produced more fair and accurate coverage than denial or obfuscation. And when reporters were developing stories about an issue that hadn't been decided or a military operation still in the planning phases, we could usually persuade them to withhold or delay publication so as to avoid needlessly complicating our work, and especially to avoid endangering the troops.

I found that, when working with professionals at this level, I could generally expect fair treatment for the department. But in today's world, where the press is a distressed industry, that kind of professionalism is unfortunately becoming rare. The collapse of the old business model in which newspapers were supported by reliable streams of advertising revenue has forced editors to cut costs drastically, with predictable consequences for the quality of reporting.

I found that even some news outlets with impressive journalistic histories, such as the *New York Times*, had been forced by budgetary concerns to focus their government reporting mainly on the White House and the State Department. Coverage of the Pentagon was not as robust as I would have hoped. Some of the best defense reporters I'd worked with in my previous jobs had become editors, supervising younger reporters with minimal knowledge and understanding of defense, many of whom seemed to come and go as members of the Pentagon press corps. In talking to those in the press room or aboard my plane during a foreign trip, I had to be mindful that half the reporters there needed to be filled in on basic information before they could cover the story of the day.

Some of these green young reporters were would-be scandal mongers in search of stories they could sensationalize; others were just looking for clicks, tweets, and a twist of the day's story that would get them noticed among readers and their peers. Their questions were often transparently designed to lure me into revealing something they planned to write about anyway, whether relevant to the day's news or not. It often seemed as if half the press corps was trying to outdo one another in the cleverness of their "gotcha" questions.

The rules of the game would change with the political climate. During my first year as SecDef, the most popular sport was to try to find and highlight some disagreement between me and President Obama; during my final year, it was to find space between me and one of the presidential candidates.

Some of the established news outlets had also cut back on their coverage of the major war zones. Rather than sending reliable reporters, they relied on local stringers—freelance contributors—without seeming to realize that these stringers were often biased supporters of some local faction with a slanted view of regional politics. There was also a strong tendency for the media to emphasize negative stories about American military operations. Prior to Vietnam, good news from the battlefield would be reported just as fully as defeats or failures, and the historical record shows that fiascos were often hushed up, sometimes by official censorship but more often by editorial consent. That era has long passed. So when things were going well with the counter-ISIS campaign, for example, there were almost no stories telling of Iraqi forces gathering strength and courage with the support of American troops. On those days, the papers would simply be devoid of war news. Only when the inevitable setbacks occurred did the coverage resume. The motto of the media seemed to be, "Good news doesn't sell."

Budget cuts and a natural bias for newsworthy negativity in the newsroom aren't the only sources of bad reporting. The acceleration of the news cycle under pressure from the Internet and the twenty-four-hour cable networks poses other problems. The velocity of the news media is now so great that some reporters file stories without adequately checking on their accuracy or fairness. They also repeat stories they've heard from one another rather than doing independent reporting or research. Once reported, a falsehood becomes its own kind of truth. And even though most fake news stories vanish from the headlines in a day or two, they live forever on the Internet.

I don't want to imply that smart, responsible reporting about government, and about defense in particular, is a thing of the past. As I've mentioned, there are still many excellent, seasoned journalists who do a fine job of covering DOD. Many of their younger colleagues with less experience are working hard to try to develop the same level of skill and expertise. And it must be said that many journalists take on significant personal risk when they cover events in the world's war zones—writing about the troops, which is a lot more important than writing about me. Some of these brave reporters have given their lives for the cause of an informed public. For this, they deserve our respect and gratitude.

Still, the changes we've seen in the world of media have made it harder for journalists to ply their craft at a consistently high level of excellence. That means a SecDef—like other leaders in the public eye—must be more vigilant than ever about his interactions with press and public.

Staying Clear of Bad Reporting in Tricky Circumstances

The combination of declining professionalism in many sectors of the news media and the increasingly extreme partisanship of our politics has created a world in which it sometimes seems that every day brings a new media frenzy, often centered on some supposed "scandal" with little or no real substance. The media addiction to scandals—often inconsequential or misreported—creates the risk that when truly scandalous behavior occurs, a public numb to the daily bombardment of spurious accusations will ignore or dismiss the news.

I hope I'll see the day when the scandal machinery that has become such a powerful part of our news media is dismantled. In the meantime, those of us in the public eye have no choice but to find ways to avoid it, even as we continue to inform the public fully and accurately about the work we're doing on their behalf.

The best way I've found to avoid scandal is meticulous planning and preparation for any consequential public act. There are a number of examples throughout this book. But even actions that are of modest importance in themselves can get magnified out of proportion in the press. Learning to avoid such distortions is also important, as a story or two may demonstrate.

In January 2013, President Obama nominated Senator Chuck Hagel to serve as SecDef. I'd been deputy secretary for a number of years and had enjoyed the job immensely, and I agreed to stay on under Hagel. In fact, Obama didn't give me much of a choice. He called me to the Oval Office, where he'd arranged for us to have lunch in his side study. Without giving me the name, he said he had decided he was going to name "a politician" to succeed Leon Panetta and that he regarded me as "part of the deal." He therefore wanted me to stay on as deputy.

I had no problem with the request, both because it came directly from Obama and because for a deputy to depart at the same time as a secretary is to irresponsibly leave a department without experienced officials in its top two positions. I promised the president I would give six months to help the new SecDef get up to speed.

A few days later, I learned that the choice was Chuck Hagel. I didn't know Chuck well at all, but I certainly knew his reputation, both as a soldier wounded in Vietnam and an independent spirit on Capitol Hill. I had no idea how unpopular he was in the Senate until a vicious campaign against his confirmation began with a number of Chuck's colleagues turning sharply against him.

I tried to help Chuck manage the confirmation process by offering the help of Pentagon staff and advisors. But Chuck was a proud man and confident that, as a long-standing senator, he needed no one's help in managing the Senate. He turned down my offer to help him practice before the confirmation hearing, with disastrous results. Republicans successfully filibustered the nomination—a first for any SecDef nominee—and delayed Chuck's confirmation for two weeks. He was finally approved on February 26, 2013, and sworn in the next day.

By August 2013, I'd been working with Chuck for six months. I began thinking about how and when I would make my own departure from the Pentagon. I expected Chuck to serve out the rest of Obama's term, which would allow plenty of time for a new deputy to have a good run. I didn't want to stay much longer and thereby cut into the time my successor would have on the job.

Stephanie and I went out to the West Coast for our usual summer holiday. As was also our habit, we visited the lakeside home of Bob Gates and his wife, Becky. I was looking forward to an evening of salmon on the grill and good conversation with an old friend and counselor. As Stephanie and Becky worked in the kitchen, Bob and I went out to the grill, and then settled into two chairs looking over the lake with glasses of Grey Goose. We looked at each other and both knew we had the same thought in mind.

Bob Gates is a man of great wisdom, vast experience, and a kind of decency and civility that seem increasingly out-of-date today. He is also a careful Washington tactician. We both knew that it was important for me to control the narrative surrounding my departure from what I expected to be my last job in Washington. Like the moment of confirmation, the moment of resignation is a moment of vulnerability—a time when people feel free to take a shot at you knowing they can do so with impunity. All kinds of frustration and recklessness can come to the surface.

Bob and I talked through how I should handle the challenge. We decided that I would write a letter to Chuck when I got back to D.C. in September. I wouldn't beat around the bush or give any phony reason like "I want to spend more time with my family." Not that I don't love my family! But nine times out of ten, the government official, elected or

COMMUNICATING WITH THE PRESS AND THE PUBLIC   167

nonelected, who offers this as the reason for his departure from Washington is simply avoiding some more honest and less self-flattering explanation.

Instead, I would use the opportunity to recall the basic facts of my career in national defense—long service, bipartisanship, and dedication to the troops and the mission. I would flatly state that I intended to leave the department in December, which I hoped would preclude any attempt by the president to talk me into staying longer. I would be careful to praise both Obama and Hagel in the letter, which I hoped would discourage people from attributing my decision to leave to frustration or conflict.

Finally, Bob and I agreed that it was essential for me to maintain absolute secrecy. The last thing I needed was for an advance story to be written based on a leak by someone with an ax to grind. I also wasn't looking for a puff piece. There was no drama to report—just the departure of a longtime public servant who'd tried to give his all. It seems like a small thing, but in today's media environment, even small things can require care to get right.

When I got home in September, I wrote out the letter in longhand. Then Stephanie typed it on her private laptop and printed it on the printer in her office. But I delayed delivering it because the end of the fiscal year was coming. With the government facing the usual drama of continuing resolutions and a possible shutdown, Chuck really needed me to help him handle the budget situation. Under the circumstances, I didn't want to do anything to weaken my ability to help him. So week after week, as the budget drama progressed, the letter remained at my home, unseen by anyone.

Finally, by early October, the budget situation had cleared, and I was ready to go. I wrote to Denis McDonough, Obama's chief of staff, late one night and asked if I could see him first thing in the morning. This would give him minimal time to wonder what was up, but it meant I wouldn't take him completely by surprise. I knew that I could count on Denis to be discreet, and I felt I owed him and the president some advance notice of my plan. Denis wrote right back and asked me to stop by his office at seven a.m.

The next morning, Denis invited me into his office and closed the door. "I've been wondering all night what this is about," he remarked. I silently slid the letter across the table.

He read it and said, "Should I walk you right down the hall to the Oval Office?"

"No, Denis, my mind is made up. But please ask the president not to share the news until I've had a chance to deliver the letter to Chuck." Denis agreed.

Unfortunately, Chuck had a full calendar of outside activities that morning. I nervously fidgeted in my office, waiting for his return. When he arrived late in the morning, we met privately in his office, and I slid the letter to him across the table.

I was taking Chuck entirely by surprise. He has a temper, and I was worried he might respond with an explosion of anger. Instead he blinked, paused for a moment as if to digest the news, then raised his head slowly and deliberately, and said, "Thank you, Ash. I know I wouldn't be where I am without you." It was a magnificently graceful moment for Chuck Hagel, and it made me admire him even more.

With that, I returned to my own office and gave the letter to my own loyal, long-standing staff. I wanted it to be distributed immediately so that my words would be the first version of the story to circulate in gossipy Washington. It was the first time I'd kept such a big secret from my staff members, and I know they were disappointed and hurt. But the secrecy I'd imposed had been essential.

My careful management of the process paid off. The reports about my departure were straightforward, with minimal speculation and no political potshots. A number of people said to me afterward, "Very few leave Washington with a higher regard than when they came in, and you are one." Chuck gave me a magnificent sendoff in the Pentagon auditorium in December, and I went off to what I thought was my permanent post-Washington life.

I was pleased I'd been able to handle a risky moment in the public spotlight so adroitly. But even with the greatest care, it's impossible for a public figure like a high government official to avoid running afoul of the media now and again. When that happens, the way you react to a burgeoning media frenzy can make a big difference.

Toward the end of 2015, almost a year into my tenure as SecDef, Peter Cook came into my office with some worrisome news. The *New York Times*, which had been reporting extensively about Hillary Clinton's use of a private email server while she was Secretary of State, was planning to publish a story about my own use of email. They had been told by someone that, during my first months as SecDef, I'd communicated extensively with my staff members using the personal email account on my own phone rather than the official account on my government Black-Berry. The messages were stored on the DOD email servers, but the *Times* reporter also wanted to know whether classified information was involved, which, if true, might even have put military operations and troops at risk.

The story was partially true. I'd used my personal email not only to exchange messages with friends and family, but also to communicate with my new Pentagon staff. This was the wrong thing to do—a sloppy violation of the strict and appropriate rules against mixing government and personal information systems. But I was certain there was no sensitive or classified information involved. They were mostly messages about when I expected to arrive at the office in the morning—administrative information like that.

Still, against the backdrop of the Clinton email controversy, my staff and I knew we had a problem on our hands. We had to decide how we would deal with it.

Peter, the DOD's general counsel, and my chief of staff, Eric Rosenbach, took the time to go over all the emails on my personal account written during the relevant time frame—a painstaking task that involved individually reading every single message I sent or received during those months. They found that no classified or sensitive material had been involved, and they had that confirmed by non-political security experts in the department.

Of course, this didn't mean I wasn't in the wrong or that I was home free. The press was barbecuing former Secretary of State Clinton over a different but related email issue, which meant they couldn't afford to ignore my misbehavior. After thoughtful discussion, my team and I agreed that the best response was for me to be totally transparent—to admit that

I had made an error and that I was prepared to take the full weight of criticism.

A few days later, I was traveling to our Special Forces outpost in northern Iraq, from which I was then intending to expand our counter-ISIS campaign in Syria. This was a pretty big piece of national security business, which meant that I was accompanied by a larger-than-usual complement of Pentagon press. But by then, the *New York Times* had broken the email story, and I knew that it would be the first thing I'd be asked about.

The occasion arose in the form of an on-camera interview with Charlie D'Agata of CBS News. We were in an austere location in Iraq with camouflaged tents in the background and helicopters and aircraft taking off and landing as we talked. And, of course, the very first question was about my emails.

I had carefully planned my response, which would be to explain my misdeed and answer questions. I looked directly at the camera and explained that, despite being warned about the importance of email security, I'd continued to use my personal iPhone. I noted that my emails had never contained any classified information. Still, I said, "It's a mistake, and it's entirely my own. . . . I have to hold myself to strict standards, and I didn't in this case."

My candor went over better than I had reason to expect. On *Morning Joe*, Mika Brzezinski ran a clip of me and made a comment to the effect of, "This is the way people should react when they've done something wrong." The whole thing blew over in twenty-four hours.

To this day, I'm convinced that if I'd tried to obfuscate, shift the blame, or point to extenuating circumstances, I would merely have given fresh life to the issue and helped it become a lasting blot on my reputation. Maybe this story illustrates the fact that many in the press are able to resist the temptation to drum up scandal for scandal's sake—especially when no serious harm is involved, and when those in the spotlight are forthcoming and willing to work with them on getting the truth out sooner rather than later.

Over time, my instincts for avoiding needless controversies became finely honed, extending to matters some people might consider trifling.

During my years at the Pentagon, the White House Correspondents' Dinners became increasingly glitzy affairs. I was invariably invited by one of the major news outlets, and I was expected to attend. But as Hollywood stars and other celebrities became more and more prominent participants, I became more and more uncomfortable. I didn't want to appear to the troops to be shirking our serious duties for this sort of thing.

In April 2015, I was scheduled to attend the dinner, and, as usual, my press secretary advised me beforehand about the people who would be at my table as well as the foreign dignitaries I might run into. I was also warned, "There's one guest you definitely don't want to be photographed with. CNN is hosting Jane Fonda, and she'll be escorted to the dinner by Wolf Blitzer."

I didn't need to be warned about avoiding a picture with her. Like many of my DOD colleagues—as well as countless veterans—I could never forgive Fonda for posing for photos astride a North Vietnamese antiaircraft gun at the very time American aircraft like the one piloted by John McCain were flying overhead.

In the event, avoiding the photo proved trickier than I expected. At some point in the evening, Blitzer came over to me and said, "I'd like you to meet my guest, Jane Fonda." I couldn't simply refuse, so I walked over quickly, keeping my head low, quickly mumbled a curt greeting, turned my back, and walked away—doing the minimally polite thing without being conspicuously rude.

I hoped and prayed that the moment hadn't been captured on anybody's iPhone. It must not have happened, since I never heard any more about it.

"Don't Jam Me": Protecting the President's Freedom to Decide

Some of the most consequential communications decisions that a SecDef makes revolve around things he must *not* share with the world. When those decisions are mishandled, they can thwart the administration's plans or even rob the president's freedom to make his own decisions. In such cases, communications can control substance, which is exactly backward.

As I've mentioned, in our earliest conversation about my becoming his Secretary of Defense, President Obama said to me, "If you have something to tell me, come and see me. I don't want to read about it in the newspaper. Don't jam me."

Obama and his close aides had become convinced that certain people in DOD had repeatedly leaked their military recommendations to the press before the president had decided whether or not to follow those recommendations. In this way, they had boxed Obama in, putting him in a position where he would be forced to publicly defend himself if he chose not to accept the DOD's advice.

There was more than one side to this story. While there were many leaks, the Pentagon's propensity to leak was somewhat exaggerated in the White House version of events. And on many occasions when the White House complained about a DOD leak, our press officers concluded that someone at the White House itself had actually been the source of the leak.

Still, the unhealthy dynamic in which internal policy debates were being conducted in the press had left wounds that still smarted, six years later. So I promised Obama that I would always give him my recommendations, as well as the professional military advice to which he was entitled as commander in chief, in private and without leaking it to the press. I did this both because the president deserves such courtesy (indeed, he can't function without it) and because I knew this professional approach would increase the chances that my advice would be accepted by a thoughtful leader like Obama.

I was pleased that, as SecDef, I was always able to keep my promise to avoid jamming the president. Both of the chairmen of the Joint Chiefs who served with me—Marty Dempsey and Joe Dunford—recognized the importance of this principle and honored it, as did all the combatant commanders we worked with.

Here's an example of how it worked. In late 2015, it became clear to me, Joe Dunford, CENTCOM's Joe Votel, and Afghanistan commander General John "Mick" Nicholson that the then-current plan to reduce U.S. forces in the country to 6,500 by the end of 2016 was imprudent. The long transition from the presidency of the mercurial Hamid Karzai to that of Ashraf Ghani had resulted in eight months lost for the Afghan government, which meant the Afghan forces were not yet ready to operate independently. They would also need an extended period of allied air support, due to delays in delivery of aircraft as well as crew training. Having found in Ghani a president of Afghanistan who was willing and eager to work with us—at last—we couldn't risk letting the country backslide into terrorism by pushing ahead with the planned troop reduction.

But how could we win the agreement of a president who had campaigned and won, in part, on his promise to end two lingering wars in the Middle East—especially as we were ramping up the anti-ISIS campaign? We knew the internal debate had to be handled with the utmost professionalism—and especially without leaks to the press.

Joe Dunford and I decided to make our recommendations in two steps. First, we asked Obama to expand General Nicholson's authority to use the U.S. forces that we already kept in Afghanistan. These forces were supposed to let Afghan forces take the lead in fighting, coming to their aid only in extremis. Sometimes, however, coalition forces had arrived only after the battlefield situation had deteriorated too greatly. Joe and I asked the president for permission to give Mick the authority to act more proactively with the troops in country so they could intervene in a conflict before the situation reached the emergency phase, but not so early as to take the initiative away from the Afghans. We made this recommendation in one of our private discussions rather than the leak-prone setting of a Situation Room meeting. It never appeared in the press until after Obama had agreed to the new authority.

The second step was to recommend keeping about 8,500 troops in Afghanistan rather than the 6,500 in the drawdown plan. Again, we kept a tight seal on the issue. When we presented our case to the president, only Dunford, Votel, Nicholson, and I were aware of the proposal and the numbers attached to it. After a thorough discussion, Obama agreed with our plan—a tough political decision that took courage on his part. He was helped by the fact that we'd kept the secret secure and refrained from jamming him.

A press conference in the Roosevelt Room of the White House was scheduled for Obama to announce the change. Moments before, Joe

Dunford and I joined the president in the Oval Office while reporters gathered next door. With evident satisfaction, Obama remarked, "They have no idea what I'm about to say. Only the three of us know."

The principle of providing advance warning about any significant event or initiative didn't always work the other way, from the White House to the Pentagon. There were occasions when the White House made a move of consequence without previously informing the DOD or other agency heads. This was rare, and it seldom bothered me, so long as the decision involved general foreign policy rather than military operations—for example, the president's closely held decision to reopen diplomatic relations with Cuba.

And sometimes, I admit, I surprised the White House, too—as when I revealed my decision about opening all military positions to women. In that case, I deliberately kept the president in the dark until just half an hour before I stepped to the Pentagon podium to make the historic announcement. I'll recount the whole story, and explain the reasons behind my secrecy, in a later chapter.

Communicating openly with the public can be a powerful leadership tool—and so can secrecy. There's an art to understanding which tool is the right one for a particular moment in the decision-making process.

Connecting with the Troops and Their Families

As SecDef, I knew that my most important audience was not the White House, Congress, the press corps, or even the general public. It was the troops and their families. They were the ones who bore the brunt of the mission. And they were the ones who needed, more than anyone, to understand and embrace the strategies underlying that mission. They were the first people I thought about when I woke up in the morning and the last people I thought about before falling asleep at night. It was important to me that the troops and their families knew that.

For this reason, while traveling the nation and the world to conduct the Pentagon's business, I always tried to set aside time to talk face-to-face with the troops and their families. That's also why I became the first

SecDef to create a presence on social media. In a world where millions of families stay in touch every day through Facebook, YouTube, and other websites—especially when separated by vast distances—it made complete sense for me to be visible on the same pages, sharing news about our efforts, explaining our goals and strategies, and conveying the nation's gratitude for their service. I wasn't looking to create an online presence, burnish my image, or collect a large number of followers. My core purpose was to express my personal dedication to the troops.

Social media, of course, also offered the advantage of being direct and unfiltered. I didn't have to rely on a reporter, editor, or producer to convey my message accurately and completely. Nor could anyone hearing my words wonder whether they'd been taken out of context or distorted. For better or worse, it was all me. And millions of military families seemed to appreciate what they saw.

I was fortunate to have the help of Stephanie Dreyer, a social media expert on my staff, in navigating this new landscape. With her support, I found it surprisingly easy to use social media to connect with thousands of people in the department, uniformed and civilian alike, as well as their loved ones and many others with an interest in our work, such as Washington journalists, members of Congress and their staffs, and so on. A few photos from my latest trip—usually surrounded by proudly grinning men and women in uniform—and a few sentences from me, and the result was a social media post that would circulate widely among a service member's unit mates, family, and friends.

One of the big social media successes that Dreyer helped organize was the first-ever SecDef Worldwide Troop Talk, held on September 1, 2015. Broadcast live on Facebook, YouTube, and Defense.gov, the talk allowed me to answer questions from troops around the world, submitted via social media (for example, using the Twitter hashtag #ASKSECDEF), by Skype or satellite, and from a live studio audience at Fort Meade, Maryland. The questions arrived from such varied and far-flung locations as Kuwait, Okinawa, Guantánamo Bay, the demilitarized zone in Korea, and Thule Air Base in Greenland. And they dealt with topics ranging from the practical ("What changes in our retirement compensation should we be expecting?") to the strategic ("What's next in the battle against ISIS?") to the fanciful ("Who is your favorite U.S. president?"). For the record, I chose George Washington as my favorite president—after all, he is perhaps the preeminent example of a soldier-statesman in our nation's history.

Another memorable social media moment came during my first holiday tour as SecDef. I made a point of traveling overseas during each December to meet with service members, tell them how important their mission was, and remind them how much those at home were thinking of them. During that first holiday tour, Dreyer and her team arranged to record troops at each stop singing a stanza from "The Twelve Days of Christmas," and the whole rendition made its way onto Facebook, off-key notes and all. A special touch was the three sailors from the French aircraft carrier *Charles de Gaulle* whom Stephanie persuaded to sing the line "Three French hens" in their national accent. All the service members in the video were excited about having friends and family back home see it to share a lighthearted moment of holiday cheer—and we got countless happy comments from folks saying, "That's my uncle Gary on a ship in the South Pacific!" or "I spotted my sister-in-law over in Germany!"

Sometimes, of course, the connections I made with the troops and their families involved duties that were much more somber. I soon learned that every time a Pentagon official—especially the SecDef—visits a military hospital to be with wounded warriors, or travels to Dover Air Force Base to receive fallen soldiers in a ceremony called "dignified transfer," the whole force watches. Every spouse and parent with a loved one who is deployed watches as well. It's important for them to see that those who have given their all are being treated with the care and respect they've earned.

I made sure to represent the department, and the nation, with appropriate dignity and empathy on such occasions. A mostly symbolic gesture? Yes—and an essential one.

Historically, there has been no American institution more respected than the Defense Department. Even today, in an age when public confidence in government, religion, law enforcement, higher education, and the press has waned, polls show that the military continues to command broad public approval, as it has for almost two decades. But having spent a lifetime working in and around the Pentagon, I worry that the public faith in our military may be broad but shallow. As someone with a deep belief in the importance of the mission to which the troops and their families have dedicated themselves, I consider it vitally important for the American people to understand the work of DOD so that they can participate intelligently in debating it and helping to shape its future. That's why communicating with the public was no mere afterthought for me, but rather an urgent part of my job.

PART 3

TROOPS IN ACTION

CHAPTER 7

CHAIN OF COMMAND: HOW MILITARY PLANS AND ORDERS ARE DEVELOPED AND EXECUTED

Giving authority for the conduct of military operations is the most critical function of the SecDef. Such orders are transmitted via a clearly delineated process that is known as the chain of command. The U.S. Constitution makes it clear that the chain of command begins with the president. But where it goes from there is not really understood by many. In fact, I once had to explain the chain of command to a distinguished former Secretary of State who had served on the National Security Council for years.

In today's chain of command, orders for the armed forces flow from the president to the Secretary of Defense, and then to the combatant commander (COCOM) whose forces carry out the orders. The current military structure includes ten combatant commands. Most cover geographical regions—for example, Central Command (CENTCOM), responsible for some twenty nations in the Middle East and North Africa; European Command (EUCOM), which works with NATO and other partner states on security and defense issues in Europe and parts of the Middle East and Eurasia; and Northern Command (NORTHCOM), which operates in the continental United States, Alaska, Mexico, Canada, and parts of the Caribbean.

Other commands cover operational functions. For example, Cyber Command (CYBERCOM) deals with threats and operations in cyberspace; Special Operations Command (SOCOM) is responsible for a range of special operations, including small-scale offensives, unconventional warfare, counterterrorism, counterinsurgency actions, and counter-proliferation of weapons of mass destruction; and Strategic Command (STRATCOM) manages U.S. nuclear capabilities, space, global reconnaissance and communications, and efforts to combat weapons of mass destruction.

So, for example, during my tenure as SecDef, when President Obama reached a decision about launching a particular operation as part of the anti-ISIS campaign in the Middle East, he would transmit the order to me, and I would pass it along to General Joe Votel, then commander of CENTCOM. As I'll explain later, the order would ultimately be executed by officers and troops under Votel's command, including Sean MacFarland (and later Steve Townsend), to whom overall leadership of the anti-ISIS campaign had been delegated.

Thus, the basic chain of command is a simple chain with just three links: president, SecDef, and COCOM. Just as noteworthy as those who are included in the chain are those who are *not*. For example, the chairman of the Joint Chiefs of Staff and the Joint Chiefs as a body are not part of the legally mandated chain of command. Neither are members of the National Security Council, such as the Secretary of State and the Secretary of Homeland Security. All these are important and influential figures in the world of national defense—but none of them is involved in actually transmitting battle orders from the president to the troops on the ground, and none of them has the power to countermand or interfere with any such order. This applies even to the ultimate exercise of military power, which would be a command by the president to launch a nuclear attack (via STRATCOM).

However, there are good reasons why the chain of command was designed as it is. Remember that the single most important responsibility of the chairman of the Joint Chiefs of Staff is to provide professional military advice to the SecDef and the president. If the chairman was in the chain of command, his advice could not be truly independent of those higher and lower in the chain. I find the logic of this argument compelling, which is one reason I was a stickler both for the importance of my role in ensuring the president was provided with candid military advice and for following the chain of command to the letter.

As for the legal basis of the chain of command, it traces back ultimately to the U.S. Constitution. Article II, Section 2, Clause I of that document designates the president as "Commander in Chief of the Army and Navy of the United States, and of the Militia of the several States, when called into the actual Service of the United States." The details of how this role works are spelled out in Title 10 of the U.S. Code. It defines the president's defense-related powers, outlines the command structure of the armed forces, and prescribes specific procedures that must be followed when raising troops, procuring supplies, launching operations, and performing all the other activities that the military engages in.

These regulations have evolved significantly throughout American history. Right through World War II, the U.S. military was divided into two separate cabinet departments: the Department of War, which governed the Army and, eventually, the Air Corps, and the Department of the Navy, which included the Marines. In the National Security Act of 1947, as amended in 1949, Congress unified the military services under the leadership of the new Department of Defense. However, the services still reported along chains of command that led to individual service chiefs—the chiefs of staff of the Army and the Air Force, the chief of naval operations, and the commandant of the Marine Corps. These service chiefs made up the Joint Chiefs of Staff, whose chairman reported to the SecDef.

This was a structure that led to interservice rivalries and difficulties in coordinating orders and operations that involved two or more of the services. These weaknesses were exposed in various ways during the Vietnam conflict of the 1960s and 1970s, the failed attempt to rescue American hostages in Iran in 1980, and the 1983 invasion of Grenada, provoking growing frustration among both civilian and military leaders.

Congress's response was the Goldwater-Nichols Act of 1986, which introduced sweeping changes to Title 10 and to the military chain of command. It was named after its two chief sponsors, Senator Barry Goldwater (R-AZ) and Representative William Flynt Nichols (D-AL)—a symbol of the bipartisan teamwork that formerly dominated congressional oversight and management of issues related to defense (and that now, alas, has largely fallen by the wayside).

I'd just started working on defense issues when Goldwater-Nichols was being debated in Congress. I remember Caspar Weinberger, my first Pentagon boss, fighting bitterly against Goldwater-Nichols when it was introduced by the authorization committees. He thought it intruded on the prerogatives of the SecDef and, ultimately, the president to conduct the affairs of the department as they saw fit. But in retrospect, the law and the regulations it led to were actually very effective, in large part because they were developed and implemented in an open, deliberative fashion. Thus, the department had plenty of time to make inputs into the law during its crafting, helping to ensure that the final rules were realistic ones that supported rather than hindered the work of the department.

The first and most fundamental impact of Goldwater-Nichols was to introduce and insist upon the concept of "jointness" in the armed forces. This meant that separate wars would no longer be waged by the Army, Navy, Air Force, and Marines, as in effect they had been in Vietnam. Instead, forces from all the services operating in a given theater would report to a single commander, making coordination of their efforts far easier and more effective.

To broaden the experiences of individual officers, and also to make sure that the services didn't starve the new joint structure of talent and, therefore, render it impotent, Goldwater-Nichols required all officers to serve in joint assignments, where there would be a mixture of service components fighting a war or running a command post for a theater working side by side. Thus, a Navy officer could no longer go through his entire career without serving under a joint command with Army, Air Force, and Marine officers. The law also created a system for joint procurement, enabling technological advances to be spread and shared more rapidly and efficiently among the services, a system I took advantage of when I became acquisition czar.

Goldwater-Nichols also greatly strengthened the office of the chairman of the Joint Chiefs of Staff and created a vice chairman to aid him, even as it removed the Joint Chiefs from the chain of command. It designated the chairman as the principal military advisor to the president, the National Security Council, and the SecDef. At the same time, it created the combatant commanders to direct operations in time of war. Among these, it introduced the Special Operations Command, designed to prevent future fiascos like the Iranian hostage-rescue failure. The end result was today's chain of command, leading directly from the president to the Secretary of Defense to the combatant commanders and bypassing everyone else in the Pentagon.

In theory, the clean lines in the chain of command laid out by Goldwater-Nichols provide clarity and accountability in the exercise of the most solemn duties of the government. But in practice, matters are often more complicated, as presidents, cabinet officers, and generals have often discovered in the heat of conflict. Understanding this complexity and ensuring that the right people are in place at every link in the chain are not just constitutional "niceties" that can be brushed aside in times of crisis. It's essential to avoid confusion and tragic mistakes in a confrontation—perhaps one with an emboldened, aggressive Russia or with a nuclear-armed North Korea or in a massive terror attack launched by an enemy that may be difficult to identify and pursue.

Protecting the Integrity of the Chain of Command

As soon as I was sworn in as the new SecDef, my first priority was to update myself about ongoing military operations, the workings of the White House, and the flow of orders along the chain of command. I quickly perceived some glaring deficiencies in the way things had come to be managed between the SecDef's staff and the president's staff, as well as some problems with internal DOD management. I did not know when or how these weaknesses had come to be part of the department's standard operating procedures. But I knew they had to be remedied if I was going to play the role as secretary that I intended and that I believed the president needed and wanted.

One example of these problems was the prevailing procedure for seeking presidential approval to conduct a military operation or to change the authority under which I and the commanders in the field could conduct ongoing operations. The procedure was for the secretary to send a formal recommendation to the president in the form of a concept of operations—a CONOP. (I discussed this process when addressing the issue of micromanagement back in Chapter 4.) According to the chain of command, the CONOP was to be formulated not by a member of the Joint Chiefs of Staff or even the chairman but by the relevant COCOM— that is, the military leader responsible for all operations in his region of the globe or military function. No one else was in the chain of command, certainly not the National Security Council as a body nor anyone on it (except the SecDef). Yet the procedure as it had evolved prior to my appointment called for a CONOP recommended by the SecDef to be referred to the NSC staff for "interagency review." In practice, this meant that the CONOP from the number two link in the chain of command would be vetted by a committee of middle-level officials from the NSC staff, the State Department, the Office of the Director of National Intelligence, the Central Intelligence Agency, and any other entities that might be involved.

I could not accept this procedure. I felt it was offensive to my office and against the spirit of the laws defining the military chain of command for my recommendations to the president to be scrutinized by a committee of people outside that chain. It surely would have seemed crazy to Cap Weinberger.

On the other hand, I knew that things had changed since Weinberger's day. Today, more than ever, most military operations have complex nonmilitary dimensions—diplomatic, political, and economic. In fact, it's a rare case in which the military dimensions aren't dwarfed by the nonmilitary ones. (I suppose all-out nuclear war might be an exception.) So when considering a military action with far-reaching implications, it's valuable to have the views of the Secretary of State, the national intelligence director, the CIA director, the UN ambassador, the Treasury Secretary, and others whose staffs and agencies could help gauge the prospects for success and whose parallel efforts were needed to execute the overall policy.

I therefore made a change in this procedure that was understood immediately in the bureaucracy and among my combatant commanders. Henceforth I would review a COCOM's recommendation for a CONOP and, after giving it a preliminary scrub, pass it to Susan Rice at NSC not as a recommendation to the president but as an idea that we in the department were formulating and for which I requested the input of the other NSC members. I would reserve my own recommendation to the president until after I'd received the views of other agencies and incorporated those views into the CONOP. In this way, I protected the integrity of the chain of command while making room for the value of interagency expertise in formulating operational plans.

Susan complained once or twice about the new procedure, and I waited to see whether the president would raise it with me in our private meetings. He never did, and Susan dropped her complaints.

I've already described how I worked with the White House in other ways to eliminate the irritant of micromanagement. I took on the responsibility of scrubbing the CONOPs so thoroughly that the president gradually developed a sense of trust in the plans I recommended—which made micromanagement by him unnecessary. But some additional measures were needed to correct a perceived imbalance that had developed and which my effort alone could not address.

When I arrived, the COCOMs submitted weekly reports to the SecDef concerning their activities and plans in their area of responsibility. I read these "weeklies" every Sunday afternoon. They were necessary and appropriate, since the COCOMs were my direct reports and I needed to know what they were doing and thinking. But I soon began to recognize from my discussions with Susan that she also knew the contents of the weeklies—in fact, she sometimes asked me questions about them before I had even discussed them with the COCOMs or the chairman.

It turned out that, sometime in the past, the NSC staff had begun requiring the COCOMs to submit their weeklies to the White House at the same time as they sent them to the SecDef. When I learned of this practice, I forbade it immediately. Most of the COCOMs were relieved, and the quality and the candor of the weeklies improved greatly. Susan raised it with me once, but it never came up with the president.

Another outrage, from my point of view, was that it had apparently become common for NSC staff members, or for Susan Rice or John Kerry, to call the COCOMs without asking my permission. I recalled that one of the few times I had seen Bill Perry blow his stack during his time as SecDef in the 1990s was when a White House staffer tried to issue an instruction directly to a military commander rather than working through Bill—an egregious violation of the chain of command.

The problem I was experiencing wasn't quite so serious—these were just phone calls, not orders. But I put a stop to them by telling the CO-COMs they could not accept calls from members of the NSC without my permission.

John Kerry had been the most frequent offender; the reason, I think, was that his personal communication style relied heavily on the immediacy afforded by the telephone. To soften his resentment of my crackdown, I made a point of asking Kerry several times, "Is it all right with you if I make a phone call to one of your ambassadors?" Kerry got the point, and developed the habit of asking my permission before calling one of my COCOMs.

The only calls from the White House to one of my commanders that I never objected to were calls by the president or Susan to the chairman of the Joint Chiefs. These were different, because the chairman is the president's military advisor too, not just mine. Allowing the White House free access to him was one of the ways I kept my promise to provide the president with professional military advice.

As these vignettes show, the legally mandated chain of command—like any other procedure dictated by law—does not just happen automatically. People must take deliberate steps to follow it appropriately and to defend it when necessary. I think a system that some of our finest leaders dedicated time and energy to developing, and that has served our country well for decades, deserves to be respected and protected. That's what my actions were designed to do.

Allies in the Chain of Command

Many Americans have a vague sense that our military alliances somehow represent a drain of money and other resources—that our partners in Western Europe, Asia, the Middle East, and elsewhere are freeloaders taking advantage of America's wealth and power to nestle under a security umbrella we provide at little or no cost to them. President Trump seems to share this belief. Perhaps he's influenced by his background in real estate, a business that centers on "the art of the deal." For Trump, success is measured in terms of transactions: every deal has a winner and a loser, and when it comes to America's military alliances, we are invariably the losers—big time.

Maybe President Trump wouldn't believe this if he knew how our alliances *really* work.

Our oldest and most extensive multinational alliance, NATO, links the United States with the countries of Europe in a pact designed to prevent the outbreak of another world war like the two that caused global devastation during the twentieth century. The NATO mission has been so successful that many Americans take it for granted. But to dismantle it or reduce it to a mere set of dollar-for-dollar deals could have a devastating effect on our national security.

More recently, on the other side of the globe, the United States has been carefully seeking to build a comparable network of alliances and security partnerships with countries around the Pacific Rim, from Thailand (actually America's oldest formal ally) to Australia, the Philippines, Vietnam, Indonesia, Korea, and Japan. The goal: a network of bilateral partnerships that can help keep the peace in a volatile region rife with ancient rivalries and burgeoning conflicts. The Trump administration's move to jettison the Trans-Pacific Partnership sent a signal that the United States may be abandoning this effort. This risks ceding regional leadership to China and reducing trade relations to a series of purely bilateral arrangements, which the Chinese will be sure to make coercive and predatory for smaller states.

Provided the United States is careful not to allow its partners to drag it into conflicts that do not directly affect our vital interests—for example, Saudi Arabia asking us to join its war in Yemen—these relationships are force multipliers. They amplify the formidable strength and geographic reach of the United States still further. And they reflect the attractiveness of our values, which explains why our major antagonists have few allies or none at all.

There's truth in Trump's complaints that some of our alliances—our NATO partners, for example—don't contribute their full share to the project of joint defense. Every recent U.S. administration has called our allies to task on this score. I once embarrassed my U.K. counterpart Michael Fallon by giving him a public dressing-down on the issue at a NATO meeting. (He found a way to exact revenge on me a few months later. During a joint press conference, when a question was asked regarding some embarrassing hot-potato issue for the United States, Fallon gave an answer—then pointedly added, with a smile, "Perhaps Secretary Carter would like to add something to my response.")

Most important, practically every NATO member is making some effort to raise its defense spending to the pledged level of 2 percent of GDP, and several have now reached that threshold—including Britain.

Like so many other aspects of national defense, our international alliances are complex and imperfect. They don't run themselves; instead, they require attention, support, and nurturing. But their forces supplement our own during conflicts, their bases provide valuable operating locations for which they pay much of the expense, and they provide political and moral support to American interests. Underestimating their importance and failing to maintain them would be an act of monumental folly that I hope our current and future leaders will avoid.

In a world where international alliances play a huge role in national defense, the question of how our military partners fit into the mandated chain of command is bound to arise. DOD is very selective about putting Americans under the command of non-American officers. But there are times when it's necessary—and in those cases, important rules and procedures need to be followed.

We have formal alliances with the countries of Western Europe through NATO, and with South Korea and a small number of other nations, including Japan and Australia. Our relationships with other friendly nations are not, strictly speaking, alliances, but rather partnerships, with rules and protocols that are different and less strictly defined. When we are party to a formal alliance, our allies are built into a command structure that is always led by an American. Thus, the supreme allied commander of NATO (SACEUR)—as of November 2018, Army General Curtis M. "Mike" Scaparrotti—is always a U.S. officer.

Any decision by NATO to take military action requires agreement by the heads of state of all the allied countries, now twenty-nine in number. Once that decision is made, all NATO's forces acting under that authority fall under the leadership of the supreme allied commander. However, national governments reserve the right to issue what they call "caveats," which limit what they will allow their forces to do. So, for example, some allies who participated in the counter-ISIS campaign were authorized to participate in operations in Iraq but not in Syria—or vice versa. This is an annoyance to the commander but usually not debilitating. Minor caveats are a small price to pay for the important benefits, both real and symbolic, that NATO unity provides.

In similar fashion, the head of the Combined Forces Command in Korea, which includes troops from both the United States and South Korea, is always an American. In an interesting example of how diplomatic and military interests can get intertwined, and sometimes tangled, one of my predecessors, Don Rumsfeld, agreed to transfer wartime control of South Korean forces (though not U.S. forces) to our South Korean allies. The idea was that this would shift some of the burden for defense of the Korean Peninsula to the people of Korea. However, it was a bad idea, especially given the fact that the South Koreans themselves were unprepared to accept that responsibility. For that reason, we and the South Koreans agreed to delay implementing this ill-considered plan. It remains unimplemented to this day.

The principle that "Americans command" when one of our alliances is engaged doesn't eliminate all possible complications. For one thing, there are times when Americans fighting in NATO operations are commanded by foreign officers. So even though all NATO forces in Afghanistan are under an American, the SACEUR has subordinate commanders belonging to various nations who may indeed command American units yet further down the chain.

In other cases, a country that we want to include in a multinational force may strongly object to having its troops commanded by Americans. This whole issue got quite sticky with the Russians during the Kosovo conflict. Under the 1995 Dayton Accords, which brought an end to the three-year-long war in Bosnia, an implementation force (IFOR) led by NATO was charged with overseeing and monitoring the military elements of the agreement. For a variety of reasons, we felt it was important to have the Russians participate in IFOR—partly because of our desire to bring post-Soviet Russia more closely into alignment with the international community, partly because we knew that if we left them outside the tent (as the old saying goes), they'd be tempted to piss into it.

But how could we make Russia part of a NATO operation on terms that both Russia and NATO could accept? The Russians simply could not swallow their national pride and join up like a normal ally, under the leadership of an American commander or, even worse, a commander from Western Europe.

We found a way to finesse this situation. In prolonged negotiations, American General George Joulwan, the COCOM of EUCOM and the supreme commander of NATO, and Russian General Leontiy Shevtsov worked out a scheme that hinged on the distinction between "operational control" (OPCON) and "tactical control" (TACON). OPCON refers to the selection of tasks assigned to a given unit and the rules of engagement it must follow; TACON refers to specific orders to go somewhere and do something. Joulwan and Shevtsov agreed that the overall commander (the American Joulwan) would exercise OPCON over the Russians through Shevtsov, as deputy commander for Russian forces. But TACON would be exercised over the Russian forces through General Bill Nash, an American, who would command a multinational division including Russians, Americans, and other NATO forces.

In this way, both sides could claim victory. The Americans got unified command under a U.S. general; the Russians got what they called a role "with, but not under" NATO.

Adroit management of our alliances and military partnerships with countries around the world is an important part of the SecDef's job. For me, the job was eased by the mutual respect, even friendship, that I developed with most of my counterparts in other nations. We generally found that our shared values and mutual feelings of global responsibility made it possible for us to work together effectively for the common good.

The group of defense ministers I brought together in late 2015 and early 2016 to help craft and carry out a combined anti-ISIS war plan exemplify this sense of shared partnership. Most of those from the

European NATO countries had long experience in various roles in public life, and two (Ine Eriksen Søreide of Norway and Jean-Yves Le Drian of France) have since gone on to become their countries' foreign ministers (equivalent to our Secretary of State). Interestingly, four of my seven major counterparts in Europe were women—in addition to Søreide, they included Ursula von der Leyen of Germany, Roberta Pinotti of Italy, and Jeanine Hennis-Plasschaert of the Netherlands. The United States has yet to have its first female Secretary of Defense.

The males in the group, in addition to Jean-Yves Le Drian, included Pedro Morenés of Spain and Michael Fallon of the United Kingdom. Le Drian had written a hardheaded yet humane book about ISIS called *Qui est l'ennemi? (Who Is the Enemy?)*, which did a good job of explaining the nature of Islamist extremism as opposed to Islam more generally.

Another close U.S. ally is Canada, whose defense minister was Harjit Sajjan, an Afghan war veteran and a soft-spoken, precise, and extremely capable leader. He is a Sikh, and shared his experiences with me when I was wrestling with the challenge of addressing the ban on beards and turbans imposed by the U.S. military. Sajjan told me that, as a young soldier in the Canadian armed forces, he had worked on the problem of accommodating his beard inside a gas mask and his turban inside a helmet. His example, as well as that of India's armed forces, confirmed my feeling that our rule against accommodating the religious preferences of Sikhs regarding hair and dress was unjustified, and I'm pleased that the U.S. military has begun to come around on this issue.

Some of my colleagues from the Asia-Pacific region were also active in the anti-ISIS struggle. They included Marise Payne of Australia (another female defense minister who has since become foreign minister), Ng Eng Hen of Singapore, and Hishammuddin Hussein of Malaysia. A good friend of mine was South Korean Defense Minister Han Min-goo. In past decades, I'd had good relationships with Russian defense ministers, but in the current era of heightened tensions between our nations, I found this to be no longer possible. China was an increasingly tricky partner, but here I kept trying.

Among the people I miss the most now that I've left my government post, my counterparts at defense ministries around the world rank near the top. Being SecDef is a tough and sometimes lonely job. It meant a lot to me to have a group of congenial colleagues in capital cities across the globe who understood and shared the challenges I faced, and who could be counted on to support America, and me, in difficult times.

Preparing to Fight: How War Plans Are Developed and Why They Matter

The most heartfelt desire of any SecDef is to defend the freedoms and uphold the interests of the American people without having to go to war. But we know that, in the real world, war is sometimes unavoidable. This means that a vital job of DOD is to be prepared for possible conflicts that could erupt anyplace on Earth where U.S. interests are involved. This is where the war-planning process comes in. At any given moment, the American military has a range of war plans in its kit, tailored to a wide variety of contingencies. In theory, we should be ready to respond to almost any conceivable international conflict with a military plan that matches the nature of the adversary, the theater of operations, the level of threat, and the likely strategic and political goals our nation would pursue.

Most war plans unfold like the script for a six-act play, specifying the actions that every participant on the American side would take at each stage of the conflict. In each case, the six acts of the drama are

- Phase 0, "Shape"—when our chief goal is to shape conditions to avoid war and to be favorable to the United States in the event of war;
- Phase I, "Deter"—which describes activities to show potential enemies that aggression will fail;
- Phase II, "Seize Initiative"—in which our military moves rapidly and decisively to respond once a conflict has actually begun;
- Phase III, "Dominate"—which describes how the United States will achieve overwhelming victory on the battlefield;

- Phase IV, "Stabilize"—in which we reduce or eliminate remaining forms of resistance; and, finally,
- Phase V, "Enable Civil Authority"—which describes the creation of a peaceful state after the cessation of conflict.

Of course, the precise details of any given war plan are secret, since they would provide valuable information to a potential enemy if they were known. Even the names and numbers designating the various plans are classified, although a couple have become known to the public—for example, OPLAN 5027, which was for years the general plan for a war on the Korean Peninsula. Within DOD, war plans are generally referred to as "O-plans," the *O* standing for operation.

There's always an element of unreality involved in any war plan. History shows that no conflict ever unfolds precisely as planners had imagined. Once the fighting starts, the generals and the civilian leadership inevitably have to scramble and improvise to respond to unexpected developments, leaving the pre-scripted war plans behind. But this doesn't negate the value of those plans. As Eisenhower famously remarked, "Plans are worthless, but planning is everything." The value of the planning process lies in the way it enhances both the clarity of our strategic thinking and the readiness of our forces. Detailed war plans enable the troops and their leaders to practice against a range of specific scenarios. They also help those charged with acquisition, logistics, communications, and other support services to make sure they provide all the right supplies and equipment to meet the needs that might emerge once actual combat begins.

Each of the COCOMs who reports to the SecDef is responsible for maintaining the war plans that pertain to his or her region or function. Thus, during my tenure at DOD, the supreme allied commander and head of the European command, Mike Scaparrotti, was responsible for U.S. and NATO plans in the event of a war with Russia. Admiral Harry Harris at Pacific Command was responsible for the China plan. Army General Vince Brooks, serving in Seoul as commander of the UN command, the Combined Forces Command, and U.S. forces in Korea—yes, he wore three hats—was responsible for the plans to defend South Korea against an invasion from the north. Army General Joe Votel at Central Command was in charge of various plans regarding a possible conflict with Iran. And Air Force General Lori Robinson at Northern Command— incidentally, the first female COCOM in history—had operational responsibility for defending the U.S. against incoming ballistic missiles.

There is an elaborate, formal process by which each war plan is developed, updated, and finally approved by the SecDef, all on a cycle that generally takes about two years. Input from many key leaders within the services and at DOD is incorporated in the planning process. In turn, the operations described in the war plans are taken into account in the daily activities of DOD, from setting troop levels to budgeting. For example, when I was acquisition czar, I noted how many bombs of different kinds were slated for use in each of our current war plans, and I took these requirements into account when I was placing orders for munitions. In Chapter 1, I described how DOD went about acquiring a new aerial refueling tanker. The principal way we determined the overall number of tankers needed was by identifying the biggest day for tanker use in our biggest war plan—that is, the day of fighting in the war plan script in which there was the largest number of U.S. combat and transport aircraft in the air requiring tankers. Then we made sure to buy enough tankers to fill our needs on that (hypothetical) day.

The war plans are thus extremely important for military units and DOD personnel responsible for recruitment, training, logistics, transportation, budgeting, and countless other managerial tasks. Each plan describes and enumerates all the forces, equipment, and other resources that would reinforce or flow to a given theater of conflict, thereby bringing the great weight of the American military to bear. This force-flow plan is called the "time-phased force deployment document" (TPFDD), and it's incredibly detailed: look up a particular day of action in a particular war plan, and you can usually see exactly how many cargo planes will be in the air on that day, carrying exactly what quantity of munitions to exactly which military units in specific locations around the globe. These specifications are taken very seriously by DOD as guides for planning and budgeting. In fact, "resourcing the TPFDD" is a standard preoccupation of many members of the Pentagon and command staff.

Our allies are made aware of the contents of our war plans, with the exception of some classified details—for example, plans to use certain supersecret weapons whose existence is unknown even by most Americans.

During my time as SecDef, I made sure that President Obama was exposed to each of the major O-plans. He took an active and intelligent interest in them, and while he never gave specific guidance or tinkered with details, he would sometimes make a general observation regarding how he would consider the situation from the point of view of a national leader. The COCOMs and I always benefited from that perspective.

SIOP: Planning for the Ultimate War

The options and details that would be involved in a possible nuclear war plan are contained in a set of documents known as the single integrated operations plan (SIOP).* Bound in a spiral notebook with a laminated cover, the SIOP is carried by the president's military aide in the fabled "football" that is never far from the president's side.

I first came into contact with the SIOP in the early 1980s, when I discovered that the safe in my first Pentagon office contained the records of the final set of nuclear war exercises that President Carter had participated in with his SecDef, Harold Brown. When I mentioned these to Harold at a social event, his reaction was immediate: "Oh my gosh, you must destroy them. No president's views on the SIOP should be recorded." Of course, they were promptly destroyed.

As this story suggests, the details of the SIOP are supposed to be top secret. However, the contents in general are well known. As in strategic bombing dating back to World War II, the SIOP contains the usual categories of strategic targets. Each carries a number of specific consequences in terms of escalation of nuclear war and the annihilation of populations and cities.

As with other war plans, the SIOP specifies a series of actions that will

---

* Technically, since 2012, SIOP has been superseded by a plan with the designation OPLAN 8010-12. But DOD insiders still usually refer to the nuclear war plan as SIOP.

be involved in a possible nuclear war. In the case of the SIOP, however, most of the major steps are assumed to take place within a matter of hours or even minutes, and most involve decisions by the president himself, who alone can authorize the use of nuclear weapons. Generally speaking, the options available to the president fit into a two-by-two grid, defined by a pair of variables: whether the United States is under attack with advance notice or without warning, and whether the president's response is immediate or delayed.

As most people know, the United States has a large number of nuclear weapons that are ready to attack at any given moment. However, if an attack on the United States is launched after some period of warning, it's likely that the president will have had the option to deploy additional nuclear forces to demonstrate an even more robust retaliation. An extra phalanx of bombers can be loaded with nuclear bombs and put on airstrip alert or even sent aloft, ready to respond, and nuclear submarines in port can put to sea. The SIOP includes plans for eventualities like these.

If the attack from an adversary occurs entirely by surprise, then the retaliatory options make use of the submarines that are normally and always at sea; any surviving bombers that can make it into the air with nuclear weapons before their airfields are hit in a first strike; and any ICBMs that survive the first strike as well. (In point of fact, the adversary in this case could only be Russia, since it is the only country with the ability to launch an attack that does serious damage to American nuclear forces.)

Then there's the question of whether the order to retaliate is immediate or not. It would take about half an hour for Russian missiles to arrive at U.S. targets, and about ten to fifteen minutes for submarine-launched missiles to arrive in Washington. While it is conceivable that the president could give a retaliatory order during this period and thereby make use of a larger portion of the force before it could be destroyed, I always regarded that as a pretty far-fetched scenario. In most conceivable circumstances, the retaliation would occur after the first strike had been received. And of course the whole point of the so-called nuclear triad—bombers, submarines, and missiles—is to guarantee that the United States will have plenty of retaliatory power even after a successful first strike by an adversary.

Once one of the four boxes in this two-by-two grid is determined, a number of other choices come into play involving the three categories of targets I described above. Thus, SIOP becomes a kind of Chinese-restaurant menu of options (to use a metaphor that inevitably feels rather macabre given the subject matter).

Only the president may authorize the use of nuclear weapons. The question naturally arises, therefore: "What happens if the president is killed or disabled?" This matter was treated informally within the executive branch up until the Reagan administration. At that point, President Reagan, SecDef Caspar Weinberger, and the National Security Council staff felt that the Cold War was getting dangerous enough that it was important to tackle the problem of presidential succession in the chain of command. (We now know, from Soviet records that have since become public, that their perception of heightened tensions on both sides of the Cold War was completely accurate.)

If you start with the principle that only the president can authorize the use of nuclear weapons, then the next question is, "Who is the president?" In the event of the death or disability of the president, the chain of succession is prescribed in the Constitution and the Presidential Succession Act of 1947. They say that the office of president passes first to the vice president, then to the Speaker of the House, then to the president pro tem of the Senate, and thence to the cabinet secretaries in chronological order of the creation of their offices. This means that the first cabinet office to assume the presidency would be the Secretary of State, followed by the Secretary of the Treasury, the Secretary of Defense, and then on down the line to the Secretary of Education, the Secretary of Energy, and, newest of all, the Secretary of Homeland Security.

So in the event of a nuclear showdown, if the president is dead or disabled, what the Secretary of Defense and members of the command-and-control system are supposed to do is find the highest-ranking member in the chain of succession, inform him or her, "You are now the president of the United States," and request orders.

The Reagan administration believed, I think completely rightly, that the view of all three branches of government ought to be considered in formulating these procedures. So we checked the constitutionality of this plan with the chief justice of the United States and with the congressional leadership. In the course of doing so, we developed the concept of "continuity of constitutional government," meaning that in addition to prescribing chains of devolution and survival for the executive branch leadership, we would do the same for the congressional leadership and the Supreme Court. Thus, we developed evacuation plans for key members of Congress and Supreme Court justices in the event of a nuclear war. These are highly classified, but they do exist and are considered necessary to comply with the Constitution and the rule of law.

A fine but important distinction to be made regarding the powers of the president is between the chain of succession and a possible chain of delegation.

Getting back to the presidency, the chain of devolution is different from a chain of delegation. A president may pre-delegate to his subordinates the authority to take specific actions. This has actually been done when appropriate—for example, the authority to exercise missile defense operations has been delegated to NORTHCOM.

However, any order involving nuclear release remains valid only as long as the president is alive. So President Obama could have said to me, "Ash, if I'm unavailable, you do the right thing." But if the president had subsequently died, his pre-delegation of authority to me would be judged to be invalid. As the constitutional lawyers would say, "The president may not irrevocably bind his successor." It would be up to the then-living president to give valid orders to those below him or her in the chain of command.

In practical terms, of course, having to track down people according to a complicated chain of succession would be time consuming and perhaps impossible under the intense time pressure of nuclear war. Therefore, our priority needed to be to make sure the top members in the chain of delegation would survive, so that we wouldn't end up having to track down, say, the Secretary of Agriculture, who happened to be giving a speech in Des Moines that day.

This practical necessity is one reason for the elaborate and costly travel arrangements used by high-ranking administration officials. That includes the specially equipped 747 jumbo jet that the SecDef uses for global travel, known as the E4-B—an interesting airplane with an interesting history. Its most important purpose is to serve as an aerial command center in the event of a nuclear war. It's prepared to take the place of the Pentagon, the mountain fortress built in Colorado Springs on President Eisenhower's watch, and the Omaha center of the Strategic Air Command—all presumably well known to Russia and others who might want to target the American military headquarters in time of war.

I also have a personal history with the E4-B. During my very first job in Caspar Weinberger's Department of Defense, I was charged with working on problems of nuclear command and control. One of my tasks was to develop the details of the communications suite for this aircraft.

From the outside, the E4-B looks good and proudly represents our country, with its gleaming white fuselage, its blue stripe along the side, and bold black letters declaring UNITED STATES OF AMERICA. Inside, however, the plane's decor is right out of the 1980s. The whole back half of the plane is filled with vast consoles where officers and technicians once sat in swiveling seats a bit like the one Captain Kirk used in the old *Star Trek* TV series. Those seats made it easy for them to operate the electronic gear custom-built for the E4-B by Raytheon. In the age of the Internet, that equipment has been superseded by rows of flat-screen displays, so those seats are now mostly used by the E4-B Air Force "battle staff," the Pentagon front office staff, the regional staff responsible for each stop on the journey, the SecDef's personal security detail, and the Pentagon doctor. Members of the press corps who tag along to report our doings to the world also have seats here. In front of this area are two conference rooms, where I would work with my staff and give interviews to the press—sometimes on the record, sometimes off. Way up front is a small cabin with bunk beds and a table that I used as an office while way in the back are more bunk beds where staff members can catch some shut-eye.

The members of the security force are housed in quarters upstairs on the plane. These heavily armed and intensively trained troops make an impressive and daunting sight when the jet lands. They are always the first to disembark, using a special set of stairs lowered from the belly of the plane. They come out with machine guns at the ready and confirm that the location is secure and safe before anyone else is permitted to emerge.

The principal oddity of the E4-B is its lack of windows. The fuselage is completely enclosed to protect the fragile communications devices from the powerful electromagnetic pulse that a nuclear detonation would produce. So although we may be flying over the broad reaches of the Atlantic, the historic cities and river valleys of Europe, or the breathtaking mountain ranges of the Near East, none of these sights is visible to me or to any of my traveling companions. Nor is there any indication of the time of day except for the large digital clocks mounted everywhere, indicating what the military calls Zulu time—otherwise known as Greenwich mean time.

All in all, the E4-B is a somewhat surrealistic, hermetically sealed environment that is a fitting reminder of the apocalyptic mission it was originally built to serve—and that every SecDef hopes will never come to pass.

In addition, aboard the E-4B as well as in the major command centers like the National Military Command Center in the Pentagon and the STRATCOM command center in Omaha, the current locations of all the key successors to the president are always posted. An elaborate set of evacuation plans have been devised so that there should never be any question about the survival of the office of the president—even if a large number of high-ranking officials should be killed in a massive attack.

Further details about these arrangements are secret, of course—as they must be.

One more nightmare scenario that novelists and filmmakers have toyed with is the idea of a mentally disabled president deciding to launch a nuclear attack. As I've noted, the chain of command itself is short and direct, facilitating swift action when necessary—which could conceivably increase the risk of catastrophic errors. But I personally discount the likelihood of such a scenario ever coming to pass. The military code of justice requires troops to refuse to follow orders they know are illegal. And the high-ranking leaders, civilian and military, who surround every president and would be aware of his intentions, are overwhelmingly likely to be sensible, ethical, and strong-willed individuals. I can't believe they would robotically follow the unlawful orders of a clearly deranged president and thereby condemn an unprecedented number of human beings to needless deaths.

It may seem strange that our national leaders—including me—can discuss military strategies that would inevitably involve the deaths of scores or hundreds of millions of people with apparent equanimity. Maybe it's a little less strange in my case. Remember that my very first role with the DOD involved studying potential siting choices for an entire class of nuclear missiles. My later assignments dealt with topics such as space-based missile defense and (as I detailed in Chapter 3) efforts to control the problem of "loose nukes" in the countries of the former Soviet bloc.

So I've been thinking about, examining, and wrestling with the problems of nuclear weaponry for decades. But don't assume that I or any other serious leader of national defense ever gets used to these realities. My experience over the decades tells me that just the opposite is true.

Naturally, I hope and pray that no future SecDef will ever be faced with the necessity of using such weapons. But I rest (relatively) easy at night knowing that, in all my DOD jobs, I did everything within my power to reduce the chances that they will ever need to be used. That's all that any of us living in a post-Hiroshima world can ever hope to do.

CHAPTER 8

COMBAT READINESS IN A CRISIS-PRONE WORLD

Many Americans don't realize it, but the U.S. military today is engaged in combat much more frequently than it ever was during the post-Vietnam years of the late 1970s, 1980s, and 1990s. It's a reality driven by today's complex, many-sided challenges, including state-supported terrorism, chaos generated by rogue and failed states, and the growing ambitions of a number of nations that are potential adversaries of the United States. Consequently, as SecDef, I was called upon to exercise command authority over military operations far more often than many of my predecessors. When your decisions involve U.S. lives at risk on the battlefield, details suddenly become more crucial than ever.

A lot of White House meetings, Washington gossip, and press reporting are about the formulation of national security policy. But for the SecDef, decision-making is only the half of it. Implementation—and specifically in the matter of command, the conduct of military operations—is the other half of the secretary's responsibility. That's why, in my confirmation hearing before the Senate Armed Services Committee, after pledging that I would give the president my own candid advice and access to the best professional military advice, I added, "And when the president makes a decision, I will also ensure that the Department of Defense implements it with its long-admired excellence."

Decades of experience with DOD had made me pretty proud of the department's skill in execution. I think it measures up well against any other part of the government and the rest of society's major institutions. According to surveys, American citizens seem to agree.

At the same time, I knew from my experience as undersecretary and deputy that implementation takes work and constant attention from the leadership. All too often, the urgent details needed for effectively fighting wars get forgotten in the daily bureaucratic scrum. So the system needs periodic kicks in the behind from the leadership. To ensure a constant focus on the immediate needs of the troops during the ongoing wars, I established the Warfighter Senior Integration Group, as described in Chapter 2. I also took frequent trips to war zones, and I held regular early-morning meetings to help drive the bureaucracy's agenda—all during my tenure as undersecretary. I had my able and dedicated successor, Frank Kendall, continue these practices when I became deputy secretary and then SecDef while also remaining personally engaged.

Where details of implementation matter most of all is in regard to combat operations. These are how we carry out the core mission of DOD: to protect and defend the United States and its interests, both at home and around the world. Warfighting is when the rubber meets the road. So ensuring that our forces are thoroughly prepared for combat, and then making certain that their combat missions are conducted with the greatest possible skill and effectiveness, are the ultimate leadership tests for any Secretary of Defense.

Military Exercises: Honing the Warfighter's Skills

One of the crucial ways we hone our implementation skills is through military exercises. In one form or another, these have been used since at least the eighteenth century, when the Prussian monarch Frederick the Great manipulated clockwork armies in tabletop conflicts to practice and test the effectiveness of various battlefield tactics. Today, military exercises for U.S. troops are mandated by law and form an important responsibility of the DOD.

For over thirty years, I participated in a range of military exercises and studied their results as revealed by written reports and the "after action" reviews prepared by the commanders and officers who led them. When I became SecDef, I continued to participate in exercises, now collaborating with many of the highest-ranked leaders in the nation, from uniformed officers like those in the Joint Chiefs of Staff and their chairman to powerful civilian officials like National Security Advisor Susan Rice and Secretary of State John Kerry. To the very end, I found such exercises to be valuable learning experiences and essential tools for ensuring that the military is ready for any emergency the world and our adversaries may throw at us.

Exercises serve several purposes and come in several forms. Some are very small-scale activities in which combat units or even individual soldiers simply practice their skills—for example, by firing their weapons and maneuvering as a group. Others involve larger formations carrying out a particular tactical scenario or a portion of one of the big war plans. Some are joint (or interservice) exercises that involve troops from two or more of the armed services, giving officers and soldiers the opportunity to hone and practice their collaborative skills.

The largest are combined (or international) exercises like those we carry out in Korea and Europe. These exercises, which take place on a grand scale, require complicated advance scheduling and plenty of preliminary practice by individual units, so they tend to be on a fairly fixed schedule. Examples of these regularly scheduled exercises include the maneuvers we conduct annually with the South Korean military under names like Foal Eagle and Max Thunder. (The use of code names like these to designate particular exercises is another old tradition.) Occasionally, however, the timing of regular exercises is adjusted to avoid coinciding with important local events—for example, a national election or a highly publicized visit by the U.S. president.

These combined exercises are frequently covered in the news media and often attract protests and other forms of controversy. Sometimes they are denounced, particularly by potential enemies, as "provocative" or "aggressive," as though, by preparing for the possibility of armed combat, we are somehow encouraging or hastening it. In reality, of course, the opposite is true: well-managed exercises enhance the readiness of our forces to defend against hostile attacks and thereby reduce rather than increase the risk of war.

That said, some rules and customs are followed by most countries, including the United States, when planning and conducting combined military exercises so as to avoid misunderstandings or accidental conflicts. For example, the Organization for Security and Co-operation in Europe has nonbinding rules that ask all member states—which include Russia—to provide forty-two days' notice prior to military exercises involving nine thousand troops or more and to invite international groups to observe exercises involving thirteen thousand troops or more. In regions where there are no fixed international guidelines—in the Korean Peninsula, for instance—it's simply good practice to publicly announce exercises before they begin so there's no chance they can be confused with a troop buildup preparatory to an actual attack.

In addition to the exercises of various sizes described above, U.S. troops participate in special categories of exercises designed to sharpen the skills of particular groups of military professionals in tackling unusual, complex, and urgent challenges. Special ops teams, for example, participate in exercises that simulate hostage-rescue operations or counterterrorism assaults. Airborne divisions practice landing squads of paratroopers in remote locations otherwise inaccessible to troops. And periodically, teams of high-level military and civilian leaders, up to and including the president, engage in SIOP exercises that simulate the ultratense moments when a decision regarding the use of nuclear weapons would need to be made.

Simulation exercises that force participants to make consequential choices in conditions of imperfect information and high-pressure time constraints can really test—and sometimes expose—the nerve, grit, and composure of a leader. I'll never forget the time when a high-ranking admiral, participating in an exercise that simulated the early stages of an all-out war to defend our NATO allies against an invasion by Russia, lost track of what his own forces had been ordered to do. On the third day of simulated combat, the officer announced, "I recommend you authorize the use of tactical nuclear weapons in Europe." After an awkward silence, I had to politely remind him, "Admiral, you already did that yesterday."

SIOP Exercises: Prepping for Doomsday

SIOP exercises that simulate the nuclear launch-or-no-launch decision under conditions of enemy attack are especially fraught, because they are an attempt to embody an emotionally charged dynamic that no American president and his advisors have ever yet experienced. It's impossible, therefore, to know whether or not the recorded outcomes of past SIOP exercises accurately reflect what would happen in case of a real nuclear attack on the United States.

This uncertainty has some consequences that could be very important in the crucial moments of a nuclear standoff. The nation's nuclear policy of having a survivable strategic force means we do not have to rely on launching an all-out assault in the early minutes after receiving warning of incoming missiles, but rather can hold back to give the president (or a surviving successor) time to make a considered decision. This is the reason that, as SecDef, I advocated spending hundreds of billions of dollars to maintain and modernize our nuclear triad—the three-leg delivery system of intercontinental ballistic missiles, bombers, and sea-launched ballistic missiles—to ensure its survival of a first strike. However, our command-and-control systems do give us the capability of retaliating very quickly—and so, in SIOP exercises, lower-level headquarters tend to do so, just to practice the most demanding scenario.

My own intuition is that, in reality, most American leaders would be more likely to refrain from a hasty launch decision in a moment of nuclear crisis—especially since our nuclear triad system virtually guarantees the fact that we would have plenty of forces available for powerful retaliation even after absorbing a first strike from abroad. Some scenarios in which the circumstances and facts are clear seem brutally simple to me. If Russia (or some future power) has definitely attacked the United States with nuclear weapons, then both vengeance and the need to deter future attacks clearly demand a "Go" command. Carrying this out in a SIOP exercise doesn't take a lot of practice.

Nonetheless, we ran routine, role-playing exercises practicing what was called "launch under attack," where we launched everything we could against Russia in the half hour before missiles arrived. Having participated in such exercises since the 1980s, I knew every second of the timeline intimately. It involved initial warning from satellites, followed by confirmation by radars, and, if a few missiles struck early, we also had satellites that detect the signal of a nuclear detonation.

During the SIOP exercises I participated in as SecDef, my own advice to the president (or to whoever was playing the role of president in the exercise) was to focus on ensuring his own survival, via a rapid evacuation into a secure place of shelter. Then he could take his time about making a decision regarding a military response. This struck me as the most realistic and likely scenario and therefore the one most deserving of prior practice and evaluation at his level.

I remember vividly one nighttime exercise in which Susan Rice, John Kerry, and I were the principals. Susan played the president, and John and I played ourselves. The call came through and the usual half-hour countdown began. Susan and John began discussing what to do, and it came as a little bit of a surprise to them, I think, when I emphasized that they did *not* need to make a decision within a half an hour (as their staff had obviously told them would be practiced). The whole reason we had a survivable arsenal was so that they didn't have to be in that position. "So let's take the time to think about what you ought to do," I suggested.

In addition to getting the president to a safe place—along with his team members if possible—a second priority was to get our own forces in the highest state of alert. This meant "flushing," or launching into the air, all the bombers that were ready and armed with nuclear weapons; making sure all the ICBMs and sea-based missiles were alerted; and following emergency procedures to put in-port submarines to sea quickly. There were plans in place for carrying out all these activities.

A third important step was to do everything necessary to ensure the integrity of the command-and-control system that would inform the president or his successor what had happened and carry his instructions back to the force. This consists of a complex system of communications links of all kinds along with a network of fixed and mobile command centers all equipped with communications. It also involves the warning satellites, radars, and nuclear detection (NUDET) satellites that can spot and identify nuclear detonations.

These, then, should be the key priorities for the president in the first half hour after a report of a nuclear attack—not making a hasty decision to unleash the entire U.S. arsenal. It was also important to think about how to communicate whatever we were doing to the Russians. If the Russians, for some reason, had not launched an all-out attack but a partial attack, we might want to calibrate our response accordingly. Since we couldn't know the full extent of their attack in the first half hour, this so-called escalation control, if desired, would also require waiting and seeing.

The Costs of Military Exercises

Almost all forms of military exercises require open areas of land or water—"ranges"—in which they can be conducted. These ranges are an endangered species in our increasingly populous world, and their existence is routinely challenged by economic interests and sometimes environmental ones. So protecting military access to these ranges is yet another duty of the SecDef. I spent a great deal of time trying to protect our "live fire" ranges in the Gulf of Mexico from encroachment by oil rigs. I also had to try to defend the sound of jet engines engaged in aerial exercises against the complaints of local residents. Inside the Pentagon, we called the overhead roar "the sound of freedom," but this was one case where a catchy slogan didn't win over the populace.

Exercises also involve a degree of danger. In fact, in 2017, for the first time in many years, there were more military deaths in training exercises than in combat. In the context of an active-duty military that includes 1.8 million service members, the actual number of deaths in exercises is relatively small—a total of 80 during 2017. And some of the deaths are an inevitable result of the need to simulate real-world battle conditions as fully as possible—including the dangers involved. Still, every training death is a high price to pay for readiness, and the department continually strives to minimize them.

Defining and Measuring "Combat Readiness"

The core purpose of every form of military exercise is to enhance "combat readiness"—the ability of troops to take action to defend our nation and its interests immediately if necessary. But what exactly is "readiness"?

When we talk about the readiness of military forces, we mostly mean whether they have exercised enough to do what they're supposed to do, meaning that they're fit to send to war. There's an elaborate system for ranking this readiness, one originally mandated by Congress in 1999 and subsequently amended by Congress no fewer than seven times. In addition to the level of training accomplished by the unit, the commonly used readiness metrics also take into account such considerations as whether each slot in the unit is actually filled by a service member, whether aircraft are ready to go or undergoing maintenance, and whether all the equipment the unit needs is in its possession.

As measured by these standards, readiness is an important characteristic that requires a significant commitment to maintain. It costs time, money, and other resources to provide military units with the training they need, the personnel and equipment they require, and so on. But unfortunately, these forms of investment are not very exciting or impressive—which means they tend to get short shrift when budgets are being established. Members of Congress find it much sexier to tell their constituents that they added money to the budget for a fancy new weapons system than to say that they paid the fuel costs that would enable more frequent training for helicopter pilots. Therefore, the habit of the congressional appropriators is to shave a few dollars here and there from readiness in order to provide the dollars for the shiny objects that will get members' attention back home. This makes it especially ironic that those same members of Congress frequently use "readiness shortcomings" as a bludgeon with which to criticize administrations.

In truth, department budgeteers sometimes engaged in the same behavior when trying to balance the books. It's easier to squeeze readiness accounts bit by bit than to find short-term savings by cutting personnel headcounts or major contracts.

I regularly decried this behavior in my testimony before Congress, as did the members of the Joint Chiefs I served with—as well as every other SecDef I've ever known. Defense professionals constantly pleaded with Congress to prioritize readiness spending when drawing up the budget. We like to say that "readiness has no constituency" other than the chiefs and the SecDef. But all our jawboning never really seems to do any good.

Complicating the management challenge is the fact that readiness is a more complex quality than any single measurement can capture. There are almost as many definitions of *readiness* as there are people using the term, and no two definitions are quite the same. Readiness to engage in counterinsurgency or counterterrorism activities is different from readiness to engage in combat against aggression by a great power. A unit that has just spent a year training to go to Afghanistan is obviously not going to be fully ready for a major war in Europe. If such a war was threatening, the unit would need to switch its training regimen and spend time practicing an entirely different kind of warfare.

This example also illustrates the reality that "lack of readiness" is not always, or even usually, a result of neglect or mismanagement. A unit that just got back from a year in Afghanistan won't be ready to return to combat for quite some time, because the troops need time to be with their families, to rest up, to have their equipment replenished, and to be retrained for the next mission. Similarly, after a long deployment at sea, a ship returns to port, the sailors go ashore to reunite with their families, and the ship enters a cycle of maintenance. In these cases, partial readiness by these units is part of the natural course of things.

Counterintuitively, it can also happen that a unit's readiness *declines* after it is deployed, at least as it's measured by the mandated systems. An air wing to be stationed in Kuwait, for example, will generally deploy after a period of intensive training back in the United States. During deployment, the air wing will generally be involved in periodic activities rather than constant full-spectrum combat—which means that its readiness to conduct more intensive operations will go down. Likewise, a ship at sea that is traveling from one place to another or making a politically important foreign-port call will have its readiness go down, because the opportunities for training exercises are much more limited than they are at home.

Units that are scheduled to deploy into combat zones abroad are naturally the ones that are most heavily engaged in activities to enhance their readiness. Troops that are set to rotate into Afghanistan, for example, will devote time to practicing for the role they're going to play. They study maps of the particular region where they're going to be deployed, right down to the nearby town and every marketplace, mosque, hill, and culvert it contains. They learn about the general strategy and operational concepts that govern what they're going to be doing, as well as the rules of engagement that specify the actions they may and may not take. And they practice these activities in Colorado, North Carolina, or wherever they happen to be based before they are deployed. In this way, their readiness for combat can be raised to the highest possible level before they board the transport planes that will take them to the Middle East.

Pieces on the Global Chessboard: Deployment Orders and Employment Orders

The central way that the authority of the SecDef is exercised within the chain of command is by the issuing of *deployment orders* and *employment orders*. These two processes may sound, at first, like mere "paperwork"— but they mark the steps by which young American men and women are sent into harm's way to defend our interests and, if necessary, to sacrifice their lives in the effort. For that reason, just like all my predecessors whom I knew, I always regarded them as my most important duty.

Let's start with deployment orders. These are documents mandating the overseas deployment of any U.S. forces, for whatever purpose, anywhere in the world. Without these orders, not a single American troop can set foot on foreign soil—and only the SecDef has the power to sign them.

There is an elaborate procedure for signing deployment orders, which I went through every few weeks. It takes place in the SecDef's conference room, in which I would be joined by the chairman, vice chairman, and director of operations of the Joint Chiefs of Staff, as well as a host of experts on various aspects of the deployments to be approved. All of us would gather around a huge loose-leaf briefing book that covers the entire world, theater by theater.

The procedure centers on a tab-by-tab review and discussions of the contents of that briefing book, each deployment described and explained to the SecDef by one of the attendees. For example: "Sir, as you know, you have decided to add another brigade combat team to our forces in Europe to deter Russia. By signing here, you order such and such brigade at Fort Hood to prepare for deployment on September 1." If I had questions or concerns, I would raise them. But in most cases, I had already essentially made the decision, and I would sign where indicated.

The law required my signature for the overseas deployment of even a single sailor, soldier, airman, or marine. Indeed, sometimes enlisted men or women were deployed as individuals—in which case I might be presented with an order sending a single nurse's aide to work at the Guantánamo Bay Naval Station. And until I signed that deployment form, he couldn't get on a plane.

The signing of normal deployment orders would take perhaps forty-five minutes. Then the room would be closed, and a separate book with a multicolored cover with lots of obscure code words printed on it would be brought in. These were the deployment orders for secret forces. A smaller group of us would go through this with a different set of briefers who would cycle in for each deployment one by one, since most of them were not cleared to hear about anything but their own particular decision.

Deployment orders are just the first step in the process of sending troops into battle. Employment orders are the second step and another major responsibility of the SecDef—perhaps the gravest. These authorize forces to actually be used. They cover a specific place, time frame, and a set of "authorities" defining what the troops can do. For example, an "authority" might be to conduct air operations against ISIS oil facilities, including wells, refineries, and transportation systems, subject to a set of specific limitations involving efforts to minimize civilian casualties, advance notification when appropriate to the government of Iraq, and so on. Sometimes these authorities are set by the SecDef, sometimes by the president; sometimes they bind the COCOM, and sometimes they delegate authority within specific boundaries to subordinate commanders.

The only authority that never needs to be specified is the authority to take the steps necessary to defend oneself against an enemy attack. Every American service member and military unit has an inherent right to self-defense and requires no orders or authority to act accordingly.

Responding When Crises Strike

The SecDef's involvement in employment orders basically falls into two categories: those in which the United States takes the initiative, and those in which we are reacting to actions by others.

In the first instance, which might involve launching a strike against an enemy base or a rescue mission to save the lives of Americans or citizens of an allied nation, the commander will create a concept of operations. The CONOP proceeds up the chain of command until it reaches the SecDef, and I've described the process by which I scrubbed and scrutinized CONOPs before sending them to the president for his approval, if required. Of course, very risky operations would get an extra level of attention from me, and sometimes from the president. For example, when we were conducting a hostage-rescue operation, I would go down to the National Military Command Center and monitor the radios and surveillance cameras while the operation was in progress. On occasion, the president himself would take part in such direct, real-time observation, a classic example being the bin Laden capture/kill mission.

The second type of employment order is one that would be quickly issued in response to an unanticipated incident—for example, an attack on U.S. forces or a diplomatic facility. Incidents of this kind were among the most taxing challenges I faced as SecDef.

Most often, sudden attacks would take place at awkward times, such as in the middle of the night or while the president or I was traveling

overseas. However, as SecDef, you quickly learn how to shake off the
cobwebs of fatigue when a crisis demands your attention. You learn how
to make rapid connections with your entire decision-making and support
network, no matter how far from the Pentagon you may be. In time, you
also discover that there's a pretty standard rhythm when it comes to dealing with crisis situations, even the most serious—a playbook that has
been developed over the years, containing steps you can take to quickly
get command of the problem and prevent it from spiraling out of control.

Take, for example, a provocation or confrontation between troops
from the North and the South somewhere in the demilitarized zone in
Korea or the waters near the Korean Peninsula—the kind of event that
occurs with fair frequency in that tense corner of the globe. When one of
these standoffs occurred, I would always be informed immediately, and
I'd confer promptly with our commander on the ground. Our core objective would be to handle the matter in a cautious, deliberate fashion, ensuring that neither our South Korean allies nor our North Korean
adversaries did anything inappropriate that might inflame the situation
needlessly.

It would also be absolutely vital that the defense minister of South
Korea would hear from my office within hours of such an incident. This
could happen by way of a personal telephone call (time-zone differences
permitting) or by my issuing a public statement regarding the incident.
The purpose wasn't to exchange information, because the commanders
on both sides would have kept us both fully informed. The real purpose
was to enable my South Korean counterpart to tell his president and the
Korean press, "I have been in touch with the U.S. Secretary of Defense
and we are addressing this matter together." Being able to make such a
statement has important symbolic meaning in Korean culture and
politics—an example of the subtle yet critical protocols of international
relations that a SecDef must observe.

In a similar way, any incident involving U.S. service members on the
Japanese island of Okinawa must be handled with extreme diplomacy.
There have been a number of terrible cases involving the sexual assault
of a local citizen by an American service member, which, it goes without

saying, must be dealt with swiftly and firmly; not just for reasons of international relations but because it is the right thing to do.

Almost equally politically sensitive are issues relating to the safety of U.S. military helicopters on Okinawa. American military choppers are operated in some congested urban areas on Okinawa, in part because the United States has been unable to arrange to move our helicopter base to a more remote area. The people and press of Okinawa have become so sensitized to this issue that even a bumpy helicopter landing has been known to garner headlines—which meant that it was incumbent upon me as SecDef to place a phone call to the Japanese minister of defense when such an incident would occur.

Unfortunately, there are times when a budding crisis can't be contained simply by following a standard playbook. That's when higher-order skills for information gathering and decision-making must come into play—and quickly.

One of the most challenging elements in dealing with an emerging crisis is the lack of clear information. Those moments when it's difficult or impossible to define precisely what has happened and why are often when a SecDef is under the most intense pressure to make a quick decision—with the president demanding a recommendation, the press reporting rumors and clamoring for action, and American allies and adversaries alike scrutinizing your every word. Here are some of the rules of thumb I've developed over the years for handling such situations.

First, I force myself to remember that, in the early hours of a developing situation, at least 20 percent of what I am hearing is probably false—and at least one time in four, the level of false information is more like 90 percent. Those are not good odds for making rapid decisions. So my first rule of thumb is simply to take a deep breath and refrain from making any hasty decisions. Otherwise I may slip into the kind of mistake that my former colleague Air Force Secretary Mike Donley used to call "getting caught speeding."

Next, when the people around you are pressing for a decision—send troops? recommend a bombing attack? issue an ultimatum? impose a blockade?—stop and ask *when* a decision is actually required, and *why*.

In many cases, those clamoring for a decision are rushing matters need-lessly: the situation is such that taking an extra few hours or even a couple of days to assess the facts and consider your options isn't likely to make a meaningful difference.

Once you turn down the temperature in the room, you'll find that, quite often, what your team members really need from you is not an im-mediate decision but simply a sense of clarity and an orderly process. Let them know that you are aware of the problem, that you are gathering in-formation, that you are examining options, and that a decision will be made when one is needed. A message to this effect is often all that's re-quired to restore a degree of calm to the organization. It also helps if you can give your team members tasks to handle in the meantime—relevant, meaningful jobs like collecting information and readying forces, not mere busywork. Giving people assignments that let them contribute to the emerging decision helps defuse their anxiety and reduces the likelihood they'll feel you are simply being indecisive or dragging your feet.

Just as I always wanted a clear explanation of the reasons for a par-ticular decision timeline, I tried to extend the same courtesy to the pres-ident. I avoided asking for a decision at a certain time just because it would be convenient for me or because the people around me were get-ting antsy. Instead, I would tie the requested timetable to one or more specific practical requirements: "We need a decision by noon tomorrow in order to be able to move troops to the region by six p.m.," or "The U.S. ambassador is going to be on Iraqi television in fourteen hours, and he needs a clear statement of American policy that he can articulate in re-sponse to this morning's attack."

Buying time to make the right decisions is doubly difficult when the crisis has already been publicly reported. In today's fast-paced media world, the pressure to respond quickly to every twitch of the news cycle is particularly intense. At one time, when many of the top Washington press jobs were held by veteran reporters with a sophisticated under-standing of government, it was widely understood that the information circulating in the early hours or days of a crisis was likely to be wrong. Therefore, a decision-maker's statement to the effect that "the depart-ment has X under investigation and will make a decision when one is necessary" would be accepted as reasonable and prudent. Today, such a statement is more likely to be treated as prevarication or stonewalling. It may get quoted on cable news—only to be followed immediately by a panel of talking heads speculating about the issue (usually based on few facts or none at all), questioning your competence to deal with it, and theorizing about the reasons you are "refusing to take a stand."

Handling these moments of media-induced pressure requires a huge dose of patience and inner strength. It also helps to "feed the beast" with whatever morsels of information and policy background you can safely provide. After all, as the saying goes, "You can't beat something with nothing," so it is better to fill the news vacuum with content that reflects your perspective and your values rather than leaving a void to be filled by America's adversaries or people who may be well meaning but ill-informed.

Here's an example of how a SecDef has to grapple with gaps and uncertainties in the information available to him while a crisis is unfolding in real time. It dates back to October 2015, when the news media exploded with stories about an air attack by U.S. forces on a hospital in Kunduz, Afghanistan.

I was aboard my 747 en route to some other part of the world early on Sunday morning, October 4, when video images of an attack on a clinic operated by the international nonprofit Médecins Sans Frontières (MSF, or Doctors Without Borders) popped up on the worldwide news. It was the first I'd heard about the incident, though sketchy reports had actually surfaced during the night, and Peter Cook had issued a noncommittal statement of behalf of DOD. But now the story had morphed from words into pictures, making it far more accessible, and powerful.

We turned on the television onboard the airplane and watched the footage on CNN. We were indisputably seeing a hospital in flames—markings on the roof clearly showed its medical function. There were witnesses saying that it had been bombed. And based on battle activity in that region of the country, war planes operated by the United States or its coalition partners were the most plausible explanation.

But experience had taught me that this did not mean there was an open-and-shut case for U.S. responsibility. There are always people in terrorist groups as well as adversaries from countries like Russia or China trying to suggest that American forces have done something that they didn't do. In some cases, the United States is blamed for crimes the ac-cusers themselves committed. And of course, the fog of warfare often conceals other possible causal chains. It was important to verify the facts before jumping to a reaction in any direction—either by denying U.S. involvement or by taking full responsibility.

Here I was at a moment when I knew nothing but what was on my television screen—but it sure looked as if there was an elephant in the room. Spokespeople for MSF moved quickly to denounce the attack; one even used the phrase "war crime" during a television appearance in the early hours after the incident. An American officer on the ground in Af-ghanistan issued a brief, unsatisfactory statement that provided no infor-mation and expressed no sense of urgency or concern. When emotions are running high, that sort of response from a U.S. official can do more harm than good.

The press, of course, was clamoring for me to say something. Evi-dence was mounting that U.S. forces had in fact been responsible for the attack. And under the circumstances, with horrific footage of a hospital in flames being broadcast around the world, we couldn't get away with a bland statement about "studying the matter," even if we'd wanted to. Tak-ing a stance that could be perceived as defiant or callous risked provoking a serious international backlash, perhaps including a loss of support from our allies in the region or even a violent uprising.

To his credit, my chief of staff, Eric Rosenbach, was adamant about insisting that I had to respond publicly, and to do so sooner rather than later. And I had to respond in a way that reflected the seriousness of the incident and the readiness of the United States to take responsibility for its actions—even though the precise nature of those actions was unclear in this case.

I followed Eric's wise advice. The statement I issued said, in effect, "The attack shown on cable television appears to be the result of a mis-taken U.S. air strike on a hospital. Such an attack is clearly a very serious matter. Therefore, I intend to take the following actions." I went on to briefly describe how DOD investigates any apparent case of needless civilian casualties and how we deal with cases in which casualties are caused by U.S. error, negligence, or deliberate action. Thus, I described actions under way, rather than asking people to just "wait and see."

Over time, the facts emerged, thanks largely to an investigation mounted by CENTCOM itself. Afghanistan commander John Campbell took steps to ensure that this investigation was thorough and unbiased, including removing responsibility for it from his direct chain of command. The CENTCOM commander, Joe Votel, released the final report. It turned out that the special operations unit involved in the attack had lacked proper advance clearance. Then the American gunship crew, misled by an inaccurate visual description provided by Afghan troops, had misidentified the clinic as a nearby government building controlled by the Taliban. In addition, our airmen had failed to consult their no-strike list, which would have informed them that the building was a clinic run by MSF. Furthermore, malfunctioning electronic equipment on the plane prevented the crew from receiving corrective warnings until after the attack was over.

All these details were made public in the report we issued. This kind of openness is one big difference between the American military and our counterparts in some other countries, particularly those ruled by authoritarian regimes like Russia, which regard the flow of information as simply a tool to be manipulated for the benefit of those in power.

This tragic series of errors led to the death of an estimated forty-two people and injuries to another thirty. President Obama personally apologized to the president of MSF, and the United States made some 170 condolence payments to the families of the victims, as well as contributing $5.7 million to rebuilding the hospital. Sixteen members of the military were disciplined for their contributions to the mistaken attack. And in the long run, the relationship between the MSF and the U.S. military actually improved as a result of the lessons learned from this terrible event.

The Kunduz hospital-strike story illustrates the difficulties involved in responding to a fast-moving crisis in times of uncertainty. We all wish that the attack had never happened, of course. But given the reality that it did happen, I think DOD handled it about as well as it could have been handled. We managed to balance the sometimes-conflicting demands of forthrightness, speed, and accuracy and so prevented creating an impression of callousness on top of grave error. That's not by any means a justification for what happened, but under the circumstances, it is the best that was possible.

When Every Moment Counts

The crises I've just described involve situations in which the United States must respond to unpredictable events, including aggressive acts by potential enemies. As I've explained, in most cases it is possible to buy time to make a thoughtful and considered decision about how to react—and it's important to do so.

However, there are three kinds of crisis scenarios that unfold on very rapid and predictable timelines. These require different kinds of action and authorities. In escalating order of risk, they are authorizing the launch of missile defense interceptors against a foreign rocket; shooting down a civilian airliner that appears to have been hijacked and is heading for a high-value target like the Capitol or the White House; and responding to a massive nuclear attack from an adversary like Russia or China. I've described some of the considerations involved in the third scenario as we would play them out in the SIOP exercises. Now I'll explain how the first two scenarios would, and should, be handled.

An ICBM launched from North Korea in the direction of the United States would take about a half hour to reach U.S. territory. Satellites would detect the launch moment, because the bright exhaust plume could be seen from space as soon as it broke cloud cover. A series of radars we have deployed in the region, including several on ships and one on a barge, would detect and track the missile.

In response to this observation, the United States would have to decide whether to activate our missile defense interceptors, deployed in Alaska and California. In my role as acquisition czar, I received some criticism for accelerating the deployment of these defenses, which critics considered needless. But today, as the North Korean threat has grown, we're happy to have them deployed. They are constantly at the ready, but they can be spun up to very high readiness when a North Korean launch is imminent or under way. Considering how long it would take the interceptor to fly into space and intercept the incoming missile, there would be a window of only a few minutes to make a decision.

This decision is in the hands of the NORTHCOM commander. In principle, the choice could be escalated to the Secretary of Defense and the president, but in practice this couldn't be counted on. Accordingly, the NORTHCOM commander has authority to authorize the interceptor launch on her own, or even to delegate it to her subordinate commanders. This delegation to lower levels would be appropriate, since the interceptor wouldn't hurt anything except the incoming missile.

The second scenario, and by far the most troublesome for the SecDef, involves the question of whether to shoot down a civilian airliner that appears to have been hijacked for use in a hostile attack. This is the principal task for which Operation Noble Eagle (ONE) was created in the wake of the 9/11 attacks. It involves fighters on hot alert at bases throughout the continental United States with air-to-air missiles slung under their wings. It also involves some missile defenses based on interceptors and other techniques, especially surrounding Washington, D.C.

Under ONE (pronounced oh-en-ee), the president has reposed authority to shoot down airliners in the Secretary of Defense and, if he was unavailable, in the deputy secretary of defense. But that authority was supposed to go no further down the chain of command, unless, for some reason, they absolutely couldn't be reached. Therefore, it's the duty of both the SecDef and the deputy to make sure that at least one of them is always reachable. Having served in both jobs, I can tell you that I always knew when I was the designated reachable official. Being ONE was a little like being "it" on the playground—your status as the person who might be called upon to make a rapid life-and-death decision was never far from your mind.

I found that the problem of civilian aircraft violating airspace restrictions and therefore inviting a possible defensive attack arose rather frequently. Particularly troublesome was the air bubble that the Federal Aviation Administration (FAA) would put around the president when he was traveling. These so-called restriction zones were posted by the FAA and were supposed to be observed by all civil aviators and airline pilots in the vicinity. Unfortunately, the civil aviators routinely violated the zones. It was common for such pilots—say, a dentist going for his weekend flight in his private Cessna from his little airfield near home—to blunder into the region of airspace around the president. The result would be an ONE teleconference involving the ops centers of the FAA; the air-traffic controller in the sector involved; the FBI, CIA, and other federal agencies; and, of course, most important, the NORTHCOM commander and the SecDef.

We'd have to make a decision within moments. Should we err on the side of caution, hoping that the pilot was harmless? Or should we shoot down an unidentified plane, which might be an airliner with hundreds of people onboard? This was not a pleasant choice.

The most memorable of those ONE events for me occurred just a few days after I became Leon Panetta's deputy secretary of defense. Leon was traveling and had given me ONE. I was sleeping in my apartment in Washington when, in the middle of the night, the security officers who lived in an apartment near mine hammered at my door to wake me. I found myself with a secure cell phone being stuck in my face. On the phone were the NORAD ops center plus all the relevant players. It was ONE.

The situation was rapidly explained to me. An airplane scheduled to land at Baltimore-Washington International Airport had overflown BWI and was heading south toward Washington. Its flight path would take it directly over the U.S. Capitol. A check revealed that the airplane was foreign-flagged and foreign-crewed, and it was large enough to do serious damage. We had just a few minutes to react.

F-16s from Andrews Air Force Base and Langley Air Force Base in Virginia were already in the air. They soon made visual contact with the plane and flew alongside it, trying to warn the pilot that he should change direction. Radio communications were attempted, but received no response. The fighter jets fired flares in front of the cockpit to alert the pilot to the fact that he was being escorted. No response.

Finally, one of the F-16s maneuvered itself right in front of the airliner so that a blast from its jet engine would shake the aircraft. This is called *bumping*. It's a dangerous maneuver, but it's authorized in a situation like this.

At last, the pilot responded and changed course. The aircraft, which turned out to be a large cargo plane, was escorted to a small airfield nearby. When the pilot was questioned by the FBI, it turned out that he had been alone on the flight deck and had fallen asleep!

It always ticked me off how lightly the FBI and the FAA let off the pilots who were responsible for incidents like these. Recreational pilots are a powerful lobby, so airspace violators routinely get a slap on the wrist rather than the heavy fines or even jail terms I think they deserve—which would underscore the seriousness of the problem. But I never got anywhere with the FAA on that issue.

As the stories in this chapter illustrate, a big part of the job of the SecDef is to make sure the entire vast array of people, organizations, weapons, equipment, and other resources that make up DOD are ready to spring into action when the need arises because of some externally driven event—an attack by an enemy, a natural disaster, a terrorist incident. But there are other times when circumstances on the global stage call for the U.S. military to take proactive steps against adversaries—to plan and launch a campaign to stop the depredations of countries or groups that mean to do harm to America, its allies, and to the peace and freedom of the world.

One such campaign was perhaps the single most dramatic episode of my tenure at the helm of America's military.

CHAPTER 9

CLARITY OF PURPOSE: DEFEATING ISIS

On December 11, 2016, just before my time as Secretary of Defense would end, I stepped off a C-130 transport plane onto a cold and dusty patch of northern Iraq that had been on my mind for more than a year: an Iraqi military airfield called Qayyarah West. Q-West, as it was known to the American military, was a talisman of progress on one of the defining issues of my time as secretary, the fight to defeat ISIS. A year before, General Joe Dunford and I had briefed the president on a plan to energize the counter-ISIS fight. We had laid out a series of military tasks in Iraq and Syria that would lead us to the liberation of ISIS strongholds in Mosul, Iraq, and Raqqa, Syria. Q-West was a fulcrum of that plan. Ejecting ISIS and turning the airstrip into a logistics hub was essential to seizing Mosul, just forty miles to the north.

Standing next to Lieutenant General Steve Townsend, the commander Joe and I had selected to lead the fight, I told a small group of reporters: "I wanted to come here to Qayyarah West personally, particularly at this holiday time, to thank our troops who are out here at a pretty austere location that was in [ISIS] hands not long ago. . . . That has been part of our plan for more than a year now. This very airfield was part of our plan of more than a year ago."

That plan had become reality, and I was there to see it yet again in person. Iraqi forces, with the support of a U.S.-led global coalition, had seized Q-West just as planned. In fact, the campaign plan that had unfolded on the battlefield was the same one that I had presented to President Obama the previous December. I had been looking at Q-West on campaign maps for a long time.

226

The story of how we got there is one of a little good fortune and a lot of skill and bravery on the part of young men and women from many nations—and, I think, some key decisions and recommendations that I and the department's leadership made, and that President Obama consistently approved, to change a fight that had been going poorly.

The Emergence of ISIS

Understanding the campaign requires going back to my time as deputy secretary of defense. By the time I left in 2013, Abu Bakr al-Baghdadi, the barbaric head of a terror group called the Islamic State of Iraq, had no large base of territory or power but was seeking to gain power and influence by merging with other extremist groups. In the year I was out of government, between leaving the deputy secretary role and becoming Secretary of Defense, Baghdadi's group had emerged, suddenly and unexpectedly, as a major threat. Shortly after I left the Pentagon, Baghdadi's forces shocked the world by seizing control of Fallujah.

Baghdadi had taken advantage of the power vacuum and sectarian strife in Iraq that followed the departure of U.S. forces in 2012—a departure that, as Leon Panetta's deputy, I had argued against, along with Leon, undersecretary for policy Michèle Flournoy, and the joint chiefs. An agreement reached with Iraq during the Bush administration called for withdrawal of all troops by the end of 2011.

Over Christmas 2011, as that deadline approached, I participated in conversations with the White House and State Department to try to preserve some sort of U.S. military presence that could remain engaged with Iraqi forces. Iraq was refusing to grant legal protection to U.S. troops who would stay. My own view was that the legal debate was made more difficult by the fact that a pullout was politically popular in both countries. On Christmas Day, I had called Leon, who was in California. I apologized for bothering him on the holiday. He said it wasn't a problem—"I'm just cooking sausages."

I had to tell him, "Boss, I'm not getting anywhere with this." Leon told me to hang in there and do what I could. At one point in the discussions, the State Department declared that it intended to "normalize" its embassy in Baghdad, making it more like embassies in India or Saudi Arabia, where our major national security focus was arms sales. I pointed out the difference between those countries and Iraq: We hadn't invaded India or Saudi Arabia. As the clock wound down, I remember being asked by another senior administration official, incredulous, "Don't you get it?" The message: There would be no residual force. I needed to move on.

I believed then, and still believe, that if the governments of Iraq and the United States had been able to reach agreement on a small but meaningful residual force, it is possible that we could have averted much of the violence that followed. Such a force, to advise and assist Iraqi forces in keeping order, could have provided some ballast to an Iraqi military that dissolved under ISIS pressure. But one cannot say for sure, because many other powerful factors contributed to that failure, including sectarianism abetted by Prime Minister Nuri al-Maliki and Iranian meddling. Ultimately, Iraq's government failed to meet its basic obligations to its people in allowing ISIS to rise. But leaving when we did, combined with these and other important factors, made ISIS's emergence more likely.

By December 2014, when President Obama asked me to become the new SecDef, ISIS had rapidly expanded its reach. It had seized Mosul, Tikrit, and wide swaths of northern Iraq, key oil and gas fields, the cities of Raqqa and Tabqa in Syria, and important border crossings that secured its ability to move forces, money, and matériel between Iraq and Syria freely. It had openly declared an Islamic caliphate in Iraq and Syria, and announced its intention to expand into Yemen, Saudi Arabia, Egypt, Algeria, and Libya. Tens of thousands of foreign fighters had streamed into Iraq and Syria to bolster its ranks. And in an era of gruesome terrorist attacks, it had set a new bar for brutality, as evidenced by the savage executions of American journalist James Foley and British aid worker David Haines, its enslavement and mass murder of ethnic and religious minorities such as the Yazidis, its imposition of violently repressive rule over millions of Iraqis and Syrians, and its use of social media to foment hate and inspire violence around the world.

In public statements at the time, military officers described ISIS as "halted" and militarily "in decline." While the United States had begun conducting air strikes against ISIS in September 2014, and had begun advising Iraqi ground forces, ISIS was not yet halted. Over the next four months, ISIS would capture At Tanf and Palmyra in Syria and Ramadi in Iraq—a "battle" in which a small ISIS band chased away a much larger Iraqi force that simply refused to fight, a fact I bluntly stated publicly. The news was not all grim: as I was awaiting confirmation, Kurdish forces had ousted ISIS from Kobane, Syria—but good news was the exception.

Meeting the ISIS challenge was clearly going to be a big part of my job.

The Need to Change Course

Two days after I was sworn in as SecDef, I flew to Kuwait. In a secure conference room at Camp Arifjan, I assembled all the military commanders, diplomats, and other civilian leaders from across the U.S. government—everyone associated with the problem. CENTCOM commander General Lloyd Austin was there, as well as his subordinate commanders, including Lieutenant General James Terry, the commander of what had been designated Operation Inherent Resolve just months before. So were combatant commanders from EUCOM and AFRICOM; presidential envoy John Allen and his deputy Brett McGurk; U.S. ambassadors from the region; and senior intelligence officials. We informally called this the "Team America" meeting. (We agreed to keep the phrase private after my staff reminded me of an irreverent film with the same title.) The goal was to hear not just what we were doing, but why—how the pieces fit together into a coherent strategy. The United States was bombing ISIS targets and trying to strengthen the Iraqi security forces (ISF), but I was deeply concerned by the state of the effort.

I gradually concluded that the United States and its coalition partners lacked a comprehensive, achievable plan for success. Also lacking was a way to talk about the effort that could inspire the confidence of the American people or the publics of European allies who were at even greater risk from ISIS terrorism. The coalition lacked both useful tools to fight ISIS and a realistic assessment of the tools at our disposal, and was almost totally bereft of accurate intelligence about the enemy. It lacked clearly articulated objectives and a coherent chain of command for the operation. An American public stunned by ISIS successes, European nations concerned about ISIS terror attacks by their own nationals, a business community with rising concern about the effect on tourism and commerce—all these constituencies saw no plan to defeat ISIS and had little confidence in the campaign's success.

What would follow over the next twenty-three months was a massive reorganization in the planning, execution, and communication about the counter-ISIS campaign. As I look back on this period, it divides into clear stages. From my confirmation in February 2015 until late that summer, we were still struggling to get a handle both on the operation and on how to talk about it with confidence. It's fair to say that we took longer than we should have to get our act together. In fits and starts during this time, the department began with slow but increasing success to address the weaknesses in the counter-ISIS campaign. In the second half of the year, we began introducing "accelerants" to the campaign that increased the pressure on ISIS and helped shape the events to come. In the final weeks of 2015, Joe Dunford and I put a detailed military campaign plan before the president that offered a clear path to retaking Mosul and Raqqa. From that point, there was a clear public message on the strategic goals and methods of the campaign. From then on, the job was aggressive implementation of the campaign plan, as city after city would be liberated from ISIS in accordance with the plan Joe and I had recommended to the president.

Talking About the Fight: "Lasting Defeat" and the "Combat" Question

My first task in the counter-ISIS fight—before I could actually do anything—was to change the way we talked about it. Officials spoke of the need to "degrade, and ultimately defeat" our enemy. While that phrase conveyed the reality that beating ISIS was a process and would take time, I wasn't sure it fully spoke to the urgency of the task. I wanted language that made clear we were in for the long haul, but that, without chest-beating or braggadocio, projected purpose.

During my Senate confirmation hearing on February 4, John McCain asked if we had a strategy to defeat ISIS. He had a point in pressing me.

I answered by describing our goal as a "lasting defeat" of ISIS. I used the phrase "lasting defeat" eleven times in my confirmation hearing and hundreds of times in the months to follow. I chose both words carefully. "Defeat" was more fitting than "degrade" and other weaker verbs—an enemy like ISIS, violent and without conscience, had to be defeated.

"Lasting" reflected the lesson of the Iraq and Afghanistan wars of the years before, and contained what would be a centerpiece of our strategy. As I told our own troops over and over in the two years to come, I had no doubt that they could have marched into Raqqa and Mosul and ejected ISIS. But sending them to do so would have been a strategic blunder. First, the United States would have done so alone—there was a coalition to defeat ISIS, but no coalition willing to re-invade Iraq or invade Syria with us.

Militarily, such a strategy would also cede our unique advantages in technology, firepower, intelligence, and logistics to play on ISIS's turf—infantry fighting in the streets of Iraqi and Syrian cities. Such an approach could well backfire and strengthen our enemy: large U.S. formations back in the Middle East would undoubtedly have pushed some Iraqis and Syrians willing to assist in the fight, or at least to stay on the sidelines, into ISIS's arms. And had we overcome all those disadvantages, the problem would have remained: How would areas liberated from ISIS have remained free? A defeat of ISIS by a U.S. force of arms would be fleeting unless communities taken from ISIS could rebuild and secure themselves to prevent such extremism from once again threatening the Americans it was my job to protect. America's experience with conquering Middle Eastern countries was not encouraging to such a strategy.

Another seemingly rhetorical puzzle with deeper significance would occupy a great deal of my time—the "combat" question. "Lasting defeat" required enabling local forces to reclaim territory from ISIS and hold it rather than attempting to substitute for them. That meant focusing U.S. forces on training, equipping, enabling, and often accompanying them. All this involved risk and—of course—the possibility that U.S. troops would be in combat. Explaining a strategy that assigned primary responsibility for seizing ISIS territory to local forces while also remaining clear about the danger and heroism involved for the U.S. forces enabling them, was a challenge. The president clearly wanted to reassure the American people that we were not involving ourselves in large-scale ground combat, and the people of the region did not want invasion-size forces to return, either.

But the avoidance of the word "combat" risked minimizing the risk and sacrifice of U.S. and coalition forces. With the press and, above all, with the troops, this hairsplitting didn't fly. The press, eager to play got-cha, constantly searched for any hint of U.S. troops in "combat" roles or that they had moved closer to the front lines. There was fodder for such claims. It included a massive air campaign in which U.S. and coalition aircrews were in combat every day, as well as ground operations that couldn't be fully discussed for security reasons. I saw no point in pre-tending that we weren't involved in combat.

In October 2015, when Army Master Sergeant Joshua Wheeler be-came the first U.S. service member to lose his life in direct ground action against ISIS, the issue came to a head. The raid in which Master Sergeant Wheeler lost his life was an example of the kinds of operations we wanted Iraqi forces to conduct with our support—and of the risks inherent for the troops in training, assisting, and advising anti-ISIS forces. Wheeler's unit was advising a Kurdish Peshmerga special forces unit that planned to assault a location where ISIS was holding prisoners and readying them for execution. The plan called for Wheeler's unit to transport and sup-port the Kurdish forces that would assault the compound, but to remain outside it. When the assault force arrived and Kurdish troops began to engage ISIS forces in their target building, they came under fire from a nearby building in the same compound. Wheeler did just what you would expect a brave, competent, highly decorated American soldier to do—he went to the aid of comrades in trouble. In giving his life, he helped rescue seventy ISIS prisoners whose graves the terrorists had already dug.

When asked by a reporter about Wheeler's death, I replied honestly: "Of course he died in combat." I was proud of his actions, and I told the press I was proud.

Some in the Pentagon press corps might have been tempted to report that this honest acknowledgment contradicted our stated strategy. They never fully conveyed that, even in a supporting role, the troops faced real risks every day. Other journalists, including those more familiar with how special operators train, advise, and assist allied forces, apparently thought we didn't recognize the danger—that we considered such missions a risk-free way to conduct the fight. But the dangers the troops faced were always on my mind. Being forthright about this reality was another element in the rhetorical shift we had to make as part of a revised anti-ISIS strategy.

Muddles Inside the Pentagon and Out

One factor that made our public statements on the ISIS fight so cloudy during my first year back at the Pentagon was that we still could not describe the actual steps we would take to achieve "lasting defeat." The anodyne messaging I inherited revolved around nine "lines of effort." Two of these lines of effort were the Defense Department's responsibility: denying ISIS safe haven and building local partners' capacity. Other lines of effort belonged largely or entirely to other agencies: strengthening governance in Iraq; negotiating a political transition in Syria; combating ISIS's illicit financing and media messaging and the flow of foreign fighters; gathering intelligence; providing humanitarian support; and disrupting terror threats to the United States.

In congressional testimony in the early months after my confirmation, I sought to weave these nine lines of effort into a coherent message that Congress and the public could understand and support. I had little success. All nine were important tasks, but they were far too numerous and "in the weeds." It was a list, not a strategy.

The "lines of effort" approach was no easier to handle behind closed doors than it was to talk about in public. At my suggestion, I met a number of times with Secretary of State John Kerry to manage and track their implementation, including the seven lines of effort outside DOD's responsibility. However, with Kerry's attention dedicated to the important Iran nuclear deal and other matters, and State's comparatively limited role in the fight, the meetings proved largely unproductive.

Further clouding the picture was the creation, before I became secretary, of a position for a special State Department envoy on ISIS issues. When I returned to the Pentagon, retired General John Allen had been in the role for five months. John is a good man, a good friend, and a great partner in years of work together on the Middle East and Afghanistan. Unfortunately, the position he was in confused everyone, at home and abroad, about who was in charge. It badly blurred the responsibilities of the Defense Department, State Department, and White House, and was a nuisance to the chain of command. As the expression goes, the Allen role "filled a much-needed gap."

By December, Allen had stepped down after doing his usual best in an awkward role. But the lines of responsibility remained blurry. I saw this on my first visit to Baghdad as secretary in July 2015. Landing in a country where the United States was engaged in a tough military campaign against a barbaric enemy, I was greeted not by a uniformed commander, but by State Department diplomats, who transported me in State Department vehicles and State Department–contracted helicopters (which, we would learn when the State Department sent us the bill, were really expensive) and who planned most of my itinerary. The overwhelming impression was that the State Department was running the show and sidelining the military just to prove a point. This was not the State Department I had worked with for thirty years at its best. That relationship— and much more—needed to change.

Compounding our problems was the fact that intelligence on ISIS was almost entirely lacking. We did not understand who our enemy was, where he was, or what he would do next. ISIS's capture of Ramadi, with zero warning, three months after I returned to the Pentagon and months after we had launched counter-ISIS operations, epitomized the paucity of intelligence in these months—a problem we only gradually solved.

Our military planning for counter-ISIS operations was also a problem. While in Kuwait for the Team America meeting, I was briefed in private by CENTCOM Commander Lloyd Austin on a plan to retake Mosul. I admired Austin's desire to take the fight to the enemy, but the plan he presented to me was entirely unrealistic, relying on Iraqi army formations that barely existed on paper, let alone in reality. To make matters worse, a CENTCOM official had already told Pentagon reporters in Washington that we planned to launch operations to retake Mosul by March or April, adding an imaginary timetable to the imaginary forces that would carry it out. Building the kind of Iraqi force that could retake Mosul would ultimately require the better part of a year. Had we launched these aspirational operations without sufficient resources and planning, the failures would have set back the counter-ISIS campaign—and increased the already intense pressure on the White House.

Attempts to train and equip counter-ISIS forces across the border in Syria were another embarrassing failure. The plan I inherited when I took office was to constitute whole anti-ISIS units from scratch by recruiting individual fighters, forming them into units, providing them training and equipment in Turkey and other Arab countries, and reinserting them into the fight in Syria. This would have been difficult under any circumstances, but we were hampered by the requirement for ironclad assurances to Congress that troops we trained and armed would fight only ISIS, and not engage in the bloody civil war to unseat Bashar al-Assad—a Solomonic compromise between those who wanted to get more involved in Syria and those who wanted no part of it. It made little sense in real-world Syria, where almost all the real fighters were already part of ad hoc groups and wanted to fight Assad as well as ISIS. Mike Nagata, the able Army two-star in charge of the effort, had no real chance to succeed.

I failed to recognize just how badly the effort was going until it became a minor scandal. In July 2015, I had to acknowledge to the Senate Armed Services Committee that despite spending several months and millions of dollars, we had trained and deployed only about sixty dependable anti-ISIS fighters in Syria. There were also reports that some units we had trained and equipped had handed over U.S.-supplied equipment to al-Nusra, al-Qaeda's Syrian affiliate. All that saved me from a massacre by the astounded committee members was my candor.

In a subsequent meeting with the president, I acknowledged to him that we had let him down. To his credit, Obama said that the error was "more in conception than execution," which was another way of saying that Nagata's most able efforts hadn't stood a chance. Gradually, we would adopt a more effective method of equipping and training local forces to fight ISIS in Syria—but the success came only after much stumbling.

All these problems were in part a reflection of the fact that no one person was really in charge of the counter-ISIS campaign. The senior officer in Baghdad when I became secretary was Army Lieutenant General Robert Caslen, a capable officer who nonetheless had almost no real authority to influence the fight and was mostly there to oversee arms sales to the Iraqis. Another Army officer, Lieutenant General James Terry, the land forces commander for U.S. Central Command, was overseeing the counter-ISIS fight—not from Baghdad, but from Kuwait, and he too lacked clear authority. Terry was only tenuously connected to the Air Force three-star who managed the air campaign that had begun in August 2014, and none of them was properly tied into what special operators were doing. General Austin and the CENTCOM staff were trying to provide operational leadership from Tampa—difficult if not impossible to do while simultaneously confronting Taliban forces in Afghanistan, Iranian misbehavior, and instability in Yemen, among other problems also on CENTCOM's plate.

We needed to build a military campaign, and a campaign needs a single commander.

From "Lines of Effort" to Concrete Steps

It would take months to properly address these shortcomings. But we didn't have months to make progress against ISIS. Every day, ISIS was brutalizing civilians in Iraq and Syria, spreading its influence via affiliates in Libya, Afghanistan, and elsewhere, and plotting attacks in Europe and North America.

Over spring and early summer 2015, ISIS continued seizing territory—Palmyra, At Tanf, Ramadi, even Sirte, Libya. The U.S.-led air campaign continued, but we were far from having the effects on ISIS operations that we wanted and needed. In May, when ISIS seized Ramadi, the capital of Iraq's al-Anbar province, I caused a stir when I told CNN's Barbara Starr that Iraqi forces defending the city had "just showed no will to fight. . . . They were not outnumbered. In fact, they vastly outnumbered the opposing force, and yet they failed to fight. . . . That says to me, and I think to most of us, that we have an issue with the will of the Iraqis to fight ISIS and defend themselves." That needed to be said to the Iraqis and acknowledged to our own troops, who appreciated that someone had finally spoken the truth. General Marty Dempsey, the chairman of the Joint Chiefs put it even more pithily: "The ISF was not driven out of Ramadi. They drove out of Ramadi."

Fielding Iraqi forces who were not just well trained and equipped, but who also fought with will and determination, would be a months-long process.

We gradually began to identify and take advantage of opportunities to speed up our progress. In mid-May we launched a raid targeting Abu Sayyaf, the head of ISIS's lucrative oil and gas operations. We hoped to capture him, but he was killed in the raid. His death complicated ISIS's effort to support its operations with petroleum revenue. More important, we got valuable intelligence about ISIS leadership from others captured in the raid, including Abu Sayyaf's wife and a slave who was freed in the operation, as well as from documents and electronics that we seized.

Helped in part by that intelligence, over the course of the summer and fall, special operators undertook several raids or air strikes targeting senior ISIS figures. Each raid required approval from me, President Obama, Iraqi Prime Minister Haider al-Abadi, and Kurdish President Masoud Barzani, since such operations could pose political risks for each of these leaders. Thankfully, President Obama never wavered in his support. Whenever Marty Dempsey and I saw an opportunity to do more, Obama never declined a single request for additional resources or authority.

A key turning point came on July 6, when President Obama visited the Pentagon for a National Security Council meeting in which he encouraged DOD to present him with broader and more creative options for accelerating the fight. This was just what we'd been hoping to hear. Over the next several months, we recommended and received approval for additional forces and authorities to intensify the fight. The pacing items we'd use to trigger the increases were steadily improving intelligence, more and better training for local forces, and the growing confidence of Abadi and Barzani. All these factors steadily created battlefield opportunities that we could exploit, doing more and more and getting more and more. Contrary to popular belief, our pacing did not depend on matters like the rules of engagement or the need to get permission from President Obama. It annoyed me when people who didn't understand how things really worked misunderstood the real pacing factors and consequently dismissed our approach as "incremental."

Later that July, I traveled to Iraq to assess the campaign, and in particular plans to recapture Ramadi. After once again sensing too many cooks in the kitchen, I directed General Dempsey to draft plans for consolidating the campaign under a single operational commander.

That commander would be Sean MacFarland. He was not fully in place until September. But finally, there was one (exceedingly competent) officer responsible for the entire campaign—in the air and on the ground. I knew Sean best from his stint as deputy commander in Afghanistan years before, when I was equipping and supplying the war there as the acquisition czar. But it was his experience as a brigade commander in Iraq that made him so effective in fighting ISIS. Sean had deep knowledge not just of Iraq's physical geography—he had walked the streets of Ramadi and Mosul—but of what the military calls "human terrain": the tribal relationships and political rivalries that drove so much of what happened there. He was also an exceptionally effective public spokesman for the campaign. His briefings to reporters back in Washington, and his appearances with me when we would brief the traveling press, conveyed plainspoken reassurance.

Sean's exceptional skills would pay off in the months ahead as the fight accelerated and grew more complex—on the battlefield and in terms of the tangled politics of the region. When Sean's tour was up in August 2016, I chose Lieutenant General Steve Townsend, another excellent officer whom I also knew from the days of the Afghan surge and who had also served previously in Iraq, as his relief. Steve performed his command, which ended in September 2017, with the same great skill.

Key roles in the campaign were also played by the "Two Erics"—Eric Rosenbach, my chief of staff, and Marine Brigadier General Eric Smith, my senior military assistant. Eric Rosenbach's expertise, experience, and clear thinking—he is a former Army intelligence officer who cowrote an excellent book on the transformation of U.S. counterterrorism policy after 9/11—made him an invaluable sounding board and advisor on all the challenges we faced, and in particular on planning the counter-ISIS campaign. Eric Smith was handpicked by me for his combat experience, leadership acumen, and wide-ranging knowledge of military affairs. They will both go far in the years ahead.

Most of all, the march to defeat ISIS was led by men and women of bravery and skill willing to place their lives on the line to protect ours: Iraqi security forces, Kurdish Peshmerga, Syrian Arab, and Kurd fighters, coalition partners, and, of course, the incomparable troops of the U.S. military. As always, nothing we could do from conference rooms in Washington or Brussels or Baghdad could substitute for their competence and courage.

Accelerating the Campaign

The same month that Sean MacFarland took command, General Joseph Dunford would be sworn in, at my recommendation, as chairman of the Joint Chiefs. One of the best leaders I have ever known, Joe was an invaluable partner on the ISIS campaign. He described the items the president approved over the summer and fall as "accelerants" for the campaign, a useful coinage that I quickly adopted.

In October, the president approved a series of accelerants to replace the failed train-and-equip program for Syria. We received authority to deploy a small group of special operators into Syria, where they established contacts with members of the Syrian Arab Coalition (SAC), a group of Arab fighters organized under the umbrella of Syrian Kurdish groups. The existence of the SAC—revealed to us when our operators came out of Syria saying, "We can work with these guys"—was one of many lucky breaks we got during the campaign. The president authorized us to begin training and equipping the SAC, as well as local anti-ISIS forces in southern Syria. However, working with groups so closely tied to Syrian Kurds sparked immediate tensions with Turkey, which never went away.

Our commanders and I identified more specific steps we could take. We deployed A-10 and F-15 aircraft to Incirlik Air Base in Turkey, where the Turks had, after months of delays, finally given permission for us to launch anti-ISIS missions. The president also authorized us to employ AH-64 Apache helicopters, if Abadi requested their use, for the fight in Ramadi. Each of these accelerants would strengthen the local ground forces we were supporting.

As winter approached, these accelerants were bearing fruit. A strike in November killed Mohammad Emwazi, the British extremist known as "Jihadi John," who had participated in several brutal executions. Kurdish Peshmerga liberated Sinjar in northern Iraq, cutting off one main route of ISIS communications with Syria. And we were having more and more success targeting the network of oil facilities that provided ISIS hundreds of millions of dollars in illicit revenue.

But elsewhere in the global fight against ISIS, the battle wasn't faring so well. On November 13, ISIS operatives carried out a deadly attack in Paris, setting off a bomb outside a soccer match and wantonly shooting civilians at venues including a concert hall. In all, 139 people died. Hours after the attack, I had a wrenching phone call with Defense Minister Jean-Yves Le Drian, a stalwart of the campaign whose nation had been shaken by the attack. Then, less than a month later, an ISIS-inspired couple killed 14 people in San Bernardino, California. These attacks were painful reminders that every day that ISIS ruled wide swaths of Iraq and Syria was a day it could execute or simply inspire deadly attacks against us and our allies.

We'd made a lot of progress in the fight. We had a command structure. We had gone from vague "lines of effort" to specific steps, and had buy-in from the president for those steps. But we didn't have a way of showing how the steps would get us to our destination. And I didn't have the full backing of the president for an integrated, specific campaign. Both would come in December.

"Two Red Arrows": The Christmas Campaign Plan

At the start of December 2015, I testified before both congressional defense committees, where I outlined some of our progress. For example, I reported how Iraqi forces with our support had begun to make progress in retaking Ramadi and had demonstrated resilience in dealing with ISIS counterattacks in the area—a notable change from the ISF's retreat from the city in May. At these hearings, I also announced another accelerant for the campaign: the deployment of an Expeditionary Targeting Force (ETF) of special operators to conduct high-impact operations in Iraq. Though we did not often discuss the ETF's operations publicly after that announcement, it achieved major results both in killing and capturing ISIS leaders and in gathering valuable intelligence that fed future operations.

At the Senate hearing, John McCain grudgingly praised our progress in Iraq but derisively claimed that our strategy on the Syrian side looked "more like a hope." The only way to answer such criticism was with results. The campaign plan taking shape would demonstrate the soundness of our approach.

In the previous weeks, I had been working with Joe Dunford and others to develop the campaign plan that would lead to capturing Mosul and Raqqa. By the time the president traveled to the Pentagon on December 14 for a National Security Council meeting on the ISIS campaign, we were ready to brief him on our plan. We met around the long table in my conference room—the president, vice president, Joe Dunford, and I at the head, and the NSC members arrayed down the sides.

The president opened the meeting, then turned to me to speak. I started by pointing out that ISIS was targeting everyone in the room, including me and my family. I turned to the president and said, "To hell with that." And then I told him what we wanted to do about it.

I knew we needed to go from concrete steps to a clear path toward an end state. I took inspiration from World War II newsreels that represented the relentless march of the Allies across Europe and the Pacific with big, sweeping arrows. I showed Obama a map with two bright red arrows pointing to Mosul and Raqqa. And then Joe and I told him how we would get there, step by step, tracing the path of each arrow using a methodical plan to gather and employ the local and coalition forces needed at every step.

In Iraq, the coalition would assist the ISF in retaking Fallujah, in part to help ease the pressure of daily terror attacks in Baghdad. At the same time, the ISF would advance, step by step, to the isolation and liberation of Mosul. Iraqi forces would move north, up the Tigris River from the area north of Baghdad into ISIS-held territory, first along the right bank, into Makhmur, southeast of Mosul, and then Iraqi forces would bridge the Tigris to move farther north against the airfield at Qayyarah West. Q-West, just a short drive from Mosul's southern outskirts, would become a logistics hub for the daunting task of building up a massive Iraqi-led force for the assault on Mosul. Subsidiary operations would eliminate ISIS strongholds in Iraq's western desert such as Rutbah and Hit, liberating oppressed communities and complicating ISIS's logistics by cutting off routes between Iraq and Syria. After a period of rest, refitting, training, and equipping additional Kurdish and ISF units necessary for the task, the Pesh and the ISF—never comfortable together, now indispensable to each other—would cooperate to first isolate, and then assault, Mosul, Iraq's second largest city.

In Syria, we would leverage our link to the Syrian Arab coalitions' Syrian Democratic Forces (SDF), building their combat power as we had the ISF's. The coalition would support SDF operations to clear ISIS-held territory in the north, focusing on Ain Issa, Shaddadi, and then an ISIS-held pocket, centered on the town of Manbij, between two Kurdish-held territories, as well as Dabiq. Dabiq is a small town west of Manbij that held outsize importance in ISIS's ideology as the prophesied location of an apocalyptic battle; ISIS even named its propaganda magazine after the town. These operations would begin to isolate Raqqa, both in preparation for assaulting Baghdadi's stronghold and, just as important, to protect

In 1974, age twenty, I was working at the Fermi National Accelerator Laboratory as a physicist—my career before becoming involved in national defense. I am adjusting the detectors that counted subatomic particles created in high-energy collisions, sending signals down the green cables before me—all part of the quest for mysterious elementary particles called quarks and W bosons.

COURTESY OF THE AUTHOR.

A historic 1981 meeting of U.S. and Soviet weapons scientists at the headquarters of the Strategic Air Command in Omaha, Nebraska. In the front rows are Wolfgang Panofsky, who flew in the instrumentation plane above the Trinity atomic bomb test in 1945; Richard L. Garwin, who designed the first thermonuclear bomb; Michael M. May, director of the Lawrence Livermore nuclear weapons lab; future Secretary of Defense Bill Perry; and Evgeny Velikhov, Soviet bomb designer, later charged with managing the Chernobyl meltdown. I am in the back, right in front of the missile, smiling to find myself in such distinguished company.   COURTESY OF THE AUTHOR.

As assistant secretary of defense, I ran the Nunn-Lugar program, which consolidated and dismantled "loose nukes" after the breakup of the Soviet Union. Here I am in Ukraine in 1994 with my boss, Secretary of Defense Bill Perry, in front of an SS-19 missile, designed to carry six nuclear warheads targeted at the United States, that is being prepared for dismantling.

COURTESY OF THE AUTHOR.

In 1996 at Pervomaysk, Ukraine, the same site as the previous picture. Crops are being planted where nuclear weapons were once sited. Wielding shovels are the Russian, Ukrainian, and U.S. defense chiefs. I look on, smiling (far right, in Pentagon jacket). COURTESY OF THE AUTHOR.

Having been appointed Secretary of Defense in 2014 by President Barack Obama, here am I at work in my Pentagon office. The desk belonged to General John "Black Jack" Pershing, commander of the U.S. expeditionary forces that helped to win World War I.   COURTESY OF THE DEPARTMENT OF DEFENSE.

My predecessor from the 1960s, Robert S. McNamara, working in the same Pentagon office. Not much has changed—the big desk, the carved side table, and most of the other furniture remains the same today.

GETTY/JOSEPH SCHERSCHEL/CONTRIBUTOR.

As the number three official in the department—the "acquisition czar"—I used this chart to make fun of the over-complex bureaucratic system for buying weapons. I made it my mission to simplify the tangle—or, when necessary, to bypass it.   COURTESY OF THE DEPARTMENT OF DEFENSE.

When General Stan McChrystal reported he lacked sufficient drones to track enemy movements during the Afghanistan surge of 2010–2011, we came up with an ingenious solution: a big surge of aerostat balloons like this one being launched in Kabul, equipped with cameras. I am in the white shirt.

COURTESY OF THE DEPARTMENT OF DEFENSE.

Testing various models of bomb-defusing robots in the Afghan desert in summer 2010.
COURTESY OF THE DEPARTMENT OF DEFENSE.

Inspecting a new model of MRAP about to be shipped from Texas to the troops in Afghanistan. Quickly developing and deploying vehicles like this to protect U.S. soldiers from improvised explosive devices was my highest priority as weapons czar. Thousands of lives were saved as a result. COURTESY OF THE DEPARTMENT OF DEFENSE.

As Secretary of Defense, I met with President Obama in the Oval Office for weekly one-on-one reviews of current Pentagon activities and challenges. Joe Dunford, chairman of the Joint Chiefs of Staff, would usually join us.

A meeting with the "big four" leaders of the Pentagon, joined by aides. At the table: Deputy Secretary Bob Work (back to camera), Chairman of the Joint Chiefs Joe Dunford, and Vice Chairman General Paul Selva. Seated behind, from left: trusted Chief of Staff Eric Rosenbach, Special Assistant Ylber Bajraktari, Assistant Secretary for Legislative Affairs Steve Hedger, and Senior Military Assistant Eric Smith.

Briefing members of the press during a foreign trip aboard the Secretary of Defense's aircraft, the E4-B. Seated to my right is the department's talented press spokesperson, Peter Cook.

COURTESY OF THE DEPARTMENT OF DEFENSE.

Maintaining open communication with the troops was one of my most important duties. Our first-ever worldwide troop talk was broadcast to military bases around the world. Today's troops, and especially their families, mostly keep in touch via the Internet.

COURTESY OF THE DEPARTMENT OF DEFENSE.

The "Pacific Pivot" in action: Making a surprise visit with Philippine Secretary of Defense Voltaire Gazmin to a naval task group that had just completed a "freedom of navigation" operation in the South China Sea.

Catching up on paperwork in my windowless office aboard the E4-B, equipped to serve as an airborne Pentagon in the event of a nuclear war. The digital display on the wall offers the only clue as to the time of day outside.

Escorting President Obama from the Pentagon in July 2015, after briefing him about the proposed plan for an accelerated anti-ISIS campaign. As he stepped into his car, the president told me, "Let's do this." COURTESY OF THE DEPARTMENT OF DEFENSE.

Flanked by CENTCOM commander General Joe Votel and Assistant Secretary Elissa Slotkin at a July 2016 briefing for foreign defense ministers regarding the progress of our military campaign to defeat ISIS. To Slotkin's right is Saudi Prince Mohammed bin Salman; to Votel's left, France's Jean-Yves Le Drian.

COURTESY OF THE DEPARTMENT OF DEFENSE.

A Pentagon briefing for President Obama and Vice President Biden on the campaign to defeat ISIS. By this time—August 2016—we could afford to smile, because the key cities of Mosul and Raqqa were surrounded and would fall to coalition forces within months.

June 2015: Speaking to members of a U.S. armored unit newly deployed to Germany as part of our enhanced strategy to stand strong against aggressive moves by Putin's Russia.

The business end of a Minuteman III nuclear missile. By the time I became secretary, it was time to modernize and rebuild the nuclear triad—the bedrock of U.S. security—after twenty-five years of restraint.   COURTESY OF THE DEPARTMENT OF DEFENSE.

Conferring with our South Korean allies during a visit to Panmunjom on the demilitarized zone. A North Korean soldier looks on.

COURTESY OF THE DEPARTMENT OF DEFENSE.

Awarding prizes to the winners of the first-ever Hack the Pentagon contest, when we invited friendly hackers to expose—and help us fix—the vulnerabilities of our computer networks. Looking on is Chris Lynch, director of the Defense Digital Service (in red hoodie).   COURTESY OF THE DEPARTMENT OF DEFENSE.

Building bridges to Silicon Valley: Reid Hoffman, founder of LinkedIn, was a member of the Defense Innovation Board I founded to help ensure the Pentagon had access to the most up-to-date tech expertise—in Hoffman's case, his advice on attracting a quality all-volunteer military.

COURTESY OF THE DEPARTMENT OF DEFENSE.

Amazon CEO Jeff Bezos (second from left), another member of the Defense Innovation Board, visits with me and Chris Lynch at the Pentagon office of the Defense Digital Service.

COURTESY OF THE DEPARTMENT OF DEFENSE.

General Joe Dunford and me on one of our countless helicopter flights together. Recommending Joe for chairman of the Joint Chiefs of Staff was my single best decision as Secretary of Defense.

COURTESY OF THE DEPARTMENT OF DEFENSE.

None of my duties as secretary was more important—or more enjoyable—than spending time with the troops (here some sailors in Bahrain), making sure they understood the importance of their mission and conveying the nation's gratitude for their service.

U.S. troops in far-flung locations appreciated my visits to them, but they enjoyed meeting my wife, Stephanie, even more. Her presence and warmth made a direct connection between my family and theirs.

In October 2015, Army Master Sergeant Joshua Wheeler became the first American soldier to lose his life in direct combat against ISIS. I participated in the "dignified transfer" ceremony for his remains at Dover Air Force Base.

COURTESY OF THE DEPARTMENT OF DEFENSE.

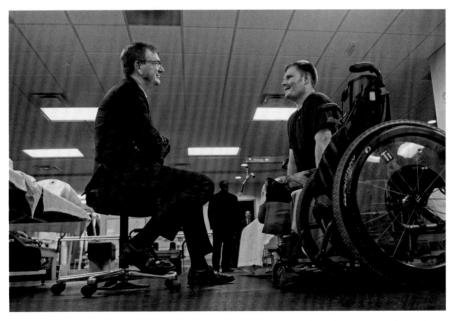

A duty both sad and uplifting: one of my many hospital visits with wounded warriors. The undaunted spirit of these service members and their families always amazed me.

COURTESY OF THE DEPARTMENT OF DEFENSE.

Stephanie and I paid our respects to the fallen at Arlington National Cemetery on the morning of my first day as Secretary of Defense—and I made the same visit on my way home after my last day in office in January 2017.

A serious moment in the Situation Room. Participating in some of the most consequential decisions of the U.S. government was a sobering responsibility—and an opportunity for which I'll always be grateful.

publics in Europe and the United States by interrupting the flow of terrorist operatives from Syria through Turkey to the West.

I told the president he should be ready for a steady stream of requests for more U.S. forces, their precise numbers not fully predictable, to support our growing operations as the campaign unfolded. The president understood, and I think the fact that we had outlined a detailed plan gave him confidence that our requests would be tied to specific objectives. Obama asked me to work with Ben Rhodes, his deputy national security advisor and chief communications coordinator on national security issues, on a plan for communicating the campaign to the public. I replied that that image would be the two red arrows.

Finally, I felt, we had the complete campaign plan and the approval to carry it out.

After the president made a brief statement to the press, I walked him to his motorcade at the Pentagon's river entrance. Before he got in his car, he turned to me and said, "Let's get this done." It was time to go on the offensive. From then forward, step by step, month by month, we would methodically execute our plan. That very afternoon, I left for Iraq.

Winning Support for the Plan

One key element was achieving a political understanding with Abadi and Barzani. I had met with both men multiple times, and knew that while each had domestic political considerations to attend to, we could work with both of them.

In Baghdad on December 16 and in Erbil the next day, I outlined the campaign plan to each man, and what we needed from each government in order for it to succeed. The plan required significant arms deliveries and funding to the Peshmerga to conduct operations around Mosul. This was a tender spot for Abadi and the Iraqi government, which constantly feared an independence bid by the Kurdish Regional Government (KRG), as well as Kurdish designs on Mosul itself.

Similarly, we needed a massive ISF force to take the city—

predominantly Arab, and by necessity largely Shia, because the reincorporation of Sunnis into the ISF was proceeding slowly. To approach Mosul from multiple directions, thousands of ISF troops would need to pass through Pesh lines and assemble in KRG territory to prepare for the assault. This would trouble Barzani and the Kurds, for reasons of politics and history. The Kurds took seriously any threat to their autonomy and would reject a heavy permanent presence in Mosul of forces controlled by Baghdad as a threat to that autonomy—but such a presence was absolutely necessary to liberate Mosul.

An even greater concern, not only for the Kurds but for the United States, would be for Iranian-affiliated Shiite militias to enter Mosul. On top of all this, memories of the Iraqi military's violent suppression of the Kurds—including Saddam Hussein's use of chemical weapons—were painfully fresh. Literally, the last time Baghdad's forces had set foot in some of the places they would be going, it was to hunt down and kill Kurdish fighters.

My pitch to both men was simple: ISIS was a threat to each. Its defeat required steps they might not ordinarily support, but these were not ordinary times. Each would receive equipment, training, funding, and support to help defeat a common enemy. But Mosul could not be a battleground for Iraq's internal rivalries. It could not become an extension of Kurdish authority nor of Shiite militias' political power. I told both men that they "would not get to keep what they took"—that Mosul would return to its pre-ISIS status quo as a multiethnic city. The militias would stay on the sidelines; Abadi would need to ensure this. And regular ISF troops would need access to Kurdish territory—that was the only way to approach Mosul from multiple directions. This was what defeating ISIS would take.

I was relieved but not surprised that they both agreed. Each had the wisdom to do what was necessary—something that could not be said for many others in Iraqi politics. Over the summer, as the Mosul operation approached, these issues never went away—in fact they required constant attention. But both agreements held. Kurdish and ISF forces cooperated more closely than they ever had, to defeat a common enemy. On a later stop in Iraq, I would speak with Iraqi and Kurdish helicopter crews who were operating together on the same airfield in Erbil—something impossible to imagine not long before.

After my visits with Barzani and Abadi, I paid a quick visit to the French aircraft carrier stationed in the Gulf, deployed there after the Paris attacks to demonstrate French resolve. Then I sat in the cabin of the E4-B on the flight back home and began work on a memo to the president submitting the formal campaign plan for his approval. I wrote the plan out myself, longhand, on five sheets of cardboard (my favorite writing surface), with the map of the two red arrows attached. The president had taken to calling the specific operational items in the campaign plan "plays," like a football coach scripting the first ten plays of the game, so I listed the first ten plays of the campaign plan down the side of the map, with the locations shown by corresponding numbers.

On January 13, when speaking to members of the Army's 101st Airborne Division at Fort Campbell, Kentucky, I outlined the campaign in as much detail as I could share publicly—appropriately, in front of the troops who would carry it out. About four hundred troops from the Screaming Eagles were preparing to deploy to Iraq to serve as the ground-component headquarters for the campaign. I talked of three strategic goals: dealing ISIS a lasting defeat in its homeland of Iraq and Syria, thereby eliminating the cancer's parent tumor; combating metastases in places like Libya and Afghanistan; and protecting our homeland from ISIS terror. This simple three-part formulation replaced the "lines of effort" muddle. Over the next year, I repeated these phrases endlessly—"lasting defeat," "parent tumor," and "metastases"—until the ears of everyone around me were ringing from the repetition. I persisted even when a Georgetown oncologist complained to the media that "parent tumor" was the wrong phrase (cancer experts prefer "primary tumor").

I told the soldiers of the 101st, "The Iraqi and Peshmerga forces you will train, advise, and assist have proven their determination, their resiliency, and increasingly, their capability. But they need you to continue building on that success, preparing them for the fight today and the long hard fight for their future. They need your skill. They need your experience. Often, they will need your patience." And I told them to keep their eyes open for things we could not see in Washington. "Tell your commanders so they can tell me." I shook hands with each of them and thanked them for their courage and skill.

A week later I was in Paris. Minister Le Drian and I hosted defense ministers from six key coalition nations—France, the United Kingdom, Germany, Australia, the Netherlands, and the United States. In November, I had written a letter to each of the coalition defense ministers, asking for more support: airpower, police, and military trainers, special operations units, financial assistance, more of everything. I was blunt about the need for everyone to do more—including the United States in that—which was tough for some of them to hear. The letter leaked, causing more of a stir than I liked. But the needs were real, and now we met to review the campaign plan in detail.

For the coalition members, the campaign plan wasn't just a planning document but a confidence booster and political enabler. Having a coherent, logical plan we could explain to leaders back at home—a path along the two red arrows that everyone could visualize—was tremendously important. For many coalition partners, military deployments required parliamentary approval, a process that could take months, and the detailed campaign plan allowed them to look ahead, anticipate requirements, and begin the process of seeking political approval.

Three weeks after the Paris meeting, in Brussels, we convened a larger meeting with twenty-six coalition partners. I have attended many international meetings, and often, the signal-to-noise ratio is extremely low. I told Elissa Slotkin, the acting assistant secretary for international security affairs who was organizing the meeting, that we needed a productive session, not a gabfest. One of the tools she used to ensure this was the "Chiclet chart," which Elissa created with the military planners from CENTCOM. It was a grid listing the categories of assistance required for the campaign—say, trainers for Iraqi police forces or logistics support— and the contributions of each coalition member, shown on squares marked in green, yellow, or red, like pieces of Chiclet gum. The colors reflected varying levels of performance—the "grades" of each coalition partner—and revealing these to the coalition members proved to be highly motivating. We displayed the Chiclet chart in future meetings, moving many coalition partners to step forward with increased contributions in order to change their red or yellow squares to green.

The discussions in these meetings were direct and unvarnished, focused on the truth about the work ahead of us and what we needed to do to complete it. We also took time to build camaraderie, one day singing "Happy Birthday" to Norway's defense minister, Ine Eriksen Søreide, and another listening to Jean-Yves Le Drian speak passionately about the impact of the November attacks on his country. I'd built a strong relationship with Le Drian, and during these meetings I developed important friendships with other partners, including Michael Fallon of Great Britain, Ursula von der Leyen of Germany, Roberta Pinotti of Italy, and Pedro Morenés of Spain.

Surprisingly, given all the high-level leaders in these meetings, none of the discussions ever leaked. It was a sign of the deadly seriousness shared by this close-knit group of war leaders.

Executing the Plan: A Year of Constantly Growing Momentum

No plan is perfect, and no campaign goes perfectly according to plan. But in the year between approval of the campaign plan and the end of the Obama administration, the plays unfolded on the battlefield largely as we had envisioned them. They continued to do so as the Trump administration took over, with the recapture of Mosul and the envelopment of Raqqa at the end of those two red arrows—exactly according to the 2015 plan.

Soon after the adoption of the campaign plan, we introduced the latest set of accelerants. They included the April announcement of more than 200 additional troops for Iraq, as well as the authority to advise and assist smaller Iraqi army units, down to the battalion level. The president also authorized 250 new special operations forces to deploy to Syria, increasing our presence by a factor of five and providing invaluable support to the SDF.

Washington critics continued to complain that these sequenced accelerants amounted to "incrementalism," smacking of Vietnam-era mission creep. This characterization missed the point. The "increments" largely represented requirements that we foresaw, and planned for, well ahead of time, now being deployed as they became tactically relevant. We also needed to ease Prime Minister Abadi into accepting more U.S. forces (which was controversial for him at home) and to condition each U.S. movement on his and Barzani's continued adherence to their own side of the bargain. This approach also had practical benefits at home: It kept tours short, and gave units the time they needed to prepare. And it let us add new capabilities to the fight based on continually emerging new opportunities on the ground and new intelligence.

In May, Iraqi forces liberated the town of Rutbah, a desert junction on the main road from Baghdad to the Jordanian border, and a month later, the ISF completed a long and difficult operation to liberate Fallujah. That event had symbolic resonance not just for the Iraqis, but for thousands of U.S. troops who had fought to free and secure Fallujah in 2005. It also freed ISF formations to begin moving north for the assault on Mosul.

The seizure of the Q-West airfield in July allowed us to begin reconstructing the base as a logistics hub. Q-West is just west of the Tigris River, and the bulk of Iraqi forces in the area were around Makhmur, on the opposite side of the river. With no standing bridges in the area, we had known for months that we would have to help ISF engineers build a temporary span. Bridging a river in a combat zone is among the most complex tasks an army can undertake. Months earlier, Elissa Slotkin and Frank Kendall, the undersecretary for acquisition, had done the work to ensure that floating bridge sections would be on hand when the time came. U.S. engineering troops advised the Iraqis on the bridge's construction and on how to protect it from attack from land and from the floating explosives ISIS used to try to disrupt supply lines. The bridge was just one example of the complex logistics task the Iraqis had taken on—bigger than any the Iraqi military had performed in decades.

Moving thousands of troops along with their food and water, fuel, arms, and equipment was a major effort. And at that floating Tigris bridge, at Q-West, and elsewhere, support from U.S. and coalition engineers, logisticians, and other technical experts was essential.

Days after Iraqi forces captured the airfield, I was in Baghdad, where

I announced we would deploy an additional 560 troops, mostly to support logistics operations at Q-West. More troops later in the fall would further strengthen logistics operations, provide additional train-advise-assist teams, and help sort through the flood of intelligence materials we were recovering in formerly ISIS-held territory. One major source of that intelligence was the Syrian town of Manbij, seized by the SDF in August after difficult, block-by-block combat. ISIS had used the town as a way station for foreign fighters entering Syria, and for external-attack plotters trying to move in the opposite direction across the border into Turkey and beyond. The intelligence gleaned from the dozens of ISIS safe houses and other facilities that the SDF captured was of high value, especially in halting ISIS terror attacks in Europe and the United States.

The assurances of cooperation I'd received in December from Abadi and Barzani continued to hold, but not without regular attention. In a late-summer conversation, Barzani once again expressed his concerns about Iraqi troops in the Kurdish region. Remembering Saddam's forces coming north to kill Kurds, he asked me how he could be certain the ISF would depart his territory as promised. I told Barzani, "I'm not asking you to trust Baghdad. I'm asking you to trust us." That, apparently, was good enough.

By October, Prime Minister Abadi was ready to announce the start of the operation to free Mosul, in keeping with the timeline we had projected the previous December. And by mid-January, as Inauguration Day and the presidential transition approached, the battle for Mosul was full-on. ISF units had nearly liberated the eastern bank of the Tigris in Mosul, and had begun penetrating neighborhoods in the much denser western half of the city. SDF troops were on the way to Raqqa, and its fall was a matter of time. Though still dangerous, ISIS was clearly on the path to losing its capitals in Iraq and Syria.

It was not possible to complete the job on President Obama's watch. But as I departed the Pentagon, I was handing to my successor a military campaign plan capable of dealing ISIS a lasting defeat. Sure enough, despite the promise by candidate Trump of a "secret plan" to defeat ISIS, the coalition campaign under the current administration basically followed the same track we laid out for it over Christmas 2015. By summer

2017, Mosul had been free from the last remnants of ISIS for several weeks, and the majority of Raqqa was in coalition hands. Air strikes had weakened ISIS in its few redoubts not already under assault, in western Iraq and eastern Syria. As a result, ISIS's battlefield leadership and coordination noticeably suffered. By the time I left the Pentagon, Abu Bakr al-Baghdadi was the last senior leader of ISIS to survive—and he was forced to operate from a posture of deep hiding.

In short, the plan we'd created and launched for handing ISIS a lasting defeat had been successful.

Spoilers and Fence-Sitters: Russia, Iran, Turkey, and the Gulf States

Our coalition partners played a major role in making the campaign plan a reality. But others in the international community couldn't seem to get off the fence on the counter-ISIS fight—and a few actively sought to impede our efforts.

In September 2015, just as our accelerants were beginning to have an effect, the Russian air force began conducting air strikes within Syria. The Russian defense minister, Sergey Shoygu, called me to discuss the first such strike. Shoygu told me that Russia was entering Syria to fight terrorists and end the civil war. He told me that they were there not to preserve Assad "as a person," but to save Syria as a country—to preserve its "state structures," he told me in a Soviet-style locution. He told me he would call again before Russian forces took any action. He never did. That was one of many lies the Russians told about their involvement in Syria.

Russia's real ambitions were to keep Assad in power, to secure Syria's Mediterranean port at Tartus, to refine its military capabilities, and to demonstrate its weaponry for the global arms market. But from that first moment, Russia sought to associate us and the counter-ISIS campaign with what they were doing in Syria—constantly telling the world of their desire to coordinate and cooperate with us, and asking to share targeting and intelligence information.

I argued strongly against any association between our campaign and theirs, which would have been ill-advised, strategically and morally.

Strategically, it would have baffled our coalition partners—the Europeans, the Jordanians, Turkey, and the Gulf States—none of whom thought that Russia's siding with Assad would do anything but fuel the civil war they all wanted to end. Because Russia was so closely aligned in Syria with Iran, any cooperation with Russia would have strengthened Iran and its proxies in Baghdad, undercutting Abadi's resolve to work with the United States and to exercise multi-sectarian rule. And it would have naively granted Russia an undeserved leadership role in the Middle East.

Morally, cooperating with the Russians would have implicated us in the inhumanity of their campaign. While our forces made extraordinary efforts to protect innocent lives, the Russians actively sought to increase the suffering in rebel-held areas of Syria through air strikes that were clumsy and indiscriminate. Their brutal, months-long bombardment of Aleppo, including the intentional targeting of health care facilities, was especially inhumane.

John Kerry, who was shocked, as all of us were, by the carnage of Syria's civil war, tirelessly sought to end that carnage with a series of cease-fires. None held for long, because Russia and Syria showed no interest in observing them. But what Russia asked for, time and time again, was military cooperation with us. This was a Russian obsession, and Kerry tried to use it to entice their participation in a cease-fire.

In meeting after meeting with the president and his team, I argued strenuously against such cooperation without strict conditions—principally, that Russia stop worsening the tragic conditions in Syria and commit to a political transition in Damascus. I pressed hard for the president to instruct Kerry that any agreement must require Russia to fully meet these conditions. President Obama agreed; those were Kerry's instructions, and in the end, the Russians never met these conditions.

Still, in July 2016, agreement on a cease-fire including a joint planning cell was reached—essentially, a baby step toward cooperation if Russia could meet our conditions. The Pentagon and CENTCOM staff ramped up to make it happen. But once again, the Russians and Syrians never upheld their end of the deal, the cease-fire never really started, and the planning cell never materialized. The whole episode struck me as a serious blunder. Later that fall, as the extent of Russia's meddling in the U.S. election became clear, the folly of trusting the Russians became even more apparent. History will show that by imposing strict requirements on any agreement with the Russians, President Obama prevented us from entering a moral and strategic tar pit.

We kept our distance from the Russians in Syria. A narrowly tailored memorandum of understanding on avoiding incidents in the air led to regular video conferences with Moscow led by Elissa Slotkin and a hotline between military headquarters, helping to prevent any collisions in the crowded airspace above Syria. I insisted that these talks be purely professional and characterized accurately as "deconfliction," not "cooperation." And spokespeople in Baghdad and Washington repeated constantly the fact that our fight in Syria was against ISIS, and that it had nothing to do with what the Russians were doing.

Like Russia, Iran would have loved to derail our efforts against ISIS and extend their influence in the region, but in this they were largely unsuccessful. Abadi succeeded in controlling the Iranian-backed militias in the liberation of Mosul. He co-opted the more moderate and effective Shiite militias into something called Popular Mobilization Forces, under his control, cutting out the Iranians. Other forces—those armed and directed by Iran—Abadi referred to as outlaws. Despite lavish gifts of Iranian equipment, these forces never actually seemed to do anything. Some were detailed to subsidiary operations that would keep them out of the way without creating problems with the Kurds or others in the region. But most were good mainly at holding press conferences in Baghdad and driving around the dusty highways of Iraq in impressive convoys, waving their sectarian flags, safely behind the front—not so good at accomplishing anything on the battlefield.

Some commentators have argued that the campaign against ISIS has handed Iraq over to the Iranians. This is not only wrong; it is nearly backward. Iran has had virtually nothing to do with the liberation of Iraqi territory, and every Iraqi can see that. Winning the counter-ISIS campaign is good for us and good for multi-sectarianism in Iraq, and it is bad for Iran, confounding its ambition for a Baghdad totally aligned with

Tehran and offering unfettered use of a "land bridge" to southern Syria and on to Damascus and Lebanon.

In the end, it was a NATO ally that caused the most complications for the campaign. Turkey's internal politics and its obsession with suppressing Kurdish power—born out of hard experience—were recurring distractions.

After long months of dithering, Turkey had eventually joined the counter-ISIS coalition, allowed air strikes from Incirlik, and taken steps to close its lengthy border with Syria. In 2016, we assisted Turkey in clearing the border region around the Syrian town of Jerabulus, which had been under ISIS control.

However, Turkey was less interested in fighting ISIS than in preventing Kurds in eastern Syria from linking up with those in the town of Afrin, less than one hundred miles away from Manbij, which would give the Kurds control of a continuous stretch along the Syria-Turkey border. Turkey grudgingly agreed to plans for the Syrian Arab Coalition, which operated under the umbrella of the Kurdish-led Syrian Democratic Forces, to seize Manbij, just twenty-five miles from the Turkish border. In return, the Turks demanded assurances that Kurdish elements of the SDF would immediately withdraw to their positions east of the Euphrates River once Manbij was freed. When the SDF didn't move as quickly as the Turks wanted, Turkey's own proxy forces began shelling SDF positions. Likewise, Turkey regularly and publicly erupted at the thought of the SDF leading the drive on Raqqa. Turkey claimed—in the absence of any evidence—that fighters it supported could take Raqqa instead. But in repeated meetings with the U.S. military, the Turks never produced an actual plan to field such forces. Turkey was also a problem in Iraq. It established a base north of Mosul and conducted air strikes against its Kurdish opponents in Iraq, which understandably angered the Iraqi government.

Tensions reached their height in the weeks after an attempted coup against President Recep Tayyip Erdoğan in July 2016. Turkish aircraft from Incirlik had participated in the plot, and in the aftermath, utilities were disconnected from our portion of the base. It took days of patient diplomacy by Joe Dunford and others to cool things down, but from that point on, the Turks were always ready to misinterpret any thread of information as evidence of U.S. complicity in the coup. I found many in the U.S. government far too cowed by Turkish threats to withhold support from the counter-ISIS campaign or to align more closely with Russia. I considered such threats hollow. The more we waffled, the worse the problem became. At some point, we needed to call Ankara's bluff.

In part because of Turkish sensitivities, the Obama administration never fully resolved the question of how to constitute the force that would assault Raqqa. At the Pentagon, at least, we understood from the start that the one force capable of taking Raqqa was the SDF, and in the fall, I made the case that we should provide the training and equipment they needed to do so. However, the decision was delayed until, in the administration's final weeks, the White House simply decided it was a decision the next administration should make. The Trump administration took longer than should have been necessary to make the choice, but when it did, it made the only choice available. In May 2017, it decided to arm Kurdish elements of the SDF. By then, the envelopment of Raqqa was already well under way.

As for the Gulf States, they had plenty of incentive to aid the campaign, but contributed relatively little beyond talk. Like the Iranians, the Gulf States were active in lobbying and PR that somehow never translated into battlefield action.

I recall one conversation with a senior member of Congress, who recounted a meeting she'd just had with a senior diplomat from one of the Gulf States. "He says there's a Sunni army of seventy thousand ready to storm across Iraq and Syria and defeat ISIS," the senator said.

I told her that I was familiar with that claim. "Why didn't you take him up on the offer?" the lawmaker asked.

I replied, "Did he tell you that sixty thousand of them were Sudanese?"

That apparently hadn't come up in the conversation. The idea that a mercenary army from Sudan represented a good-faith effort on the part of the Gulf Arabs to deal with ISIS was unfortunately typical of their level of commitment.

There were reasons for this. Many of the Gulf countries had little usable military capability beyond their air forces. There were also deep historical reasons why the Gulf Arabs were reluctant to be too visibly active in Syria and Iraq, and why such efforts would not have been welcomed by the local forces and populations. These factors would not, however, prevent the Gulf countries from assisting in the political and economic restoration that is essential to a lasting defeat of ISIS. Regrettably, the Gulf countries have so far fallen short in these areas as well.

Beyond the Red Arrows: The Aftermath

Important work remains to be done in eliminating ISIS's metastases outside Iraq and Syria.

In Libya, ISIS had seized on the chaos following Moammar Qaddafi's ouster to establish a stronghold in the country. The lack of an effective government there also complicated our response. President Obama and allies such as Italy, with the most at stake, felt strongly that we needed Libyan government support before we took action in Libya. The emergence, and eventual UN recognition, of the Government of National Accord (GNA) made this possible. With our air support, GNA-backed forces ousted ISIS from Sirte in December 2016. But continued instability in Libya creates the kind of ungoverned spaces in which ISIS can reconstitute itself.

Afghanistan presents another challenge. It was messy enough there before ISIS entered the picture; ISIS has made matters even worse. It's important for us to maintain our close strategic partnership with the Afghan government. Both President Ashraf Ghani and his main political rival, Chief Executive Abdullah Abdullah, are supportive of long-term engagement with the United States—a tremendous boon that we mustn't squander.

Because ISIS seeks a foothold in the Asia-Pacific region—which actually has a larger Muslim population than the Middle East does—our Southeast Asian partners have to confront ISIS as well. Many are eager to do so. Because Malaysia is a majority-Muslim nation, its public embrace of the fight against ISIS had major significance. Singapore's highly professional military contributed imagery analysts and an aerial refueling tanker to the fight, and Australia brought immense capability and determination to the fight (as it has so often done).

Meanwhile, the future of Iraq and Syria themselves lies mainly in the hands of the people of the Middle East. Our successful military campaign has set the stage for a lasting defeat of ISIS. But for the defeat to last, ISIS's rule of terror must be replaced by stable, effective, legitimate governance. This will require sustained diplomatic, economic, and political support from the United States and the rest of the international community. However, responsibility for long-term security in the region falls first on the people and governments that are directly affected. Too many nations in the region sat on the sidelines while ISIS grew, and too many remained on the sidelines while an international coalition assembled to defeat the ISIS menace. Middle Eastern nations need to take some responsibility for securing the victory against ISIS—and for preventing the next extremist threat from emerging.

One of the most persistent threads in the vague sense of malaise many Americans feel about today's military is captured in the word *quagmire*. Since Vietnam—perhaps even since Korea—the wars in which the United States has become engaged have tended to be long-term struggles in distant countries in pursuit of elusive goals against hard-to-define enemies. The clear, decisive definition of *victory* that Americans recall from the two world wars—ending with a joyous homecoming, a triumphant ticker-tape parade, and a nationwide return to peacetime pursuits—no longer seems to apply. Under the circumstances, many Americans feel disconnected from the seemingly endless, indecisive battles the troops appear to be waging in battlegrounds far from home. And older people, in particular, can be heard asking, "Aren't we allowed to *win* wars anymore?"

It's still true today that there is no substitute for victory. And though the complicated political and military situations we often face in today's complicated, multipolar world make the definition of the word less simple than it once appeared, America's military must never settle for anything less. That's why we must always have a president, a SecDef, and a Pentagon leadership team with the wisdom and fortitude to define *victory* clearly and realistically, and to pursue it relentlessly. I believe the story of our success against ISIS offers one model for future leaders to study and learn from.

PART 4

THE BIG PICTURE: DEFENSE STRATEGY IN A TIME OF TRANSITION

CHAPTER 10

STRATEGIC TRANSITION: MAJOR ADVERSARIES ON THE GLOBAL CHESSBOARD

One of the most significant jobs of the Secretary of Defense is to publicly articulate the national security strategy of the United States. People around the world, from ordinary citizens to national leaders, look to the leaders of the United States for a clear vision of how the most powerful country on Earth intends to promote freedom and secure the peace.

Accordingly, as SecDef, I began talking about the fact that the United States faced no fewer than five major strategic challenges: Russia, China, Iran, North Korea, and the threat of terrorism. I never tried to turn this straightforward list into a fancy strategic theory, nor did I seek explicit approval for it from the president or the National Security Council. It just seemed like common sense. Who could object to naming the challenges we face in the world?

Nevertheless, naming these five adversaries—real or potential—proved to be an unconventional, even controversial step. For a long time, the norm in U.S. policy statements had been an anodyne vagueness designed to offend and alarm nobody. As a typical example, the official *National Security Strategy* document for 2010, issued by the U.S. government and signed off on by President Obama, referred merely to China and Russia as two countries in a list of "other 21st century centers of influence" with whom the United States sought to "deepen our cooperation." Another paragraph that named no countries at all referred even more vaguely to "adversarial governments" with whom we sought "engagement." A reader might get the impression that actually naming these governments would violate some unwritten rule of diplomatic etiquette.

Similarly, the *Quadrennial Defense Review Report* of 2001 declined to name names, saying outright that it "cannot predict with a high degree of confidence the identity of the countries or the actors that may threaten [U.S.] interests and security." Five years later, in 2006, the next review referred to "countries at strategic crossroads"—again, without naming names.

Against this backdrop, my frank listing of four countries and one global threat—terrorism—that posed concrete challenges to American interests seemed to strike a note of bracing honesty. I knew that it had an enormous effect on the members of my own department, both uniformed and civilian. To them, it represented clarity and consistency, two traits that the culture of the DOD values highly. My colleagues in the department noticed the difference in my speeches, in which I frequently repeated the point, and many of them commented on it favorably.

One day soon after I began talking about the five challenges, I was chatting with one of the senior combatant commanders who kept referring casually to "crickets." Over the years, I've become fluent in the complicated lingo of defense, but it wasn't obvious to me what he meant.

I later asked one of my staff members, "What are these crickets people are talking about?" I was told, "That's the name the joint staff has come up with for your five challenges: CRIKT." Thus does common sense become transformed into national strategy—complete with acronym.

The CRIKT formula sent some clear signals that helped people at DOD and beyond make sense of other strategic and organizational initiatives I was championing. For example, it made clear that my advocacy of more high-technology systems, in areas ranging from drone warfare to cybersecurity, was driven by concrete strategic threats, not just a vague sense that the passage of time required technological improvements.

Beyond 9/11: The Strategic Transition

The CRIKT formula also clarified the fact that the United States was, and is, in the midst of a great strategic transition—one that has so far gone little noticed yet that is profoundly significant. It's a transition from an era in which our core security concerns were centered on counterterrorism and counterinsurgency—an era that began with the 9/11 attacks—to a new era of renewed rivalry among major world powers. Unlike the Cold War era that ended in 1991, this new era is not about a bipolar world dominated by two rival ideologies—communism and capitalism. Instead, it involves a multipolar world in which the United States is confronted not just by global threats from Russia and China but, to a lesser extent, by major regional challengers like Iran and North Korea. The transition requires our nation to reorient fifteen years of strategic thinking, budgetary priorities, and leadership training. It's a process we've barely begun.

The challenge for the U.S. military is particularly acute. To defend America successfully in the twenty-first century, the giant battleship that is DOD must somehow learn to maneuver as swiftly and flexibly as our multifarious adversaries can.

Consider, for example, how Russia's behavior has changed under President Vladimir Putin. Rather than working to join the international order and support its work of promoting global peace and economic progress, Russia now appears intent on undoing decades of progress in healing the Cold War. It has committed aggression in Ukraine and Georgia, fueled the continuing tragedy in Syria, violated arms control treaties and other international agreements, and conducted attacks in cyberspace aimed at undermining American democracy. To protect itself and its allies, the United States must not only counter these moves but also take steps to deter a war with Russia that could quickly spread to all of Europe and the Middle East. As I'll explain, I took a series of steps to deal with these challenges during my tenure as secretary, including the creation of the first new war plan for responding to a Russian attack in twenty-five years.

On the other side of the globe, the United States welcomes the emergence of a stable and prosperous China. But we must also be concerned with China's willingness to accept and even provoke regional friction as it pursues its national self-interest. With their actions on the seas, in the global economy, in cyberspace, and elsewhere, the communist dictators who govern China are undercutting the international rule of law that has helped fuel their nation's economic growth. As a communist dictatorship, China is able to bring to bear on individuals, companies, and allies a combination of coercive tools—economic, military, and political—that these independent entities generally cannot withstand. The result is a power that is able to pose a major strategic threat to the United States and its allies.

In response, as SecDef, I took actions, both practical and symbolic, that were designed to underscore the tricky balancing act we need to perform: continuing to strengthen our partnership with China while refusing to cede technological superiority or regional hegemony to this rising economic and military power.

Success in navigating this new world of multipolar rivalries will require flexibility, creativity, and the ability to turn on a dime—qualities not always associated with the bureaucracy of the Pentagon or the rest of the U.S. national security establishment.

The Two-Wars Fallacy

Unfortunately, much of the formal strategic analysis that the Pentagon has engaged in over recent decades has been increasingly stale and arid. A classic example is the assumption that the U.S. military must be designed and funded around the need to fight and win two major wars at the same time—an assumption that has come to dominate and control much of the strategic thinking that goes on in and around the DOD.

The problem is that this two-wars strategy really makes no sense. Here's why.

Each of the ten combatant commanders who oversees American military power in a particular theater of operations devises a war plan for likely contingencies in the region for which he or she is responsible. As I've explained, these plans are very detailed and generally impressively done. So during my tenure as SecDef, General Vincent K. Brooks, commander of U.S. forces in Korea, came up with well-designed improvements to the long-standing plan for war on the Korean Peninsula while General Mike Scaparrotti, commander of U.S. forces in Europe, developed a plan to defeat a Russian invasion.

So far, so good. But the problems start with the fact that each of these plans calls for the deployment of many of the same forces. So by definition, there is no way that two of these plans, as normally written, can be carried out simultaneously. And the same is true for the other pairs of war plans we've duly created and approved.

This might suggest that the United States needs a larger military. Perhaps we do, but the two-wars strategy doesn't address that issue one way or the other. If the force was larger, the problem would remain: every commander developing a war plan would understandably want to use every asset they could lay their hands on.

The two-wars strategy, then, is inherently self-contradictory. It owes its existence to an accident of history.

Throughout the Cold War years, U.S. military strategy was dominated by the possibility of an all-out war against the Soviet Union and its Warsaw Pact allies. They represented by far the largest potential adversary that the United States faced anywhere in the world. We built a military establishment that would be capable of winning such a war. And, of course, that military was also capable of prevailing in any war against another adversary—which by definition would be a smaller conflict that should be easier to win. A U.S. military able to beat the Soviets would also be able to beat the Chinese, the Iranians, the Iraqis, the North Koreans, or other regional powers. (In strategy-speak, all these other rest-of-the-world threats were described as "lesser included cases.") So our strategy was "Prepare to beat the Russkies," and this would take care of everything else.

But when the Soviet Union collapsed in 1991, this strategic rationale collapsed along with it. That posed a big problem for Dick Cheney, then SecDef, and his chairman of the Joint Chiefs, Colin Powell. They felt in their bones that they needed to justify the current size of the military establishment, or at least something close to it. They had no desire to dismantle the U.S. military—to slash the defense budget by, say, 50 percent, to eliminate or drastically scale back dozens of multimillion-dollar procurement projects, and to tell hundreds of thousands of Americans in and out of uniform, "We don't need you anymore—good luck finding new jobs." Not only would this be tremendously disruptive to the national economy, but it could leave the country vulnerable if some unforeseen danger was to suddenly arise. I would have shared many of their concerns.

So the two-wars concept was developed as a way to forestall a total collapse of the defense budget. The logic it was based on was speculative—something like the following: "Suppose we get tied down in a war against Iran. Iraq might see its chance to make a big aggressive move—or Korea or China might. We need to be able to handle two threats at once."

This became the DOD's new strategic doctrine—and the doctrine in turn drove future decisions about personnel, equipment, and other resources. The idea birthed for good reason by Cheney and Powell became, over time, a monster. (And, ironically enough, despite this, Dick Cheney was actually the SecDef who ended up presiding over the largest sustained budget decrease in the history of the department.)

Today, this two-wars doctrine has ended up hamstringing U.S. strategic thinking. Neither the Pentagon bureaucracy nor the leadership on Capitol Hill is easily able to escape this box. If a SecDef was to confess in a congressional hearing that he presides over a DOD that is *not* capable of winning two major wars at once, he would be massacred for his honesty. Similarly, if a commandant of the Marine Corps was to respond to a question in a hearing by saying, "I only have enough forces to win one war, not two," the gasps would be audible all over Washington—and the demands to expand his portion of the military budget would begin immediately.

At the same time, however, neither the citizens of the United States nor, to be fair, the members of Congress really want to devote additional hundreds of billions of dollars to increasing the size of the military. A Pentagon given the power to grow with no reasoned limit would inevitably eat up an unsustainable share of the nation's wealth—and the truth is that no one wants that to happen.

To his great credit, President Obama quickly saw that he was not trapped by the two-wars fallacy—at least in the real wars he might have to conduct as commander in chief, if not in the budget wars fought on Capitol Hill. As Obama rightly observed, in the real world it would never be necessary for the United States to fight two major wars at precisely the same time. If we were at war with, say, Iran and a crisis developed on the Korean Peninsula, the United States and its allies are smart enough to develop a holding strategy to keep one adversary at bay while the other is being dispatched.

Furthermore, in his logical way, Obama reasoned that if we were really serious about the notion of being prepared to engage every major threat—and to tackle them all simultaneously—we would have to budget and plan for five wars, not just two, since that is the number of adversaries included in the CRIKT list. This reality is the final piece of evidence, if any more was needed, concerning the fundamentally dead-end nature of the two-wars doctrine.

The problem is that the true purpose of the two-wars concept was never to guide strategy formulation for the real world. It was to serve as a tool and a cudgel for political and bureaucratic battles. And unfortunately, much the same can be said about a lot of what passes for strategic thinking about national defense. That includes, for example, the claims (as of 2018) by the current administration and its supporters in Congress that the Obama administration "decimated" America's military and that the DOD budget increases they are demanding will "rebuild" and "restore" the capabilities we need. As I've already pointed out, the Obama administration requested *more* money for DOD than Congress approved in every year but one. The modest increases enacted by Congress during the first year of the Trump administration will buy some helpful additional equipment (since this is what Congress likes to do) but do little to improve actual readiness. And as I write, a year later, the defense budget is again being scaled back. So, unfortunately, there is much more politics than strategy in the defense budget.

One of the major challenges faced by a SecDef who wants to engage in some serious thinking about the strategic challenges we face is to try to ignore, or bat down, the purely political posturing that constantly threatens to distract policy makers from the real issues.

My approach to injecting some realism into the serious business of war planning was to ask each COCOM to prepare not one but two war plans for their theater: the traditional one that assumed theirs was the *only* major war going on, and a second plan that assumed their war broke out when another was already under way. Thus, we could at least bring some reasoned military foresight to this scenario. This was not a trivial request, because the amount of work that goes into even one plan is enormous and takes the efforts of the whole department. Given the multiyear nature of O-plan development, I was not able to see this through, but I hope it continues.

Strategy in the Obama Era: "Better Than It Sounded"

The joke that Obama's strategic thinking was "better than it sounded" contained some truth. Obama's instincts regarding foreign policy and security issues were largely sound. But his strategic attention seemed to be focused more on avoiding the kinds of mistakes made by some of his predecessors, such as the disastrous war in Iraq, than on enunciating an overarching strategic vision of his own. Thus, he often expressed his disdain for the standard geopolitical playbook while failing to articulate a set of alternative principles to take its place. As a result, I worried that his foreign policy speeches were too few and too arid, which meant that the public, Congress, and the press didn't always see the overall picture of his strategy. Governments abroad weren't always convinced they had it right about the American policy line.

Furthermore, as I've noted, the workings of Obama's National Security Council, other than Susan Rice and a few truly good professionals, didn't make it easy for the rest of his team to provide him with our best advice in broad strategic context. We formulated and implemented an effective counter-ISIS strategy. But there were few White House meetings on overall Russia or China policy, and the president rarely gave wide-ranging speeches on our relationships with these potentially threatening powers. Susan herself gave few speeches, as is normal for a national security advisor, and John Kerry was focused on the important trade, Iran, and climate negotiations. Thus, my colleagues in the administration didn't provide much of a springboard for my promulgation of defense strategy as SecDef.

Many have said that the closest thing to an "Obama doctrine" was the president's own admonition, "Don't do stupid stuff" (using a cruder four-letter term in place of "stuff"). If so, Obama himself did a fair job of living up to it. The administration may not have offered a powerful overarching vision, but neither did it lead the nation, or the world, into any new strategic quagmires. In today's world, that's no mean feat. Avoiding "stupid stuff" is important. Nonetheless, despite the lack of forceful strategic communication from others on the president's team, I felt compelled to speak about strategy for Asia, Europe, the Middle East, nuclear deterrence, and other topics in the broadest terms. I had to give the COCOMs, the troops in various theaters or preparing to deploy, and our allies and partners a clear description of, at a minimum, what DOD was doing. In addition, the world thinks that the SecDef is the Great Karnak—an all-knowing source of profound secrets—and if you are not clear about your messaging, people will draw strange inferences both from what you say and from what you don't say.

Thankfully, I was pretty confident I could formulate strategy well, I knew my own viewpoint after so many years of working on some of America's top national security challenges, and I write easily. So I gave first-principles speeches on many topics, usually with just a few available Obama words to insert. At the same time, he neither overrode nor rebutted my speeches, nor did he fiddle with my drafts or bawl me out once I'd delivered them. (I always gave the president copies of recent speeches in our weekly one-on-ones, though I knew perfectly well that his staff kept him abreast of what his SecDef said in near real time.)

By far the biggest need from my point of view was to devise and convey clear defense strategies for Russia and China. The post-9/11 period's preoccupation with terrorism and counterinsurgency had made both Bush and Obama teams focus elsewhere. But neither Russia nor China had stood still strategically. And in fact, each had been trending in a direction very different from what America had hoped for before 9/11.

My Decades of Engagement with Russia

When I was asked to assume leadership of the DOD in this time of strategic transition, I had a unique advantage. During my previous decades of work in and around the DOD, I'd had many opportunities to engage with our potential adversaries in Russia and China, and so I'd developed a deep sense of the political, economic, and military challenges they posed—as well as the cultural and psychological patterns that impact the nature of our rivalries. I'd also gotten to know many of the leaders in both countries, some of whom I considered friends.

The most far-reaching geopolitical shift of my lifetime was the end of the Cold War—a shift that involved not just a moment in time but a series of symbolic events that ushered in the change from an old world to a new one. The most obvious of these events were the collapse of the Berlin Wall and the reunification of East and West Germany. These changes opened the way for millions of Europeans to experience the end of the Cold War in more personal ways: through family members no longer separated by militarized borders, young students free to study abroad, and citizens casting their first votes in a truly democratic election.

For me, as an expert on nuclear weapons, missile defense, and command-and-control systems, the Cold War ended when the last nuclear weapon rolled out of Ukraine. I was there in Pervomaysk that summer day in 1996, along with U.S. Secretary of Defense Bill Perry, Ukrainian Minister of Defense Valeriy Shmarov, and Russian Defense Minister Pavel Grachev. We stood watching as a landscaping crew began planting sunflowers in a field where a Soviet missile silo had previously stood. It was a profound moment, because it demonstrated that the world could change for the better—that despite the deep-seated insecurities and fears felt by all people in a dangerous world, nations can willingly give up the awesome destructive power of nuclear weapons, placing their trust instead in a world order dedicated to peace and a powerful America dedicated to international partnerships.

I was fortunate enough to play a central role in that historic denuclearization program. It grew out of a project known as *preventive defense*, which my friend and boss Bill Perry and I had developed and popularized as an outgrowth of the tumultuous events of the 1990s.

During those years, debates over geopolitical strategy had been dominated by such humanitarian catastrophes as the Balkans crisis and the genocide in Rwanda. Meanwhile, in the wake of the collapse of the Soviet Union, the kinds of great-power conflicts that had long dominated strategic thinking seemed to be in abeyance. But Bill and I believed that this period of "B-list" and "C-list" crises would not last forever—that the time would come when frictions among great nations like the United States, Russia, and China would again seize the spotlight. In thinking about how to prepare for this future shift, we became convinced that the world's defense capabilities could play an important geostrategic role— not just by deterring aggression, but also by preventing conflicts through the development of communication channels and cooperative projects among potential adversaries. Programs of this kind, we believed, could help build an international environment in which trust might flourish. Perry and I further theorized that joint exercises, scenario planning, and sharing of technology could help focus potential antagonists on common interests and allow them to join forces in mutually beneficial operations when the opportunity arose. This, in a nutshell, was the concept we dubbed preventive defense.

After we left the Clinton administration, Perry and I launched a program to explore this concept, which was housed in Harvard and Stanford universities and supported by a number of foundations. As it developed, the project ended up focusing on three countries that were potential military opponents of the United States: Russia, China, and North Korea. The preventive defense project developed activities with all three. These were initiated and promoted through what are called Track II dialogues with leaders of those nations (as opposed to the usual diplomatic engagements between government officials, which are referred to as Track I negotiations). The existence of Track II channels for informal discussions makes it possible for new ideas to be put on the table without any official commitment, creating the potential for creative breakthroughs.

Bill Perry and I were well positioned to engage in such Track II dialogues. In office and out, we'd established many contacts with our counterparts, both inside and outside government, in nations around the world. For example, I had traveled to Russia and the other states of the Soviet Union many times, going all the way back to the early 1980s, when I visited Russia with a delegation that included Brent Scowcroft, former chairman of the Joint Chiefs David Jones, and former Army chief of staff Edward "Shy" Meyer. After that, I met with Soviet delegations both in

Russia and in the United States many times, and I had close personal friends in both their scientific and policy communities. While assistant secretary in the 1990s, I attended a number of U.S. summits with Boris Yeltsin, during which I noticed a young Russian staff member sitting with his back to the wall, taking detailed notes of everything that was said and done—a then-little-known security officer named Vladimir Putin.

Perry and I used our many overseas contacts to launch Track II dialogues about concepts of mutual interest—always keeping officials from the U.S. Defense, State, and other relevant departments fully informed about what we were doing. The main purpose of our Track II dialogues with Russia was to explore cooperative efforts for European security against the backdrop of the expansion of NATO, which the Russians hated and feared.

These dialogues made possible the Nunn-Lugar program, which secured the nuclear weapons of the Soviet Union after the breakup of that vast empire, as I recounted in Chapter 3.

Responding to Putin and the New Russian Threat

By the time I became President Obama's SecDef, I'd worked with the Russians in a number of settings on a wide range of issues over an extended period of time—which meant I had a pretty good idea of what to expect from that complicated relationship, on both the positive and negative sides. That was important, because one of the core features of the strategic transition we now face is the reemergence of Russia as a serious political and military threat to the democracies of the West. The positive legacy of Nunn-Lugar has given way to a new era of renewed tension between our two countries, driven largely by the vision of one man: Russian President Vladimir Putin.

In my view, Putin is a man consumed by three bitter beliefs: that the end of the Cold War was not a rebirth for Russia and its people but a humiliation; that the United States had made a mess of things by destabilizing countries and unhorsing their leaders, and would do the same to

Russia and him if it could; and that, therefore, thwarting the United States around the world must be a central objective of Russian foreign policy.

I can understand the first two beliefs or at least why Putin holds them. But the third view makes it almost impossible to build a bridge to today's Russia. There's no way the United States can collaborate in the frustration of its own policies. Thus, Putin's attitudes toward the United States place our two countries on course for continual friction, including potential military conflict.

In Europe, Russia is behaving in a manner reminiscent of nineteenth-century great-power rivalries, rather than one befitting a responsible member of the modern international community. Russia has used its political, economic, and military power to undermine the sovereignty and territorial integrity of Georgia and Ukraine, flouting accepted international principles such as nonaggression as well as violating international agreements to which Russia is a party, such as the UN Charter, the Helsinki Accords, and the NATO–Russia Founding Act. It has sought to intimidate Sweden, Finland, and the Baltic states, as well as other countries along Russia's periphery, and used an array of tactics, including disinformation campaigns, in an effort to foster division in Europe and undermine institutions such as NATO and the European Union.

Russian actors have also violated important international principles in other areas, notably in cyberspace. Russia directed the 2016 hacking of emails from American political organizations, including the Democratic National Committee, in an effort to interfere with the U.S. electoral process—the essence of our democracy—and undermine Americans' faith in our own political process and institutions. This is not a unique occurrence: Russia has repeatedly used similar tactics across Europe.

Alongside this troubling behavior, Russia has also been aggressively modernizing its warfighting doctrine and its military capabilities, and is using those capabilities in provocative and destabilizing ways. Russia has carried out major military exercises on the borders of its neighbors, reintroducing large-scale no-notice, or "snap," exercises designed to sow fear and intimidation on the continent. Its aircraft have repeatedly violated the airspace of countries around the periphery of Europe, and its personnel have conducted unwarranted and unsafe intercepts of U.S. and NATO ships and aircraft operating in international waters and airspace. And through the new Russian approach to warfare, often referred to as *hybrid warfare*, it is conducting information-warfare campaigns with military and nonmilitary means to destabilize a number of countries and to infringe upon their sovereignty.

Finally, and most disturbing of all, Russia is behaving irresponsibly and aggressively with respect to nuclear weapons. It has built up its nuclear arsenal, investing in new ballistic missile submarines, heavy bombers, and the development of a new intercontinental ballistic missile. Russian leaders have also made dangerous statements about using nuclear weapons in a potential war to deter or prevent us from coming to the aid of our European allies. And they have pulled out of the Plutonium Management and Disposition Agreement without warning and violated their obligations under the Intermediate-Range Nuclear Forces Treaty.

Faced with this set of disturbing circumstances, when I became SecDef, I moved to adjust DOD policy to recognize and respond to the new aggressiveness on the part of Russia.

Not everyone in the White House shared my concerns about Russia. For example, the White House staff had drafted a Russia-strategy document that I had a chance to review before it was adopted. I proposed some changes needed to make it stronger and more realistic, most of which were accepted. Unfortunately, working in haste, I didn't catch one phrase in it that I should have: the words that Russia was "not an existential threat" to the United States. This was factually nonsensical: How could a country with many thousands of nuclear weapons trained on the United States not be an existential threat? When this phrase was leaked, it was understandably derided for minimizing the inherent threat posed by a massively armed Russia.

Meanwhile, however, I was directing my DOD team to prepare a classified defense strategy for Russia that would reflect our adjustments to Russia's changed behavior as well as the gradual decline of the war efforts in Iraq and Afghanistan. I was also communicating my concerns within the cabinet and in my one-on-ones with President Obama. Thankfully, the president himself shared my concerns over the threat Putin posed, and he supported the moves I took at DOD to respond to that threat.

Those moves started with a unilateral buildup of capability. We introduced more permanently stationed or continually deployed forces into Europe—Army brigade combat teams, tanks, artillery, armored personnel carriers, and tactical aircraft. We also made qualitative improvements in technology to improve our ability to respond promptly and effectively to any aggressive moves by Russia. These included new unmanned systems, enhanced ground-based air and missile defenses, new long-range anti-ship weapons, a new long-range strike bomber, and also innovation in technologies such as the electromagnetic railgun, lasers, and new systems for electronic warfare, space, and cyberspace.

Building on the strategy document I mentioned a moment ago, we also developed formal war plans for a European conflict for the first time since the end of the Cold War. We created what I called a "new playbook" for the United States and NATO that took into account Russian hybrid and information warfare capabilities, NATO's expanded (and exposed) flanks, particularly in the Baltics, and all of Russia's own vulnerabilities.

I spoke about this repeatedly at NATO ministerials and in public speeches. Most of the NATO militaries had taken advantage of the post–Cold War period to shrink dramatically. Now they needed to do some rebuilding. I joined a long list of secretaries of defense banging their shoes on the table at NATO meetings about the need for our allies to spend more on defense—and most of them responded by taking steps to increase their military budgets (in some cases, the same increases that President Trump has now been taking credit for).

To help make sure that we and our allies would be prepared to respond promptly to new threats in Europe, in fall 2014, NATO's leaders agreed to establish the Very High Readiness Joint Task Force. It's a military force designed to be able to deploy on forty-eight hours' notice from multiple locations in Europe to any crisis on NATO territory. More important, while I was SecDef we increased our forces committed to Europe for the first time in decades, including tanks, heavy artillery, and troops in both stationed and continually rotating deployments.

There were some in the Obama administration, as there had been in the Bush administration, who didn't want to bear the political burden of developing these new war plans for Europe. Doing so required us to admit that the relationship with Russia had become largely antagonistic rather than cooperative. The president supported all the increases in spending and deployment I called for. But I was the only senior member of the administration actually describing the policy the president's actions reflected and its strategic rationale.

The administration's less-than-wholehearted pushback against Russian aggression almost led to disaster in Syria. In that broken corner of the world, Russia has been throwing gasoline on an already devastating fire, prolonging a civil war that fuels the very extremism that Russia claims to oppose. As I've explained, Russia sent forces into Syria on the pretext of fighting terrorism. Instead, its purpose was to back Assad and to help him suppress the moderate opposition to his regime.

This betrayal left me very skeptical about any prospect of working with Russia on Syria. When the crafty Russian Foreign Minister Sergei Lavrov began talking to John Kerry about the possibility of "cooperating" with Russia militarily in Syria, I smelled a trap. I urged for the creation of a disciplined process of interagency backstopping for the Kerry-Lavrov negotiations, with negotiating positions debated by the senior officials and cleared by the president in each round. This was the process we'd used in arms control talks with Cold War Russia, as well as the process Obama himself had mandated for the Iran nuclear negotiations. The president agreed.

I had some sharp debates on this issue with John Kerry. I admired his efforts to get Russia on a more constructive path, but I believed his diplomatic effort to forge a Syria cooperation pact was doomed from the start. In the end, Kerry was instructed to insist that Russia ease Assad out and promote a political transition, secure a cease-fire and humanitarian relief, and stop bombing moderate opposition groups. I was convinced the Russians wouldn't meet these conditions—and, sure enough, they didn't. We did work with our counterparts in the Russian military to develop some principles of deconfliction to prevent accidental contact between our operations. But beyond this, there was no military cooperation with Russia in Syria.

The Chinese Challenge

A second major focus of the strategic transition is the rising might of China—the *C* in CRIKT.

No piece of hardware better exemplifies America's military might than an aircraft carrier. And for more than seven decades, dating back to the brutal naval clashes of World War II, that has been especially true in the Asia-Pacific. Broad oceanic expanses, narrow straits through tropical archipelagos, and ever-expanding maritime trade make naval power the guarantor of security in the region. U.S. aircraft carriers remain the linchpin of that power.

So in April 2016, when I landed aboard the USS *John C. Stennis* as it sailed through the waters of the South China Sea, I knew the gesture would be noticed. The nuclear-powered *Stennis* is massive: longer than three football fields, the Nimitz-class carrier is essentially a 4.5-acre floating fortress home to three thousand American men and women who do everything from conduct counter-piracy operations to humanitarian assistance and disaster relief. Even before we touched down on the flight deck, the Chinese foreign ministry had issued a statement criticizing my visit as emblematic of a "Cold War mentality."

China's reaction stemmed in part from the *Stennis*'s location: it was patrolling in the five-hundred-mile stretch of open ocean between Manila and the Paracel Islands. The Paracels, less than five square miles of coral reef and sand that dot the ocean between the Philippines and China's Hainan Island, typify a series of nondescript but strategically located tropical island chains that have become major irritants in international relations. Both China and Vietnam claim the Paracels as their own. Both have taken unilateral actions in the area to bolster their claims. Unchecked, friction over the Paracels, or over the disputed Spratly Islands to the south, risks jeopardizing decades of security and prosperity in Asia.

China is not the only nation that has unilaterally claimed control over international territory. In the South China Sea, countries including Vietnam, the Philippines, Malaysia, and Taiwan have all developed outposts in recent years. But China has gone much further and much faster than any other country, claiming more acreage than all the other countries in the region combined. Given the fact that the region's waterways are critical to international trade and energy resources, this attempt to undermine free and open access is very troubling.

My visit to the *Stennis* concluded without further escalation, though Beijing said it proved "who was the real promoter of the militarization in the South China Sea." The truth, as I and many other U.S. officials said repeatedly, is that the United States had no objection to China's rise. What the United States should not accept, and should strenuously work against, is the growing Chinese tendency to undermine the pillars of peace and stability that have made possible its rise and that of its Asian neighbors.

Some astute observers fear that the United States and China are on a collision course. They include my good friend Graham T. Allison, who explains the historical pattern of conflict between rising and ruling powers, and suggests that this pattern could apply to our two nations. It's my view—and my hope—that war with China is unlikely. But a key determinant of that question will be the evolution of Chinese thinking—an evolution that I personally have witnessed over the past twenty years and that gives no reason for complacency.

Just as we did with Russia, Bill Perry and I also engaged in Track II dialogues with the Chinese during the early years of the post–Cold War era. These discussions focused mainly on the Taiwan issue, which seemed the most likely spark for possible conflict. Perry and I therefore usually made it a point to visit Taiwan at the same time we were visiting China. We also hosted the Chinese both in Washington and in Honolulu. In those days, the Chinese leaders were not nearly as aggressive and assertive as they have since become. They were still basically imitating the United States economically, and they seemed to have less confidence in the future of communist dictatorship. By the time I became SecDef, this whole picture had turned much darker.

The preventive defense projects spearheaded by Perry and me continued right up until the fall of 2008, when I was asked to join the Obama transition. During those years, the U.S. military pioneered methods for joint exercises with non-alliance countries like the NATO Partnership for Peace members India, Vietnam, and China. Informal arrangements, like officer exchanges and other joint programs, live on today. And other countries around the world have learned from the example we set; for instance, the Chinese have now begun conducting similar preventive defense activities with partner countries in various regions. So the tradecraft of preventive defense that Bill Perry and I first practiced in the early 1990s and then tried to develop further in later years has filtered into militaries around the world—and that is a good thing.

In both my governmental and nongovernment roles, I'd had the opportunity to meet with many of the top Chinese leaders, including Presidents Jiang Zemin, Hu Jintao, and Xi Jinping. I'd also had numerous encounters with People's Liberation Army (PLA) leaders, diplomats, and various scholars associated with the Chinese military, diplomatic, and intelligence agencies. Practically all these institutions are government-dominated; few Chinese institutions are truly independent, as U.S. think tanks and universities are.

These contacts revealed two conflicting tendencies in Chinese thinking. One emphasized continuing the informal system of peace and stability in the region that had served as the backdrop for China's spectacular rise from the backwardness of the Maoist era—provided this regional system would freely accommodate an increasingly powerful China.

But the second Chinese tendency was to stress China's pre-Mao "century of humiliation" at the hands of the West. Those who embraced this strand of thinking believed it was the destiny of the onetime "Middle Kingdom" to dominate Asia once again. In pursuit of this goal, they advocated the creation of bilateral security relationships between China and each of its neighbors—relationships that would not be true partnerships but would grant China a domineering role, by coercion if necessary.

During my two decades of encounters with China's elite, I watched the second tendency growing steadily stronger, especially among leaders of the PLA. Countries in the region noticed this change, too. Thus, by the time I became SecDef, it was clear that China, like Russia, was mounting a new challenge to the United States that would need to be addressed in the strategic transition process.

China never misses the chance to describe its growing power as a "peaceful rise." Though serious observers don't buy the spin, one reason Beijing can make such a claim is that since the end of the Cold War, Washington has often backed down in the face of Chinese bullying. From aggressive territorial claims to human rights abuses and brazen theft on a trillion-dollar scale, China has violated core international norms time and again with few repercussions beyond scolding American speeches.

The rationale for tolerating China's troubling behavior in the security sphere was premised on an economic policy that never made sense to me. The de facto economic relationship we have with China is that we give up skilled jobs in the United States in exchange for cheap goods made in China—which we buy with money borrowed from China. I think this has been bad for the American people. Our economic policies tend to treat China as a big version of France rather than the communist monolith it is. China's centralized control of its economy gives it tools that simply aren't available in our society. American economists have yet to give us a credible policy playbook for dealing with a country that, for example, will threaten to stop buying important South Korean agricultural goods if South Korea agrees to deploy missile defenses against North Korean missiles.

In all the decades of the Cold War, we never had a substantial trading relationship with a communist dictatorship. We had a prolonged and tense, though ultimately peaceful, strategic relationship with the USSR—but we didn't trade with them. That means we have as yet no trade playbook for China—which makes dealing with China on the diplomatic and military fronts even more difficult.

Implementing the Asia-Pacific Rebalance

Responding to the Chinese challenge must begin with an understanding of its broader context in the Asia-Pacific region—soon to be home to nearly half the world's population and economy, and likely to be the most important area of global focus for the United States for decades to come.

For seventy years, since the end of World War II, the Asia-Pacific region has enjoyed great stability and peace. In this climate, first Japan rose and prospered; then Taiwan, South Korea, and Southeast Asia. And today, China and India rise and prosper, too. This has been true despite deep wounds among the nations there dating back to before World War II—one only has to visit the capitals to grasp how deep these animosities run—and despite the absence of a multilateral security structure comparable to NATO in Europe. The critical factor in these seven decades of overall peace, stability, and economic progress has been the pivotal role of U.S. military power.

Soon after Barack Obama took office, he began speaking about the need for a strategic "rebalance" to the Asia-Pacific region. This shift was driven in part by Obama's recognition that Asia was where much of the future of America, and the world, would be written. It was also driven by his conviction that the United States had dissipated too much of its strength in the Middle East, and by his desire to "end two wars" in that region. The rebalance became a consistent theme of his administration—one that I wholeheartedly supported and that I believe will be remembered as one of Obama's most important commitments.

The rebalance recognized that the United States had long played a critical role in a rapidly changing, fast-growing Asia-Pacific region—a role that had enjoyed bipartisan support here at home. The rebalance called for us to continue to play this role by making the adjustments demanded by changing times. I spent a lot of my time as acquisition czar, deputy secretary, and SecDef on the military implementation of the rebalance.

The rebalance meant, first, shifting combat power from the western hemisphere and the Middle East to the Asia-Pacific area. Henceforth, 60 percent of the U.S. Navy would be dedicated to the Pacific, upending the historic preference given to the Atlantic. The newest resources of air power, like the F-22, F-35, P-8, and Global Hawk, would be stationed there, too. Ground forces from the Army and Marine Corps that had been tied up in Iraq and Afghanistan could return to bases in Japan, Guam, the Marianas, Hawaii, Alaska, and California, where they would train for new Asian contingencies while other forces would be sent to new locations in Australia, Singapore, and the Philippines.

As with the renewed emphasis on defending Europe from Russian aggression, the Asian rebalance occasioned many technological innovations, with the aim of catching up after a decade of emphasis on counterinsurgency and counterintelligence. These included the new stealth B-21 bomber, undersea and anti-ship weapons, lasers, and hypersonics; new capabilities for electronic warfare, space warfare, and cyber warfare; and naval technologies aimed to check high-end military capabilities of the kind China is building.

The rebalance also included a growing set of military-to-military linkages, both unilaterally and with our historical treaty allies Japan, South Korea, Australia, and (despite some local complications) Thailand and the Philippines. We also began new activities with important nations that are not treaty allies: India, Vietnam, and China itself.

In a series of speeches, I called this U.S.-led but not U.S.-dominated security system the "Principled and Inclusive Security Network." I considered this network the broad strategic context for the rebalance. It was *principled* because it embodied not power or coercion but the peaceful resolution of disputes through legal means in accordance with international law. And it was *inclusive* because it excluded no nation. That last point was aimed at China, which I hoped would join the rest of the region in supporting the network and contributing to the region's continued security and stability

Unfortunately, I was the only senior U.S. official delivering such speeches, although the president and Susan Rice read them—usually in advance, though not always, because I fine-tuned my speeches right to the end. In any event, they never complained about my speeches and never publicly contradicted them. John Kerry was usually deeply involved in Middle East issues, and he traveled less often to the Asia-Pacific. And while Rice tended to the periodic meetings between Obama and Xi Jinping, the principal objective set for those discussions was usually to secure what the Chinese most valued—a "successful meeting" free of rancor.

The Chinese leaders themselves have long been eager for closer ties with the United States. When I became SecDef, General Fan Changlong, one of China's most senior officers and then vice chair of its Central Military Commission, came to visit me immediately. I had known Fan for some years, and he surely expected a warmly cordial conversation between old friends, perhaps including an elaborate banquet to honor our relationship. Instead, I hosted a little no-frills dinner in a drab Pentagon dining room. When General Fan presented me with an elaborate gift of a decorative platter adorned with my image, I refused to smile in any of the ceremonial pictures.

More important, I confronted General Fan privately but pointedly on a number of issues, including China's unilateral actions in the disputed South China Sea island chains, its support for the increasingly provocative action of the North Korean regime, and the recently disclosed theft of some four million records from the U.S. Office of Personnel Management, in which a Chinese national had been implicated. I made it clear that I was angered by these aggressive actions, and that our personal relationship would continue to be positive, but it couldn't outweigh my duty.

Fan was taken aback. I'm sure he was dismayed that he would not be able to report to his superior about a "successful meeting." He went home disappointed but with no ambiguity about the standards we expected the Chinese to uphold.

I also made a point of being the only defense secretary during President Obama's two terms *not* to visit China—despite repeated invitations from the Chinese leaders, including Xi himself, as well as President Obama's urgings that I should go. This was one of just a small handful of requests from Obama that I did not honor. But then, it's probably just as well that I didn't go to Beijing, since the president always added that, when I went there, I should be sure to avoid "banging pots and pans." If I had gone, I would surely have banged a few. After all, I'd seen how the Chinese had deliberately attempted to embarrass my predecessor Bob Gates by rolling out their first stealth fighter during his visit to China. They would probably have staged something provocative to embarrass me as well—for example, landing a ship on a disputed island. I wouldn't have taken such treatment lying down.

A Way Forward if China Continues Its Self-Isolation

For more than two decades, I worked alongside scores of other U.S. and allied officials to strengthen military and diplomatic ties with China, hoping China could be encouraged to join the network of relationships that has served as the backbone of Asia-Pacific security since the end of World War II. I would have liked to use my time as SecDef to reinforce those efforts.

That was not to be. In my statements as SecDef, I warned that China risked erecting a "Great Wall of self-isolation" if it succumbed to its domineering, unilateralist tendencies. Unfortunately, it seems that this has happened. China's actions in recent years show that this strain in its policies appears to have triumphed over the strain that values partnership and integration—at least for now.

What does China's choice mean for U.S. policy? First, it means the U.S. military rebalance begun under President Obama must continue. We must continue to invest in the innovative systems and ideas required to counter China's military capabilities, as we've done by launching development of the B-21 bomber and by developing new war plans for a possible conflict with China. And we must ensure that we have the quality and quantity of forces necessary to prevent Chinese aggression if we can, and counter it if we must, as we've done by shifting resources of the Navy and other armed forces from the Atlantic region to the Pacific.

We must also continue to build stronger military partnerships in the region, with established allies such as Japan, South Korea, and Australia, as well as newer partners such as Vietnam and India. Partnership is at the heart of the principled, inclusive network, and the stronger the ties among the United States and its partners, the better off we all are. We're doing this by conducting more joint exercises and training programs with Australia, Vietnam, Malaysia, the Philippines, and Indonesia; by providing modern equipment and infrastructure support to many of these regional partners; and by modernizing and upgrading our ability to respond rapidly to crises and emerging threats. These deepening ties are enabling us to improve our cooperation in areas ranging from maritime security to disaster relief. And if it becomes necessary, they'll also enable us to stand against aggression by any nation that might choose to attempt it.

Under Obama, one major response to the Chinese economic challenge was developed: the Trans-Pacific Partnership (TPP) trade deal. I strongly supported TPP on strategic grounds, since it reflected the principled and inclusive security network in the economic sphere. TPP would have bolstered security in Asia by offering companies and countries an alternative to one-on-one contests of strength with China, which they are overwhelmingly likely to lose. For this reason, I've often described TPP as "just as important strategically as an aircraft carrier." President Trump's decision to withdraw from participation in this agreement damaged our national security in the region.

Beyond TPP, however, the failure to develop and articulate a coherent policy for economic relations with China has been a continuing problem for the Obama and Trump administrations. In some ways, that failure was understandable. Many in the U.S. financial community were perfectly happy with our existing economic relationship with China. But China's anti-competitive practices, strategic manipulation of key industries and resources, use of coercion in bilateral affairs with other countries, theft of intellectual property, and dictatorial control of the Internet pose a serious challenge to U.S. businesses and the international system they depend on. American businesses don't want their government to be confrontational, but they do want their government to use national power to stand up for their interests. The Obama administration never fully solved this dilemma.

Unfortunately, in this area, the Trump administration has floundered. Its rejection of the TPP made the fundamental error of ceding the field to the opposition, thereby creating an opening for China to become the dominant economic force in the region. And the administration's tariff measures, launched in April 2018, represent a seemingly dated response to a real need to counter the genuine problem of Chinese trade manipulation, focusing as it does on commodities more than on manufacturing, digital technologies, and biotech—the sectors that will largely define our children's future, rather than steel and aluminum. It's important to transform these policies to protect our security and our prosperity.

If China has chosen isolation over partnership, the United States, too, has a choice. The Asian security network has served our interests well, and it can continue to do so—but only if the United States continues to believe in it and to support it wisely.

The Ultimate Deterrent: Updating the Nuclear Umbrella

The strategic transition we're now making, from an era dominated by concerns over terrorism and insurgencies in failed states to a new era of great-power competition, may strike some as a kind of return to the Cold War. That would be an inaccurate reading of the facts. The world has changed in too many dramatic ways to expect a simple reprise of the pre-1991 era. But one aspect of the Cold War era that remains important and that, indeed, has taken on renewed urgency is the value of nuclear weapons as the ultimate deterrent against a major enemy attack.

Remember that nuclear weapons came of age during the burgeoning Cold War between the Western nations, led by the United States, and the nations of the Warsaw Pact, led by the USSR. When the Soviet Union took advantage of the closing months of World War II to expand its communist empire into several nations of Eastern Europe, many feared that the stage was being set for a vast new war over control of the remainder of Europe. Fueling these anxieties was the fact that the Warsaw Pact nations, in combination, boasted greater military manpower than the NATO alliance. In addition, the Soviet bloc countries were right on the border of the nations of Western Europe, not separated from them by an ocean as the United States was. It was easy to imagine the USSR mounting a surprise attack that would enable them to rapidly sweep across Germany, France, Italy, and the rest of Europe.

Part of our answer was nuclear weapons. Our advantage in this technology served as an "offset" against the Soviet Union's capabilities—a term used to refer to an asymmetrical advantage that compensates for some other advantage held by an adversary. Even after the Soviets detonated their own first atomic bomb in 1949, the value of the nuclear offset remained enormous, because the relatively greater size of the U.S. strategic arsenal gave us the capability of decimating our Russian adversaries should they dare to attempt an assault on the West. Among other benefits, this allowed President Eisenhower to keep U.S. military spending under control, since a robust nuclear deterrent was cheaper to create and maintain than a vast standing army would have been.

Highly motivated for both ideological and nationalistic reasons, the Soviets worked intensely to match American nuclear technology as well as the size of our arsenal. By the 1970s, when the scope of the U.S. nuclear offset was no longer clear, Harold Brown, President Carter's SecDef, declared the administration's intention to outcompete the USSR in new technological areas. The idea was that American superiority in designing and deploying devices such as precision-guided weapons, stealth technology, and space-based systems for communications and navigation would more than check the threat posed by Soviet nukes, no matter how numerous the latter became. This concept became known as the "second offset."

Nuclear weapons remain a crucial element of our national defense today.

Designed to deter an attack by a major adversary—chiefly the world's other great nuclear power, Russia—America's nuclear arsenal rests on a complicated human-intensive and technology-intensive system. This system has many pieces, starting with the three delivery tools of the so-called triad. There's also our fleet of dual-capable aircraft, those select fighter jets that extend a nuclear umbrella over our allies.

Equally critical is the network of tools that enable nuclear command and control, communications, and intelligence: satellites, radar systems, ground stations, command posts, control nodes, communications links, and others. Thousands of individuals, in uniform and out, have important roles to play in maintaining this vast system and keeping it safe— thereby protecting Americans, and the world.

However, after a period of relative stability in the global system of nuclear deterrence, recent years have seen unsettling changes that are forcing the United States to respond.

As I've noted, Russia has recently been engaged in building new nuclear weapons systems. Russia is investing in new ballistic missile submarines, new heavy bombers, and the development of a new ICBM. In combination with Russia's aggressive moves elsewhere on the security chessboard, these weapons investments raise serious questions about Putin's commitment to strategic stability and the profound caution that Cold War–era leaders on both sides of the Iron Curtain showed with respect to brandishing nuclear weapons. At the same time, North Korea has been engaged in its own set of nuclear and missile provocations. In addition, other countries, including China and Pakistan, have also been enhancing their nuclear capabilities, though generally in a more responsible and less aggressive fashion than Russia and North Korea have.

These moves by other nuclear powers—including some potential adversaries—can't be ignored. And they haven't been. Under Obama, the United States acted to sustain deterrence by taking steps to ensure that all three legs of our nuclear triad do not age into obsolescence. The administration's 2017 defense budget began a process of correcting decades of underinvestment in nuclear deterrence by targeting $19 billion for weapons upgrades—part of a five-year, $108 billion plan. These funds have gone to sustain and recapitalize the nuclear force and its associated strategic command, control communications, and intelligence systems, providing increased funding for manpower, equipment, vehicles, and maintenance. The money also supports technological efforts that will help sustain our bomber fleet and other delivery systems—for example, by replacing old ICBMs with new ones that will be less expensive to maintain. It will keep our strategic bombers effective in the face of more advanced air defense systems by replacing our aging air-launched cruise missile with a more effective long-range standoff weapon; by replacing the F-16s in our dual-capable aircraft fleet with F-35s and the B61-12 gravity bomb; and by building replacements for our Ohio-class ballistic missile submarines.

These aren't aggressive moves. They're defensive moves intended to shore up the system of deterrence that has kept the world's nuclear peace for more than seven decades.

If we don't replace these systems, they will continue to age and become unsafe, unreliable, and ineffective. The fact is, most of our nuclear weapon delivery systems have already been extended decades beyond their original expected service lives. So it's not a choice between replacing these platforms or keeping them; it's really a choice between replacing them or losing them. That would mean losing confidence in our ability to deter, which we can't afford in today's volatile security environment.

Some have objected that recapitalizing the U.S. nuclear arsenal will stimulate others to follow suit, fueling an arms race. Those who make this argument do not have history on their side. For a quarter century, the U.S. fielded no new nuclear weapons systems, yet during those years, nuclear programs churned along and accelerated in Russia, China, North Korea, Pakistan, India, and (until recently) Iran. Those countries have already been engaged in an arms race; it's past time for the U.S. to act to sustain its own deterrent arsenal.

Doing this will cost money, of course. But funding for the nuclear enterprise is and will remain a relatively small percentage of total defense funding. This is one aspect of offset theory that has continued to be valid since the days of Eisenhower: nuclear weapons are a bargain, in that they provide a big dose of deterrence at a relatively small economic price. That's why, as we work through today's strategic transition to a new age of great-power rivalry, one of the oldest tools in our defense tool kit remains one of the most essential.

CHAPTER 11

THE WORLD'S HOTTEST HOT SPOTS: IRAN, KOREA, AND BEYOND

Navigating the challenges posed by China and Russia would be enough to keep any SecDef busy. But the world doesn't let us pick and choose our adversaries. I also had to dedicate significant time and energy to the next three letters of CRIKT: *I* for Iran, *K* for North Korea, and *T* for terrorism and other threats to the U.S. homeland. None of these dangers is going away, and the Defense Department will need smart plans and programs for addressing them for the foreseeable future.

Iran in the Context of a Volatile Middle East

On July 14, 2015, the Joint Comprehensive Plan of Action (JCPOA)—referred to colloquially as the Iran nuclear deal—was formally announced. The deal had been negotiated mainly by three people: Secretary of State John Kerry; Secretary of Energy Ernie Moniz, a fellow physicist whom I knew I could count on to assure the technical aspects were nailed down; and Undersecretary of State Wendy Sherman, with whom I'd worked in the 1990s on North Korea.

As written, JCPOA verifiably put a stop to the major aspects of Iran's nuclear program, essentially cutting off its pathways to accessing fissile materials needed for manufacturing a nuclear weapon. The agreement included not just the United States and Iran but a broad array of other world powers, including the other permanent members of the UN Security Council (the United Kingdom, Russia, France, and China),

Germany, and the European Union. As SecDef, I was a willing supporter of the deal, and I continue to support it to this day, despite the current administration's rejection of it. The reason is that it verifiably and at least temporarily took off the table a big potential headache for me as SecDef—an Iranian bomb. Without the treaty, I'd need even more forces to deter and more defenses to defend against Iranian aggression.

On the other hand, the JCPOA was not and could never have been a "grand bargain" that settled all the problems we had with Iranian behavior. For this reason, when I spoke with Marty Dempsey, chairman of the Joint Chiefs of Staff, on the day after the announcement of the treaty, my message to him was, "There should be zero change in our policy toward Iran." We would continue to update our finely honed plans for the so-called military option—a strike designed to destroy Iran's nuclear infrastructure. We would maintain our full military posture in the region, aimed at deterring aggression and defending our allies, especially Israel. We would continue to defend freedom of navigation in the Gulf, both in words and in actions. In short, we would continue to serve as a check on Iran's many malign influences in the Middle East and elsewhere.

If the Iran nuclear deal was a valuable step toward protecting the peace in the Middle East—as I believe it was—then why was it so important for the United States to continue to stand firm against Iranian ambitions in the region? And how does that objective fit into our overall strategy in the Middle East?

There's a common perception that American involvement in the Middle East has generally been characterized by "quagmires" in which vast amounts of U.S. resources—including the lives of service members—have been expended for no good reason. Some citizens with just a passing knowledge of the Middle East and its history are understandably weary of hearing about America's long, sometimes painful engagement in support of peace and stability in the region. Many are tempted to throw up their hands and say, "Why don't we just get out of the Middle East altogether and let them fight their own battles?"

There are plenty of reasons this alternative isn't a realistic one—and, contrary to conventional wisdom, the oil resources of the region do *not* head the list. In today's rapidly evolving energy landscape, the economic power of Middle Eastern oil is steadily diminishing.

To understand the true significance of our role in the Middle East, consider the three goals of our successful anti-ISIS campaign as crafted in 2015: to hand ISIS a lasting defeat in the territories it held in Iraq and Syria; to crush its metastases into other regions in the Middle East and Africa; and to protect the U.S. homeland from terror attacks sponsored, guided, or inspired by ISIS and ISIS affiliates. All these goals were and are essential to U.S. national interests. A Middle East roiled by conflict and dominated by extremists would spell danger for U.S. allies (especially Israel) and pose a real threat to peace in neighboring regions—North Africa, West Asia, and Europe. It would endanger the safety of shipping lanes that are essential to international trade connecting three continents. Above all, it would provide a vast recruiting network, training ground, and launching pad for terrorist assaults on the United States and on Americans around the world. It's absurd to imagine that the United States could be indifferent to these possibilities.

That's why the three goals of the ISIS campaign were so important. And none of them could have been achieved without the leadership of the United States. Indeed, it's abundantly clear that no other nation could have brought to bear the resources, assembled the coalition, and led the execution of the comprehensive campaign that America marshaled. The result has been no quagmire but rather a clear victory for the United States and its allies, driven largely by local forces enabled by the United States. That successful combination needs to be the key to our strategic approach in the region in the years to come.

Our role in the Middle East is also *not* centered on nation-building. Following the invasion of Iraq in 2003, the United States has had a decade and a half of education concerning what an outside power can do in a country torn by internal strife—and what simply isn't possible. We learned some important lessons that have left us with a more realistic view of what our national goals should be in the region. As I put it in a PBS interview in 2016, "We don't have to make Iraq and Syria perfect. We don't have to put order in the Middle East. We understand it's a complicated place. But we're clear about what our interests are. We need to protect our people."

In effect, I was saying that "fixing the Middle East" is not an American strategic objective, nor was it my job as SecDef. We can't allow ourselves to be baited or seduced into getting involved in regional conflicts that don't directly impact our national interests. But when our interests *are* involved, we have no choice but to act.

How, then, should America's national interests in the Middle East be defined? I'll answer this question by discussing our relations with three countries in the region that are particularly important for us: Afghanistan, Saudi Arabia, and Israel.

Afghanistan—a potential safe spot in a bad neighborhood. The war in Afghanistan has become the longest war in American history. In my roles as the number three, number two, and number one official in the Pentagon, I participated in it for half its duration, as I discussed in Chapter 2. I got to know every corner of the country, and I visited with way too many wounded warriors and grieving families. I had a lot of heart invested in the war in Afghanistan. But it's more than sentiment that makes me care about the success of our campaign there.

Most people say that the purpose of our war in Afghanistan is to make sure the country never again becomes a launching pad for terrorist attacks on the United States. That's true, but there's another argument that is seldom made. Take a look at the globe and consider the neighborhood in which Afghanistan sits. The United States has few close friends in the region. Pakistan is an uncertain security partner, to say the least. It's very useful to have a friendly nation in the neighborhood. After all, we couldn't have conducted the raid that killed bin Laden without a presence in Afghanistan. Under the circumstances, isn't it important for the United States to have a security partner in the region that will be willing to host our forces for the foreseeable future?

This argument stands on its head the understandable but misguided view you'll hear people offer from time to time: "That part of the world is a mess. Why don't we just get the hell out?" The correct response is, "Yes, it *is* a mess—and that's the very reason that we need a presence there. Not to try to fix the mess, but to protect our interests from the bad guys who want to turn the neighborhood into an anti-American stronghold."

When I became SecDef, President Obama's plan was to drastically reduce the U.S. presence in Afghanistan on a rapid, predictable schedule. I thought this plan unwise, favoring instead the maintenance of a larger force in the country in the long run. Ultimately, the arguments Joe Dunford and I offered convinced President Obama to agree to slow the build-down and actually to increase the number of forces in country for the final year of his presidency and a short time thereafter—an unpopular move, but, I believe, the right one. I believe that the mission can succeed in strengthening the Afghan security forces so that they can keep a modicum of order in the country, thereby providing some protection to American interests there.

A reason for optimism in Afghanistan is the replacement, in September 2014, of Hamid Karzai as president by Ashraf Ghani. The continual turmoil associated with Karzai had retarded the progress of our effort to build the Afghan security forces. Karzai himself sowed a spirit of discord and mistrust between the United States and the Afghan people through his actions and statements. For example, he repeatedly disrespected the American forces who had sacrificed for his own people (and whose support was responsible for his remaining in office—to say nothing of remaining alive) by calling them "invaders and occupiers."

I had to keep my composure in his presence, but President Obama did not. He once cleared the Situation Room during a Natural Security Council meeting attended by Karzai so that he could tell the Afghan president exactly what he thought of him. Obama's language on that occasion was scathing, caustic, and richly deserved.

By contrast, Ghani was a breath of fresh air. I will never forget his first visit to Washington. I hosted a reception for him in the center court of the Pentagon, where he met a number of people who'd served in Afghanistan, including wounded warriors and families of the fallen. When I turned the podium over to President Ghani to speak, he started by saying, "I just want to say to all the Americans who've given so much for my country, thank you."

I got a bit choked up. We'd never heard words like that from an Afghan leader before. With Ghani in power, we quickly got back on track in the process of building the Afghan security forces. I hope and believe that American patience with this long twilight struggle is now being rewarded with the creation of a regional partner that can be a useful friend in a dangerous part of the world.

Saudi Arabia—time to rebalance. The story of our relationship with Saudi Arabia is very different—much longer and much more fraught. This is not the place to try to recap that complicated story. But I share what seems to be the growing conviction among many U.S. foreign policy experts: that while Saudi Arabia remains an important partner of ours in the Middle East, it's long past time that we rebalanced our relationship. In fact, this is a position I've long held.

As SecDef, I found Saudi Arabia to be a frustrating partner to deal with, particularly in regard to the most important initiative I launched in the Middle East, the invigorated campaign against ISIS. Despite continual requests from me and continual promises by them, the Saudis made essentially no contribution to the victory against ISIS in Iraq and Syria. They never contributed any ground forces, and their participation in the air war was tiny. They would not drop ordnance in Iraq (only in Syria), and the number of sorties they flew was a minuscule fraction of the number they devoted to their ill-starred and incompetently conducted campaign in Yemen.

Eventually, having given up on the Saudis being of any military help, I urged them to provide some financial help to the reconstruction of the Sunni areas devastated by ISIS. Saudi Arabia is an enormously wealthy country, but it contributed next to nothing to this cause.

Finally, after leaders of other Muslim countries around the world urged Saudi Arabia to become more active politically and morally against ISIS, the young crown prince Mohammed bin Salman (MBS) abruptly announced that his country had formed a coalition of Muslim countries to stand against ISIS. Immediately, a host of other important Islamic countries informed reporters that they had no idea what this coalition was, had not been consulted about it, and had not agreed to join it. It was a typical Saudi military initiative—an idea without a plan.

As this story illustrates, the Saudis have consistently failed to prove themselves good military partners. Their military has some impressive qualities, but it's very uneven: their ground forces, their special forces, and the integrated air and missile defenses they operate with their neighbors are all rather weak, while they lavish their big-ticket investments on their air force and navy. Their few really capable ground forces are dedicated to protecting the monarchy, not fighting their external wars, for which they tend to rely on hired mercenaries. These weaknesses greatly diminish the value of Saudi Arabia as a potential military partner to the United States.

This is one of the reasons I favor rebalancing our relationship and demanding more in exchange for the benefits we provide them as one of our main friends in the Middle East. Another reason is the declining importance of oil in the world economy and that of the United States. Saudi Arabia still has the power to impact global oil prices through the choices it makes about its own oil sales, but our own reliance on Saudi oil is just a small fraction of what it once was. We no longer need to behave as if the Saudis hold the key to the world economy. They simply don't.

I don't advocate a complete break with the Saudis. We remain essential to their security, and they remain important players in the Middle East because of their size, their strategic location, their wealth, and the fact that they host the two most holy sites in Islam. But we must be realistic about the extent of their importance to us, and not be swayed by their skills as propagandists and lobbyists (the Saudi leaders ply U.S. politicians, journalists, and think tanks with abundant cash).

As for the sale of U.S. arms to Saudi Arabia, which seems to loom so large in the thinking of President Trump, I support them. But U.S. arms sales are not a gift we give to the Saudis, nor are they an act of generosity on the part of the Saudis. They are simple transactions of mutual and balanced benefit, and they should be regarded as such—no more and no less.

Today, the eyes of the world are on the controversial Mohammed bin Salman. I got to know him quite well, starting when he was defense minister and then deputy crown prince. My efforts to win his support for the counter-ISIS campaign were basically unproductive. When he first came into office, his knowledge base about his region and about the Saudi security relationships with other states, including the United States, was very rudimentary. MBS was the first major Saudi foreign leader who had been educated entirely in Saudi Arabia rather than in a major Western university, and his parochialism was apparent. He would say—and apparently believe—things about history that were simply untrue. MBS was obsessed with the threat from Iran almost to the exclusion of anything else, including ISIS. He could be arrogant at times and tended to act impulsively, and I noticed that his military leaders were extremely ill at ease with him.

Having said all this, I'll give credit to MBS for learning quickly. After I left office, he initiated efforts to consolidate his power, hiring a large number of American consultants to help him reform his country economically and politically. Perhaps he will mature into a more seasoned leader over time. But the controversy over the murder of dissident journalist Jamal Khashoggi has justifiably made the relationship between our countries even more difficult.

Whatever happens to MBS, our relationship with Saudi Arabia is likely to remain a troubled one—two partners that share some values while being deeply conflicted over others, yoked uneasily together by the mutual need for friends in a part of the world where friends are hard to come by.

Israel—an enduring friendship with occasional rough spots. Historically, our relationship with Israel has been an entirely different matter. I've always considered Israel a rare example of shared values, overlapping security interests, and admirable military competence in a region where all three are in short supply. For these reasons, I've always considered our friendship with Israel as our one real anchor in the Middle East, a view I believe most Americans share.

Much of the security relationship between the United States and Israel, which I tended as SecDef, resides under the waterline and is not visible to the public in either country. It includes some highly sensitive matters, including cybersecurity and cyber-intelligence, other forms of intelligence collection and analysis, joint development and mutual deployment of defenses against ballistic missiles, and so on. With a much larger and more powerful military, the United States has more to offer Israel in these areas than vice versa. But my experience showed me that the relationship is far from one-sided. In particular, as undersecretary, I learned a lot of valuable information about bomb-sniffing dogs and techniques for armoring vehicles against IEDs from the Israelis.

One complex matter that I spent a lot of effort on was guaranteeing Israel's qualitative military edge. It's a concept embedded in U.S. law that is shaped by the strategic realities of the Middle East. Because Israel is smaller than the potentially antagonistic states that surround it, its ability to defend itself cannot rely on a quantitative military edge, such as a larger army. Instead, the United States has undertaken to guarantee that Israel will retain a qualitative military edge, both to protect Israel itself and to keep the peace in the region. This means selling to the Israelis some of our best and most up-to-date technology, and excluding that technology from arms sales to other states in the region, like Saudi Arabia and the United Arab Emirates. The details of these rules are highly technical and ultrasecret, known to just a handful of officials in the government of each country.

Despite our long-standing friendship with Israel, there have been periods of disagreement between us, and during my time as SecDef, a strong divide that was both personal and policy-driven opened up between President Obama and Prime Minister Benjamin Netanyahu. It led to Netanyahu's openly campaigning against a security initiative promoted by a U.S. president—namely, the JCPOA with Iran—and even working with the U.S. opposition party in the process.

I got caught up in this controversy when I prepared to visit Israel shortly after the conclusion of the Iran deal. This trip was fraught with political peril. I knew Netanyahu would try to make me take the brunt of the full fury of his anger at President Obama. I needed to stick up for my government's decision while also assuring Netanyahu that the JCPOA was not intended to resolve all the problems posed by Iran. Thus, all the work done by the United States and Israel on planning for possible conflict with Iran would continue and grow ever stronger. My goal was to deliver this message and thereby ease the tensions between our two countries. But I worried about Netanyahu's instinct for drama, especially since the press in both Israel and the United States were fanned into high flames waiting for a shootout. In fact, the day before my arrival, Netanyahu had made international headlines by embarrassing two high-ranking officials of the United Kingdom in a long, tense press conference. I didn't want the same thing to happen to me.

I did not know Netanyahu well, although I had first met him thirty years earlier at a dinner when I was at MIT. A bit of research revealed that, while living in the United States as a teenager, he had attended a high school near mine in the suburbs of Philadelphia, though he was older than I was.

Our meeting, on my second day in Israel, began with our staff members and the U.S. ambassador in attendance. Netanyahu spent about the first half hour thundering and berating me. I just sat across the table staring at him with what Ron Lewis, then my senior military assistant, used to call my "assed-up" look—a mixture of annoyance and feigned boredom.

Finally, in an effort to change the tone, I pointed out to Netanyahu that we'd gone to neighboring high schools in Montgomery County, Pennsylvania. He dropped his bombastic style, grinned at me, and offered a glimpse of what must have been his teenage personality: "Yeah, we used to beat you in sports."

Two could play at that game. I shot back, "That's not how *I* remember it! What sport did you play, anyway?"

"Soccer," he replied.

"Well, soccer wasn't a real sport in America back then."

After this exchange of playful barbs, things got a lot more relaxed and more serious. Netanyahu gave a heartfelt explanation of the Holocaust and the duty he felt never to allow anything like that to happen to Israel again. Of course, as a human being with a commitment to decent values, I was able to relate to this message, and the mood in the room continued to soften.

Then the prime minister brought me and Eric Rosenbach into his office for a private discussion with him and his aide Yoshi Cohen. The conversation turned to more practical topics, including the many military programs our two nations were engaged in together, especially those designed to maintain intense pressure on Iran. The whole meeting ended up on a much more businesslike note.

After this meeting, Defense Minister Moshe "Bogie" Ya'alon of Israel and I went to Yad Vashem, the site of the World Holocaust Remembrance Center, where I was able to lay a wreath. It symbolized the mutual commitments of our two nations, so much more enduring than the argument we were having at the moment. Similarly, just before Christmas 2016, during my final weeks as SecDef, I timed my last visit to Israel to coincide with the delivery of the first F-35 Joint Strike Fighters to Israel—a monument to the lasting bond between our countries, and a moment of personal pride for me because of the role I'd played in helping to make the JSF program successful.

Our friendship with Israel plays a key role in defining American interests in the Middle East. Because Israel is our closest ally in the region, a country that shares our democratic values, and a reliable partner in international affairs, the United States is committed to helping ensure Israel's freedom and safety. That means providing support to Israel's own formidable self-defense capabilities. And it also means doing what we can to help turn down the temperature on potential conflicts throughout the region, whether driven by sectarian, ethnic, ideological, or political forces.

The United States is not and cannot be the policeman of the Middle East, nor can it resolve differences that have been centuries or even millennia in the making. But it can play a role as a stabilizing force to help prevent a war that might not only wipe out a close ally but also could easily threaten to spread far beyond the region.

These brief accounts of our relationships with three important Middle Eastern countries—Afghanistan, Saudi Arabia, and Israel—help suggest why the Middle East is a complicated and challenging place for American diplomacy and defense. Security relationships there have never been defined by a formal, NATO-like structure spanning the entire region. That's why the DOD's engagement in the region has most often been through bilateral relationships—many of them lasting half a century or more. Our security cooperation with Saudi Arabia, for example, goes back to over six decades of building institutional capacity, honing interoperability, and combating mutual threats. Bahrain, too, is a venerable partner in the Gulf, being home to one of America's oldest defense relationships in the region. Bahrain hosts our Navy's Fifth Fleet and the headquarters of U.S. Naval Forces Central Command, helping ensure maritime security not only in the Gulf but also the Arabian Sea, the Red Sea, and parts of the Indian Ocean.

Moving beyond the Gulf, Jordan is also among our oldest security partners and one of the U.S. military's most steadfast, invaluable, and capable allies in the region, especially its special operations forces. And Jordan also hosts the largest military exercise in the region, Eager Lion, with some three thousand rotational U.S. troops participating each year.

We've also had a long history of engagement with Lebanon. After Syrian troops withdrew from Lebanon in 2005, the DOD's security assistance for Lebanon's military and special forces advanced a range of interests to help counter the spread of ISIS and al-Nusra, and stem the influence of Iran and Hezbollah. And there are also deep roots to our security cooperation with Egypt, a historical leader in the region, with an important strategic role in stability here.

The United States has newer partnerships with other countries in the region, including Kuwait (a relationship that took shape during the 1991 Gulf War), Qatar (which hosts our Combined Air Operations Center, critical to managing the coalition air campaigns over Iraq, Syria, and Afghanistan), and the United Arab Emirates (with one of the most capable militaries in the Middle East).

These partnerships between the United States and a range of Middle Eastern states are not without friction, as our disagreements with our Saudi friends illustrate. But the network of American connections in the Middle East has, on balance, been a force for stability and peace in the region. Our concerns about the threat posed by Iran must be understood in that context.

One of the largest and wealthiest countries in the region, with both a proud history dating back to the Persian Empire and a modern industrial base, Iran has unfortunately chosen to position itself as a promoter of extremism and unrest throughout the Middle East. It was the first

Islamist state dedicated to spreading its radical religious and political views internationally. Iran supports the violent dictatorship of Assad in Syria, backs the terrorist-supporting Hezbollah in Lebanon, undercuts the Baghdad government in Iraq, and exploits disorder in Yemen, all while continually directing hostility and violence toward U.S. ally Israel. These and other dangerous behaviors—along with a constant stream of threatening rhetoric aimed at the United States and its allies around the world—mean that we have no choice but to take steps to deter Iranian aggression and to be prepared to defeat it in the event of war.

How might a war involving Iran break out? The two most likely causes would be Iran's taking a step too far in its support of proxy military forces in Iraq, Syria, Lebanon, Yemen, or elsewhere, sparking a confrontation with a U.S. ally or with U.S. forces themselves; or Iran's interfering with freedom of navigation in the air or at sea in the Gulf region, for example, by mounting an attack on U.S. vessels.

Such a war would run the risk of quickly becoming a regional conflict, with the United States and its allies, including some of the Arab countries and Israel, getting drawn in. The results would likely include both widespread violence by Iranian proxy forces around the world and, eventually, the destruction of the Iranian armed forces. However, the countries arrayed against Iran would be unlikely to attempt to invade and occupy Iran. The country is simply too vast and complicated for any outside force to want to control it for any length of time. The result would be a dangerous period of instability and potential chaos within and around Iran—posing further dangers for the region as a whole.

A wild card in any of these scenarios is the danger of Iran trying to use nuclear weapons. That's the risk that the United States tried to reduce with the JCPOA. If the Iran nuclear deal was still being verifiably implemented, no nuclear weapons would be available for Iran to use in a regional war. Unfortunately, however, the narrowness of the deal was confusing to many Americans and to some of our friends in the region; the idea of a treaty that sharply reduced one threat while leaving others unchanged seemed contradictory to many. What's more, the Obama administration's failure to adequately explain the surrounding strategic context gave ammunition to the deal's many critics. That included

Donald Trump and many of those who would later become key decision-makers in his presidential administration.

As the world knows, President Trump announced his intention to withdraw from the deal in May 2018. At the moment, it's unclear what will happen next. As of now, the remaining signatories to the deal, including our allies in Europe, continue to support it. But if the deal collapses and Iran restarts its nuclear weapons program in full force, as it has already threatened to do, all bets for the future are off.

The North Korean Dilemma: Dealing with a Rogue State

North Korea rounds out the list of nations included in the CRIKT formula. It's another country I've dealt with extensively in the course of my career.

In 1994, as assistant secretary of defense responsible for strategic issues, I was focused on issues of loose nukes and proliferation. As I've explained, this gave me jurisdiction over the Nunn-Lugar program in the countries of the former USSR. But it also required me to focus on North Korea's nuclear program, which was already viewed as posing a potential threat to the region.

In that capacity, I spent about half my time in 1994 planning a possible air strike on the facilities housing North Korea's nuclear program. These were centered on a plutonium reactor at Yongbyon, about sixty miles north of the capital of Pyongyang, which the regime claimed was solely for electricity production, but which was really a staging ground for their development of a nuclear weapon. The reactor had been in operation since 1986, which meant that its fuel rods had been irradiated to produce enough plutonium 239 to make a bomb. Our belief was that the North Koreans were planning to remove the fuel rods and transport them to a nearby reprocessing facility, where the plutonium could be chemically separated for military use. Additional reactor fuel would be produced at a fuel fabrication facility in the same vicinity.

Destroying this string of facilities would not have been easy—particularly the plutonium reactor. Experts say that if you drop a bomb on an operating reactor, it's likely that the core will be breached, causing a meltdown. The ensuing fire in the graphite "moderator" will break out, causing a plume of radioactive material to flow downwind—basically what happened at the site of the Chernobyl disaster in 1986. To try to avoid this possibility, I worked with a supersecret Air Force planning team on devising a way to bomb the reactor so as to cause its roof to collapse into the core, smothering it and preventing a meltdown. I was confident this plan could work if a bombing of the site became unavoidable.

At the same time, I was working on the war plan for the defense of South Korea in response to the attack from the North that would almost surely have followed a Yongbyon strike. All this work on possible military options was viewed as an important fallback measure in support of the negotiations then being conducted by the State Department under President Clinton's direction.

In the end, the need for an air strike at that time was eliminated, thanks to the unexpected success of negotiations. Former President Jimmy Carter—an indefatigable freelance negotiator, and thus a persistent thorn in the side to President Clinton—showed up in Pyongyang to talk with Kim Il-sung, North Korea's founding communist dictator. Deploying his personal knowledge of nuclear technology (Carter had worked on the fledgling nuclear submarine program as a Navy commander under Admiral Hyman G. Rickover), he persuaded Kim that the United States could help him build less-dangerous, larger nuclear reactors for the production of peaceful power if he gave up his weapons program. This was the basis of the so-called Agreed Framework of 1994.

Of course, no deal with a rogue regime like that of North Korea can ever be taken at face value. Both countries abided by portions of the Agreed Framework, but the United States soon began to accumulate information showing that the North Koreans had covertly launched a uranium program elsewhere in the country, a possibility only elliptically covered by the Agreed Framework. We demanded a more extensive inspection regime to verify compliance, which led to a cat-and-mouse game involving an extensive network of underground tunnels and bunkers that the North Koreans had built. Their clever negotiators even tried to make the United States pay some $300 million in fees before they would agree to let us inspect a highly suspicious site known as Mount Kunmyungmi—which turned out to feature nothing but a honeycomb of empty tunnels.

Concern over North Korea's aggressive intentions reached new heights in 1998, when the regime launched a ballistic missile on a trajectory that passed directly over Japan. Of course, this provoked outrage and fear in Tokyo, Seoul, and Washington. Under pressure to take action, President Clinton named Bill Perry as a special coordinator of overall North Korean policy, and Perry asked me to serve as his deputy. This led to "the Perry process"—an intensive two-year mission in which Perry and I worked closely with Wendy Sherman, a State Department official appointed by Madeleine Albright, to pull together an overall approach to North Korea, in coordination with Japan, South Korea, and China. Others from Bill Cohen's Pentagon and George Tenet's CIA supported us as needed. My experience with Wendy Sherman during this period gave me great confidence in her when she negotiated the Iran nuclear deal for John Kerry many years later.

Perry, Sherman, and I made a number of journeys to Japan, South Korea, and China, hammering out a common negotiating strategy that could win the support of all four members of this informal negotiating block. The Perry process culminated in 1999 when Perry, Sherman, and I traveled to Pyongyang for the first high-level negotiations with North Korean leaders since the armistice of 1953.

We flew into North Korea on a U.S. military aircraft. However, we did not dare approach North Korea from a U.S. military base in South Korea or Japan, because those were the flight routes against which North Korean air defenses were targeted, and we were afraid someone out in the field might not get the word that Americans were arriving on a peaceful mission. Fortunately, the Russians gave us permission to fly over their territory, which was the only remaining option.

After landing at Pyongyang's small, little-used airport, we drove into the city. While the worst days of the 1990s were over, the country's poverty was evident: military trucks made up most of the vehicular traffic, and the roadsides were filled with emaciated people traveling on foot, some obviously over distances of many miles. In the heart of the city, the wide boulevards were also practically empty. Yet each intersection was staffed by a female traffic attendant who whirled around at the approach of our motorcade as though she were stopping traffic, before ceremoniously waving us through.

We visited the most famous Pyongyang sights, each absurd in its own way. We visited Juche Tower, a monumental fifty-story structure topped with an electric candle flame; it symbolizes the North Korean political concept of *juche*, or self-reliance, which is more central to the national philosophy than communism. From the top of the tower, we looked out over all of Pyongyang. There were no cars on the streets and no lights visible in most of the buildings.

However, as we were peering down to the street, a red bus pulled up below the tower. Out spilled some forty adults, who proceeded to link arms and dance in a circle in a desultory fashion. I asked my North Korean "minder" what was going on. She looked me straight in the eye and straight-facedly replied, "Spontaneous popular masses!"

We also visited what we were told was the leading pediatric hospital in the city, for which we'd brought a box of children's medical supplies as a gift from our country. We were greeted by the head nurse, who told us solemnly, "When the children learned that Americans were coming, they wanted to leap from their beds and fight you." But when we entered the ward, we found it filled with children three or four years old. We doubted they'd been indoctrinated in anti-Western sentiment at that tender age, even in North Korea.

The next day, we had our first meeting with Kang Sok-ju, who would remain the lead North Korean negotiator until 2016. The North Korean negotiating style involves sitting wordlessly across the table from you while you make your opening statement. When you're finished, they go away and replay the tape they've made. Once they decide what to say in response—which may be a day or two later—they return and deliver it to you.

So Bill Perry laid out our opening statement, a comprehensive historical and strategic review of the situation, and a description of the goals that the United States was interested in pursuing. When he finished, Kang said simply, "Now you are going to the circus."

Perry asked, "When does it start?"

"When you get there."

Sure enough, when we arrived at the Colosseum, every single seat was filled with North Koreans neatly dressed in the standard style: men in black suits and white shirts, women in similar black-and-white work clothes, and schoolchildren in white shirts with red kerchiefs. We took our seats, and the show began.

On our last day, we had a meeting with the top officer in the Korean People's Army. He treated us to a long tirade, relentlessly belligerent and hectoring in the style of North Korean propaganda. One of the highlights came when he recited the standard North Korean threat, "We will turn Seoul into a sea of fire and Tokyo into a sea of fire!" At that point, he paused and asked Perry, "Where are you from, Dr. Perry?"

"I'm from Palo Alto, California."

The general didn't skip a beat. "We will turn Palo Alto into a sea of fire!" he declared.

Despite these theatrics, the negotiations went rather well. They resulted in a suspension of North Korean missile tests and the beginning of detailed talks about the country's burgeoning plutonium and uranium nuclear programs. We believed that progress along these lines might well be able to continue right up to the point where the pledge that all the parties had made to completely denuclearize the Korean Peninsula, back during George H. W. Bush's administration, would finally be realized.

Unfortunately, as frequently happens, the Clinton administration was overeager to complete this process before it left office, and the effort became politicized during the election campaign of 2000. The political opposition was turbocharged by a visit Secretary of State Madeleine Albright made to Pyongyang, in which she toasted Kim Jong-il, then the leader of North Korea. Pictures of this unfortunate gesture played into partisan hands and solidified the feeling in Republican circles that talks with North Korea should be cut off. That's exactly what happened after George W. Bush took office in 2001. In the wake of 9/11, he declared North Korea part of an "axis of evil" and cut off talks with the regime.

It wasn't until 2005 and 2006 that Condoleezza Rice and Colin Powell restarted talks with North Korea. A "Six-Party Talk" framework was devised, involving the United States, South Korea, and Japan, as well as

North Korea, China, and Russia—the right idea and the right group of participants. But the ensuing years had given the regime plenty of time to make progress on its nuclear program, and in 2006 the North Koreans exploded their first underground nuclear bomb.

In the years since then, the North Korean nuclear threat has gradually worsened.

Having consolidated his grip on power, Kim Jong-un, the son of Kim Jong-il, appears intent on advancing North Korea's ballistic missile, nuclear, and submarine programs. In particular, he seems intent on developing the missile technology that could allow him to target not only our key allies in the region—particularly Japan and South Korea—but also the continental United States. The regime's nuclear tests and missile launches have been highly provocative acts that undermine peace and stability on the Korean Peninsula and the wider Asia-Pacific.

With this behavior, North Korea has gone from being a persistent annoyance to a direct threat—a cause for serious concern for our allies, a prospective danger to our homeland, and a source of irritation in U.S.-China relations.

My involvement in the Korea issue as undersecretary, deputy secretary, and SecDef during the Obama years was focused on strengthening defenses, including missile defenses. This included improving the quality of missile interceptors, then deploying forty-four interceptors at Fort Greely, Alaska, and Vandenberg Air Force Base, California. These are capable of intercepting any North Korean ballistic missiles aimed at the United States. Mind you, we didn't believe they'd yet developed missiles capable of reaching our mainland, but I thought it was better to be one step ahead of them. We also deployed more and better Patriot missile defense systems, both in Asia and afloat, against short-range missiles; the theater high-altitude area defense, against medium-range missiles; and new and improved radar systems in Japan, Hawaii, and Alaska, and at sea aboard ships and seaboard platforms.

As a deterrent to any attack, we also maintained our permanent presence of 28,500 U.S. forces on the Korean Peninsula—the same number we've had in place for some decades.

Extremely important during my time was work on our war plans, which were updated and improved in accordance with regular Pentagon schedules during my eight years with the Obama administration. We developed plans not just for all-out war, but also for a possible collapse of the North Korean regime or an accidental initiation of a war through an incident at the demilitarized zone. Also brand-new was the explicit possibility of a role for Japan, as well as involvement by China. Finally, we developed various plans for precision strikes against North Korea and the use of classified weapons programs that cannot be discussed publicly.

Where do matters stand today? Is Kim Jong-un bent on provoking a war with South Korea and its allies—chief among them the United States? Probably not. But North Korea's aggressive behavior certainly increases the chances that a war could break out. There are two plausible scenarios for a war with North Korea. One would be a missile test that—perhaps mistakenly—landed on the territory of the United States or one of its allies. The other would be an incident between North and South Korea on the demilitarized zone or near the Northern Limit Line that escalated out of control because of miscommunication, mismanagement, or sheer hubris by one or more parties.

The United States would not enter a war on the Korean Peninsula unprepared; in fact, we've planned for it during sixty-four years of armistice. The combined forces of the United States and South Korea would surely win, destroying the North Korean military and taking Pyongyang. But the intensity of violence would be of a level not experienced since the last Korean War. Hundreds of thousands of residents of Seoul and its northern suburbs would be subject to sustained artillery bombardment by more than ten thousand North Korean artillery pieces that could not be silenced by U.S. airpower for several days. North Korean army advances could likely be stopped before Seoul fell, but nuclear and biological attacks by the North Korean regime before its collapse are likely.

What passes for conventional wisdom on North Korea—a forced choice between option A (diplomacy) and option B (war)—is the wrong way to think about the threat. A better approach—one that is, frankly, the least-bad option from a menu of unappealing choices—is what I call "coercive diplomacy." This approach, which combines elements of option A and option B, would involve tough measures (such as intensified international sanctions) that inflict noticeable pain on the regime of Kim Jong-un, combined with hard-nosed talks aimed at strictly limiting his ability to further develop and deploy nuclear weapons.

Coercive diplomacy would force our potential adversary to make the hard choices that can lead to either war or peace—while making it unmistakably clear that the path to war would mean utter destruction for his nation.

As for the negotiating process itself, the first important ingredient would be to involve the other countries that are of necessity implicated in the risks of war on the Korean Peninsula. We did this in the 1990s under the Clinton administration, as did Colin Powell and Condi Rice when they created the Six-Party Talk rubric. It's the right approach, in part because it allows the five countries facing North Korea to pool their carrots and sticks, creating more opportunities for the strong negotiating package that can help lead to an agreement.

Next, any agreement has to be incremental or step-by-step. There should be a series of prescribed steps for North Korea to take, each of which is rewarded in a balanced fashion by the United States and its partners. For example, in return for an agreement by North Korea not to test any long-range ICBMs, the United States might agree to take a step relaxing some economic sanctions. It's important that one proceed in increments, because progress simply can't be made overnight, even in the best of circumstances—and when dealing with an untrustworthy opposite number, progressive steps are advisable.

Patience is the most critical ingredient in such negotiations. Even in the case of the Nunn-Lugar program, where cooperation between the two sides was essentially total, and where the United States was funding most of the effort, the whole process of denuclearizing the former Soviet satellites took years to complete. A North Korean denuclearization would take just as long.

Finally, three big caveats. First, I would never trade U.S. military exercises on the Korean Peninsula for progress in North Korean denuclearization. Those exercises are crucial in improving our readiness to help South Korea defend itself against a North Korean attack. Even a nonnuclear North Korea is a formidable foe, with chemical and biological weapons and a vast military just a few miles from Seoul. To provide a strong deterrence of conventional war, we need forces that are ready to respond, and exercises are the way to guarantee that.

Second, I would never agree in advance to an overall peace agreement with North Korea. Such an agreement could be the ultimate outcome of a step-by-step process leading to a completely denuclearized North Korea. We should never give something that big upfront in return for small initial steps by North Korea.

Finally, I would never agree to a presidential summit with the North Korean leader except to sign a completely buttoned-down final agreement. A summit with an American president has been a long-sought desire of the North Korean leaders, and it shouldn't be given away free.

Sadly, all these warnings went unheeded as the Trump administration made its initial moves, including the summit meeting between the two leaders. President Trump either got none of this advice or chose to ignore it. Mistakes like these make the path to successful negotiations even more difficult, and unlikely.

On the Home Front: Protecting America from a Range of Terrorist Threats

The *T* in CRIKT stands for *terrorism*. Unlike the other letters in my strategic acronym, it designates not a country but rather a wide range of threats that could harm Americans here at home. The possibilities include lone-wolf attacks with guns, explosives, or even just cars; carefully planned assaults by teams of operatives aimed at hijacking or destroying planes or trains, or sabotaging water, electrical, or communications networks, directly or via cyber attack; and, most frightening, the use of weapons of mass destruction (such as nuclear, chemical, or biological devices) to produce enormous casualties and widespread panic in our cities.

If coping with the challenges posed by China, Russia, Iran, and North Korea is complicated, the task of protecting Americans against the range of potential terrorist attacks—and the wide variety of extremist groups and individuals who might launch them—is even more complicated. Terrorism is a "forever problem." As long as human depravity exists—and world history dating back to the dawn of civilization suggests that it will never disappear—then the urge to inflict violence on the helpless will always persist. And modern technological developments, from biological and chemical weapons to cyber-warfare, have given small groups of individuals access to destructive capabilities once monopolized by powerful nation states. We can never expect to eradicate terrorism, only to deter, control, and punish it.

Terrorism was not a major responsibility of the job of assistant secretary of defense for international security policy when I occupied that office from 1993 to 1997. My portfolio there was major strategic affairs, including Russia, nuclear weapons, missile defense, and other supposed big-ticket items. Terrorism was then considered among the regional portfolios, and it supposedly had less importance. However, the first attack on the World Trade Center in New York (1993), the Oklahoma City bombing (1995), and the attacks on Khobar Towers (1996) and the USS *Cole* (2000) made it clear to me—and to many other defense experts—that terrorism was taking a new and deadly turn.

My immediate concern was the possibility that terrorism would escalate from these relatively contained though dangerous and frightening events to much larger events involving loose nuclear weapons or biological, chemical, or radiological weapons. These risks took center stage in a body of work I began in 1998 in my private capacity. For example, I served on the DOD's Threat Reduction Advisory Committee from 1998 to 2002, which provided the first major input on the terrorist threat to the U.S. government before 9/11 and made a serious difference, at least in the Department of Defense.

This led to further work with John Deutch, who had been CIA director, and with Philip Zelikow, a former member of the NSC staff. The three of us published an article in the November–December 1998 issue of *Foreign Affairs* in which we urged the creation of a national terrorism intelligence center and warned of the possible impact of a major attack on U.S. soil:

Such an act of catastrophic terrorism would be a watershed event in American history. It could involve loss of life and property unprecedented in peacetime and undermine America's fundamental sense of security, as did the Soviet atomic bomb test in 1949. Like Pearl Harbor, this event would divide our past and future into a before and after. The United States might respond with draconian measures, scaling back civil liberties, allowing wider surveillance of citizens, detention of suspects, and use of deadly force. More violence could follow, either further terrorist attacks or U.S. counterattacks. Belatedly, Americans would judge their leaders negligent for not addressing terrorism more urgently.

To our dismay, this warning would prove prescient within less than three years. Zelikow himself would later author the famous report of the commission that investigated the 9/11 attacks, explaining how failures by the CIA and the FBI had helped make those attacks possible.

In the aftermath of 9/11, I continued to advise the U.S. government on terrorism. I served on the Defense Science Board policy board and on Condi Rice's foreign policy advisory board, I testified before Congress, and I participated on a panel of the National Academies of Sciences on technologies for countering terrorism. Within the context of the preventive defense project, I worked specifically on the problem of nuclear terrorism. I wrote about "the day after," which tackles the potential threat we feared most intensely in the days after 9/11—a nuclear detonation in downtown Washington or another major American city.

I was also involved in the formation of the office of the homeland security advisor Tom Ridge, as well as the subsequent establishment of the cabinet-level Department of Homeland Security (DHS)—which I believed misguided, and said so. Countering terrorism, like many other jobs of government, can be accomplished only by the collective action of various departments with different specialties. You can't create a new agency for every cross-cutting issue; the right managerial approach is coordination, not aggregation.

My reasons for that opposition have, unfortunately, been borne out in the sixteen years since the department was formed. DHS collected a lot of the agencies involved—border controls, customs, airport security, and other pieces. But defense, law enforcement, intelligence, and foreign policy still resided elsewhere. The various agencies from which DHS was constituted have never come together into a coherent whole, and the department leadership has never found a way to make the differing activities of its units cooperate so as to produce enhanced safety and security for the American people. I was more favorably disposed toward the creation of the Office of the Director of National Intelligence, and I have been good friends with all the directors, including, most recently, Jim Clapper, who filled that role under President Obama, and his successor, Dan Coats, appointed by President Trump.

Later, during the Obama administration, when I served as the third-highest and second-highest official in the DOD, my participation in the ongoing effort to prevent terrorism continued. I was involved in support of the drone, intelligence, and capture/kill counterintelligence operations of those years, as well as the wars in Iraq and Afghanistan.

I've already explained that a core purpose of our anti-ISIS campaign was to severely limit the capabilities of our enemies abroad who seek to sponsor, launch, and inspire terrorist attacks on the United States and its allies. The success of that campaign therefore represents an important step in the effort to reduce the terrorist threat. But in the aftermath of the ISIS campaign, there's much still to be done to reduce the regional and global dangers posed by extremist forces in the Middle East.

We need to continue to counter foreign fighters trying to escape and to renew their efforts to launch attacks on the West, as well as ISIS's attempts to relocate or reinvent itself. To do so, not only the United States but its coalition of allies must remain engaged. In Iraq in particular, the coalition must provide sustained assistance to Iraqi security forces to consolidate security over the rest of the country and carry on our work to train, equip, and support local police, border guards, and other forces to hold areas cleared from ISIS—as always, with the full support and permission of the government of Iraq and partners in Syria.

Beyond security, there are still towns to rebuild, services to reestablish, and communities to restore. Those aren't military matters, but they're part of how, after winning the battle, you win the peace—not by trying to build a new democratic nation, but by taking steps to safeguard a security environment that protects U.S. interests and increases the chances for peace and stability. This is an area where countries in the region can really do some good.

There also needs to be continued political support for an inclusive and multi-sectarian Iraq. In a region where sectarianism is on the rise, the threat of ISIS has brought people together against this common enemy. That's certainly true in Iraq—where, thanks to the unity and leadership of Prime Minister Abadi and Kurdish Regional Government President Barzani, cooperation between the Iraqi security forces and the Kurdish Peshmerga in the battle to retake Mosul reached a level that would have been unthinkable in the past. In Syria, however, even with the seizure of Raqqa and defeat of ISIS, the violence won't stop until an end is put to the tragic civil war there—a war that, as I've noted, Russia has helped inflame, prolonging and worsening the suffering of the Syrian people.

It's crucial that we continue to combat ISIS's metastases around the world, thereby helping to protect our homelands and people. The U.S. military has taken strong actions in support of capable, motivated local forces in Libya and Afghanistan. In Libya, we've provided air support to the Government of National Accord and its forces to isolate and collapse ISIS's control over Sirte. As a result, ISIS has been ejected from Sirte. And in Afghanistan, U.S. forces are proactively assisting and enabling our Afghan partners in strategic operations while the United States also continues to maintain its financial commitment to the Afghan National Defense and Security Forces.

In addition, the Defense Department has been working closely with partners in intelligence, homeland security, and law enforcement both at home and abroad, conducting operations to gather intelligence with a particular focus on destroying ISIS's external operations cadre. As a result, during the Obama administration, we not only killed the chief of ISIS's external operations but also took out over thirty of ISIS's external plotters.

I hope that in the years to come, both the DOD and the administration as a whole will maintain a sharp, smart focus on the many sources of terrorist threats to the United States. There's always a risk of complacency as well as the possibility of being distracted by other dangers, whether real or illusory—for example, the terrorism dangers supposedly posed by immigrants from across the U.S. southern border.

It would also be a mistake for Americans to believe that a large-scale "Muslim ban" would serve as an adequate replacement for intensive, well-managed intelligence and security efforts designed to identify and target specific individuals and groups who are plotting acts of violence. Our efforts to protect Americans must be clearly aimed at those with the desire and ability to do us harm, rather than being diffused and diluted by a broader, vaguer concern with hundreds of millions of people who simply happen to belong to particular ethnic or religious groups.

When the Danger Comes from Nature

No book about the Pentagon would be complete without some acknowledgment of the fact that the DOD is often called upon to protect Americans against dangers that don't involve foreign armies or even terrorists. These can include massive outbreaks of violence—for example, insurrections or large-scale rioting. But more often they center on helping states and localities deal with hurricanes, floods, earthquakes, forest fires, and other natural disasters. Most military leaders and SecDefs don't especially relish these assignments; they're not what we are trained for, and so we don't regard them as among our core tasks. But we also understand that they are important and necessary, and so we handle them with all the professionalism and skill at our disposal.

During my time as deputy, managing these "second-order operations" was my responsibility. During and after Hurricane Sandy in October 2012, DOD's ability to provide transportation, power generation and restoration, and other critical functions to stricken communities in New York, New Jersey, and Connecticut was essential. We were also important in helping contain the Ebola and Zika outbreaks, providing equipment and logistics such as airlift and field hospitals on an urgent basis.

The military manages the Army Corps of Engineers, which handles a wide range of domestic functions, including flood control. In August 2012, drought in the Midwest drastically lowered the water level in the Mississippi River, preventing barges loaded with grain from reaching the Gulf of Mexico—a potentially crippling economic blow to the region. Investigators found that there was actually enough water in the North American watershed to provide adequate flow in the Mississippi, but the states north of the grain belt were unwilling to open their reservoirs, and, according to a 150-year-old law, were not required to do so.

The Army Corps of Engineers was called in. They started by dredging the river bottom, sucking up sediment in an effort to enhance the channel depth. When they reached the level of bare rock, they planned to dynamite the rocks. Fortunately, the rains came, and the flow of water in the Mississippi was naturally restored to its normal level. I was relieved to see an end to the uncomfortable spectacle of an arm of the Department of Defense detonating explosives in the middle of our own country.

The frontline force for most of the disaster-relief functions of the DOD is the National Guard, not the active-duty military. Few people realize that the origins of the National Guard can be traced back to the French Revolution. Under the monarchy, the French military was regarded as a tool of the nobility, so during the French Revolution, an army of the people, or National Guard, was formed as a counterweight. The founders of the United States, influenced by French thought, incorporated the same idea into our Constitution. The National Guard was thought to be a check against abuse of the states by the federal government, since the National Guard resides in the states and is under the command of the governors. It joins the active duty in service of the nation only when it is "federalized" by the president.

National Guard bases and the forces associated with them are scattered all over the country. The deployment of these assets is somewhat inefficient, and I and other secretaries of defense have failed in various efforts to impose more economical systems for managing them. But in general, the National Guard operates effectively. It certainly came through for us in the Iraq and Afghanistan wars, providing troop numbers that the active-duty forces couldn't provide for these prolonged conflicts with their rotating deployments. The Guard plays a vital role in helping to keep Americans safe, not only from our external enemies but also from the threats periodically posed by the forces of nature itself.

As these two chapters on the CRIKT threats have shown, the world remains a complicated and often dangerous place. For each of the potential adversaries we face, there's a complex history and a set of difficult political, social, economic, and cultural factors that make peaceful resolution of the differences between us challenging. And, of course, we can never discount the possibility of unexpected dangers erupting from unpredictable quarters at any time.

For all these reasons, it's crucially important that the shaping of the U.S. security strategy never be permitted to become just a bureaucratic activity driven by institutional goals—bigger budgets or a more impressive organizational footprint. Nor should it be a merely partisan activity aimed at inflaming public opinion and winning elections. Making choices about what we must do to deter and, if necessary, defeat the biggest dangers America faces is too important for that.

CHAPTER 12

MAINTAINING AMERICA'S HIGH-TECH EDGE: A NECESSITY FOR STRATEGIC SUCCESS

D avid Dworkin doesn't wear a uniform or earn a government paycheck. When I got to know him, he hadn't even graduated from high school. But David Dworkin made America's military stronger and the country safer. In May 2015—between studies for his high school Advanced Placement exams—Dworkin participated in Hack the Pentagon, the first-ever "bug bounty" project conducted by a federal department or agency. Its aim was to test for vulnerabilities in the DOD's public websites by crowd-sourcing the effort to 1,400 registered white-hat hackers, with cash prizes for those who succeeded.

Within thirteen minutes of the program's start, the first bug was found. By the end of day one, 137 more were discovered, including several by Dworkin. Incentive programs like this one are common in the private sector. Dworkin says he has found and reported vulnerabilities for Netflix and Uber, among other well-known companies, during similar bug bounties. Usually he does it for the chance to win some money or a T-shirt. But when Hack the Pentagon was announced, he signed up out of a sense of duty and patriotism.

The pilot project cost the DOD a total of $150,000, mostly in organizing expenses. The prizes awarded were modest; the prestige involved in hacking the Pentagon was the main draw. Hiring an outside firm to conduct a comparable security audit and vulnerability assessment would have cost several times as much. In addition, it freed the department's talented in-house cyber-specialists to spend more time fixing problems rather than finding them, and it showed them how to streamline their efforts to defend our networks and quickly correct vulnerabilities.

Perhaps most important, it underscored how solutions to even the Pentagon's trickiest technology problems can come from anyone and anywhere among America's tremendous human, corporate, and institutional resources—provided we're willing to seek out our brightest talents and open our doors to them.

Technological superiority is an absolute necessity if the U.S. military is to be successful in carrying out its strategic missions around the world. It's not enough to have well-crafted war plans for defending Western Europe from a Russian assault; if the communications systems the troops depend on should become vulnerable to being infiltrated or shut down by enemy hackers, our superior military power may be drastically undermined. The same applies to other areas of technological vulnerability, from advanced radar-blocking devices on jet fighters to enhanced systems for intercepting nuclear missiles. In all these areas, American technology superiority is not a birthright. It must be earned again and again in today's rapidly changing and fiercely competitive world.

At the start of my own career in national security decades ago—which began with projects related to missile basing and space-based defense technologies that were considered high-tech at the time—the United States had an unquestioned edge over the rest of the world when it came to technology. In the decades following World War II, most new technological breakthroughs originated in America, and much of the leading-edge research was being sponsored by the federal government, particularly the DOD.

Today, the Pentagon is still a major sponsor of important research in fields ranging from electronics to biotechnology to nanotechnology. But the relative balance of power has shifted dramatically. Commercial businesses and research labs drive a far greater percentage of today's technological research; both the research programs and their practical applications are increasingly global; and countries in Europe, Asia, and elsewhere have dramatically accelerated their pace of innovation, relying both on new inventions from their own labs and off-the-shelf products available on the open market. Today, as access to high-end military technology has diffused, it has become increasingly available to regional powers like North Korea and Iran, and even to non-state actors. And as our own reliance on technological systems like satellites and the Internet has grown, we've developed vulnerabilities that our adversaries are eager—and increasingly well equipped—to exploit.

For all these reasons, if the CRIKT acronym encapsulated my strategic thinking as Secretary of Defense for today, technology was at the center of my work as Secretary of Defense for tomorrow.

A Great Transition

As I've explained, a great strategic transition was needed from the post-9/11 era, with its nearly single-minded focus on counterterrorism and counterinsurgency in Iraq and Afghanistan, to the broader and more complex priorities of CRIKT. This necessitated a parallel transition in technologies. Aided by my own professional background in science and technology, I made driving this tech transition a high priority for the department.

This is not the first such transition the U.S. military has experienced. My superb deputy Bob Work possesses, among his other talents, a gift for military history. Bob has captured U.S. post–World War II history in terms of three eras, using terminology that is both accurate and catchy, and that therefore has been widely adopted.

The first of these eras was the early Cold War of the 1950s and 1960s. It was characterized by an overwhelming reliance by the United States on nuclear weapons to deter a possible attack by the Soviet Union and to "offset" the Soviet superiority in troop strength and other conventional military measures.

However, once the Soviet Union caught up in nuclear weapons, and the dangers of overreliance on nukes became increasingly apparent, the search was on for another way to offset Soviet military mass. The 1970s and 1980s brought a second era dominated by the application of superior U.S. computers, sensors, and advanced design to neutralize the vast numbers of Soviet troops and tanks in Europe, rather than forcing NATO to rely on the deterrent effect of nuclear weapons alone. The new technologies powering this "second offset" included high-tech systems such as the B-2 bomber and the F-117 Nighthawk stealth aircraft, precision strike weapons, satellite-based systems for electronic warfare and surveillance, and other innovative systems, many deriving from the breakthroughs in information technology then erupting from the United States and not yet available to the Soviet Union. These tools greatly increased the accuracy and lethality of the weapons in our arsenal, and ultimately helped the United States to win the Cold War and to defeat regional enemies like Saddam Hussein in the first Gulf War.

Now, as Bob puts it, a "third offset" is needed for the era of CRIKT and a return to the focus on big-power competition. This era requires a special emphasis on the high-end, high-tech tools of warfare—tools for cyber-warfare, biological defense, space-based weaponry, and more.

In between the eras of the second and third offsets lies the period from the end of the Cold War to the beginning of my most recent stint in the Pentagon, roughly 1990 to 2010. This was a strategic and technological interregnum, in which grand strategy took a backseat to other concerns. American military dominance and democratic values were unchallenged, Russia was reeling from the disintegration of the Soviet Union, and China seemed to be embarked on a peaceful rise from a backward start. During this period, defense efforts were initially focused on peacekeeping in the Balkans and elsewhere; then, after 9/11, the focus shifted to counterterrorism and counterinsurgency in Afghanistan and Iraq. All these challenges put a strong focus on interagency marshaling of all parts of the U.S. government alongside the military and required their share of agile inventions to deal with threats ranging from airline hijacking to improvised explosive devices. Such low-tech dangers called for ingenuity and persistence, but not a transformation of the military itself.

Redefining High-Tech Innovation for the Age of CRIKT

One way I tried to push high tech for the transition to the CRIKT era was by relinking the Pentagon to the vibrant commercial tech base through novel approaches like the bug-bounty project. But a lot would also be accomplished by orienting the department's huge traditional in-house tech machinery to the needs of the new strategic era. Even though the commercial tech base around the world has burgeoned in recent decades, the DOD is still a leading hub of technology development. The department's first budget during my time as SecDef called for $72 billion in research and development spending, more than double what Apple, Intel, and Google were spending on R&D combined.

Much of this R&D money is expended outside the DOD, both at the for-profit defense companies that build weapons and at universities. The Army, Navy, and Air Force also have labs staffed by military and civilian employees who do their own research aimed at giving the services a future edge. Another stream of R&D money flows to nonprofit research establishments funded by the government, many of which were created shortly after the launch of Sputnik. The DOD spawned a family of such labs, including MIT's Lincoln Laboratory and the MITRE Corporation, while the Department of Energy gave rise to the Los Alamos National Laboratory and the Lawrence Livermore National Laboratory, both dedicated to nuclear weapons research.

The lion's share of DOD's R&D budget is dedicated to developing specific weapons, and especially to injecting new tech into legacy ships, planes, armored vehicles, and networks. Such upgrades may sound mundane, but America's installed base of military equipment is worth trillions of dollars, and it makes sense to transform it without rebuilding it when that's possible. However, the CRIKT transition really emphasized the new frontier technologies around cyber-warfare, space warfare, electronic warfare, undersea dominance, lasers, hypersonic vehicles, biotech, and biodefense, and these are the areas into which I increasingly steered our R&D dollars.

The DOD's R&D budget of more than $70 billion is a lot of money, but I believed it would still leave some big gaps in our technology needs. These gaps arose from three basic causes. First, there was the tendency of the Pentagon's R&D system to focus on meeting specified requirements defined by the warfighters in the services. These are important, but they leave no space for brand-new, revolutionary technologies or concepts that today's warriors are unlikely to envision on their own.

Second, the system was slow, based on a lengthy process of defining the requirement and then a five- to fifteen-year program for building a system to meet it. My experience with the wars in Afghanistan and Iraq had shown me that this approach, inherited from the Cold War, was no longer adequate.

Third, a dangerous gulf had emerged between the Pentagon's in-house innovation culture and the commercial, global world of tech.

Each of these three gaps required a different solution. As undersecretary, deputy secretary, and SecDef, I set about to narrow all three.

The legendary Defense Advanced Research Projects Agency pioneers daring new research into technology and weapons. It, too, was created in the fertile post-Sputnik moment, and it has continually delivered break-throughs, of which the Internet, stealth technology, and the global positioning system (GPS) are just a few. DARPA is not a laboratory or a testing facility; it's just an office building in suburban Washington. And DARPA doesn't do scientific work; it gives out grants to scientists. What makes it special is the program managers, themselves scientists at the top of their game, who decide where the funding goes and how it will be used. They typically join DARPA to contribute their unique expertise for a few years, then return to the laboratory bench.

DARPA reports to the undersecretary of defense. But it is so success-ful that it didn't need much from me when I filled that role, nor in my incarnations as deputy and SecDef. However, I did have to appoint a good director who could select top-flight program managers and then refrain from micromanaging them. I found two fine directors in Regina Dugan (who served in the role from 2009 to 2012) and Arati Prabhakar (from 2012 to 2017). Occasionally I needed to defend DARPA's staffing approach, which looked like a revolving-door system with grant givers and grant receivers swapping roles in a potentially incestuous fashion. In reality, however, it had careful controls to minimize conflicts of interest.

The biggest challenge was connecting DARPA's breakthroughs to real military hardware. The "valley of death" that separates R&D from production is an age-old problem in technology, and bridging it is a vital challenge that every senior tech manager must tackle. So imagine my astonishment when the congressional armed services committees wrote a law shortly before I left the SecDef office that divides research and engineering from acquisition in two separate organizations! This was one of the most wrongheaded of all the amateurish tinkerings by Congress I witnessed. You might as well write a statute repealing the laws of thermodynamics (which explain why a perpetual motion machine is impossible). I hope the lawmakers will recognize their error and undo this mistake before it produces much damage.

DARPA, then, was a successful way of doing frontier research that didn't require much help from me besides funding. By contrast, the Strategic Capabilities Office (SCO) was an innovation I founded in 2012 during my time as undersecretary to meet urgent near-term needs for faster solutions to immediate battlefield problems. The issue had been gnawing at me for some time when one day I received a briefing from the Missile Defense Agency. The content was interesting, but the young man presenting it struck me as extraordinary. His lucid explanations demonstrated total mastery of the technical details, and when questioned, he could drill down through layers of additional depth.

His name was Will Roper, and he was a Rhodes scholar physicist (as I'd been years earlier). I promptly stole him for my own R&D staff. And when I decided to launch the SCO to address the challenge of agile innovation for quick results, I selected Roper to run it.

We started the SCO small, as an experiment. I told Roper to ask the COCOMs what they'd regret lacking in the way of technology if they had to carry out their war plans tomorrow, and then to ask the joint chiefs for their advice as to how he could help them quickly provide what the COCOMs wanted.

The results were phenomenally successful. Here's an example. One challenge SCO tackled was the problem of protecting stealthy aircraft like the F-35 and the new B-21 bomber from detection by enemy radar at short range, when the stealth system isn't enough to conceal them and they are close enough to the air defense to be shot down. The standard electronic warfare response would be a jammer that could drown out the return signal bounced off the aircraft. But SCO's unique contribution was to forgo the option of an expensive, high-powered jammer, which had to operate from a long way off so as to avoid being itself shot down, in favor of a clever and much simpler approach. Their idea was to use a swarm of tiny, toylike microdrones, each equipped with a small battery-powered jammer. These would be dumped out the back of a distant aircraft and would fly right up into the radar beam, where their small jammers would still be effective. These microdrones would also be so numerous that the enemy could never shoot them all down.

This example illustrates the SCO's special genius: devising brand-new upgrades for existing weapons like fighters and bombers, thereby creating new capabilities while saving time and money, and simplifying the logistics and training processes.

Here's another illustration. The Navy had a superb ship-to-air missile designed to shoot down Iranian, Russian, or Chinese cruise missiles attacking ships. SCO figured out how to enable the same missiles and launch systems to destroy enemy ships, too. Suddenly the American missile became a double threat, both on offense and on defense. The idea may sound simple, but like many elegant inventions, it simply hadn't been imagined before. In a similar spirit, SCO figured out ways to fire missile defense interceptors out of artillery barrels, to launch anti-ship missiles from Army rocket launchers, and to drop huge loads of small bombs from cargo planes. In all these cases, SCO wasn't pushing technological frontiers. Instead, it was bridging the valley of death by bringing existing technology rapidly to the battlefield.

I take special satisfaction in spotting young people with talent. In Will Roper, I hit a gold mine.

Building Bridges to Silicon Valley

The Pentagon has a long history as an incubator of technological breakthroughs, and as I've explained, DOD is investing heavily in developing the new high-tech weapons of war that changing circumstances demand. But experience shows that it's risky to assume that the technologies conceived inside the five-sided box will be enough to guarantee American supremacy. This is the third big gap we needed to bridge to achieve the technological transition demanded by the age of CRIKT.

Consider, for example, the story of the digital-radio frequency memory (DRFM) chip that I recounted back in Chapter 2. This electronic technology with a host of applications was originally developed in the United States—though not mainly in the Pentagon or even at a defense contracting firm. Instead, it was originally applied in consumer products like cell phones and Wi-Fi devices, which is why the Chinese had access to them. Not until the People's Liberation Army began using DRFM chips as ultrasophisticated jammers did the DOD realize that we needed to begin deploying them as well.

The lesson is clear: if the American defense establishment is going to maintain a technological edge over the world's other great military powers, we need to do a better job of staying connected to the global innovation engine that is driving breakthroughs in every sphere of technology. That means that we need to nurture strong connections between the private sector and the DOD. Otherwise, we run the risk that many more breakthroughs like the DRFM chip may end up getting snatched from under our noses by an overseas adversary—and used against us on the battlefield.

To ensure that the DOD has the ability to stay at the forefront of technological change, one of my core goals as SecDef was to build—and in some cases to rebuild—solid bridges between the Pentagon and America's technology community. The effort started with a visit to Silicon Valley that I made early in my tenure as secretary. (Later I discovered that I was the first SecDef to make that trip in almost twenty years.) Subsequently, our department redoubled its efforts to forge new connections with America's many unrivaled hubs of innovation—not only in Silicon Valley, but also in technology strongholds including Seattle, Boston, Austin, and places in between.

In 2015, I created the Defense Innovation Unit—Experimental (DIU-X)—to help build bridges between the Pentagon and commercial technology firms, including start-ups. Initially, I allowed DIU-X to be organized and staffed by the Pentagon's research and engineering arm. This quickly proved to be a mistake. The first director was one of the DOD's best in-house technology leaders but had little history with Silicon Valley or the commercial tech community at large. As a result, in its early days, DIU-X tended to be seen as dedicated to training freewheeling techies in the government way of doing things—just the opposite of my intent.

As the techies would say, it was time to declare a "fast failure." I rebooted DIU-X with a new director and a direct reporting line to me as SecDef, with Eric Rosenbach helping to ensure that urgent issues got through to me promptly. The director of DIU-X 2.0 was the remarkable Raj Shah, a successful entrepreneur who was senior director of strategy at Palo Alto Networks, a firm based in Santa Clara, California. Shah is also a former F-16 pilot in the Air National Guard.

Shah had the right stuff we'd been looking for. Under the leadership of Shah and his deputy Doug Beck, a naval officer and executive vice president at Apple, within months DIU-X had conducted events in nine states and connected with companies in twenty-two more. DIU-X closed five project deals within three months—light speed by traditional DOD standards—and it had another twenty-two projects in the pipeline. DIU-X had solicited proposals for funding in such categories as microsatellites and advanced analytics, leveraging the ongoing revolutions in commercial space and machine learning to transform how the Pentagon uses space-based tools and advanced data processing to provide critical situational awareness to forces around the world and add resilience to our national space architecture. In all these ways, DIU-X had expanded the DOD's access to the creative brilliance of Silicon Valley—an essential complement to the research we continue to do internally at agencies like DARPA.

Before his departure from DOD in early 2018, Shah had gone on to expand DIU-X from a single outpost in Silicon Valley to include offices in Boston and Austin.

As of August 2018, DIU-X is no longer officially considered "experimental." The DOD issued a statement in that month saying, "DIUX has generated meaningful outcomes for the department and is a proven, valuable asset." So the word *Experimental* and the letter *X* have been dropped from the group's name, which is now known simply as the Defense Innovation Unit (DIU).

In April 2016, I launched another bridge-building program. This was the Defense Innovation Board (DIB), comprising a group of prominent technology leaders chosen for their records of innovation and their ability to suggest new approaches that might be applicable to defense. The members I recruited included, among other brilliant thinkers, Eric Schmidt, executive chairman of Alphabet (parent company of Google); Jeff Bezos of Amazon; Reid Hoffman, cofounder of LinkedIn; Walter Isaacson, CEO of the Aspen Institute and biographer of Albert Einstein, Steve Jobs, and Leonardo da Vinci; Jennifer Pahlka, founder of Code for America; Admiral William H. McRaven, who commanded the special ops raid that led to the death of Osama bin Laden; and Eric Lander, human genome mapper.

The impetus for creating DIB came from a couple of major shifts in the culture of the American tech community over the past few generations. These shifts have impacted the relationships among the technology sector, the business sector, and the defense sector.

We talk a lot these days about "disruptive" technologies like the Internet. But the scientists of the Greatest Generation were proud to have created the original "disruptive" defense technology: nuclear weapons. That technology had ended World War II and deterred a third world war through almost fifty years of an East-West standoff. But the flipside of that coin was an existential danger to humanity. Recognizing both bad and good, those same scientists—coming at the challenge from various ideological and political directions—accordingly devoted themselves in the years following to developing arms control and nonproliferation as new fields of innovative endeavor; to missile defense and civil defense; to making strong contributions to the intelligence systems that were needed to monitor arms control agreements; and to reactor safety to make the accompanying revolution in nuclear power safer. This culture, combining technology with public responsibility, is the one I saw around me when I entered the world of physics.

The generation of tech leaders that came shortly thereafter was very different. Today's tech culture, including what is most associated with Silicon Valley but is actually pervasive in digital tech (though not the rest of tech), grew out of the counterculture and libertarian movements of later decades. This is a very different kind of social impulse from the one that guided the Manhattan Project generation. It is inherently distrustful of government and believes that public good and public purpose will somehow emerge through a popular and supposedly freer mechanism.

I won't pretend to understand or share this ethos, but it is still the prevailing one among not only the founders, but also many (though by no means all) of the employees of the tech companies today. It contributes to a gap between the Pentagon and Silicon Valley that has weakened our ability to take full advantage of the newest technologies with potential defense applications. I wanted to reach across this gap.

Another, related shift has impacted the attitudes of business leaders to the American defense establishment.

During World War II and into the Cold War era, most major companies in the United States behaved as if helping to defend the nation was an integral part of their corporate mission. Businesses like Ford and General Motors, DuPont and Westinghouse, Bell Telephone and Intel did not need to be told that their help was needed to defeat the Axis and deter the Soviet Union.

Today, we don't face a national emergency on the scale of World War II. But we continue to face threats from a hostile world, and technological tools to respond to those threats are as important as ever. Yet there's no longer a clear understanding that U.S. companies have some obligation to support the nation's defense effort. With their multinational reach, most high-tech companies naturally don't view themselves as solely U.S. companies, and their CEOs often come from a post-Vietnam generation that knows very little about the DOD and its operations.

That's why I brought people like Eric Schmidt, Reid Hoffman, and Jeff Bezos into the Pentagon and said, "Get to know us. In return, we'll be respectful of your culture, too." I arranged for these executives to spend time with airmen in Nevada, sailors aboard ships, soldiers and special operators on the East Coast, and troops deployed to the Middle East.

As a result, they developed a deeper appreciation for the importance of the DOD and its mission. They already recognized that the blanket of security we provide to them (and to the entire U.S. economy) is what makes it possible for them to operate in peace and safety in their enclaves in California, Massachusetts, Texas, and other locations, focusing on imaginative consumer uses for the latest technology. If they hope to continue to enjoy a stable and peaceful environment in which to operate, they can help us by providing their advice and ideas, and by giving us access to some of their most creative and brilliant thinkers.

To mix it up further between commercial tech and the Pentagon, I also sought to create a variety of on-ramps and off-ramps to stints in the Pentagon, as well as stints in tech for "guvvies." For example, we adopted an idea originally suggested by President Obama with the help of Todd Park and D. J. Patil, who became tech advisors for me as well. This was the Defense Digital Service (DDS), which invited brilliant geeks to take on top-secret challenges in fields like cyber-warfare. DDS was assigned an office suite in the E ring of the Pentagon. Each volunteer came in to do a tour of a few months or a year, and they were given permission to import their Silicon Valley culture into their corner of DOD. It was interesting to see young people in ponytails and gray hoodies walking through the halls of the Pentagon alongside ramrod-straight officers in their uniforms.

To run this program, I recruited Chris Lynch, an entrepreneur who had founded three successful tech companies. Now in his third year at the Pentagon, Chris is helping to guide the development of a cloud-based data system for DOD, which he has dubbed the Joint Enterprise Defense Infrastructure (JEDI). As you might guess from the acronym, Chris is also a devoted *Star Wars* fan.

Maintaining and expanding our partnerships with companies and individuals from the world of commercial technology will require sustained effort and openness on the part of the DOD. Since the department and the technology community have different missions and somewhat different perspectives, there are likely to be culture clashes from time to time. Leaders on both sides of the divide should expect and tolerate disagreement, but work together nevertheless for breakthrough ideas and real transformation in service of a common public purpose.

From an Airplane to a Network Node: Designing the New Stealth Bomber

A more traditional but still signature technology project of the CRIKT era that I spent a lot of time on as undersecretary is the design of the new stealth bomber. The venerable B-2 stealth bomber, still in service today, was designed back in the 1970s. The new stealth bomber, currently designated the B-21 Raider, is expected to be ready by 2025. It will have a useful lifetime of a few decades; and as technology evolves, it may end up being the last generation of stealth bomber—just as the Joint Strike Fighter I worked on may end up being the last generation of tactical aircraft. But in the meantime, the B-21 is essential to strategy in the CRIKT age, and very different from earlier bombers.

As undersecretary, I had a dream team working with me on the conception of the B-21 program. It included Vice Chairman Sandy Winnefeld; systems analysis head Christine Fox; the Navy and Air Force acquisition executives Sean Stackley and Dave VanBuren, both world-class experts at their craft; and my principal deputy, Frank Kendall. Since the Air Force will own and operate the aircraft, critical participants were General Mark Welsh, an air warfare expert whom I later named chief of staff of the Air Force; and Dave Hamilton, who ran the Air Force's stealth office.

Since there were very few people with security clearance for this project, a lot fell on us, and we met frequently to go through all the details. The first big challenge involved the air frame itself. Making an aircraft stealthy (that is, virtually undetectable by radar and other surveillance systems) is less a matter of grand design than of meticulous attention to countless details. Every seam where two parts fit together and every corner of the inlets of the engines is a potential radar-reflecting giveaway. The whole aircraft needs to be looked at from end to end to eliminate these potential flaws. What's more, this inspection must be done at all radar frequencies and from all angles. And since aircraft will increasingly be detected by telescopes as well, their visible and infrared signatures have an importance that they never had before.

Other ingredients were just as important and just as difficult to engineer as the air frame. These included jammers and other electronic warfare tools to fool radars and complement the plane's basic stealthiness by blinding or fooling enemy radar systems and missiles. They could be onboard, aboard separate vehicles flying near the stealth aircraft, or trailed on a wire behind the bomber.

In addition, the new bomber needs to be in touch with all the many intelligence sensors that can help it, whether they be aboard other aircraft, on satellites, or in the great intelligence processing centers back in Washington, D.C. All this information has to get to the bomber in flight, which means it needs to have stealthy, but very high bandwidth, communications. We experimented with using lasers rather than satellite radios for this purpose. And finally, in today's air defense environment, you can't just drop a bomb out the belly of an airplane and expect it to survive to the target. Defenders will shoot down the individual bombs or missiles fired from the airplane, so these, too, must be stealthy, as well as being smart, super accurate, and, in some cases, designed to penetrate buried targets.

Given the importance of the digital connections that make the new stealth bomber so powerful, it might better be described as a node in a network rather than a traditional airplane.

You might ask why we didn't opt to develop an unmanned bomber using the new powers of artificial intelligence (AI). The answer is that the time for such an approach has not yet come. Given the complexity of tasks involved in gathering intelligence, processing electronic warfare information, keeping track of navigation and battle plans, diverting to targets that move during flight according to real-time intelligence, and much more, replacing the pilot with an artificial intelligence system is not possible today. That will require something more like what specialists call "general AI," which has all the suppleness of the human mind, rather than "narrow AI," which is limited to performing one or a few specified tasks.

One day, that will be possible—and when it happens, the U.S. military will need to lead the way. But for the B-21 generation, AI assists the air crew, but cannot replace it.

Cyberspace: The Newest Battlefield

Another technology challenge that I particularly focused on during my tenure as undersecretary, deputy, and SecDef was the threat of cyber-warfare. It's an unfortunate reality that the relative de-emphasis of high-end military technology development by the United States from 1989 to 2010 created an opening for potential adversaries to play catch-up—including in cyberspace. Chinese and Russian programs to deploy information technology aggressively against American interests have followed, including, most notoriously, attempts to interfere with U.S. elections. But even before Russia's meddling in 2016, it was clear that we mustn't let such efforts go unchallenged.

I divided the cyber issue into three parts: defense, which focused on making sure that DOD networks were not penetrated and DOD information was not compromised; offense, which referred to using cyber as a weapon, especially against military and command-and-control targets; and homeland defense, which was about supporting civil authorities in their efforts to provide cybersecurity for the United States as a whole, including businesses, critical infrastructure, other government agencies, and ordinary citizens.

I'll start with cyber-defense. It's an extremely difficult problem to solve, because the core items that make up cyber-systems, right down to the design of microchips and the basic protocols that govern the Internet, were not designed with security in mind. This helps to explain why nobody is really any good at cybersecurity, as you can tell from seeing corporations routinely hacked despite the millions they spend on security consultants. Offense, not defense, is dominant in cyber-warfare.

Moreover, the DOD, like many big corporations, maintains a patchwork of hundreds of networks, all of different vintages and run by people with varied levels of technical talent and sensitivity to their vulnerabilities. The department's information technology workforce numbers almost one hundred thousand people. Most are not deeply knowledgeable regarding defensive preparations. But all these networks are linked, meaning that the weaknesses of the most decrepit and vulnerable can affect the whole. The audits and surprise checks we did during my years at the Pentagon, in which a "red team" would be dispatched to try to penetrate a network, routinely showed ridiculously high levels of success.

As SecDef, I never used the desktop terminals in my office that connected me to the classified, secret, and top-secret gateways of those networks. Instead, I used a specially secured telephone and conducted as many of my conversations as possible in person. The main reason was that my words would inevitably be forwarded (often with good intentions) to many "interested" recipients that I didn't intend to have privy to my thinking. But I was also constantly aware of the dangers of malicious leaks and of enemy penetration of our networks, which I always assumed might be vulnerable to such assaults.

I'd begun to focus intently on cyber-defense when I was deputy secretary in 2011 and 2012. Luckily for me, the assistant secretary of defense for global security and homeland defense at that time was Eric Rosenbach, a noted cybersecurity expert and author of books and articles on the subject—the same Eric Rosenbach who later became my chief of staff.

One of the first cases that Eric and I worked on together involved extensive Chinese hacking of American industry, making technology theft possible. The implications for our defense companies were clear. Eric managed to maneuver DOD into the position of leading the first-ever interagency group to tackle this problem. He also authored our department's first cybersecurity strategy.

One key assumption of our cybersecurity strategy was the recognition that it was simply impossible to stop all penetrations, given the inherent vulnerability of computer networks in general and our ramshackle "network of networks" in particular.

An example of the problem was the Navy's network. The Navy had been one of the first services to go digital in the 1990s, which made it very forward-looking, but as a consequence, its network infrastructure at the root level was badly outdated. It became clear to Eric sometime in 2013 that Navy networks had likely been compromised by a foreign nation. The Navy set about trying to clean up the problem, but this was a complex and slow process.

The issue came to a head the night we were scheduled to carry out a strike on Syrian chemical-weapons facilities. In my role as deputy secretary, I was tidying up every last detail of the plan when Eric came to me with a disturbing thought. What if the attackers of the Navy network took down the network in an effort to complicate the strike? This might be the day when the vulnerability of the Navy network suddenly assumed real-world operational consequences.

I called in the head of Navy cyber and the head of CYBERCOM, which was the joint subcommand charged with addressing conflict in cyberspace. I asked them for their assessment. To my dismay, both said they did not have one. It was a sad testament to our lack of preparedness.

In the end, the strike on Syrian chemical facilities never happened. This was the famous instance in which President Obama decided not to enforce his Syria "red line," because the Russians had secured Syria's agreement to destroy all its chemical weapons, which Obama believed was a better alternative. As deputy, I was not watching the diplomacy that night; instead, my job focused on the strike itself, which I thought was very likely to occur. The vulnerability of the network didn't hurt us that time, but the potential for such harm was still undeniable.

It was clear that better cyber hygiene and defenses were essential. To drive this home, I used one of the tactics I've relied on to get people's attention: namely, calling everyone together on a Saturday. This is a pain in the neck for everyone, and I did it deliberately to underscore that I was deadly serious about the issue. I asked all the joint chiefs, the combatant commanders, and the commanders of the major field agencies to come to my conference room to examine the state of hygiene of their respective networks.

In advance, I created a matrix-style tracking chart. The rows were the various networks used by the people in the room, and the columns were the fifteen to twenty major items of network hygiene that any good IT system manager would know—for example, whether firewalls were in place, whether network administration and exfiltration of data were carefully controlled, and so forth. Each box was colored red, yellow, or green, representing the quality of security features on each factor for every incorporated network.

The first meeting showed a bleak canvas of red in one row after another. This made the officials in the room very nervous, which was exactly the effect I'd intended. When the meeting ended, I announced that we were going to conduct follow-up meetings every quarter. "Everybody in this room is responsible for turning all the red squares green," I declared. "I want to see steady progress."

I'm sure this approach was annoying to many. But it was the only way to drive home the importance of the challenge—and it did produce results.

A second approach to reducing vulnerability besides hygiene is to train forces to operate through a cyberattack on warfighting networks. Thus, I instructed the commands to practice blacking-out parts of their networks in the course of conducting operations to see how military effectiveness could still be retained despite the loss or disruption of these networks. Perfect performance is not possible here, but with some practice a lot can be achieved.

I also advocated using deception to undermine the confidence of those who steal information from our less-than-perfectly secured networks. This is easily done by creating some attractively titled files that contain information contaminated in subtle ways—for example, by changing occasional digits in numbers, moving decimal points, or mixing up miles and kilometers in a list of distances. When our adversaries realize that some of the information has been tampered with, they come to doubt the accuracy of all the information they've stolen.

I first became intrigued by this technique back in 1993, when I was establishing defense and intelligence relationships with the fifteen brand-new countries carved out of the old Soviet Union. At a reception in one of these new capitals—I believe it was in Belarus—a drunken colonel staggered up to me and angrily announced, "Your boss Bill Perry ruined my career." The story, as I pieced it together from what the colonel told me and the details that Bill later provided, was this: Back in the late 1970s, when Bill was the acquisition czar, he became aware that the Soviets were clandestinely trying to procure advanced computers made by Digital Equipment Corporation for use in their nuclear weapons program. Bill decided to let them acquire the computers, but to infect the software with what today would be called a virus. After the computers were smuggled back into the USSR and installed in a secret weapons lab, they began spitting out rubbish.

The colonel at the reception had been in charge of that covert acquisitions system, and the American trick had cost him any hope of a future promotion. It may be an old trick, but it's still an effective one that should be part of our ongoing efforts to defend against cyber-infiltration.

The last element of defense is the problem of the insider threat, exemplified most spectacularly by Edward Snowden, the CIA employee and contractor who stole and published classified information about U.S. surveillance programs. Today he is living in Moscow to escape the criminal charges he would face in the United States.

The Snowden case was an example of gross and completely idiotic violations of basic network security protocols. Snowden had much more access than was necessary for his job. He also used tricks to obtain passwords and system-administrator accesses to which he was not entitled. And he was able to remove enormous quantities of data from the network without being detected. All this violated basic security principles designed to minimize insider threats.

This infuriated me. I thought it was a lapse of command responsibility by the leaders at CYBERCOM and the National Security Agency. In 2007, after missiles with actual nuclear warheads were accidentally flown from one base to another in the belief that they contained only dummy training warheads, Bob Gates fired the Air Force secretary and chief of staff—an example of an officer being held appropriately responsible for a serious error on his watch. But nobody was held accountable in the Snowden case or in several subsequent cases of insider compromise less publicized than Snowden's but also damaging to our national interests. I advised President Obama, with the agreement of DNI Jim Clapper, to hold the NSA director responsible, but he did not.

Just as infuriating to me is the fact that some people consider Snowden a "whistle-blower" and even a hero. This is absurd. There is a body of thinking regarding ethical whistle-blowing that I respect, but Snowden abided by none of its principles. He revealed that the United States tries to collect information on potential antagonists and criminals, and that it does so using cyber-tools as well as other means. Of course it does. We would be derelict in our duties if we did not, and it's ridiculous to think that this came as a surprise to any serious observer of world affairs. An ethical whistle-blower might question aspects of how this is done without publicly exposing any and all of our methods.

Furthermore, a true whistle-blower who is concerned about potentially illegal or unethical behaviors would first have attempted to call attention to them through legitimate channels, seeking correction of the problems. There's no record that Snowden ever made any such effort. Instead, in an act of supreme arrogance, he simply chose to violate a public trust without any warrant from the 330 million Americans who gave him that trust.

The result was real harm to national security, to U.S. international diplomacy, and to U.S. companies. By every test, Snowden fails the standard for ethical whistle-blowing. And, for what it's worth, I have held top-secret communications intelligence clearances since 1980, and I have never seen or heard about foreign intelligence collection being used for coercion or repression or to embarrass an American.

As SecDef, I once got a letter from a university professor seriously offering to host a debate between me and Edward Snowden. She actually thought that the Secretary of Defense might agree to a debate with a fugitive traitor who would be subject to jailing the moment he set foot on U.S. soil.

My assistant laughed and said that she would obviously decline the invitation. I said, "No, don't do that. Instead, say that the secretary accepts with pleasure an invitation to debate Edward Snowden, but it must be in person in the United States." That was the end of that idea.

Cyber-offense—the Pentagon's second mission in cyberspace—was a different matter. When I was undersecretary and deputy secretary, it was a sensitive topic verging on taboo. But the new cyber-strategy I released early in my tenure as SecDef—authored mainly by Eric Rosenbach—made it clear that DOD would henceforth regard cyber-offense as a crucial tool for protecting U.S. security. Eric and I agreed that this was long overdue. The strategy document included a lengthy discussion of the concept of deterrence as it applied to cyber, including the sensitive issue of how to retaliate and respond if someone else attacked us first.

Later, when the combatant commanders seemed reluctant to develop cyber-offensive capabilities as part of their war-planning tasks, I directed that $300 million to $400 million in the budget be taken from other purposes and dedicated to cyber-offense capabilities. In effect, I forced the strategy upon the commanders.

People sometimes ask me whether a cyberattack on the United States is a "real" attack or not. My answer is simple: An attack is an attack. If harm is done to this country, I don't care what the method is. In my judgment, the United States should always retaliate and inflict punishment on the source of the attack.

As for the nature of the retaliation, that shouldn't be limited to the same methods used in the attack. After all, the 9/11 terrorists flew airliners into our buildings, but we didn't respond by flying airliners into their buildings. We bombed and invaded the country that gave them safe haven, and we hunted them down around the world. In the same way, I would not rule out any means for punishing a cyberattack on the United States, so long as the retaliation is proportional to the severity of the attack itself.

The third element in DOD's work on cybersecurity is support to civil authorities in defending the homeland from cyberattacks. This can be tricky because DOD has powerful capabilities in this area at NSA, CYBERCOM, and, especially, the cyber-units of the four armed services, but generally lacks the legal authority to use them. That authority rests with particular nondefense agencies, depending on how one classifies a particular event. Is a cyber-breach an attack? A crime? A disaster? A regulatory issue? The answer is often unclear.

Because of this tangle of jurisdictions, DOD needs to cooperate with our sister agencies—just as we do, for example, when we provide helicopters and uniformed personnel to assist the Federal Emergency Management Agency in the wake of a devastating flood or hurricane. If an event is deemed a matter of critical infrastructure, disaster management, or regulation, authority generally rests with the Department of Homeland Security. If it is deemed a criminal act, responsibility rests with law enforcement agencies like the FBI. Other harms are handled by departments that have responsibility for particular elements of our national infrastructure—for example, the Department of Energy, which deals with the electrical grid and the atomic laboratories at Livermore and Los Alamos. As in any situation where authority and responsibility are diffused, coordination and clarity in dealing with cyber-challenges are difficult to achieve. My guidance to the DOD was always, "Don't contest the authorities. Just help out in such a way that the impact on readiness for war can be minimized."

Probably the most outrageous cyberattack the United States has suffered from overseas is the 2016 Russian assault on the security of the presidential election. This involved both leaks of stolen emails and the exploitation for propaganda purposes of social media platforms like Facebook and Twitter, which looked the other way while these misdeeds were occurring. In my role as SecDef, I watched this attack unfold and participated in discussions about how the administration ought to respond.

Beginning in the late spring and building through the summer and fall of 2016, a very considerable body of information relayed by Director of National Intelligence Jim Clapper, CIA Director John Brennan, and FBI Director Jim Comey showed with absolute clarity that the Russians were, indeed, trying to hack the U.S. election and that most of their efforts were directed against Hillary Clinton, if not explicitly promoting Donald Trump. This included some highly sensitive items indicating direct complicity by Putin himself.

Joe Dunford and I were among a small group of people with whom this information was consistently shared. We never thought that enough was being done to protest these actions, either privately or publicly. Political considerations played a significant role, and in those discussions Dunford and I were (appropriately) not included. For example, Denis McDonough had shared some of this information with Speaker Paul Ryan and Majority Leader Mitch McConnell and asked for a bipartisan condemnation of the Russian behavior. Unfortunately, leaders in both parties appeared to judge that revelation and action could backfire on them. They insisted that the statement be watered down, and by the time it was finally released (on September 29, 2016), it was too late to have sufficient impact on our efforts to protect the election.

For this and other reasons, the Obama administration didn't do enough, in my opinion. So far, the Trump administration hasn't done enough, either. Neither has Congress. And as the potential for future assaults looms over the 2020 election, the fragmented nature of our national systems for conducting and protecting elections has complicated the challenge of responding. Without strong, determined leadership from Washington, it's hard to see how coordinated and effective actions can be mounted by an array of actors that includes fifty separate state election agencies, a multitude of privately run databases and communications networks, and the giant social media companies like Facebook and Twitter, which have been weaponized by foreign entities eager to sow discord and disinformation among the electorate.

We're far from having solved the problem of cyberassaults on American democracy.

Organizing Cyber Command

One managerial issue related to high-tech warfare that I didn't finish solving was the structure of Cyber Command. When I became SecDef, CYBERCOM was a subordinate part of Strategic Command, or STRATCOM, and had been so since it was created back in Don Rumsfeld's time. CYBERCOM and the National Security Agency, though separate, were both run by a single four-star general or admiral. Increasingly, the officer in charge of CYBERCOM had tended to act and be treated independently of his nominal boss at STRATCOM. So I was frequently asked, why not elevate CYBERCOM to be a combatant command in its own right?

I didn't think that CYBERCOM's subordination to STRATCOM mattered much in practice, since the Maryland headquarters of CYBERCOM (and NSA) did have de facto freedom from STRATCOM's Nebraska headquarters. I was more concerned about the issue of who was in charge of these two security agencies.

I was also concerned about the possibility that the elevation of CYBERCOM might trigger calls for a separation of CYBERCOM from NSA. I didn't want that, since, for now, we didn't have enough good cyber-experts to populate two separate organizations. Also, I feared that separation might give rise to the suggestion that NSA be given a civilian rather than a military leader, like most other national intelligence agencies. I favored maintaining military leadership of NSA, since this would guarantee that its communications intercepts and the language and cyber-skills would be fully dedicated to the needs of commanders and troops on the battlefield.

I was concerned about what I'd seen happening at most of the other national intelligence agencies—for example, the National Reconnaissance Office, which develops spy satellites; and the National Geospatial Intelligence Agency, which operates satellite and drone photography. These agencies have civilian directors, and as a result, they sometimes give similar weight to battlefield needs and important but distracting nonmilitary needs—for example, attending White House meetings on broad foreign-policy issues. I thought that the director of national intelligence could handle these tasks. Important as the politico-military collection and analyses are, a lot of the day-to-day resources were needed for military plans and operations.

Moreover, to the extent that the elevation of CYBERCOM would signal confidence in the command and its leadership, this was not warranted. CYBERCOM had failed to deliver much help in the campaign against ISIS. And then there was the terrible job that the leaders of CYBERCOM and NSA had done in preventing multiple security disasters caused by insiders like Edward Snowden. Another of several examples, this one fully disclosed: the case of Harold T. Martin, a longtime NSA analyst arrested by the FBI, who had some of the most sensitive hacking tools of the U.S. government on his home computer because he wanted to be able to work on weekends without having to go into the office! From there they had been stolen by foreign cyber-actors and strewn over the Internet. These and other flagrant security compromises were endemic in NSA. I hesitated to elevate CYBERCOM until its leaders improved their performance.

But despite these hesitations, I finally decided to recommend the elevation of CYBERCOM to President Obama, along with some moves to strictly focus the leadership of CYBERCOM and NSA on security and counterintelligence. At first, I set out to manage the reorganization on my own, but the president brought me up short and insisted—appropriately— that I get Director of National Intelligence Jim Clapper to agree, which he did. But by then the 2016 election and a presidential transition were looming, and the clock ran out.

However, the Trump administration, using the planning that Joe Dunford and I had done, decided to go ahead with elevating CYBER-COM to a full and independent combatant command, and the change took effect in May 2018. It has not yet led to calls for CYBERCOM to be separated from NSA or for NSA to have a civilian director separate from the military commander of CYBERCOM, so my concerns on that front have not been realized. The elevation of CYBERCOM to a full combatant command seems to have gone smoothly.

A Space Force?

While the CYBERCOM/NSA management issue bubbled, another proposal kept surfacing year after year: the idea of a Space Force. Military use of space was one of my early specialties in defense technology work. I had space program security clearance starting in 1980, and I even made a little extra money by teaching a course on space technology to NSA employees in the 1980s.

During my tenure as SecDef, military space operations, like cyber operations, were subordinated to STRATCOM. Shortly after I left office, Congress passed a law (part of the National Defense Authorization Act for fiscal year 2019) pulling them out from under STRATCOM and creating around them a new combatant command, SPACECOM, which would take its place alongside the other regional and functional CO-COMs, just as was done with CYBERCOM. I supported this move. It's the rare case of a congressional tinkering with the organizational chart that does more good than harm.

But there were always persistent calls from a small group of Capitol Hill and Air Force civilians to go much further and create a Space Force—a fifth armed service alongside the Army, Navy, Marines, and Air

Force. In the military lexicon, a command and an armed service are completely different things. While a COCOM writes plans for and commands wars and other operations, a service recruits, trains, and equips forces and then supplies them to COCOMs. For example, the Army supplies ground units for service in Iraq to CENTCOM. Turning SPACECOM into Space Force would turn a "force user" into a "force supplier."

This is almost the opposite of what is needed—which is why it is so unfortunate that the advocates of Space Force apparently got to a less-experienced President Trump, leading to a sudden tweet. President Obama had been repeatedly tempted by the same idea. He held several meetings about it in the Situation Room during 2016. Every time I thought I had dissuaded him from creating a Space Force, another meeting on the topic would pop up on the calendar.

It's easy to see why the idea would have some appeal to both President Obama and President Trump, and I wholeheartedly shared their enthusiasm for giving more emphasis and coherence to military uses of space. But precisely what is lacking to meet this objective is more *integration* of space capabilities with war plans and operations—COCOM business—not *segregation* into something separate. That's why a Space Force is not the solution to inadequate military use of space—in fact, it heads in exactly the opposite direction.

It's worth noting what "space forces" are and are not. Of the thousands of military spacecraft deployed by all nations, virtually none are weapons per se: they are support systems, providing ground sea, air, and submarine forces with services such as communications, navigation (GPS), mapping, meteorology, and warning of missile launches. So the satellites are, for the most part, not forces in their own right.

Since space systems support air, ground, and naval forces, each of the services has its own space program. Most of the expenses involved are not for satellites but for terminals and ground stations. The Army, for example, flies few of its own satellites but makes huge expenditures on ground terminals at fixed bases and on vehicles.

The SecDef manages two space programs, the "white" space program and the "black" space program. White space, managed through the services, covers activities that have traditionally been publicly acknowledged, like communications and navigation. Black space covers intelligence satellites of all kinds, whose very existence was formerly unacknowledged and which are still mostly classified. Black space is managed through the National Reconnaissance Office, over which the SecDef shares responsibility with the director of national intelligence.

While most of the military space effort is support, there are a few true weapons for use in or against satellites. Russia and China both have rockets that can climb into orbit and smash satellites. The United States could easily build such capabilities, though in general it is faster and more cost-efficient to negate an enemy satellite by blinding or confusing it from a transmitter on the ground.

The key point of managing military space operations is integrating all these capabilities with war plans and operations. For much of the history of the space age, these capabilities were seen mostly as peacetime aids. Little thought was given to their wartime use and vulnerabilities. As a result, space was too segregated from the mainstream military for my liking.

Take a hypothetical conflict with China over Taiwan, for example. Detailed plans for the use of every U.S. aircraft, ship, and brigade were included in the relevant war plans, and all these resources would move and fight with support from space. But what would happen if China neutralized critical communications satellites over the Pacific? And how would we counter Chinese satellites being used to target our aircraft carriers? Answers to these questions required Pacific Command to integrate space into its operations and its planning.

Rather than creating a Space Force, which emphasizes segregation instead of integration, we need an institution more like the Joint Interagency Combined Space Operations Center (JICSPOC) I established in Colorado Springs when I was deputy. Headed by a talented space engineer I'd spotted, JICSPOC contained a small number of our best military-space thinkers charged with working through the major war plans in painstaking, minute-by-minute detail, helping the COCOMs use relevant space capabilities and planning around their possible vulnerabilities. It has since been renamed the National Space Defense Center.

Another problem with the Space Force idea is that new Pentagon bureaucracies always spend too little time and resources on the "tooth" of military operations and too much on the "tail"—designing offices, crafting organizational charts, and organizing meetings. The ensuing complications would verge on the comical. Members of Congress would vie to have the headquarters built in their district. There would be a new anthem to compose and new uniforms to design (although all the best martial colors are already taken, unfortunately). All this would be amusing but also costly and distracting—yet another reason I hope, and believe, that Congress will not create a fifth armed services but instead a CO-COM dedicated to space.

Ethical Issues Regarding AI and Robot Warfare

People appropriately raise questions about the ethical dimensions of applying new technologies to defense. Viewing myself as an heir of the scientists who developed nuclear weapons—and then dedicated themselves to decades of work designing systems to reduce the likelihood that those weapons would ever be used—I take such questions seriously.

Consider, for example, the issue of how artificial intelligence can and should be used in warfare. In my last year as SecDef, the question I would get most often in a wide-open press availability would be about autonomous weapons. How could and should these weapons be used? Does their use reduce the sense of responsibility that humans rightly feel when they make the choice to take a life?

In response, I would inform people that, way back in 2012, I had promulgated a directive on that subject that governed the conduct of DOD. It stated that for every system capable of executing or assisting the use of lethal force, there must be a human being making the decision. That is, there would be no literal autonomy. That doesn't mean that computers won't aid decision-making and carry out tasks, or that a human will be "in the loop" like another line of code. It means that the design must enable human accountability and responsibility. So that is how things stand on the books.

I was motivated to issue that directive, in part, by imagining myself standing in front of the press the morning after, let's say, an air strike that had mistakenly taken the lives of civilian women and children. Imagine further that I tried to deflect responsibility by saying, "The machine made a mistake." I would be crucified—and rightly so. We can foresee similar questions being raised about a driverless car that kills a pedestrian.

I believe that accountability and the transparency to promote it are the key issues for the designers of artificial intelligence systems. Some will say that AI systems may not enable the tracing of the method of decision that underlies an algorithm's recommendation. This is in fact a very deep question, since machine reasoning may differ in kind from human reasoning. The justification for an AI-assisted lethal decision will require building it into the system design. Some scientists are sure to object. But I've been involved for a long time in the management of complex technological systems, and I've often heard the words "It can't be done" used where "We never thought of that" would be more appropriate. To AI innovators, I would urge that if you want your algorithm to be adopted, you had better make it transparently accountable. If this requires an adjustment in design, then make that adjustment.

I also need to say something about U.S. companies or their employees who resist work on artificial intelligence for the DOD. This happened recently at Google, where the company leadership simply gave in to the employee complaints. I imagine what I would say to these employees in a Google town hall or if I was part of the Google leadership. I'd tell them they should think about and reconsider their decision.

First of all, they should understand that the American military is governed by the memorandum I have described. Our nation takes its values to the battlefield.

Second, and more fundamentally, who better than technologists like them, who are immersed in this technology, to steer the Pentagon in the right direction? Shouldn't they be like the atomic scientists and help find solutions rather than sitting on the sidelines? If they opt out, they may not like the people who end up making the decisions in their place.

Third, I'd ask them whether they're comfortable working for the People's Liberation Army. Because Google does indeed work in and for China. China is a communist dictatorship in which boundaries between the private and public sectors scarcely exist. There is no getting around the fact that working in China is working indirectly for the People's

Liberation Army or that all of Google's work is available to the PLA. And the Chinese state is openly applying AI to the tasks of mass surveillance, "social scoring," and repression.

Finally, I'd point out that their company is headquartered in the United States. Their business is protected by U.S. law. They drive on U.S. roads, are protected by U.S. police and firefighters, benefit from the U.S. systems of health and education, and enjoy the freedoms that the U.S. military helps to guarantee. Does none of this instill a smidgen of responsibility in the employees of Google?

I respect the ethical concerns that drive the tough questions that the Google employees ask. But I would also submit that working for the U.S. government and particularly the U.S. defense establishment can be a powerful way of contributing to the betterment of human society— certainly more than some of the other programs that most tech employees work on without a second thought.

Because of my background as a scientist, focusing strongly on modernizing and enhancing the technological tools used by DOD came easily to me. It's an area in which we've let our long-held advantage be whittled away by determined and increasingly sophisticated foreign powers. During my years in the department, we did a good job of renewing our efforts to make sure that the U.S. military is second to none when it comes to using advanced technology to deter and defeat our adversaries.

Going forward, all the new long-term investments in technology that DOD has made must be cultivated and allowed to bear fruit. In times when the government is cash-strapped, there will always be the temptation to uproot new projects to protect established, more traditional defense spending. DOD leaders of today and tomorrow must resist that temptation. The payoff will be powerful new weapons systems and warfighting capabilities that will play a huge role in preventing—and in winning—the battles we'll face tomorrow.

PART 5

PEOPLE MATTER MOST

CHAPTER 13

CHOOSING LEADERS

When journalists, pundits, and ordinary citizens talk about the Department of Defense, they tend to focus on issues like spending, big weapons systems, and war strategies. Less widely discussed is the real secret behind the DOD's unmatched capabilities: its people.

With 2.8 million direct employees (and millions more in ancillary organizations, like defense contractors), the Pentagon is a huge employer. With the draft a thing of the past, all these employees must be recruited in the competitive marketplace for talent. Many are asked to give far more than employees of any other organization—and they overwhelmingly respond to this challenge. This helps to explain why whenever I listed my three highest priorities as SecDef—beginning with my acceptance speech in the Roosevelt Room of the White House—the first one I mentioned, even before the president, was always "the troops."

So it's appropriate to close this book with three chapters that focus on the people of the Pentagon, because they are the force that truly drives the greatness of this institution.

One of the most important jobs of the Secretary of Defense is to hire— and, when necessary, to fire—our nation's senior military leaders. There are sixteen crucial positions on that list, beginning with the chairman and vice chairman of the Joint Chiefs of Staff. Then there are the chiefs of staff themselves (chief of staff of the Army, chief of naval operations, commandant of the Marine Corps, chief of staff of the Air Force, and chief of the National Guard), and the commanders of the various combat

commands, from the Northern Command (NORTHCOM), which protects the security of the U.S. homeland, to the Transportation Command
(TRANSCOM), which controls the flow of people, supplies, and equipment wherever in the world they may be needed.

The tenures of these officers are fixed, so, barring a firing, the schedule on which promotions need to be made is predictable. When I became
SecDef, a glance at the calendar showed me that I would be naming officers to fill fifteen of these sixteen jobs before Obama left office. So I
knew from the start that picking the right candidates would be one of the
most consequential tasks I would face.

Therefore, at one of our earliest one-on-one meetings in the Oval Office, I suggested to the president how I would make my recommendations
to him. I told him I would give him my choice during one of our regular
meetings, allowing plenty of time for him to reflect on it. I further told
him that I would bring a second and third choice, and my reasons for
ranking the candidates as I had.

Obama agreed, and that's how we did it through each of those fifteen
appointments. For each candidate, I would present a short bio and a picture, and then walk the president through the candidate's experience and
qualifications. It is a tribute to the depth of the military bench that I was
able to bring the president three choices each time, though sometimes it
was a stretch to get a third candidate in the league of the first two. I was
never in doubt about my own recommendation, and in every case the
chairman of the Joint Chiefs of Staff shared my judgment—a detail that
Obama always asked about.

In every case, too, the president accepted my recommendation—
sometimes on the spot, occasionally after a few days of reflection. I imagined that, when it took a few days to get a decision, Obama's staff was also
researching the officer I recommended to make sure there wasn't anything questionable in the record. Of course, similar vetting had already
been exhaustively done by the services and my staff before I would even
think of bringing a candidate to the president.

Once I got the word from the president, I would call the candidate
and say, "I have recommended you for the job of X. Let me tell you the
reasons I gave the president for why he should approve you. You can

expect a call from him. Be yourself and tell him what you think. Call me afterward."

The only hiccup in this process during my tenure involved Joe Dunford. When people ask me about my best decision as SecDef, I say it was picking Joe Dunford as chairman of the Joint Chiefs of Staff. Joe was a Marines' Marine, having risen steadily through the ranks from his Dorchester, heart-of-Boston background. At the time I picked him, Joe had served as commandant of the Marine Corps for just a few months, so it meant upending both his life and the Corps', but I thought Joe was far and away the best officer to help me and the president make decisions about war and peace, and then implement them.

I had known Joe best when he was our commander in Afghanistan. It was a miserable period in the war. The leader of Afghanistan was Hamid Karzai, a narrow, paranoid, and spiteful man who not only displayed ingratitude for the U.S. and NATO presence in his country—without which he would have been dead within twenty-four hours—but openly disrespected U.S. troops. This was very hard for me to take and, as I've mentioned, it once even provoked a well-earned tongue-lashing from the normally self-controlled Obama.

Meanwhile, Joe had to work with the Afghan military and intelligence services to prosecute the campaign despite their appalling leadership. This took amazing diplomatic skill and the patience of Job on top of his battlefield acumen. It was a magnificent accomplishment on behalf of the country.

Saying yes to my request that he become chairman was not so easy for Joe. He loved being commandant of the Marine Corps, and his wife, Ellen, loved her role as the commandant's wife. Moreover, Joe had only recently returned from his hard tour of duty in Afghanistan. He was still working on reestablishing his life with Ellen and their daughters, and Ellen's mom was also going through a serious illness at the time. The grueling life of chairman, with its frequent travel, wasn't something he relished. He and Ellen accepted the call, but with real reluctance.

All this showed when it came time for us to meet President Obama in the White House for the announcement of Joe's selection. As Joe, Ellen, and I huddled with the president in the Oval Office, Ellen was a bit overwhelmed by the mixed emotions she was feeling. The president glanced at me, wondering whether she was okay. I nodded assurance, but Joe settled the matter. He gave Ellen a comforting hug, she smiled back at him, and the four of us went before the cameras and made the announcement.

The painful hiccup I referred to came the day after Dunford's nomination was announced. A reporter wrote a story suggesting that Joe was not my and the president's first choice. This was totally untrue—in fact, there was no one close to Joe Dunford in my estimation.

I was outraged at this story. Imagine how Joe, Ellen, and their family must have felt when they heard about it. My press aide confronted the reporter and his editor, only to get a weaselly reply saying that the information had come from "a source." This was a lie, since no one but Eric Rosenbach, Marty Dempsey, Susan Rice, and the president had known who I recommended, and none of them would have any reason to make up a story like this. I took pains to make sure that Joe knew the story was a complete fabrication, and Peter Cook made the same point with the other members of the press corps. Thankfully, no other reporters chose to repeat this nonsense.

Adjusting the Promotional Escalator

Picking the right people for the highest roles in the armed forces has never been easy. In an era of dramatic change, when traditional military culture needs to evolve without losing its historic strengths, the challenge may be trickier than ever. Happily, my three-plus decades of experience in the Pentagon were helpful to me when it came to navigating the promotional system of the U.S. military. I'd observed it in operation, understood how it worked, and knew when and how it needed to be tweaked.

When left to its own devices, the military promotional system works like an escalator: talented young leaders get on the bottom step and hope to ride to the top. Of course, as in any pyramidal organization, the number of positions available becomes smaller the higher you rise; the Army has fewer colonels than majors, fewer generals than colonels, fewer two-stars than one-stars, and so on. Those who aren't selected for promotion at a particular level understand the signal that is being sent, and many of them depart for civilian life, where most of them find that their military experience is considered a valuable asset. This so-called up-or-out process for weeding out talent is not a bad thing, because the departure of some candidates opens spaces in the hierarchy for others and so ventilates the entire system.

However, just as an escalator runs at a prescribed speed and no faster, the promotional system in the armed services tends to elevate officers at a predetermined rate. This means that even young leaders with outstanding track records have little opportunity to rise to the top more quickly. Add in the fact that the world of the officers' corps is relatively small and made up mostly of people who have known one another ever since attending one of the service academies together, and you get a system that is rather predictable—sometimes too much so. When a high-ranking slot opens up, there is often a widespread understanding that "it's Officer So-and-So's turn to get the next promotion." This sense of inevitability can sometimes overshadow the importance of selecting the *right* person for a key job, not just the next one in line. So occasionally, an unconventional, outside-the-box appointment is needed. It brings in a candidate who is right on the merits while also shaking up the system and injecting some fresh thinking.

Most SecDefs find it difficult to make such against-the-norm choices because they haven't been around long enough to develop an intimate personal knowledge of the individual candidates' strengths and weaknesses. I didn't have that problem. I'd known almost all the candidates for years, sometimes decades. In many cases, I'd worked with them in one capacity or another. There's no substitute for having actually watched someone rise through the ranks, facing challenges and problems along the way, and seeing how they responded.

The level of personal acquaintance I had with most of the top officers in the armed services made it possible for me, as SecDef, to recognize when an unexpected choice might work better than the conventional one.

For example, when it came time to pick a new chief of naval operations to replace submariner John Greenert, the Navy brass and the secretary of the Navy were heavily influenced by the need to choose a candidate from a different Navy "tribe." In the U.S. Navy, there are three dominant tribes: the aircraft carrier aviators, the submariners who captain the attack submarines and the nuclear ballistic missile submarines, and the surface warfare officers (SWOs) who command and drive the surface ships.

Since the outgoing chief was a submariner, the expectation was that an aviator or SWO would be chosen next. However, it just so happened that moment coincided with something that affected the entirety of one of the tribes, the SWOs—the so-called Fat Leonard Scandal.

Fat Leonard was a Singaporean wheeler-dealer whose firm did a lot of work for the U.S. Navy. His specialty was supplying ships with repairs, food, and other supplies and finding berthing or anchorage in ports around the Pacific. Because a senior Navy officer traveling around the Pacific is required to meet with politicos and business leaders to help ease the access of Navy ships to local ports, a majority of the senior SWOs who had been deployed in the Pacific over the previous decade had at one time or another rubbed up against Fat Leonard. Unfortunately, it turned out that at least a few of the Navy's logistics officers had been awarding contracts to Fat Leonard's firm in return for kickbacks, parties, vacations, flings with prostitutes, and other favors. And while only a handful were guilty, countless officers had to be investigated—a Kafkaesque nightmare that, among other things, meant they would be ineligible for promotions until they'd been finally cleared. Under the circumstances, it would have been hard for me to find a fully qualified SWO to nominate as chief of naval operations.

Fortunately, I had a fine option in John Richardson. John was the quintessential submariner, an inheritor of all the rigor and discipline of Admiral Hyman Rickover, the founder of the nuclear Navy, without any of Rickover's vanities and idiosyncrasies. His assignment, at the time, was a plum one for a U.S. naval officer, which was to serve as the number two official in the National Nuclear Security Administration (NNSA), which is the successor to the Atomic Energy Commission. Formally part of the Department of Energy, the NNSA is responsible for much of the nuclear weapons complex as well as the nuclear reactors aboard Navy submarines and aircraft carriers—exacting work of the kind at which Richardson excelled.

I knew it would be a difficult call to my friend Ernie Moniz, the Secretary of Energy, to tell him that I intended to pull John back to mother Navy. But Ernie took it well, simply asking me to make sure I sent him a good successor, which I did. Some of the more narrow-minded noticed that Richardson was the second submariner in a row to serve as chief of naval operations. But I didn't think that mattered nearly as much as his quality.

Another unconventional but totally successful choice was when I chose General Joseph Votel to command CENTCOM. Joe's core experience was as leader of the Joint Special Operations Command, an elite force charged with highly classified missions. Military tradition had generally dictated that "a special ops guy" should be permitted to run only a special ops unit. But I knew Joe well, respected his talents, and realized that special ops would play a huge role in CENTCOM's work, especially the war on ISIS. So I went ahead and gave him the job—and he has performed exceptionally well.

Another unconventional choice I made was appointing Lori Robinson as the first woman to lead a U.S. combat command. There had been previous women to achieve the rank of four-star general, but combatant command is very special. In the words of Tammy Duckworth, a member of Congress from Illinois who once flew helicopters in Iraq, "In the military, a combatant command is the ultimate job. It's the pointy tip of the spear, overseeing the people carrying the rifles and flying the aircraft." So naming General Robinson as leader of the Northern Command (NORTHCOM), which is charged with defending the U.S. homeland against attack, was a big deal.

As with most of the officers I appointed to combatant commands, Robinson was someone I'd known for years. As a candidate, she had it all. Her background was wide ranging—handling budgets for the Joint Chiefs as a two-star general, working on strategy and war planning at the highest level of the Pentagon, and then managing operations in the air war in the Mideast as vice commander of the 405th Air Expeditionary

Wing, leading more than two thousand airmen in operations Enduring Freedom and Iraqi Freedom.

In many ways, then, despite her groundbreaking status, Lori Robinson was a natural choice as commander of NORTHCOM. Perhaps the most counterintuitive thing I did in her case was refrain from focusing on her gender, either when I proposed her to President Obama or when I made the official announcement of her nomination. After all, I reasoned, why should I go out of my way to point out that Robinson was a woman? When nominating her male peers to similar roles, I never went out of my way to mention that they were men! Instead, I wanted to quietly send the message that Robinson had been selected not as some kind of diversity gesture but purely on merit—which of course she had.

I think General Robinson and her colleagues of both genders understood the subtle, unspoken message—and they appreciated it.

When a Leader Goes Wrong

Over time, those senior military leaders and I became a close and deeply collegial group. We shared the enormous and complex mission of recruiting, training, and equipping the armed services—a force of millions of people—and of wisely allocating and spending hundreds of billions of dollars every year, all in the service of providing the best military possible to protect and defend the people and institutions of a proud, 240-year-old republic, today and for the distant and uncertain future. This shared burden, along with our shared histories of years or decades of service in DOD, had fused us into a tight-knit group of people. (Past SecDefs would have written "a tight-knit group of men," but by the time I became secretary, that limitation had happily been overcome.) I had shared with these DOD colleagues a range of challenges, from political contretemps to moments of crisis on far-flung battlefields, and I'd come to trust and admire them. And the connections among us had deepened to include our loved ones. My wife, Stephanie, for example, is intensely patriotic and all-in for the troops, and she forged strong connections with countless military spouses.

These close personal bonds make service in the Pentagon profoundly meaningful on a human level as well as a professional one. But they also mean that there is a heavy price to pay when an individual proves to be unworthy of the trust the country has reposed in them. This happened to me during my time as SecDef when a brilliant and talented three-star general I'd admired, befriended, and groomed for high leadership failed me—and, more important, failed the mission and the nation we serve.

Of all the stories in this book, this is the one I find most painful to tell.

I generally refrain from discussing personnel actions. But this one garnered front-page coverage in the *Washington Post* and a public report from the DOD inspector general, so I cannot pass over it.

Ron Lewis was a remarkably gifted military leader. I met him during my time as acquisition czar, when he was a colonel who had been detailed to the Defense Business Board, which advises the department on sound management practices. Born and raised in Chicago, he had attended West Point and then commanded troops in Afghanistan and Iraq, serving with distinction at each step in his career. Ron knew nothing about the acquisitions process when he became my military assistant. But he set about the task of learning it, beginning by reviewing the thick briefing books compiled for each project and mastering the countless details they contained. I was very impressed by his quick intelligence, his strong work ethic, and his ability to rapidly focus on the key issues when tackling a complex problem. I liked Lewis so much that I made a point of keeping him on staff when I became deputy secretary.

Later, when I was named SecDef, I told Army Chief of Staff Ray Odierno that I wanted Lewis to be my senior military assistant. By that time, Lewis had been promoted to the rank of two-star general (also known as major general), but the position of senior military assistant called for a three-star general (a lieutenant general). Accordingly, I arranged for his promotion. Lewis's parents attended the ceremony at the Pentagon when I pinned on his third star. And Odierno predicted that, one day, Ron Lewis would be chief of staff of the Army—he was that good. I agreed with him.

For close to nine months, Lewis played a vital role in helping me run the Pentagon. He provided me with expert analysis and advice on military matters and attended most of my high-level meetings. Ron and Eric Rosenbach made an amazing support team, and the three of us developed the intense camaraderie that arises only when people share an important mission and face its challenges as a team.

Ron and his wife, Denise, became close to me and Stephanie. Ron helped to plan my journeys to diplomatic outposts and combat zones around the world, and accompanied me on most of them. And when I was almost immobilized in the wake of a painful back surgery, Ron would even come to my apartment every morning when Stephanie was away on business and literally tie my shoes for me. Ron and I were more than just colleagues—we were dear friends.

But then it all unraveled—and rather suddenly.

Nothing blatant or obvious had happened. But Eric had begun hearing vague rumors about Lewis—rumors that were disturbing enough to make him pay attention. Then one day in November 2015, a colleague from the Pentagon came to Eric's office, closed the door, and described an inappropriate incident he'd witnessed involving Lewis. Like everyone else, this individual knew how close the three of us had become—so it took a little courage for him to step forward. But it's a good thing he did.

Armed with this information, Eric began asking questions, speaking behind closed doors with some of the people the three of us had been working with over the previous months. He got access to relevant documents, including records of payments made using government-issued credit cards. Before long, a torrent opened, involving several kinds of transgressions described by a number of different people. By the end of two days of listening, Eric had uncovered a clear pattern.

It was Tuesday, November 10, around six o'clock in the evening. Eric Rosenbach and I were at the White House, just leaving a meeting with the president—an unusually unpleasant meeting, in which President Obama had vented his frustrations regarding the issue of the Guantánamo detention center. As we stepped out of the West Wing into the raw, wet evening weather and headed toward my car, Eric said, "I need to tell you something." Something about his tone told me that my already bad mood was about to become much, much worse.

"It's about Ron Lewis," Eric added.

"Let's hear it," I said.

Eric unfolded everything he'd learned—accounts from several individuals about womanizing, inappropriate and unwelcome advances made to military colleagues and Pentagon staff members, misuse of a government credit card, and unprofessional activities during some of our official travels. It wasn't about one or two incidents, but about a pattern of behavior. And the evidence was clear—including some in writing.

My initial reaction was one of shock. How could a man I admired and respected—a leader with such promise and with such a bright future ahead of him—betray himself, me, and the nation in such a fashion? I could scarcely believe it.

Then other emotions flooded me. Anger verging on rage; if Ron had been in front of me at that moment, I probably would have wanted to strangle him. This kind of outrageous behavior diminished and disgraced the whole office. It would have been a major embarrassment if it had been discovered by others first. Fine officers had been dismissed by my predecessors for lesser offenses—and rightly so.

And then my anger was followed by profound grief. As I absorbed the reality of what he'd done, and how profoundly he had sacrificed a golden future for which he was superbly qualified, I felt heartbroken.

But none of these emotions had any impact on the rational side of my brain. That part of me quickly shook off the shock and began to focus on what I obviously had to do.

The next day was Veterans Day—an important day for the department, for obvious reasons. I was scheduled to join the president for a solemn wreath-laying ceremony at the Tomb of the Unknown Soldier at Arlington National Cemetery. Under normal circumstances, Ron Lewis would accompany me and escort the president to the site. And I knew that President Obama would be pleased to see Lewis. The two men had established a bit of a bond—two high-achieving African American men with Chicago roots. The many photographers and TV crews recording the ceremony would surely capture shots of Obama and Lewis greeting each other cordially and carrying the ceremonial wreath to the memorial.

But now I had to make sure that didn't happen. I told Rosenbach, "Arrange for a different military assistant to escort the president." He did so, and then he called Ron Lewis to inform him of the change in plans. "The secretary will speak with you the following morning," he added. I wondered whether Lewis immediately understood what that meant.

On Veterans Day, while participating in the ceremony at Arlington, I took a moment to speak privately with Joe Dunford, chairman of the Joint Chiefs. "I have a big headache," I said. "Ron's got to go." And I explained the situation in detail.

Dunford volunteered to help. "Let me handle this through the joint staff. We can get it out of your office altogether."

I appreciated the gesture, so typical of Joe. But I told him that the problem was already in my office, and I couldn't avoid dealing with it.

"All right," Joe said. "But at least I'll get in touch with Mark and explain what's happened." That was Mark Milley, the Army chief of staff. Dunford spoke to him on my behalf, lessening my burden a bit.

That afternoon, Eric Rosenbach and I called in Alissa Starzak, the Army's legal counsel, to discuss the situation. Starzak agreed that, based on what we'd discovered, I couldn't keep Lewis in his position as military assistant. Discharge from the Army and loss of rank might also prove to be necessary under departmental regulations. However, as I well knew, these further punishments would require a thorough process of review and adjudication that would take months. That job would be turned over to Glenn A. Fine, the acting inspector general (IG) of DOD, who did his usual expert and professional work. This was both the appropriate way to handle such a case and essential to ensure the integrity of the investigation. After all, it was possible that I had been negligent in my supervision of Lewis. If that had happened, it would have been important for it to be fully investigated and made public by an independent investigator. Hence the value of turning over such cases to the IG's office.

The next morning, a somber group assembled in my Pentagon office: Joe Dunford, legal counsel Alissa Starzak, Eric Rosenbach, and me. In response to my summons, Ron Lewis came in. I'm sure that, as soon as he saw who was in the room and the grave expressions on all our faces, the realization of what was happening was immediate. No greetings were exchanged. I read aloud a one-paragraph statement that our counsel had provided, informing General Lewis that he was discharged from his position in the Office of the Secretary of Defense. He listened in silence. Then he left the room.

That was the last time I saw Ron Lewis.

If I'd had any doubts as to whether I'd handled Lewis's case appropriately, they vanished almost as soon as I walked out of my office later that morning. One of the noncommissioned officers who sat outside, greeting visitors and handling administrative tasks—a woman—looked up at me with damp eyes and smiled a silent message of "thank you." And before the day was through, six other officers—four female, two male—who'd worked with Lewis came to my office to privately thank me as well. They'd all been wrestling with their growing awareness of various parts of the story, some of which affected them directly. They were gratified and relieved that it had been dealt with firmly.

Due to the public nature of Lewis's role, the story of his dismissal, including a fairly complete recounting of his offenses, appeared promptly in the media, including a front-page account in the *Washington Post*. Months later, a detailed report was published by the Office of the Inspector General, as is normal in such cases. A few outside the military expressed dismay about the publicity; some said they thought the matter should have been handled more discreetly. But I don't think I had any choice but to act as I did. In any organization—civilian or military, governmental or private—there's no place for a leader who uses his position to take advantage of his subordinates and to misuse resources for personal enjoyment. And in the military, such offenses are doubly unacceptable. They are a violation of the warrior's code and destructive of the bonds of trust that must exist between an officer and his troops. Given the fact that the U.S. military—like many other organizations of all kinds—has been grappling with a long-standing problem of sexual misconduct, it was especially important for me to act swiftly and decisively, with no hint of favoritism for an officer with whom I'd been particularly close.

The last I heard, Ron Lewis and his wife were living in Virginia, where he was starting a business. I'll always be grateful for the things he did for me, and I wish him success in the future. But I'll never forget how he let me down. It was, for me, an indelible reminder of the truth that being a leader doesn't exempt you from the sorrows of being a human being.

I'm refraining from recounting several other cases of misconduct that occurred during my tenure as SecDef (and, for that matter, under the leadership of other secretaries I've served). In each case, similar offenses have resulted in similar sanctions, as duty demands.

Ron Lewis's offenses were a blot on the record of the DOD. But as I write these pages, we're witnessing worse behavior than his from those at the highest levels of government: shameless cases of adultery and sexual misconduct, hate speech, flagrant dishonesty, abuse of office for personal gain, and more. In the military, all these are firing offenses—and they should be. Any kind of public office must be founded on honor and trust, and this applies especially to the profession of arms. How else to share a foxhole?

What Makes a Secretary of Defense?

Given the fact that I spent so much of my time as SecDef in choosing, evaluating, and grooming high-ranking leaders for America's military, it's natural that I have developed some strong opinions about leadership in general—and especially about how the leadership of the U.S. defense establishment ought to be organized and staffed.

One interesting question regards the type of background that best prepares someone to be SecDef. Bill Perry, Harold Brown, and I were all originally scientists. Chuck Hagel, Leon Panetta, Don Rumsfeld, Bill Cohen, Dick Cheney, Melvin Laird, and Les Aspin had served as congressmen or as senators. Several had served in the White House, including as chief of staff. A few, like Caspar Weinberger, had been active elsewhere in public life—in Weinberger's case, as chairman of the Federal Trade Commission, director of the Office of Management and Budget, and chairman of the California Republican Party, among other jobs. Before joining the Kennedy administration, Robert McNamara had been CEO of Ford Motor Company, and a number of other earlier SecDefs had had experience as corporate executives.

It may not surprise you to hear that I think my own long background in science, coupled with my extensive experience within and around DOD, was as good a preparation as any. Transitioning from Congress to a cabinet role has proved difficult for some. Chuck Hagel suffered as SecDef from the personal animosity of some of his fellow senators, justified or not. Les Aspin, who had been a great chairman of the House Armed Services Committee, found it difficult to transition from the role of observer to that of leader. Thus, after American service members' bodies were dragged through the streets of Mogadishu, Aspin went to the Hill to meet with members of Congress to "kick it around." That may be an appropriate approach when you're a representative yourself, but the SecDef needs to be more than a commentator; he is supposed to know what the heck is happening and to have a plan for dealing with it. Under fire, Aspin resigned a few months later.

It might seem natural to put a retired military officer in charge of the Pentagon, but that has happened only twice since World War II. General George C. Marshall was appointed to the job by President Truman way back in 1950, and General James Mattis was appointed by President Trump in 2017. The question of whether such an appointment is appropriate has two distinct and important aspects, though the discussion usually focuses on only one: civilian control of the armed forces.

As countless constitutional experts have observed, it is critical that the military be ultimately under the control of an elected civilian leader. This is the reason for the existence of a law mandating that a military officer must have been retired for at least seven years prior to being named as SecDef. This issue was much discussed in the case of Jim Mattis, the retired general whom President Trump appointed as SecDef. However, given the fact that the president—himself a civilian—chooses the SecDef, I don't see any reason the president can't decide that a former general might be the best qualified person for the job. As a political appointee, the SecDef is "the president's guy," so anyone with the right knowledge, background, and personal gifts can provide the president with appropriate advice.

The other aspect of the question is actually more serious, though much less often discussed. Under the Goldwater-Nichols Act, both the

SecDef and the chairman of the Joint Chiefs of Staff are supposed to ensure that the president receives professional military advice. To make this possible, the generals need to focus on doing what they do best—being first-rate military officers. Rather than politicizing their work and their judgments, our military professionals must provide the president and his cabinet with the independent advice they need and deserve.

Given all the relevant factors, I supported the nomination of Jim Mattis as my successor. (To allow him to serve, Congress passed a special law waiving the requirement of seven years in retirement.) President Trump was entitled to pick his favorite candidate for the job, whether he happened to be a retired general or not. Mattis's case is nevertheless a bit odd, both because the two men had never previously met and because it appears that the president chose him mostly because he *was* a general! (Trump seemed to take delight in referring to him using the nickname "Mad Dog" Mattis, evidently relishing the image of toughness it conveyed. Jim himself disliked the nickname, sharing my view that it diminished his stature.) Trump's choices were also somewhat limited by the fact that most of the Republican foreign policy establishment did not support his candidacy, which meant that many of the usual sources of SecDefs in a Republican administration were ruled out.

In any case, Mattis was certainly qualified to serve as SecDef. He and I have known each other since 1993, when Mattis was a junior military assistant in the office of Deputy Secretary Bill Perry. We sometimes slept side by side on the floor of Bill's airplane with other staff members during long overseas trips. Mattis continued to serve Perry when he became SecDef in 1994. In 2010, President Obama named Mattis commander of the U.S. Central Command (CENTCOM), and he and I worked closely on the war plan for Iran—a sensitive matter, since the Obama administration was reluctant to admit that such a plan even existed. It included plans for destroying the facilities known to house Iran's nuclear program as well as contingencies for responding to aggressive actions such as attacks on U.S. shipping. The plan envisioned everything up to annihilation of Iran's armed forces, though it stopped short of a complete military occupation of the country.

It later turned out that this Iran war plan was indirectly involved in

Mattis's departure from CENTCOM. Mattis was viewed by some as being somewhat more hawkish on Iran than most in the Obama administration, though I did not share that perception. Then–national security advisor Tom Donilon was apparently convinced that Mattis actually wanted to implement the war plan, which I think was unfair. Sadly, it led to Jim's leaving CENTCOM under what he felt was a cloud. It's an example of the personal risks an advisor may have to take when he gives the president the best independent advice he has to offer—especially when his perspective differs from that of the president himself.

Mattis may have viewed accepting the job of SecDef under President Trump as an opportunity to redeem his reputation from what he considers the unfair hit it took back in 2013. I am sure it was challenging for him to deal with the mercurial and inexperienced president who nominated him. He and I spoke occasionally, and I offered him whatever advice I could. Ultimately, Jim chose to depart in December 2018, citing his dilemmas in a clear and vivid letter of resignation.

There's a strong tradition of collegiality among present and retired SecDefs. I've known them all well since Jim Schlesinger, and I've done my best to keep that tradition alive. We're bound by an unwritten code that includes an unwillingness to offer public opinions about the performance of a current SecDef. No former Secretary of Defense ever criticized me or even commented at all on my policy decisions, and I never gave in to the temptation to blame one of my predecessors for a problem I was facing. This attitude of mutual respect and forbearance knows no party boundaries.

One of my favorite predecessors was Melvin Laird, appointed by Richard Nixon. Mel was over ninety when I became SecDef, but he kept in touch through an occasional call or note. He once sent me a declassified version of a memo he'd received way back in 1969 from his deputy, Dave Packard, of Hewlett-Packard fame, describing the challenges they faced for the year ahead. In addition to addressing the giant ongoing issues with the war in Vietnam, the memo referred to concerns over readiness and recruiting, appointment of senior officers, the DOD's relationship with the White House, the need to work with allies and partners, and problems with big new weapons systems. Mel attached a handwritten note saying, "Ash, I'll bet that if you scratch out Vietnam and write in Iraq, and scratch out the A-10 and write in the F-35, you'll have a note you might have received yourself." Mel was dead right. Not only were the problems faced by the department largely the same, even the typeface, margins, spacing, and "top secret" stamps looked the same.

A symbol of the bipartisan comity that embraces SecDefs past and present occurred during my last month in office, December 2016. I was invited to the Reagan Library in Simi Valley, California, to receive the Ronald Reagan Peace Through Strength Award for my efforts to support and enhance America's defense system. Making the presentation was Leon Panetta while Dick Cheney received the award at the same time as me. Panetta and Cheney, of course, were two former SecDefs of the generation before me, one Republican and one Democrat.

I made a number of similar symbolic gestures of my own. For example, I awarded the Defense Distinguished Service Medal—the DOD's highest civilian award—to four former officials who were not secretaries of defense: Henry Kissinger, George Shultz, Zbigniew Brzezinski, and Madeleine Albright. These two Republicans and two Democrats represented the great arc of American strategic history, bridging generations, political parties, and national security bureaucracies.

In the same vein, I named the SecDef's conference room the Nunn-Lugar Conference Room, after the two distinguished national security leaders, and named the legislative affairs office the Levin-Warner Suite, after two others. In both cases, the names paired included one Democrat and one Republican.

The Political Appointment System: Awkward, but It Works

Effective leadership is not just a matter of specific skills and personality traits. It's also dependent on the structure and system within which individual leaders operate.

One characteristic of the U.S. security apparatus that surprises most foreign observers is the degree to which it changes every four or eight years (depending on when there's a change in the political party that controls the executive branch). In most other democracies, an electoral upheaval means a change in cabinet secretaries (or "ministers"), but not in the layers of officers below that level. By contrast, in the American DOD, not only are the secretary and the deputy secretary appointed by the president, but so are the undersecretaries, the assistant secretaries, the deputy assistant secretaries, and a host of others. Thus, career civil servants will almost always be working for political appointees; they will stand no chance of occupying a top job themselves unless they leave the civil service.

The obvious downside is that a whole raft of novices come into the government with each change of administration. Speaking in general terms, I'd estimate that, in most cases, about half of these newcomers know what they're doing at first. Another quarter are capable and dedicated people who quickly master their jobs. But another quarter never "get it" and remain an embarrassment to the department.

This is certainly a significant problem, and over the years I experienced my share of frustrations dealing with some people from that final quarter. But on balance, I think that the U.S. system of turning over government to political appointees has proved to be reasonably effective.

One reason is that practically all presidents (as well as their influential political directors) have shown a basic respect for competence in making appointments. Nakedly political appointments of ridiculously unqualified people have historically been very rare.

For senior jobs, the necessity to get Senate advice and consent provides further upward pressure on the quality of appointees. The need for bipartisan support also means that many "political appointees" are not, in fact, terribly political. Take me, for example. Why am I considered a Democrat? The answer doesn't lie in any strongly partisan or ideological convictions I hold. My Philadelphia roots made me comfortable with many of the views of the Democratic Party, especially on domestic policy. But it's also true that many of my foreign policy views are centrist ones that are shared by many Republicans.

The actual answer to the question is that the first president who offered me a political appointment was Bill Clinton, a Democrat. That would have branded me as a Democrat for life, regardless of my actual party inclination. The reality is that I got the job not because of my political contacts (I had none) but because of my reputation for knowledge and effectiveness—my competence, in short. That's an example of how a system that nominally makes appointments based on political criteria actually gives a lot of weight to more important considerations, like competence—as it should, of course.

Admittedly, the degree to which presidential administrations value competence does vary. The Trump administration seems to have a particular problem in this regard. Not only does it tend to value loyalty over competence; it insists on a narrow definition of *loyalty*—namely, loyalty to the person of Donald Trump rather than to the Republican Party or its principles. This has made it harder than usual for the Trump administration to staff its departments with highly qualified professionals. Hopefully future administrations will revert to the historical norm rather than follow the Trump team down the unpromising path of valuing personal loyalty over all.

The second reason I believe the American system of political appointments is fundamentally a good one is because of the opportunities it creates to ventilate the system with the fresh perspectives of outsiders.

Henry Kissinger once remarked that all the ideas he used in government were ideas he'd brought with him—because while he was in office, he was too busy to generate any new ones. Most of us who've served in government for a number of years have experienced the same thing. It takes time, energy, and discipline to stay current on new thinking in any field, much less to create fresh concepts out of whole cloth. But those who occupy important leadership roles in government have little time to do either of these things. So bringing in new faces—with a stock of new ideas—every four or eight years is not a bad thing, even if it produces some awkward disruptions in the process.

Two Sides of the Leadership Coin: Leadership and Reinforcement

We're living in an era when some of the traditional attributes of leaders seem to have been devalued. We've recently observed individuals being elevated to high office whose experience, temperament, judgment, and character appear very different from those once demanded for positions of responsibility. These kinds of choices are sometimes defended on the ground that "the old ways have failed" and "we have to shake things up" by turning them over to leaders who appear, on the surface, to be grossly unqualified.

Unhappily, experience suggests that, in most cases, people who appear unqualified by conventional standards usually *are* unqualified—as shown by the results they produce.

Fortunately, the U.S. military has so far resisted the temptation to discard traditional measures of leadership. The quality of the leaders in our armed forces remains remarkably high, and I've learned a great deal about what makes a true leader from my decades of observing and working with scores of them.

Over time, I've come to distinguish *leadership* from *reinforcement*—two sets of skills that are both useful in what is broadly referred to as a leader's role.

Leadership in the sense I mean is required in circumstances in which you are taking your mission and your subordinates in a direction they need to go but that they don't understand or don't want to take. Not every action taken by a person in a leadership position requires this sort of leadership—and one of the tough choices a leader must make is about when to devote time, energy, reputation, and other forms of personal capital to undertaking this kind of effort. Leading people in a direction in which they may not want to go always involves risk and the cost of opportunities forgone, and the smart leader picks and chooses his spots carefully.

The work I did as SecDef in shaping the campaign to destroy ISIS was an example of this kind of leadership. The president didn't want to go in the direction I proposed, because, having run for the White House on a platform that included "ending two wars," he didn't want to be seen as having launched yet another war—one that carried no guarantee of success. Most of the international friends and allies of the United States were adrift and didn't know what to do, so their support for the campaign was also dubious at best. The members of Congress were all over the map about how deeply the United States should get involved in an effort to defeat ISIS; many insisted that we should restrict our efforts to solely supporting local forces, who should be tasked with organizing and leading the campaign themselves. The American people were appalled by ISIS's barbarism but also understandably sick of war.

This was a case where galvanizing action by an American SecDef was essential. Without it, the campaign would not have come together. For this reason, it was an example of leadership in the sense I mean.

By contrast, what I call reinforcement is less widely recognized and heralded, but it, too, is deserving of respect. Reinforcement means bringing out the best in your subordinates—not by leading them in a new direction, but by clarifying and supporting skills and behaviors they may not have fully understood, recognized, or felt free to practice. The leader who is skilled in reinforcement sees the unrecognized value in the culture, knowledge, and resources of an organization and takes steps to help people bring that value to full fruition.

An example of reinforcement from my own career was the Better Buying Power initiative that I launched as acquisitions czar. As I explained in Chapter 1, my goal was not to create a new fad for "reforming" the acquisitions process; it was to strengthen and support the best existing wisdom about how to do acquisitions right. Thus, the chart I created and distributed that set forth the basic principle of Better Buying Power was about 80 percent a restatement of what most experienced acquisition executives would describe as their best understanding of their own tradecraft. Only about 20 percent was truly novel—and even this fraction was focused on applying traditional insights to new arenas, such as the acquisition of services.

Similarly, as deputy secretary of defense, I created a gathering called the deputy's management action group. It included all the principal leaders of the department—the service chiefs of staff or their deputies, the service secretaries or their deputies, and the undersecretaries and major agency heads. At our meetings, we discussed every major issue facing the department, giving everyone a chance to say what they thought and to present their analyses. In each case, the goal was to drive toward a decision that I would render on the spot, unless I needed to check first with the SecDef. The idea was to create and maintain forward momentum on key challenges and provide a forum where concerns could be aired and dealt with quickly.

The deputy's management action group was a new idea, but it embodied the cultural instincts of the DOD. Clarity, consistency, and conclusiveness are what people in the department crave. Therefore, creating this group was an example of reinforcement, because I was building on the department's own best instincts rather than pushing it in a novel direction.

The distinction between leadership and reinforcement sheds an interesting new light on some of the quandaries of today. For example, although President Trump is often described as a "norm breaker" and a "rules buster"—which implies that he is innovative in his leadership practices—I would actually describe him in almost the opposite terms. In my view, Trump represents reinforcement without leadership. It seems apparent that neither his candidacy nor his presidency has been informed by any prior convictions or ideas about the public sphere. Instead, he gets his direction almost entirely from his base—the portion of voters who put him over the top in the Electoral College and who represent his die-hard supporters in opinion polls. Trump does what they think they want or say they want, and he has balked at repudiating what the base wants. This is true even in cases where his advisors have sometimes persuaded him to try something else—for example, when it comes to trade disputes with countries like China. Trump's lack of true leadership skills is a major reason his administration seems to be floundering.

By the same token, a leader who practices only leadership and completely neglects the value of reinforcement is also likely to fail. Such a leader would be continually pushing against the norms, culture, instincts, and values of the people he leads and the organization they belong to. The result would be continual conflict—exhausting and likely unproductive.

Both leadership and reinforcement have their place, and the best leaders know how and when to make use of each.

Vital Ingredients: Experience and Integrity

One principle that probably shouldn't need to be defended—but that seemingly needs such defense in today's world—is the value of experience. It takes time to grow into a big job, whether in government or in any other challenging leadership arena. As my wife, Stephanie, always says to me, "Ash, if I get sick, I want you to get me a doctor with an M.D. degree. And if I'm arrested, please get me a real lawyer." Practically everyone would apply the same common-sense thinking to such challenges in their own lives. But for some reason, it has become fashionable to apply the opposite thinking to the realm of government—to say that we need to "shake up the Washington establishment" (or even "blow up government") by handing power to people with no experience.

Thus the long list of political candidates who have "run against Washington," many of them successfully—with Donald Trump, of course, as the most remarkable example. He is alone among presidents in U.S. history in having occupied no public office whatsoever prior to becoming president. It is painfully clear at times that Trump has no idea of the complex history behind key issues or even the details of how the government actually functions. As a result, there have been a number of cases in which President Trump has pronounced a diktat that has been only incompletely or grudgingly implemented by members of his own team—or been thrown out by courts as illegal or unconstitutional. Only time will tell if Trump can overcome these deficiencies.

Another lamentable example was Rex Tillerson, the former Exxon CEO who served for fourteen months as Trump's first Secretary of State. I have no reason to doubt Tillerson's general intelligence or his good intentions when he took on the assignment. He obviously had his hands full, perhaps impossibly so, with the challenge of "managing upward." But his performance in the State Department gives the lie to the preposterous myth that running a business provides the experience needed for running a major government agency. Tillerson evidently believed that he could run a foreign service charged with managing the diplomatic relationships between the United States and scores of foreign nations in the kind of manner that business consultants prescribe when asked to help a corporate middle manager achieve a cost-cutting target. According to the accounts of people from within the State Department, the damage Tillerson did to the department is lasting and probably only partially reversible, showing neither good managerial ability nor any real understanding of the institution that he was appointed to run.

As for the idea that the heads of government agencies ought to copy the managerial styles of corporate executives, I can only cite the comments I would hear from businesspeople when I invited them to visit DOD. After a day or two of meeting with my colleagues—usually these corporate chieftains' first extended interaction with federal employees— they would often remark, "I wish I had a team around me as skilled and capable as yours!"

The same dynamic can be seen in the hundreds of businesses that have eagerly hired talented veterans. The same primitives who carelessly blather about "government incompetence" are constantly hiring and promoting people trained and polished by government!

Another traditional idea that, sadly, seems to be on the defensive these days is the notion that integrity, decency, and respect are fundamental requirements for anyone in a position of public trust.

In addition to theoretical physics, my academic training was in medieval history—a fascinating field that offers important insights into the events and forces that helped shape our modern world. In sweeping terms, much of the history of the Middle Ages is a record of a centuries-long struggle to establish societies in which all human beings could live lives with a modicum of order, trust, justice, and simple dignity. This root yearning underlies most of the institutions that define the societies of today, from representative government and the rule of law to the nation-state itself. There's no point in entering public life if you don't start with a sense of awe concerning those principles and a deep feeling of gratitude for the social and political structures designed to uphold them.

Of course, human nature being what it is, there have always been public servants who have failed to live up to these principles. Graft, self-dealing, dishonesty, and corruption are ever-present dangers that must be rigorously guarded against, zealously exposed, and harshly punished. I worry that we may be entering a time when cynicism, opportunism, and political polarization become so intense and pervasive that many people—including high-ranking officials—are willing to overlook or excuse dishonesty and corruption when they serve political ends.

The founders did a masterful job of crafting a constitution that used principles like the separation of powers, checks and balances, and the guarantee of rights to make it hard for any individual or group to seize and maintain control of government while flouting these principles of integrity, honesty, and respect. They worked hard to design mechanisms to restrict the inordinate power that could be wielded by a king as well as the unruly passions of the mass of people they called "the mob."

However, the founders couldn't predict an era of mass media and social media, in which candidates for office can leapfrog "the establishment" of political parties, statesmen, and experienced leaders by appealing directly to "the mob." It's interesting to speculate about how the founders might have altered their constitutional design if they'd been gifted with such foresight—but it's also ultimately futile.

Like an individual reputation, the pillars of a decent shared society take decades to build, but they can be destroyed in a moment. It rests with us to reassert the principles of honorable leadership that long guided this country, and that we perhaps came to take for granted. We can take them for granted no more.

CHAPTER 14

FORCE OF THE FUTURE

By any imaginable standard, young Joseph Riley was an employer's dream. In 2012, as a senior cadet in the Reserve Officer Training Corps (ROTC) at the University of Virginia (UVA), he was majoring in Mandarin Chinese, attending the university's honors program in government and foreign affairs, and coauthoring a book on Sino-American relations. He'd already completed an internship at the National Ground Intelligence Center, done field research on Chinese mining industries in Africa, and attended the Army's Airborne and Air Assault schools. In his spare time, he served in student government, led a group to raise funds for the Wounded Warrior Project, and helped found the Alexander Hamilton Society, a national organization to promote foreign policy debates on campus.

Riley's remarkable combination of attributes—academic achievement, leadership potential, and spirit of service—lifted him to the number 10 ranking out of 5,579 candidates in the ROTC's National Order of Merit List. He graduated from UVA in 2013 and was proudly commissioned as a second lieutenant in the U.S. Army. He then headed off to England, where he'd been awarded a Rhodes scholarship to pursue a master's degree in international relations at Oxford. His professor of military science at UVA, Lieutenant Colonel Mike Binetti, observed that studying at Oxford would be an ideal preparation for Riley's future career as an Army officer: "He will not only feel comfortable but be academically qualified to be an infantry platoon leader or [to] work in a general officer's strategic initiatives group."

Imagine Riley's shock two years later when the Army informed him that his studies at Oxford were now considered a black mark against his record. Viewing Riley as lagging behind his peers because of his time away from the service, the military personnel system told him he would not be promoted to first lieutenant alongside 90 percent of his peers. Instead, he would soon be facing a separation board to determine whether he should be asked to leave the Army altogether.

It's no wonder that when Army Chief of Staff General Mark Milley heard the story from Riley himself, his immediate response was to exclaim, "You're killing me, Lieutenant!"

Milley exercised his influence as the Army's most senior officer by intervening to salvage Riley's career. Today Riley continues to wear the uniform. But the protocols that almost led to his leaving the Army are an employer's nightmare. When contending for talent in a competitive world, no organization—let alone the largest employer in the world, charged with some of the most urgent tasks on the planet—can afford to lose employees like Joseph Riley. And Riley's story is far from unique. As SecDef, I rarely got through a day's mail without reading a letter from a member of Congress sharing a complaint about a young man or woman in the member's district who felt needlessly jerked around by one of the services. Sometimes the complaints were unfounded. But all too often they had at least a grain of truth.

One of my highest priorities as SecDef was not only to avoid such aberrations but to make sure that DOD implemented policies of talent management that would guarantee our ability to attract and retain the smartest, toughest, and most capable young people in the country, today and for decades to come.

Talent-Management Challenges in an Ultracompetitive World

Americans with little direct connection to our men and women in uniform often harbor misconceptions about them. One of those misconceptions is a vague sense that today's troops somehow don't measure up to the highest standards. That's flatly wrong. The fact is that, by every measure, the move from universal service to an all-volunteer force in 1973 enabled the United States to significantly upgrade the qualifications of new recruits, so that America's military is now more highly skilled and better trained than ever. In fact, only 30 percent of Americans of service age are capable of passing the rigorous tests for intelligence, skill, physical fitness, and character applied to all would-be recruits. The quality of our people is the core reason that America's military is the finest fighting force the world has ever known.

The need to maintain these high standards is the main reason I would oppose the reinstitution of a draft for military service. The numbers tell the story. Roughly speaking, the number of young Americans who turn eighteen every year is about sixteen times as large as the number of military recruits needed by DOD. The majority of these military-age citizens are simply not qualified for service. Many are obese; many would fail our intelligence tests; others are serving time in prison, or have problems with drugs or alcohol. As for the qualified remainder, I suspect that any SecDef would have the same attitude as I did: I want to choose the recruits I hire rather than having someone else (like a local draft board) choose them for me. For all these reasons, it's clear to me that DOD is far better off without a draft, instead competing for talent in the open market like every other employer.

However, as the world keeps changing, so do the challenges of attracting the best young people to serve in the armed forces. The talent-management issues faced by the DOD are very different—and much tougher—than those faced by any corporation. As SecDef, I worked with the joint chiefs and the individual military services to launch a plan we called Force of the Future. Its purpose: to make the DOD more open, more flexible, and more attractive to America's finest young people, as exemplified by soldiers like Joseph Riley.

Here again, my lengthy history in DOD proved to be a valuable asset. Having gotten to know the department in great depth—its culture, its history, its strengths, and its weaknesses—I had the germ of the idea for Force of the Future fully formed before I took office. That enabled me to hit the ground running.

Shortly after I was sworn in as Secretary of Defense, I went to my old high school in Pennsylvania to outline my vision for the Force of the Future. By giving it a name, I was signaling loud and clear that this would be a big theme of my tenure as SecDef. I told the students there how we in the Pentagon must "think outside our five-sided box" to make ourselves better at attracting talent from a new generation of Americans. This was the first time I used the phrase that would become one of my favorites.

In the months that followed, I traveled the country, hearing from companies like LinkedIn, Google, and Boeing, and also from our own innovative troops and military leaders about what they're all doing to compete for talent in the twenty-first century, and what we can learn from them to improve our own talent management. And I talked with them and with management experts about some of the challenges we currently face that make our job increasingly difficult.

First, there's the highly competitive labor market in which the U.S. military must find ways to hold its own. To achieve our complex array of missions, the Force of the Future must attract America's finest young people, wherever or whoever they are. But as SecDef, I was concerned about the gap between that aspiration and the reality of our recruiting. One problem is that the geographic origins of our recruits are significantly imbalanced. For example, the nine states that make up the Northeast region of the United States have about 18 percent of the nation's eighteen- to twenty-four-year-olds, yet they produce fewer than 13 percent of our new recruits. By contrast, the eight states of the South Atlantic area (plus the District of Columbia), which also have about 18 percent of our young people, produce almost 24 percent of recruits.

There are simple explanations for this imbalance. The states with an outsize representation among our recruits tend to have greater-than-average numbers of military bases and, living nearby, military families, retirees, and veterans, all of whom serve as role models for young people seeking a path in life. Relatives of service members often make good service members themselves.

The real significance of this lopsided recruitment pool is that, in many parts of the country, we have not made an adequate appeal to Americans graduating from high school, entering college as potential ROTC candidates, or considering applying for slots at one of our military academies. We have not enticed the majority of young Americans to consider public service, nor have we given ourselves the best chance of convincing those who are qualified to join our ranks. That makes the job of ensuring that we get our fair share of America's smartest and most capable young people that much harder.

This failure runs the risk of narrowing our talent pool and thereby reducing the potential of our military teams. When a disproportionate fraction of our recruits comes from a relative handful of states—many from families with a tradition of military service—it means we are missing out on gifted young people from differing backgrounds with their own unique skills to offer. A white male from the South whose father, grandfather, and great-grandfather all served in the military is likely to make a fine addition to the force. But the same could be said of a Latina woman from New Mexico whose parents came to the United States just a decade ago . . . a teenager of Asian American descent who grew up in a college town in New Hampshire . . . a white youngster from an industrial town whose father enjoyed a lifetime job in a business that has since shut down . . . and an ambitious young African American high school graduate from a Rust Belt city who wants to continue his education but isn't sure how he can afford it. We need to make sure that our recruiting efforts are tailored to appeal to all these kinds of people, and many others.

Another challenge has been the military's own personnel policies, as illustrated by the story of Joseph Riley. Like any great institution with a long and proud history, the U.S. military sometimes gets caught up in its own customs, culture, and traditions. Rather than adjusting nimbly as changing times demand, we fall into the trap of doing things a certain way just because that's the way they've always been done. In a fast-changing, competitive world, that won't fly. We need to combine the best elements of our established personnel system with the most valuable innovations from today's talent-management practices. In particular, we need to modernize our retention, promotion, and compensation policies so that they are attractive and satisfying to the kinds of people who might make the best service members and are easily employable elsewhere.

When it comes to retention, a key factor is that the U.S. military is, on balance, a married force. Statistics show that the percentage of married people among military service members is higher than in the general population, including 70 percent of officers and 50 percent of enlisted members.

For this reason, it's not surprising that an array of issues related to family needs was mentioned to me over and over again by service members and their families. I remember a visit with members of the Army's Tenth Mountain Division, stationed at Fort Drum in upstate New York. I got the chance to have lunch with ten young military couples—troops and their spouses—who were beginning to ponder the question of how long they would stick with Army careers. After getting to know them, I asked them point-blank, "When you have to decide whether to stay or go, what will make the difference?" Nearly all of them said, "When we're ready to start a family, we're going to want to settle down. But we know that Army families can expect to get moved every year or two. That's awfully tough to take."

There's an old saying among military recruitment professionals: "You recruit a soldier, but you retain a family." My session at Fort Drum reinforced for me the truth in that saying, reminding me that we needed to do a much better job of making it possible for military families to feel as enthusiastic about their soldier's service as he or she does.

These kinds of problems have been emerging for many years, and previous SecDefs had been aware of them. But the DOD hadn't done a great job of focusing on them in a comprehensive, aggressive fashion. When I returned to the Pentagon in 2015, I felt the time had come to stop fighting a rear-guard battle against change, and instead to go on offense— to launch a positive program that would show the world that the U.S. military was ready to become one of today's most attractive employers for young people. This determination was the basis of Force of the Future.

Building the Force of the Future

One step I took to support the Force of the Future program was to bring in a good manager named Peter Levine to serve as undersecretary of defense for personnel and readiness. A lawyer who had previously served in the office of Senator Carl Levin, he was calm, self-assured, an adroit executive, and a strong communicator—just the sort of person I needed to implement the program I envisioned. It took a bit of finesse to get Levine into the slot where I wanted him. He'd previously been earmarked for a different Pentagon job specially created for him by legislation. But when I explained to Levine what I had in mind, he enthusiastically switched assignments, and he ended up doing an amazing job.

The changes that Levine helped spearhead included a thorough updating and improvement of our recruiting system. We redoubled our outreach efforts to young people, particularly in the forty-four states where enlistments have lagged. We also developed a new advertising and marketing campaign that borrows some of the smartest practices from consumer-goods marketing. For example, DOD now uses predictive analytics and microtargeting techniques to identify likely recruitment candidates and to reach out to them using tools like social media.

Of course, we continue to use some of the traditional recruitment methods that the military has used for decades, including dedicated officers who nurture strong personal bonds with talented potential recruits and their families. I've seen these officers in action, and the one-on-one attention they provide is remarkable. They often develop close friendships with the young people they meet, learning about their long-term dreams and aspirations and helping them think about their best options for future learning and growth—even when those options may not be centered on military service. They spend hours talking with moms and dads, allaying their concerns, educating them about the realities of today's military, and explaining what their son or daughter can expect from their time in service. When necessary, they'll even sit with a recruit and help him or her fill out the complicated paperwork, line by line.

But the Force of the Future program is about much more than changes in how DOD recruits new members. During the year after my arrival as SecDef, I announced a series of links to the Force of the Future— adjustments in our talent-management system designed to help ensure that we continue to have the world's finest fighting force.

The first link created what I refer to as new on-ramps and off-ramps to service. These are new and easier ways for people to enter and leave jobs at DOD, designed to encourage participation by a wider array of individuals with hard-to-find-skills and to support DOD lifers in developing varied and creative careers.

The new on-ramps include programs that let people from outside DOD come in for a while and contribute to our mission—maybe for a prescribed period of time, maybe just for a single project. For example, I expanded the Secretary of Defense Corporate Fellows program, which lets business executives, chosen competitively, come into the SecDef's office to observe and contribute. Another example was the Defense Digital Service, which organizes short tours of service by young engineers from the leading tech firms.

The new off-ramps provide ways for more people pursuing military careers to spend time studying at a leading university or working at a private corporation. These kinds of outside activities can serve as a valuable substitute or supplement to time spent at a military-run war college, helping service members gain skills they can bring back into the force to make it better.

The second link focused on increasing retention by improving the support that DOD provides to military families. A critical moment in the lives of such families comes when the service member is nearing the end of one recruitment period and is considering whether to re-up. It's a critical moment for the military as well, because by this point, DOD has invested heavily in the service member—typically to the tune of hundreds of thousands of dollars—and the service member in turn has proved his or her worth to DOD. So when he or she decides to leave, perhaps spurred by dissatisfaction on the part of a spouse or by concerns over the needs of a growing family, it's a considerable loss to the service.

To minimize the chance of that happening, the department wants to make it easier for our best people to stay. We can't remove the deployments, the danger, the sacrifice, and the frequent moves we ask of service members and their families. But there are things we can do. As part of this second link, we expanded maternity and paternity leave as well as extended child care hours on base. We created 3,600 rooms dedicated to nursing moms in DOD facilities around the world. We offered more military families, in exchange for a few more years of service, the possibility of staying in the community where they're stationed for a bit longer before being reassigned. And we improved the array of professional education opportunities available to troops, a benefit that's particularly attractive to our most talented members. The modest costs of these and other policy improvements were more than offset by the value created by experienced service members who chose to prolong their careers with DOD.

The third link focused on improving the talent-management programs in the military, especially in relation to officers and how they're promoted. To make it possible for more service members to fulfill their career aspirations, we infused our management systems with greater flexibility and choice while also ensuring that our merit-based promotion process rewarded performance and talent as fully and fairly as possible.

These enhancements required changes to the Defense Officer Personnel Management Act of 1980, the law that governs DOD policies in regard to human resources. I sent Congress a legislative proposal to this effect, which was passed in 2018. The changes make it possible, for example, for officers to pursue advanced skill development through activities like a doctoral degree or a tour in a civilian high-tech industry without being penalized by the traditional promotion system, which counted years spent in a certain rank.

The fourth link focused on civilian talent management. Remember that, in addition to over two million service members in uniform, the DOD also employs more than seven hundred thousand civilians. Contrary to popular perception, these are not mere "desk jockeys" operating out of offices in Washington, D.C. In fact, 85 percent of them live and work outside the D.C. area. They include the people who fix our planes, build our ships, and staff our scientific laboratories. To attract more of the best civilian talent, we streamlined our job application process so that a college student nearing graduation can get a quick job offer. In the past, many new graduates had to take jobs they found less attractive because they couldn't afford to tread water while the ponderous gears of the DOD turned. We also expanded our scholarship-for-service programs in science and technology fields, as well as instituting other changes designed to make it easier for DOD to attract top-notch civilian talent.

Any talent-management program must include making sure that

compensation policies are fair and competitive. This is mostly not a problem at DOD, though there are a couple of exceptions to the rule that I'll explain in a moment.

Throughout the post-9/11 period, military pay has risen steadily and quite handsomely compared with salaries in the rest of the economy and the overall cost of living. In fact, the typical response by Congress to the DOD's annual pay raise proposal is to add a percent or two, then pass it. This means that, over time, pay rates have become much higher than the services think are warranted. Of course, this is an emotional issue for the troops and their families. When I would gather the chiefs to discuss military compensation, we had a tricky balancing act to manage. We all recognized that we couldn't give the soldiers, sailors, airmen, and Marines the moon. But we also knew that the troops would be furious if we seemed to be trying to shortchange them.

When it came to officers' pay, however, it was fashionable for Congress to be much less generous. Make no mistake, our officers are quite well compensated. They receive generous retirement benefits, and, of course, they get their health care and their housing free of charge during all their assignments. (In many cases, their total compensation greatly exceeds mine as a cabinet secretary.) But in recent years, Congress has been zealous about restraining the growth of senior officers' pay. They didn't dare cut it, but they just froze it for a number of years.

However, it is civilian pay that represents the true scandal. Congress loves to hate federal employees, and civilians in the DOD are no exception. Civilian pay rates were capped by Congress during six of my last eight years in the Pentagon. This is a formula for driving good civilians away from the department. And lest you think this might be a good thing for the national budget, consider the fact that paying a uniformed military member to do the same job a civilian could do will cost, on average, twice as much—while paying an outside contractor will cost three times as much. Besides, we don't want a *Beetle Bailey* military, with soldiers doing odd jobs like painting rocks and picking up cigarette stubs from pathways. We want troops training to fight and pull triggers, which civilians can't do. Being stingy with civilian workers in the Pentagon represents the worst kind of false economy.

Retirement compensation is one more item that's a big deal for service members. There's an idiosyncrasy of the military retirement system that is worth noting. It is virtually the only retirement system in the entire country that involves what's called *cliff vesting*. Rather than having retirement benefits gradually vested over time, service members get nothing until their twentieth year of service, then become eligible for full benefits. One result is that younger members are discouraged from staying with the service for ten or fifteen valuable years, because in that time they won't accumulate any benefits. On the other hand, it becomes almost impossible to get rid of a poorly performing service member after about the seventeenth year, because they'll hang on tenaciously waiting for that twentieth year.

To fix this dysfunctional system, we made a momentous change during my time as deputy and SecDef. We changed the cliff vesting system to a partial vesting system, in which service members gradually accumulate increasing benefits over time. We made the new system compulsory for new service members but gave serving members the option of choosing the system they preferred. This helped ensure that the change would be accepted by the troops, and the transition seems to be working successfully.

These points don't exhaust the steps we took to update DOD's approach to talent management. We expanded and enhanced our recruitment efforts in underrepresented communities across the country, a first step toward addressing the geographic imbalance I described earlier. And we took advantage of opportunities to highlight our modernization of America's armed forces. For example, in 2016, we celebrated two notable milestones in the history of the ROTC program: the one hundredth anniversary of the founding of ROTC, and the return of ROTC to Yale University for the first time since the Vietnam era. When Yale graduated its first class of ROTC members in May 2016, I returned to my alma mater for the commissioning ceremony and personally swore them in.

The event symbolized our determination to make sure that our armed forces draw talent from every segment of American society. To ensure that we have access to the best minds of the rising generation, we need to attract young people from every demographic category, including groups that may once have felt that military service was irrelevant or even unwel-coming to them.

The imperative to expand our talent base drove my decisions on a number of issues that might seem unrelated to the topic. For example, during my tenure as SecDef, DOD modified its rules on policies like hairstyles, tattoos, and religiously prescribed dress, while retaining the traditional emphasis on maintaining military-style discipline and deco-rum. People from every background can serve in the U.S. military with distinction—so why erect barriers against, for example, a well-qualified recruit who happens to be a Sikh for whom wearing the traditional beard and turban is spiritually important?

The same need to broaden our talent base moved me to lift the DOD's ban on transgender service members. Research showed me that thou-sands of transgender individuals were in fact already serving in the mili-tary, some openly, some not. Their commanders considered them good service members, were unfazed by their gender status, and didn't want them kicked out of the service. It was clear that there was no fundamental impediment to allowing them to continue to serve without concealment. Furthermore, the military doctors I consulted said that gender transition is a recognized medical condition that could and should be treated like any other condition.

Based on all these realities, I could see no reason to discriminate against transgender individuals already serving in the military. And hav-ing reached that decision, there was no rational way to justify keeping other transgender people who were otherwise qualified for service from joining the force. The only sensible thing to do was to open military service to all qualified people, regardless of their gender status.

Accordingly, in June 2016, I announced a new transgender policy that removed the old barriers to service and laid out a detailed implementa-tion plan to be followed over the next year. To ensure that the health and readiness status of our forces would not be compromised, the policy stipulated that new recruits must be certified by their doctor as having been stable in their preferred gender for at least eighteen months prior to enlistment.

Unfortunately, in July 2017, President Trump declared his intention to reimpose a total ban on transgender troops. That presidential tweet was uninformed and ill-considered, and would not be in the best interests of the mission of the DOD. I hope and believe that Trump's policy on this matter will never actually be implemented.

You can see that, contrary to what some people assume, my decisions on policies regarding matters like transgender troops were not driven by "political correctness" or a desire to use the military to conduct some kind of "social experiment." In fact, the exact opposite is true. My goal, in this, as in all personnel matters, was to ensure that DOD has access to the broadest possible base of talent. To exclude qualified individuals who are eager to serve their country simply on the basis of their transgender status is detrimental to our effort to recruit the best people and therefore represents the worst kind of "political correctness" run amok—a policy imposed not for the good of our armed forces but purely in service to an unrelated ideological agenda.

I'd like to see further changes in the DOD's talent-management system. For example, in areas where advanced technical skills are needed, the Pentagon should have the ability to make lateral hires of experts in midcareer, letting them enter the service with an officer's rank. This is already possible with medical doctors; the same principle should apply to other specialized fields, such as cyber-defense.

So, more still needs to be done to ensure that the U.S. military remains the world's best for decades to come. But the advances we made during my tenure as secretary were so solidly based in military logic that I believe the positive trends that emerged then are likely to continue into the foreseeable future.

Caring for the Troops: Tackling the Problems of Sexual Assault and Suicide

Sexual assault is a plague almost everywhere in society, and even more so in institutions, like the military, traditionally associated with a male ethos. When I became SecDef, I wasn't proud of our record on the issue, and I was determined to tackle it head-on. As I used to tell troops, sexual assault is offensive in any organization, but it is especially so in the military. The profession of arms is based on honor and trust, and sexual assault is a violation of both.

There are basically three parts to a strategy for addressing the problem of sexual assault: helping the victim, dealing with the perpetrator, and, most important, prevention. At DOD, we studied the best approaches developed around the world for all three elements, then implemented them vigorously.

In regard to victim care, we focused on making sure that all aspects were handled—physical, mental, and professional. We gave service members who'd been victims a choice about whether to pursue the matter through a disciplinary or judicial process, but in either case, exactly the same care would be provided to them. Each unit had to assign a senior officer within the chain of command—not somebody offline, but a real leader central to the overall functioning of the unit—to coordinate management of sexual assault cases. We trained them, and then made them practice, making clear that these duties were as important as any other aspect of their work.

With respect to perpetrators, we began by making sure all commanders understood what the uniform code of military justice says about sexual assault. We also asked Congress to make some changes in the code to bring it up-to-date on this matter. In any given case, we would move swiftly to bring relief to those affected, even before the rights and wrongs of a particular allegation were determined. For example, we'd arrange to make sure that the two parties' work did not locate them in the same place at the same time alone by adjusting hours, locations, or seating arrangements. The process might involve reassignment of one or the other, provided that it was not otherwise disadvantageous to either party, since neither the victim nor the alleged perpetrator deserves that before the truth is known and justice has been rendered.

Of course, the most important policy element is prevention, and the key ingredient here is training. Many military members are young, so a military unit can resemble a college campus in terms of the level of maturity of the individuals. Moreover, some of the young troops have grown up in environments where their family or local culture was less strict, and few have dealt directly with cases of sexual assault. All this required training so that people knew how to behave themselves and what to do when they saw the wrong thing happening.

The methodical way in which DOD took on this challenge has attracted favorable attention around the nation. When I visited the University of Texas at Austin as part of my outreach to the tech community, I was introduced to the members of the university's sexual assault team, including the chief of the campus police, several deans, and some senior officials dedicated to the problem. They wanted to thank me for the sexual assault management playbook that we'd developed at DOD, which they'd adopted as the basis for their own program. Other institutions around the country have been following suit.

I'm not proud that the DOD had to grapple with the problem of sexual assault. But I'm proud of how we did it—in the usual straightforward military way.

Suicide in the military is another tragic problem that, understandably, gets a lot of press attention. It's a genuine cause for concern. In recent years, the rate of suicide in the U.S. Army has been close to 30 per 100,000 troops, which is well above the national rate of 12.5 per 100,000 people. However, when you look across all the service branches and draw comparisons to similar age groups in the rest of society, the discrepancy is much smaller.

DOD leaders have been working to find ways to reduce the numbers of military members who take their own lives. The problem is a complex one. There's the stereotyped story of a traumatized soldier who comes home from deployment, struggles with gruesome memories, and finds that the only way out is to take his or her own life. The story has a grain of truth, but it represents only a small fraction of military suicides. Most involve people who've never been in combat who are simply suffering from the strains of personal and family life as well as their own individual hereditary strengths and weaknesses.

One factor that probably contributes to military suicide rates is access to firearms, which has been found to correlate to elevated suicide rates everywhere. The data indicates that people suffering from depression or anxiety are more likely to succumb to a passing impulse when a gun makes suicide seem faster and easier.

Another problem some surveys have surfaced is the fear among service members that their careers may suffer if they confess that they're wrestling with a psychological problem and need help. That's not true—we train our officers about the realities of mental illness, so they're prepared to let a service member "take a knee" with full support and without judgment when they're suffering. But the stigma associated with confessing "weakness" is a persistent problem, not just in the military but throughout society, that we all need to work to overcome.

Women in Service: The Story Behind a Breakthrough

The single biggest talent-management decision I made during my tenure was probably my decision to open all positions in the military to women. The story behind this decision, its announcement, and its implementation, illustrates some of the complex challenges surrounding any major policy move within DOD—particularly one that some might consider controversial. Of course, female service members themselves are at the center of this story. But here my focus is on how to effectively implement a major change of this kind.

When I became SecDef in February 2015, nearly 10 percent of all military positions—220,000 in total—were barred to women. Specific roles in artillery, armor, infantry, and some special operations units were reserved for men, despite the fact that women had been serving our country, at risk and on the battlefield, in growing numbers.

The numbers speak for themselves. More than 300,000 women have served in combat environments over the past two decades in Iraq and Afghanistan. These conflicts demolished conventional battle lines, making it increasingly difficult to exclude women from combat based on occupational specialty. Women have fought insurgents in dangerous areas as top-gunners in Humvees and door-gunners on helicopters. They have patrolled streets with machine guns, disposed of explosives, and driven trucks down booby-trapped roads. They have led convoys in combat and have flown attack helicopters. They have served on female engagement teams with the Marines and in cultural support teams that accompany Rangers, Navy SEALs, and other special operators on raids. Some women gather intelligence as members of the Navy SEAL and Army Special Forces teams. Women are, right now, flying in the skies above Syria, Iraq, and Afghanistan.

Collectively, women have earned more than 10,000 combat action badges and Bronze Stars, including at least 12 Bronze Stars awarded for acts of valor. Two women have received the nation's second-highest honor, the Silver Star, since World War II. More than 1,000 women have been wounded in action in combat operations since 2008. As of March 2018, 168 women had given their lives to our country.

This heroic level of service by women was made possible by DOD policy changes. In 1975, the department opened up the military service academies to women. In the early 1990s, Congress repealed laws prohibiting women from serving in air and naval combat units. In 1998, DOD allowed women to fly fighter jets and serve on combat ships at sea.

At about the same time, however, DOD also issued the Direct Ground Combat Definition and Assignment Rule, which prohibited women from being assigned to units whose primary mission was engaging in direct ground combat. This rule stood for two decades, until January 2013, when then-SecDef Leon Panetta partially rescinded it, opening 110,000 new positions to women.

However, Leon did not make a final decision about whether the remaining 220,000 positions would be opened to women. Instead, he gave the Army, Navy, Marine Corps, and Air Force, along with the commander of the Special Operations Command, three years to study the issue. They could recommend opening all military roles to women, or they could request exemptions. The chairman of the Joint Chiefs of Staff would review these requests, and the SecDef would decide whether to approve.

This plan effectively kicked the can down the road until January 1, 2016—one year into my tenure as SecDef. When I became secretary, I knew that the final decision would rest on my shoulders.

My instincts and experience told me that opening all positions to women was the right thing to do. But I knew that bungling either the decision process or its implementation would be a colossal setback. Long-standing questions about the risks involved in integrating women in combat positions would be reopened. The issue could easily become a political football, like so many other issues today. The fallout could have kept some positions closed to women long into the future. So the burden was on me to handle it the right way—to make the decision bulletproof.

My women-in-service decision was an example of leadership in the sense that I defined in Chapter 12—an action that involved driving change, rather than upholding the best elements of the existing culture at DOD, as one does when practicing reinforcement. Other options were open to me. I could have chosen to kick the can further down the road as had been done several times in the past, arguing that it was "too hard" or that people "weren't ready" for this move. Since this avenue was easily available to me and there was not a constant and insistent push to do otherwise, I probably could have skated through, but this was a change that I thought was worth the effort and risk. I realized that this was a time to shift into leadership mode.

Handling this challenging process correctly began with making sure that the thinking behind the decision was crystal-clear and irrefutable.

There were two pillars to my belief that women should be eligible for every military job. Both were related to one broader goal: ensuring that our all-volunteer fighting force remains the strongest in history.

First, as I've noted, I knew that finding the most qualified person to fill any position in the military requires drawing from America's entire pool of talent—not just a portion of it. Of course, the military has high expectations that must be met, so service members must earn their positions through a competitive process. But our ability to remain a highly professional and effective force depends on recruiting the best that our country has to offer—regardless of gender.

We've already seen that there are plenty of cases in which the best candidate for a job is a woman. In September 2015, I called First Lieutenant Shaye Haver and Captain Kristen Griest to congratulate them on becoming the first women to graduate from Ranger School, the Army's premier leadership course and one of the most challenging and exhausting training programs in the military. About four thousand officers and enlisted soldiers start Ranger school every year, but only two out of five earn the right to wear the distinctive black-and-gold Ranger tab on their uniforms. Ranger School graduates represent the top 3 percent of active-duty soldiers in the Army.

Second Lieutenant Zachary Hagner, who was in the same Ranger school class as Haver and Griest were, recalled a moment from training. After carrying a seventeen-pound machine gun for three days, he was bone-tired, and asked his fellow squad members for help with his burden. "I went to every single person, just in a line, no order, and they were 'No, I'm really tired, too, I'm broken.'" But when he got to Kristen Griest, Hagner recalls, "She basically took it away from me. Nine guys were like 'Well, I'm too broken, I'm too tired.' She—just as broken and tired—took it from me with almost excitement. I thought she was crazy for that, but maybe she was just motivated."

Given the chance, Haver and Griest proved that women could meet the toughest standards the U.S. military can set. And yet the policies in place at the time prohibited them from serving in a Ranger regiment. We were depriving ourselves of the chance to make full use of their proven talents and risked stalling their career progress in a way that could have caused them to look outside the military.

Every qualified woman serving in our military makes our fighting force stronger and the rest of us safer. To keep our fighting force as strong as possible, we cannot afford to pass them by.

The second pillar of my reasoning was my determination to ensure that we can recruit and—even more important—retain high-performing women in the military. This principle applies no matter what position a particular woman may hold.

Our studies indicated that, for a variety of reasons, the military jobs that had been closed to women would likely attract only a small number of female applicants, at least initially. Most women in the force are pursuing careers in other specialties. They have chosen to fly planes or repair submarines, to carry out communications or intelligence or logistics work—work that is critical to our duty protecting Americans at home and abroad.

But even though these women may not want to apply for jobs in one of the previously closed positions, it is important for them to know they are not second-class citizens in the organization to which they have dedicated their careers. When women are excluded from positions like combat arms, it has an indirect effect on both their own perceptions of how greatly they are valued and the attitudes of those around them. Combat experience is often crucial to promotion into the senior ranks of the services. So barring women from certain combat positions often means stalling their careers, making military service less appealing as a career choice. For all the women serving at lower ranks and in noncombat specialties, it also means they would never have a top commander like them.

Thus, even though the absolute numbers of women who enter the newly opened positions might be small, I believed that providing women with the opportunity would have an outsize benefit. It would help unlock the talents of *all* the women in the force as well as encourage more women to enlist. International comparisons bear out this logic. For example, through our research, we learned that since Germany opened all combat positions to women in 2001, the number of overall women in the German Armed Forces has tripled.

These two logical pillars strongly suggested to me that opening all positions to women would be a sound decision. But I wouldn't be ready to confirm that decision until we did our homework.

The DOD is a learning organization—a point of pride for me as well as a foundational characteristic of our institution. In recent years, we've studied such urgent new skills as counterterrorism and counterinsurgency, drone warfare, night raids, wounded warrior care, and sexual assault prevention and response—and we've taken on these new challenges openly and with military deliberateness and discipline.

In keeping with this institutional ethos, we carried out exhaustive studies before I made the decision. The services conducted extensive examinations of the opportunities, effects, and implementation issues inherent in opening all combat positions to women. By July 2015, the Pentagon had completed forty-one studies. We conducted surveys of the troops, male and female. We studied unit cohesion; women's health; equipment, gear, and uniforms; facilities modifications; interest in serving in combat roles; and international experiences with women in combat. We reviewed and validated gender-neutral occupational standards for combat roles to ensure none would be lowered. We studied potential effects on living arrangements and sexual assault, recognizing that this decision would put men and women into smaller, more dangerous, more tension-filled circumstances.

We looked at comparable organizations, including more than a dozen other militaries around the world that have opened "close combat roles" to women—those positions that entail engaging an enemy on the ground while being exposed to hostile fire and a high probability of physical contact with hostile forces. We looked at SWAT teams, which are mixed gender. We looked at NASA flight crews that were mixed gender and had to operate in confined quarters.

These studies yielded insights far beyond gender integration. The research and analysis conducted over two years increased our understanding of the physical and physiological demands on service members and the cultural currents that influence unit cohesion and morale. We gleaned lessons not only about the decision itself but also about how to implement it in a way that would fully harness the advantages it could offer our forces.

I received the components' voluminous analyses and reviewed every one of them carefully to ensure I took into account the many different circumstances and concerns across services. I would be the one defending this decision, so I made sure to master the details personally. I had to ensure that I could answer the question "Mr. Secretary, have you thought about this or that aspect carefully?" with a confident "Yes."

All the uniformed services were supportive of opening all positions to women—with one exception. The Marine Corps had reservations and asked for continuing exemptions that would have applied to 48,779 Corps positions, particularly in the areas of infantry, artillery, armor, and reconnaissance. The secretary of the Navy, who oversees the Corps, did not approve its request for exceptions. Nonetheless, as SecDef, I still had to consider it.

Joe Dunford was the Marine Corps commandant who asked for these continuing exceptions. As of October 2015—as the decision process was nearing its climax—he had become chairman of the Joint Chiefs of Staff. I'd recommended Joe for that position to President Obama despite knowing the judgment he'd made about the Marines. To this day, I think that recommending Joe was the single best decision I made as SecDef.

When it came to rendering his advice as chairman of the Joint Chiefs, Dunford acted as he typically does. He used his comprehensive problem-solving approach to make two critical contributions to my decision to go ahead with the policy change—despite the fact that he didn't personally agree with it in the case of the Marines. First, he recommended that whatever decision I made should be "joint"—that is, consistent across all branches of the force. In today's wars, members of various services fight side by side in a way that is different from wars of the past. As a practical matter, a consistent approach would be most effective. I followed Joe's recommendation on this matter by deciding not to make a special exception for the Marines.

Dunford's second point was that "a decision is not implementation." It was crucial that the decision be well executed. That meant training people, both female and male, to deal with the new policy properly, and ensuring that all the "little" things, like showers, bunking, and bathrooms, would be managed intelligently. I took both these points to heart in making my decision.

By fall 2015, we had done all our homework. Over Thanksgiving weekend, I took home all the binders containing the services' reports and studied them with care. I discussed the decision with two close confidants—Eric Rosenbach, my chief of staff, and Bob Work, the deputy secretary—as well as Joe Dunford.

After reviewing all the evidence, considering Joe's advice, and analyzing the decision from every perspective, I concluded that the data confirmed that opening all positions to women, without exceptions, was the right decision to assemble the strongest possible military force today and tomorrow.

And that brings us to the way I handled the announcement.

The usual thing to do would have been to wait until the long-announced deadline of January 1, 2016, walk out on that day to the podium in the Pentagon, and announce a decision to the assembled media. I did not.

Instead, I decided to make the announcement about a month earlier, when nobody would expect it.

I did so for two reasons. First, this was a professional decision that we arrived at through a deliberate, logic-driven process. I wanted the announcement to reflect that. I did not want the spectacle and controversy that would result from making the announcement on the deadline. A splashy decision may garner some praise, but it also elicits negative views that can block progress. Our surveys indicated that female service members felt the same—they did not think we should turn this decision into a spectacle.

Second, I wanted the opportunity to clearly and fully articulate the twin pillars of my argument before anyone else could put forth a competing narrative. There would be plenty of time for debate afterward. Members of Congress could respond and call hearings. Op-ed columnists and broadcast commentators could weigh in. But I would have laid out my case and preemptively addressed objections—which meant I would be in the driver's seat. Opponents would not have had the chance to distort the debate with cherry-picked examples and straw man arguments. I was confident that my argument—backed by reason and evidence—would prevail in a fair fight.

I also took pains with the wording of the announcement. I crafted a clear, straightforward statement shorn of rhetorical or ideological flourishes, focused on telling a simple story: how we'd reached this decision and why it was the right one. I wrote every word myself, by hand, giving every sentence the care it deserved.

Then there was the internal politics of the department to be considered. Joe Dunford and I had to be careful. The announcement carried risks for both of us. Opening all positions in the Marine Corps to women contradicted Dunford's stance as commandant, which by this time had become publicly known. This put him in an uncomfortable and potentially embarrassing position. So Joe and I agreed that when I made the announcement, he would *not* be at the podium with me. If the press was going to criticize the decision, I wanted them to criticize me, no one else—and I particularly did not want Joe to be caught in the middle.

To guard against leaks, I was very careful about whom I told beforehand. Joe Dunford, Bob Work, and Eric Rosenbach were the only people who knew. On the big morning, when we alerted the press corps that an announcement about women in service was coming, reporters could only guess what the decision would be. Knowing the attitude of the Marine Corps, many predicted that a number of exceptions would be granted.

Those in the dark included the president himself. An hour before I walked out to the podium, I called Denis McDonough, Obama's chief of staff: "I'm about to make an announcement opening all military positions to women, with no exceptions. I know I'm surprising you, but I think it's better this way. This is a professional decision driven by the mission and by the department's own analysis. We should be the ones to announce it and to defend it. If it looks like a White House–led decision, then it will seem political.

"That said," I told Denis, "you can put me through to the president if you want."

"No need," Denis replied. "Go ahead with your announcement."

Denis being Denis, and Obama being Obama, they both understood fully. The decision was correct, the process behind it was professional, and the outcome was too important to jeopardize by letting it get caught up in politics. I particularly didn't want the news to get leaked by a zealously supportive White House staffer tempted to turn the event into an opportunity for a "victory dance" in the media. That would only invite angry pushback from opponents—the last thing we needed.

I also refrained from alerting anyone in Congress, whether I expected them to be supportive or not. This was another way I hoped to insulate the decision from politics. I knew that high-profile decisions by the SecDef virtually always draw reactions from Congress, usually both positive and negative. Such decisions are always tough ones, often politically charged. I wanted to minimize such reactions in this case.

My well-laid plans ended up working very much as I'd hoped.

I read my statement to the assembled press corps. One of the first questions that followed was, "Why is the chairman of the Joint Chiefs not here?"

I'd prepared for that. "This is my decision," I responded. "I take full responsibility for it, and if there are any questions about why I've made it and how we will implement it, I'm the person to answer them." I went on to acknowledge what everyone in the room knew—that Joe Dunford had been a dissenter from the decision, at least as far as the Marine Corps was concerned. "As always, I sought out General Dunford's advice, which I value. In this instance, I am not taking his advice as commandant." But I also described the ways I *was* taking his advice as chairman of the whole force in regard to jointness and implementation, for which I thanked him.

The way we choreographed this somewhat delicate circumstance worked for us in two ways. First, it showed that I was forthrightly taking responsibility for the decision rather than ducking it. Most people, from the media to Congress to the troops themselves, appreciate and respect that kind of stand-up behavior from a leader. Second, it showed clearly that we'd made space for honest disagreement—but that now that the decision had been made, the military leadership were fully on board and would be carrying it out without dissension.

I also had one other circumstance on my side—as I'd anticipated I would. This was the fact that at least half of the Pentagon press corps are women. Most of them were natural supporters of the decision—a fact confirmed by the roomful of beaming smiles the moment I broke the news. All of them covered the announcement professionally and objectively—but it was only natural that, just as they wanted the chance to rise or fall on their own professional merits, they appreciated the opening of that same opportunity to women in uniform.

I took one other unusual step when communicating the decision. To supplement the usual press release and the press conference I hosted, I wrote a post for the blog platform Medium, in which I detailed the thought process behind the decision. The post was linked to the press release that was sent to reporters and posted on DOD's social media platforms. This approach let me tell the story on my terms and deliver it directly and unfiltered to those who would be impacted most: our service members and their families.

In the hours and days that followed, I received almost no backlash from Congress—a very unusual result. The same was true of the media: the decision did not become fodder for days of partisan or ideological debate. The thoroughness of our preparation and the strength of our arguments effectively shut down any controversy before it started. For once, the usual D.C. media circus simply never occurred.

Those who appreciated it the most were the female troops themselves—and many of them told me so. Rather than becoming political footballs—or casualties—they were able to quietly, professionally take advantage of the new opportunities to do what they'd always wanted to do: to serve their country to their fullest capacity.

The final step was implementation—and here, again, our thorough advance preparation paid off. Since 2015, more than 640 women in the Army have entered previously closed combat jobs, one of whom was Captain Griest, the first female Army infantry officer. In the Marine Corps, 181 women serve in non-infantry jobs in previously closed combat units. Hundreds more women are currently in the training pipeline for combat arms jobs. A 2017 RAND survey of male and female service members concluded, "Our general overall impression from the groups is that there is not a lot of opposition to the policy change in either the male or female focus groups. Many participants were either supportive or neutral on the issue."

Some open questions remain, including the recruitment, assignment, and career management of women into the new roles. For example, young men have to register for the draft when they turn eighteen, even though there is currently no military draft in the United States. Should young women be subject to the same requirement? This question arose immediately after we made this decision. At the time, I said that it stands to reason that if women are admitted to all positions in the military, they should be subject to the draft. However, the law remains that women are not currently required to register. In fact, it does not matter much to me, since I do not want a draft. I want the DOD to be able to pick who joins the military, not forced to work with those chosen by a more-or-less arbitrary draft system.

Another continuing question is how to reevaluate and adjust the standards required for all positions. In the course of our research, over many years and unconnected with the gender issue, I came to the view that we needed to modernize our standards. All the services had already come to this conclusion. I did not want to do so in association with the women-in-service issue, because it would be easily misconstrued as re-laxing standards in order to let women in—a perception I was determined to avoid. It was not the time to stress this point then, but I stress it now: in many cases, our standards are outdated. This is true of the American educational system and workplace in general. We have established standards based on a limited set of attributes, physical and otherwise, that may not fully reflect how effective a person could be in that job. Lifting artillery shells is only one aspect of the job of being a soldier or Marine in an artillery unit. But the standards for the military operational specialties that had been closed had largely remained physically focused.

I learned a different approach from Special Operations Command, where many of the positions are also physically demanding. They call their standards system a "total person" approach. This means that, in addition to your physical strength, your ability to reason through a problem, make decisions logically, work in teams, and respond to unexpected circumstances is also considered combat-relevant.

The successful implementation of this decision is far from over. But the important thing about how we rolled out this decision is that we paid careful attention to the implementation process. We sought to see all the potential complications that would arise before we made our decision. It was never an afterthought. It was critical to the decision-making process. This gave us the opportunity to proactively address these concerns in my announcement, both heading off others' objections and giving our decision the greatest chance of success after the announcement.

On July 28, 2016, I conducted the Oath of Enlistment for seven young recruits at the Chicago Military Entrance Processing Station (MEPS). There are sixty-five MEPS across the United States and Puerto Rico. Nicknamed "Freedom's Front Door," MEPS serve as a gateway through which applicants complete the enlistment process and enter the armed services. I visited the Chicago MEPS as part of my Force of the Future effort to modernize how the military recruits its people. I was the first Secretary of Defense to visit a MEPS since the 1970s. It was a complete surprise to the new recruits and their proud families.

Applicants seeking to enlist go to MEPS, where military and civilian staff screen applicants to ensure they meet all the services' physical,

academic, and moral standards to determine whether they are qualified
to join the military. This screening entails aptitude testing, career coun-
seling, a medical evaluation, and a background screening.

The process culminates with qualified applicants taking the Oath of
Enlistment, which states: "I do solemnly swear that I will support and
defend the Constitution of the United States against all enemies, foreign
and domestic; that I will bear true faith and allegiance to the same; and
that I will obey the orders of the President of the United States and the
orders of the officers appointed over me, according to regulations and
the Uniform Code of Military Justice. So help me God."

For all service members, this is the beginning of their military life.
After an individual swears the oath, she or he is a full member of the U.S.
armed forces.

Among the seven remarkable young women and men I swore in that
day in Chicago, one young woman was joining the Army. We spoke
briefly before the ceremony, and she told me that her ambition was to join
the Army's Armor Branch. It is an active combat arms branch responsible
for tank and forward reconnaissance operations on the battlefield to destroy enemy positions. It had been closed to women before my decision.

She knew she was going to have to qualify for a position in Armor—in
fact, she relished the opportunity to fight for her place. Because just a
year ago, she would not have had the chance. No matter how much she
wanted to—and no matter how capable she proved herself to be—she
would not have been permitted to join.

This young woman, and all the other remarkable women who will
follow, will make the U.S. armed forces stronger. This is why applying
reason and homework to make the right decision and then announcing
and implementing it thoughtfully were so important.

Even as we continue with implementation today, it will not all happen
overnight. While at the end of the day this will make us a better and
stronger force, there will still be problems to fix and challenges to overcome. We should not diminish that fact

At the same time, we should also remember that the military has long
prided itself on being a meritocracy, where those who serve are judged

not based on who they are or where they come from, but rather on what they have to offer to help defend this country. That's why the United States has the finest fighting force the world has ever known. And it is one other way we will strive to ensure that our military remains so, long into the future.

Welcome Home: Helping Veterans Reintegrate into Civilian Life

If treating the troops right is an integral part of building the Force of the Future, so is taking appropriate care of them when they transition away from service into civilian life. For this reason, veterans' employment was a high priority for me. I was determined that we'd never repeat the neglect and even hostility some veterans from past eras experienced. Whenever I met with a group of Vietnam veterans, I would always use the words that I'd first heard President Obama say to a group of Vietnam veterans, delivering them the message they hadn't heard when they first came home from Vietnam: "Welcome home, welcome home."

The challenge of taking good care of returning veterans was especially great because of the large force increases associated with the wars in Iraq and Afghanistan. One of the first problems I tackled was the bias against hiring veterans among many business leaders, many of whom had never served themselves. There was widespread belief that those who joined the military were people unfit for other jobs; those returning from overseas deployments were often assumed to be broken and traumatized.

These stereotypes were unfair and false. The fact is that most veterans hadn't been in combat. Whether they had or not, they'd been working in intensely demanding jobs that made them not only highly skilled but also disciplined, excellent leaders. Workers like this are hard to come by.

The best way to overcome these misconceptions was by exposing business leaders to reality. We created some high-profile initiatives with a few patriotic executives who committed to hiring a certain number of veterans. That was enough to start the ball rolling. As soon as business leaders actually met and worked with veterans, their attitudes flipped 180 degrees immediately. Every single business leader I've ever spoken to told me that hiring veterans was one of the best personnel moves they'd ever made.

We also overhauled our veterans' transition programs, which service members participate in during their final months of service. I found that these programs basically consisted of short tutorials about how to go on welfare, qualify for unemployment payments, and maximize the number of "disability points" they scored to earn the most benefits from the Veterans Administration. I thought this didn't serve the institution or the service members well at all.

We transformed the programs to cover three tracks: entrepreneurship (for example, managing a McDonald's franchise), corporate employment, and continuing education. Service members were taught how to prepare a résumé using civilian terminology to explain military skills and how to use social media in their job search. We even invited employers to participate in job fairs on military bases, like those held on college campuses.

Once service members have returned to civilian life, the job of taking care of them belongs to the VA. It's an important task. But I must say that, as SecDef, I disliked working with the VA. Despite some great leaders, I found it to be a backward, inward-focused organization whose main priority seemed to be getting DOD involved in its problems.

An example of how this dynamic played out was the issue of reforming the medical-records systems of our two health systems. DOD was operating a vast, antiquated health care system called Alta while the VA had a very different but equally antiquated system called Vista. Since Alta and Vista were both coming up for modernization at the same time, the question naturally arose whether they should be combined. The VA fervently wanted to combine them, mostly hoping to get access to our IT expertise and maybe some DOD money.

It may sound logical to merge the military and veterans' health care systems, but a moment's reflection shows you that, in medical terms, the two systems are quite different. The VA is a geriatric medical system while the DOD system is largely a pediatric system. The doctors are not in the same specialties, the medicines in the pharmacopoeia are not the same, and so on.

Furthermore, experience has shown that combining two health care systems is miserably difficult to do. Take little matters like the way prescription drugs are managed. In a normal system, the dosages will be bracketed, and departures from standard doses will require special attention and waivers, or at least be brought to the attention of the physician when the prescription is processed. But all these dosages, the units they were measured in, the names of the drugs themselves, and the methods of dealing with generic drugs were different in the two systems. And this is just one example of the complexities involved. As a result, the medical professionals were fearful of creating an error-prone "integrated" system that might end up injuring or killing patients.

Despite all this, my predecessors Bob Gates and Leon Panetta had publicly accepted a proposal by VA Secretary Eric Shinseki to create an integrated electronic health record (IEHR) program. Frankly, I think their main motivation was to get through their unavoidable meetings with Shinseki with minimal fuss.

Thankfully, while I was deputy secretary, I was able to convince SecDef Chuck Hagel to escape this commitment by making a simple proposal that got the VA, the White House, and Congress off our backs and did the right thing. We simply changed the *I* in IEHR from *integrated* to *interoperable*. This would mean that the VA and the DOD would continue to run separate health systems, simply making sure they could "operate" together. Thus, for example, the records of a departing service member could be easily transported to the VA system. This was a sensible resolution of what could have been a bureaucratic and IT nightmare.

More important have been the advances we've made in treating the serious health care problems that service members and veterans face. Here, again, the DOD's tradition of being a learning organization has proved to be invaluable. In the past few years, our doctors, nurses, and other professionals have made huge strides in improving our ability to care for wounded warriors. The so-called signature wounds of Iraq and Afghanistan include extensive burns and amputations due to IEDs—injuries found in many previous wars, but more common today because the survival rates of troops with these injuries are now much higher.

DOD physicians are experts in all the newest surgical, antibiotic, prosthetic, and other treatment approaches, and as a result many of the trauma doctors in urban medical centers around the country today are military-trained. We've also greatly improved our methods for treating post-traumatic stress.

As SecDef, my single highest priority was making sure that the troops were treated well at every stage of their connection with the DOD, from recruitment through service and into their years as veterans. Not only was this the right thing to do, but also it helped us to attract and retain the most talented people in our country, thereby guaranteeing our ability to carry out the most vital missions entrusted to anyone in America.

CHAPTER 15

THE TROOPS DESERVE THE TRUTH

Joshua Wheeler, as you'll recall from Chapter 9, became famous as the first American soldier to die in the fight against ISIS. But there's more to his story than most people know.

Wheeler grew up in a poor, troubled family in rural eastern Oklahoma, the oldest of five kids. He did odd jobs to help meet the household expenses and made sure his younger brothers and sister ate breakfast and got to school every morning. After high school, he faced the same choice as most of his fellow graduates: he could look for work in the oil business, or he could join the military. Josh chose the Army. In 1997, two years after he'd enlisted, he joined the elite Rangers and later was assigned to Army Special Operations Command, based at Fort Bragg, North Carolina.

In October 2015, Master Sergeant Joshua Wheeler was stationed in Iraq. At that point, U.S. forces were no longer doing all the fighting in that troubled part of the world. Instead, they were engaged in training and support of local forces battling against the militants of ISIS. On October 22, the Kurdish commandos Wheeler was working with had received a tip: A nearby compound controlled by ISIS contained some seventy local hostages, held prisoner for cooperating with Iraqi government officials. Now it appeared that the execution of those hostages was imminent—in fact, aerial photos showed a newly dug mass grave near the compound, waiting for their bodies.

The Kurdish commandos swung into action, supported by their U.S. special operations partners. They launched a helicopter raid on the compound, determined to rescue the hostages. Wheeler and a team of ten to twenty U.S. fighters went along, their job being to transport the Iraqi forces that would assault the compound and support them through intelligence and communications. But the raid went wrong. An effort by the commandos to blast a hole in the compound's outer wall failed. Gunfire immediately broke out. It was obvious that the commandos were in trouble.

Wheeler and his men did what American fighters do—they ran toward the sound of the guns. When the battle ended, the hostages had been freed. A few of the Iraqi commandos were injured. Only one rescuer died in the operation—Joshua Wheeler.

Days later, I met with Joshua Wheeler's wife, Ashley, at Dover Air Force Base. We were waiting to welcome her husband's remains as they came down the cargo ramp of a C-17. Ashley was an extraordinary person, filled with love and admiration for her husband. It was a marriage that had made her life whole, she said. There was no bitterness in her voice. But she did have one question for the Secretary of Defense who had signed her husband's orders—the same question many in the press were also asking: "Did he die in combat?"

I was saddened—and upset—that she even had to ask that question. But I understood all too well why she was asking.

President Obama had come into office pledging to end two wars, in Afghanistan and Iraq. That was easier said than done. Almost seven years later, Obama found himself still directing U.S. troops on the ground in both combat zones—but he was also claiming that those troops were not involved in "combat operations."

It was true, in a way. The strategy we were pursuing in Iraq was to enable and support local forces rather than substituting for them. The goal was to ensure that victory, when achieved, would stick—and the strategy was the right one. But lawyerly parsing had become the style of White House spokesmen, reflecting Obama's own tendency to speak precisely and make fine distinctions. Those distinctions reflected the admirable clarity of the president's thought processes, but they were much too fine for the press or public. They led, inevitably, to a game of "gotcha" with reporters and cable TV pundits who tried to trip up administration spokespeople and force them to make—and admit—misstatements about exactly what our soldiers were doing in the Middle East.

I was put off by the very idea of playing such verbal games. "Of course Josh died in combat," I told Ashley Wheeler. And when I spoke to the press about the incident on October 28, I repeated those words: "Of course he died in combat."

Honesty is generally the best policy for any government official to follow. Josh Wheeler's extraordinary life and death had earned him, and those who loved him, nothing less.

Speaking Truth About the Reasons for War

War has to be spoken about bluntly, especially when leaders are talking with members of families who have sacrificed everything for their country. Accordingly, I used honest language—words like "war" and "combat"— whenever it was appropriate, and ignored the "suggested edits" from the White House staff substituting other, less forthright words.

As I've noted, I also began changing the language we used to define our goals in the fight against ISIS, shifting from half-hearted verbs such as "degrade" in sentences like "We will degrade the capabilities of ISIS" to tougher words, like "defeat" and "destroy." When I met with the families of officers, I told them that history would remember their loved ones as "victorious commanders." Our intent had to be nothing less.

The most important audience for these messages about the reality of war were the troops themselves.

At every important moment of the wars during my time as SecDef, I gave a speech explaining to the troops what they were doing and why it was important. Thus, shortly after we completed the coalition military campaign plan against ISIS and the president had approved it, I traveled to Fort Campbell, Kentucky. That's where the 101st Airborne was preparing to deploy to Baghdad—the first unit to begin putting the new plan into action. I wanted them to have a clear notion of what their mission was in my own words—in words they could appreciate, and in words they could share with their spouses, their children, and their parents.

That was my goal in every troop event, wherever it was, stateside or around the world. To accomplish that, I made sure to do two things.

First, I told the troops how proud I was of them, how proud their country was of them, and how proud they should be of themselves. I said they were doing "the noblest thing you can do with your life—protecting America and making a better world for our children." I told them they were part of "the finest fighting force the world has ever known"—a phrase I used in practically every speech I made, mainly because I believed it to my bones.

Second, I told the troops precisely what we were asking them to do— what the strategy was and why it was the right one. I told them how it would fit into history. If we were meeting on a ship in the South China Sea, I would speak of the critical American role as part of a peaceful network of security in a region of the world that would have an oversize influence on the future of humankind. If they were deploying to Europe, I would tell them why NATO needed to stand tall against Russian aggression. If we were in Iraq, I would tell them how we needed to destroy the *fact* of an Islamist state based on its evil ideology in order to destroy the *idea* itself. And I would explain that they were working hand in hand with local forces rather than on their own—which would be frustrating at times—because we wanted our victory to be rooted in local conditions and culture, and therefore lasting.

Strategy and history are big ideas to these young people, many not yet out of their teens. But if my words were clear and direct, they could remember the words, they could repeat them to their mom or dad, and hopefully they could recall them proudly for years to come.

Historians of the American Civil War have studied thousands of letters written by Union soldiers to their loved ones at home—parents, friends, sweethearts. Some of the writers were farm laborers and mill workers who were barely literate; some had to dictate their thoughts to nurses or orderlies who would capture them on paper. (Poet Walt Whitman, who worked as a volunteer nurse in a military hospital, penned many such letters for wounded soldiers.) Of course the letters are filled with personal endearments and the minutiae of a soldier's day—dreary hours of marching, meals to complain about, the anxiety of facing fire.

But many also contain thoughtful and moving explanations of why the soldiers were fighting—simple but eloquent expositions of the principles of freedom and universal human dignity that sparked their patriotism.

In a democracy, every man and woman who dons a uniform in the service of the country should share that personal understanding of and commitment to the cause for which they fight. That's a basic reason it is an important part of the SecDef's job in command to talk plainly and comprehensively about war, especially to those waging it.

Addressing the Consequences

I scrubbed and gowned to enter the room of a young Marine with his dad at Walter Reed Army Medical Center a few days after he was wounded in Afghanistan. (This was shortly before the 2011 merger of Walter Reed with Bethesda Naval Hospital.) It was necessary to scrub because Mark (as I'll call him) had had both of his legs amputated "ATK"—above the knee—in this case, almost at his hips. The amputation sites were subject to infection, a constant worry in view of the several surgeries he had already undergone. We visited for a while, both Mark and his father showing the strength that amazed me every time, even though by now I had seen it all too often.

As we walked out and took our gowns and caps off, his dad followed me down the hall. "Mr. Secretary," he said, "my son wants just one thing."

"What is that?" I asked.

"He wants his dog back."

I asked for more details, and eventually the whole story came pouring out. Mark's unit had had a bomb-sniffing dog named Buckshot, and Mark had been Buckshot's handler. Buckshot had been trained to walk in front of a patrol down a path through the fields and sniff for improvised explosive devices made from fertilizer. When he smelled a bomb, he would sit down near it, circle it, or send some other recognizable signal to his handler. But one day, a bomb had gone off in the patrol anyway, injuring one of Buckshot's paws and puncturing one of his eardrums—while also mangling Mark's legs.

Now, as he recovered his strength in a hospital thousands of miles from the battlefield, this brave Marine wanted nothing more than to be reunited with his beloved Buckshot.

The next morning, I called General James Amos, the commandant of the Marine Corps. Amos was a spectacular commander, and he and his wife, Bonnie, were friends of mine and Stephanie's. I knew he'd understand the urgency of my question: Could he look into finding Buckshot?

I feared the worst. In most cases, military dogs involved in an explosion cannot return to duty. Most are euthanized as the most humane way of ending their suffering. But Jim promised to investigate, and I hoped against hope that I wouldn't have to deliver bad news to Buckshot's friend.

A little while later came back the happy news that Buckshot was alive, living at a kennel in South Carolina. The Marine Corps set about organizing a reunion between dog and handler.

A few months later, I visited Mark again, this time at Brooke Army Medical Center (BAMC) in San Antonio. He'd been moved there to receive continuing physical therapy and, crucially, to be fitted with the prosthetic legs that are one of BAMC's specialties. Again, his dad was there, taking care of his son. Again, the nurses made us scrub—which alarmed me a bit, because I'd assumed that Mark would be past any danger of infection.

But when we entered the room, my anxiety vanished. Mark was sitting upright in a wheelchair, not flat on his back in the hospital bed. When he saw me, he quickly fired up his iPad and proudly showed me a photo—a snapshot of him sharing his wheelchair with a huge black Lab. Both Mark and Buckshot were grinning broadly.

Our military hospitals—Walter Reed, BAMC, Bethesda, Landstuhl in Germany, and others—were full of young men and women with stories like this one. On weekends, Stephanie and I would visit them as often as we could, usually in Washington, where the wounded would come either directly (mostly from Bagram and Kandahar in Afghanistan) or via Landstuhl. Stephanie and I would arrive at Walter Reed and be greeted by Howard Clark, the endlessly caring and efficient coordinator for visitors. Howard would fill us in on who'd arrived that week. The peak years were when I was undersecretary and deputy secretary and the Afghan surge was in full swing. The numbers were fortunately lower during most of my time as SecDef, though they picked up as the counter-ISIS campaign gained momentum.

Sometimes Steph and I made these visits alone, but sometimes we were accompanied by friends from DOD. Two of our favorites were Pete and Beth Chiarelli. Pete was vice chief of staff of the Army—a bighearted guy who had done more than anyone else for wounded warriors. When Pete and I walked into a hospital room, no one paid any attention to me in my suit—it was the four-star general who garnered all the attention, and rightly so. Sometimes Stephanie and I were joined by another senior national security official, usually from the White House. They shared responsibility for the decisions that resulted in wounded warriors. It meant a lot to them that I'd invited them to come.

A typical scene: A big, strong young man lies in the hospital bed. In the chair next to him, his young wife and their four-month-old baby. Mom has been assigned DOD housing nearby, but the sleeping bag on the floor reveals that she and the baby have been spending most of their time in Dad's hospital room. I learn that, until the three of them came together in his hospital room, Dad had never yet had a chance to meet his tiny daughter.

"Tell me what happened," I say.

He tells me about the mission, its significance, and about how well his unit had been performing. Then came the fight in which he was wounded. "I want to get back there," he declares. "I need to help my buddies." I've heard similar sentiments from hundreds of other wounded warriors.

Meanwhile, Stephanie is talking with Mom, asking questions to gauge how this young family is coping with the shock and trauma of starting life together under these painful circumstances. Is the apartment adequate? Is transportation back and forth to the hospital working? Are you being taken care of?

I've heard enough of these conversations to realize how very rare it is to hear a single complaint. These dedicated young people are not focused on themselves. But sometimes we pick up a tidbit that we can pass on to Howard, so it can be used to make their lives a bit better, or that I can take back to the Pentagon to get people working on.

I will forever wonder at and be humbled by the hope and determination of these service members and their spouses, children, moms, dads, brothers, and sisters. The head of medicine at BAMC once told me that when he first arrived on wounded-warrior duty, he would try to provide precise answers to questions like, "Will I be able to run again? Will I be able to hunt? Will I be able to surf?" But now, he told me, he'd witnessed so many instances of fearless courage and odds-defying recoveries that he'd simply answer, "You will if you want to."

Honoring the Fallen

Sometimes the consequences of the decisions we must make at the Pentagon are even graver than the horrific injuries some soldiers suffer.

A visit to Dover Air Force Base was entirely different from a visit with a wounded warrior in the hospital. When the families arrived there for the Dignified Transfer—the solemn ceremony of transferring the fallen from the airlifter to a waiting military hearse—hope was gone.

It was usually only twenty-four or forty-eight hours since the family members had gotten notification of their hero's loss. They had spent the intervening time on planes and in buses with little or no sleep. They were dazed with fatigue and grief. Entire extended families would often be gathered in the spacious room furnished with sofas and armchairs—sometimes ten or more people altogether. They represented the gamut of family life—elderly folks, babes in arms, in-laws who might never have met before, former spouses, unwed parents, same-sex partners—the whole panoply.

Stephanie and I would have a short private word with each person there, but we would focus first on the spouse, parents, and children. I told them that I understood I could not truly know what they felt, and that I could not give them what they wanted most, which was their loved one back. I had read carefully about each service member in advance, and I briefly stated the importance of the mission they had been conducting and the reason for it. I wanted them to hear these things in my own words.

I told them it wouldn't mean much to them to hear these words on this day, but perhaps sometime in the years to come it would.

It was obvious that, for most families, the reality of what had happened didn't really hit home until the casket came off the plane and down the ramp, borne by a military honor guard. A military flag officer and I accompanied the party from the cargo bay of the plane onto the tarmac. Family members would gather to the side of the cargo bay ramp. The sounds of anguish at those moments will never leave me.

Once the twin brother of a fallen hero was there. I'd spoken to him in the waiting room. As his brother's body came down the ramp, I glanced over at him. I have never seen a face in pain like that. It was as though a part of him had been torn from his own body.

Sometimes a flash of anger would erupt. Most often, it would be a mother or father who would glower and explode in words like, "When is this shit going to end?"

The Dover staff was amazing, and the chaplain in each case would warn me in advance if I could expect an explosion. Families who especially wanted privacy were given separate rooms. The chaplain gave me the option of skipping an angry family, but I never did so unless the family positively did not want to see a high-ranking visitor who they knew was responsible for their loss.

Dover, of course, is where the sense of loss is at its most raw. No less profound is the sense of grief one experiences on a visit to a cemetery where the fallen have been laid to rest. But there, the feeling of grief is almost exceeded by the deep sense of respect and gratitude for the sacrifice made by the dead and by those who loved them.

Arlington Cemetery, right down the road from the Pentagon, has a section devoted to the fallen from the post-9/11 wars. Stephanie and I made a point of stopping there before I came into the Pentagon to begin my first day as SecDef. As the snow fell, we walked among the headstones, reading names, noting dates, and stopping to put a hand on specific stones with special meaning to us—the son of General John Kelly, the husband of our friend Jane Horton.

Many long days later, on my last day as SecDef, I made the same journey, visiting the same gravesites and many more. It seemed a fitting way to end my work as the steward of America's fighting forces—the person entrusted with the lives of the men and women who freely offer to give themselves to protect the country they love.

I think a lot about those twin journeys, and about the brave men and women—known to me and unknown—whose remains are honored at Arlington. And I think, too, about the wounded warriors and their families—those who suffered terrible physical injuries as well as those whose wounds are psychic, emotional, and spiritual. In a very real sense, their story sums up for me the central mission of any Secretary of Defense. He or she must never forget the fact that the lives of millions of people—military and civilian, at home and abroad—are impacted by every decision made in the vast halls of the Pentagon.

A TO-DO LIST FOR A FUTURE
SECRETARY

I was exceptionally fortunate in the background I brought to my first day on the job as SecDef. Having spent decades in and around the Pentagon, I'd learned firsthand how its complex bureaucracy works, how politics inside and outside the DOD impact its operations, and the varied array of managerial, technological, and strategic skills needed to run the department effectively. I'd also had the chance to watch, and learn from, a series of predecessors in the secretary's seat. I was exceptionally fortunate to enjoy such an education.

At the same time, I had to master some big areas of practice when I became SecDef for which even my level of previous experience hadn't fully prepared me. These included dealing with the White House and congressional politics, engaging on a daily basis with the news media, and an entire range of sensitive personnel and talent-management issues that fall to the secretary alone. Above all, there was the burden of having responsibility for the lives at risk whenever I ordered an operation. I'd had some limited exposure to these challenges in the number two job, but as SecDef I had to quickly master all of them. Thankfully, I had access to advice and counsel from some of the world's leading experts on these topics, including those who'd served as SecDef before me.

Grateful for all I learned from my predecessors, I consider myself an integral part of the historic fellowship of leaders of the Pentagon, with a responsibility to pass along my knowledge to those who will one day occupy the same office. That's a part of what's involved in being "Secretary of Defense for today and for tomorrow." But I hope the value of this book is even broader than that. I'd like to think that every chapter of this book has provided some insights, information, and ideas that leaders of any organization can find useful. In these last pages, I hope to offer some final thoughts that may be particularly valuable to them.

Leadership and Reinforcement: Why Both Are Essential

As I explained in Chapter 13, my experience has convinced me that both leadership and what I call reinforcement are important to running any significant organization.

Leadership is about taking your mission and your subordinates in a new direction—often one that they don't fully understand and that they may be reluctant to take. Leadership generally involves taking risks; it demands an expenditure of personal capital and a willingness to forgo other, easier priorities in favor of an often costly effort to promote change in the face of political and institutional resistance. Therefore, a wise leader is not only determined and skillful but also selective about launching projects that demand high levels of leadership and choosing the timing carefully.

Just as important as leadership is reinforcement—the art of clarifying, supporting, and amplifying the most positive values, habits, skills, and culture of an organization so that the people you lead can operate consistently at their highest and best levels. It's not enough for leaders to be able to diagnose the weaknesses in the organizations they run. They also need to be able to recognize and build on their strengths, which are often easy to ignore or take for granted. Even the most damaged organization has something to build on: a team or two with great talent and esprit de corps, an inspiring mission, an impressive history, or people who know what is the right thing to do but who have never been encouraged and supported when they try to do it. So being a great Secretary of Defense, head of state, or a leader of any kind isn't just about being willing to tear down dysfunctional systems; it's also about being smart enough to see the strength and hidden value in systems that may have been neglected and allowed to drift, and then taking steps to maximize those resources.

Anyone who assumes the helm of any great organization needs to study the leadership and reinforcement imperatives carefully and apply each where it is appropriate. The SecDef is a prime example. When I took the position, I had some priorities for change, but I also recognized that DOD was already an overall excellent organization. The SecDef is entrusted with stewardship of one of the biggest, most complex, and most powerful organizations in the world—one that has done a vast amount of good for billions of people around the world in its long, proud 240-year history . . . while also sometimes being insular and stodgy, committing its share of mistakes, and wasting opportunities to help make the world a more just and peaceful place. But the SecDef of tomorrow has a huge, rich legacy on which to build. He or she must study that legacy, master its details, and strive to bring out all that's great about it—even while undertaking to transform what needs improvement.

Practicing Reinforcement: Building on America's Military Tradition and Culture

The traditional culture of America's military includes an array of strengths that any SecDef needs to recognize, reaffirm, and adapt for the future. Practicing reinforcement means working to personally embody these traits while also transmitting them to those around you and to the rising generation of tomorrow's leaders. Here are some of the traditional strengths of our military that I'd especially commend to any future SecDef for consideration—particularly in these times when we are witnessing widespread destruction of norms and institutions.

Order, clarity, and consistency. One of the great cultural strengths of the DOD is the way members of America's military, both those in uniform and civilian personnel, tend to believe in discipline; in following lawful orders; in having written rules that provide sound guidance for responding to complicated challenges; and in having a well-defined chain of command governing the making and transmittal of decisions. Experience shows that when military leaders maximize these practices, they maximize their chances of success—understandably so, since there's no realm of human activity more volatile, dangerous, and unpredictable than warfare. It takes a calm, disciplined spirit to cope with chaos.

And so my first recommendation to any future SecDef who may read these pages is to seek, always, to operate in that spirit. Clarity and consistency are what the Pentagon craves, and if you provide these, you can lead the department almost anyplace it needs to go. Acting in this way can save lives and go a long way to enhancing the likelihood of success for every program you undertake.

A logical strategic vision, communicated with vividness. Members of America's military also recognize the value of an overarching strategic vision that makes the goals of every activity understandable to everyone involved. The smart SecDef will build on this positive trait by striving to communicate strategy as vividly as possible to people at every level of the Pentagon, as well as to political leaders, allies, and the general public. More broadly, my experience suggests that decisions stick best when they are carefully explained from the start. All my main initiatives—tech transformation, the counter-ISIS campaign plan, the Russia and China counters, Force of the Future, and women in service—were launched by making the case clearly and persuasively. Logic still matters.

Perhaps the single greatest key to this communication challenge is mastering the art of storytelling—building an instantly understandable narrative to encapsulate a given situation and the logic of the strategy developed in response to it. Experience shows that one memorable story has more power and value in winning the understanding and support of people than a dozen abstract frameworks, "four pillars of strategy," or "eight factors to consider."

One of the keys to the success of our ISIS campaign was our shift from a strategy that could be explained only through a mind-numbing list of "lines of effort" to one embodied in a story showing how we would defeat the enemy in a campaign culminating in the seizure of Mosul and Raqqa. The "two red arrows" map I used in presentations to the troops, to Congress, and to the public brought that story to life in a tangible way, making it easy for people to understand and feel confident about the path we were pursuing.

Commitment to learning. Another cultural trait that has helped define

America's military—and helped it succeed—is its deeply ingrained habit of acting as a learning organization. At every level in the DOD—including the boot camps where raw recruits are turned into troops, the war colleges at the military academies where soldier-scholars are educated, and the classified exercises engaged in by highest ranks of uniformed leadership—the Pentagon believes in and practices continual training, experimentation, and learning.

The DOD's commitment to being a learning organization is expressed in many ways. It's embodied in the almost universal practice of conducting an after-action review following any major operation, thereby capturing the insights available from the successes and failures experienced. And it's reflected in the way DOD handles problems like civilian casualties: rather than covering them up like military organizations in authoritarian societies, we launch independent investigations, report the findings publicly, and hold accountable anyone found to be responsible.

The results can be seen in the way DOD has developed brand-new skills when changing circumstances demand them—sometimes more slowly than we'd like, but often with remarkable speed and agility. In the wake of 9/11 and our engagement in wars in Afghanistan and Iraq, we deliberately and methodically set out to master new disciplines like counterterrorism, counterinsurgency, war-speed weapons development as with the MRAP, and improved techniques for treating wounded warriors, such as advanced prosthetics and enhanced therapies for post-traumatic stress. Within a few years, we'd become markedly better at every one of these challenges. The same talent will serve us well as we make the strategic transition to potential high-end opponents like Russia and China.

In a very different sphere, we also found we had to tackle the scourge of sexual assault, a problem prevalent throughout society but particularly offensive in the military. We created a multipronged program for prevention and response that is now being used as a model by other institutions. Developing and applying entire new fields of knowledge is second nature to America's military.

Nothing could be more important for any future SecDef than to respect and protect the DOD's heritage as a learning organization. The

SecDef must ensure that the DOD's leaders have freedom to reflect and a decision-making process that encourages them to take well-considered risks. That means we need to defend individuals who have taken reasonable risks, even when the results aren't optimal—because those results should be the source of important learning for the future. We also need to continue to nurture organizations within the military that are dedicated to research and innovation, such as DARPA, the Defense Innovation Unit, and the Strategic Capabilities Office.

It's also important for a SecDef to personally model the trait of valuing learning. That sometimes requires a willingness to recognize that you have a lot to learn about something. When wrestling with the issue of transgender service members, for example, I not only had no prior view as to the right policy, though I could see that the existing policies were confused and contradictory. I quickly realized I didn't know much about the topic and had a lot to learn. Growing up, I'd never known a single trans individual (that is, not that I was aware of), and the complexities of the social and medical aspects of the trans phenomenon were a blank slate to me. I went to school on the subject, consulting with military doctors, officers, and leading outside experts; reading reports; and meeting trans people who'd been serving in the military. When the time came to discuss trans policies with the leaders of the services—most of whom started out as ignorant of the topic as I had been—I was able to reinforce their own need to understand the facts, so we could work together to define and implement sound policies.

Respect for history and its uses. Closely related to the last two points—the DOD's belief in a shared strategic vision communicated through narrative, and its commitment to being a learning organization—is the department's ingrained respect for the discipline of history and its uses for decision-makers. Thinking historically is the most important practical tool used by everyone from presidents, legislators, and judges to thoughtful members of the media. Those in the DOD are among the best at using history effectively as a tool for analysis, interpretation, communication, and persuasion.

History can serve as a managerial tool in several ways. One is as a source of comparisons for current problems: *How does our counterinsurgency war in Afghanistan compare with the war in Vietnam?* Oversimplified, historical analogies can easily be abused, but when examined with care and with due respect for differences as well as similarities, they can be illuminating.

A second use of history is as a source of potential problem-solving approaches: *When faced with a problem similar to the one I am facing today, past SecDefs used processes A, B, and C.* This approach enables current decision-makers to treat the past as a kind of menu of tactics from which useful tools for today may be gleaned.

A third, very valuable use of history is as a source of insights that help explain the present: *Before I meet with the defense minister of country X, I want to study the history of the country to better understand how the military, political, economic, and social conditions there came to be, so I'll better understand the situation and thinking of my counterparts.*

Finally, history is the principal way in which argumentation is made, and therefore it can be an effective way to explain and defend your policies, either positively (*This is like the way we resolved the end of the Cold War without bloodshed*) or negatively (*That would be like Prime Minister Chamberlain at Munich*).

Any future SecDef will quickly discover—if he or she doesn't realize it already—that the department is steeped in the culture of historical analysis and argumentation. A smart SecDef will build on this strength by thoughtfully using historical analogies, comparisons, and data when forging solutions to tomorrow's problems.

Superlative team-building. Close to the center of the DOD's ethos is the commitment to comradeship—the solidarity of the foxhole in which every participant is reliant on his or her teammate for life itself. America's military has always striven to build the best possible teams of high-quality individuals and to encourage them to give their all to one another and to successful completion of their shared mission. Today's all-volunteer force exemplifies better than any other this commitment to quality. So does the powerful network of alliances and partnerships the United States has built around the globe, which enormously multiplies the reach and capabilities of our armed forces, vastly enhancing our ability to maintain the peace and defend our values.

For the SecDef, it's vital to embody this heritage of team-building by surrounding yourself with the very best people you can find. Build a support team that complements your strengths and compensates for your weaknesses. This is what I did when I brought smart, skilled people like Eric Rosenbach, Eric Smith, Peter Cook, Steve Hedger, Julie Park, and many others into my inner circle at the Pentagon. The same applies to the remarkably talented, tough, and dedicated officers I appointed as CO-COMs and members of the Joint Chiefs of Staff. Each of these leaders embodied an array of talents and knowledge I didn't have myself, and so they made me and my office far more effective than would have been possible without them.

Honor and trust. Perhaps the most essential cultural trait that any future SecDef must uphold and defend is the belief in the importance of personal conduct. The profession of arms is based on honor and trust. Only in a culture where these traits are held as sacred is it possible for people to routinely trust one another for life itself. This is why young warriors are taught to practice and hone the strength of character required to remain true to one's duty even in times of extreme crisis and danger. And because a warrior's reliability in great things is reflected in small things, honoring one's word in seemingly trivial matters—for example, by not fudging an expense account or making a misleading statement in a report—is treated in the military as a serious matter. Just like sloppy thinking, sloppy morals have no place in America's military.

Any future SecDef should take the reverence for honor and trust that is imbued in America's military very seriously. That means enforcing the department's rules regarding personal conduct even in cases involving highly valuable, talented individuals; even when people to whom you have a deep personal connection are involved; and even when it's tempting to seize on exculpatory circumstances or "fuzzy" areas of the rules. Carrying out this duty can be painful. But it's also essential to preserving this precious trait of America's military.

Of course, a SecDef must also personally uphold the departmental standards of honor and trust. Naturally this means that you must never even dream of violating fundamental codes regarding things like truthfulness, following orders, proper treatment of subordinates, sexual conduct, responsible use of taxpayer money, and the like. But it also means bending over backward to do the right thing even in seemingly insignificant or symbolic matters.

During my first week as SecDef, I traveled to the Middle East and participated in meetings, formal and informal, with a number of my counterparts from the region. One of my first conversations was with a defense minister from one of the emirates. I had just disembarked from my plane when he greeted me, and we took a few minutes to sit in the shade at the airport and chat briefly about some of the issues we'd be discussing in more detail later. I was wearing the same travel outfit I'd worn on many trips to theater as deputy secretary—khaki trousers, a windbreaker, and an open-collared shirt. I thought nothing of it when a DOD photographer snapped a few photos.

When the pictures were routinely posted on the department's website, I got a text message from a friend who had served as press secretary for one of my predecessors. "No suit?" was all he wrote.

I immediately changed my practices on matters of comportment. In later visits to the Middle East (and other parts of the world), I would step off the plane in suit and tie no matter where I was, what time of day it was, or what the weather was like. When shaking hands with hundreds of troops in sweltering conditions, in temperatures of 110 degrees Fahrenheit or higher, my staff and hosts would sometimes say to me, "Mr. Secretary, take off your jacket and tie." And even the troops themselves would say, "Mr. Secretary, relax—it's just us!"

But my response would always be the same: "I'm about to shake hands with a young recruit who is giving his all in response to orders I signed. He's going to send a photo of his moment with the Secretary of Defense to his mom back home in Minnesota or Texas or New York, and she's going to put it in her nicest frame and display it on her bedside table or on the mantel for visitors to admire. I want to make sure that mom will be proud of that picture."

That's a small example of how the commitment to conduct and honor plays out in the daily life of a leader who takes it seriously. It's not a bad rule to follow in most situations: When in doubt, act if somebody's mom may be watching.

I wish that the importance of these traditional military virtues went without saying. Unfortunately, even a glance at today's highest levels of leadership in Washington and elsewhere reveals that it's no longer so. Those of us who believe in the qualities that have made America's armed forces the greatest, strongest, and noblest in the world must reinforce and defend those qualities more fiercely than ever, lest they be undermined not only from without but from within.

What's more, those who are leaders in other realms—such as business, government, academia, and the nonprofit arena—could do worse than to study these military virtues and ponder the ways they can be reinforced in other contexts. It's not an accident that so many successful leaders in many fields have learned some of their skills during stints of military service.

Practicing Leadership: Ways Tomorrow's Pentagon Needs to Change

Even as future SecDefs need to reinforce the traditional virtues of the DOD, they will also need to move the Pentagon, when necessary, in new directions, developing traits and qualities that may have been neglected or needless in the past but that are increasingly essential in a changing world. This is the other very necessary dimension of running the Pentagon— leadership in my special use of the term.

Here are some of the areas in which my successors in the Pentagon will be challenged to practice leadership in this sense.

Getting competitive to restore American dominance. First, the U.S. military needs to regain its competitive edge over its rivals around the world. This statement may come as a surprise to those who haven't read this book. The U.S. military had a dominant position for several decades after the end of World War II. There were several interconnected reasons for this, including the fact that we escaped relatively unscathed from the physical devastation of the war, the big scientific and technological advantage we held over practically every other nation, the powerful attractiveness of our values to people from other lands, and the vast size and unrivaled productivity of our economy. As a result, many Americans were lulled into a sense of complacency. They came to regard our unmatched military might as a natural birthright. When analysts, pundits, politicians, or military leaders warned that we were in danger of falling behind other powers, many citizens pooh-poohed the message as mere alarmism, perhaps motivated by the desire to channel even more billions into an already gigantic defense budget.

However, the military, technological, and economic dominance of the United States began to be challenged even as the Berlin Wall was falling, and it can no longer be taken for granted. We are not the world's uncontested "big dog" any longer. As I've explained, our global rivals China and Russia have been developing weapons systems, cyber-war methodologies, and geopolitical strategies for which we have as yet no neat and clean response. At the same time, regional powers like Iran and North Korea have been maneuvering for advantage in their own corners of the world—and sometimes succeeding in pushing U.S. policy makers back on their heels. Our loss of the unchallenged dominance we once held over the rest of the world is largely an inevitable result of major economic, demographic, and political changes. But it's a trend we must recognize and respond to, rather than hiding our heads in the sand.

In this book, I've described the steps I took in my roles at the Pentagon to defend America's position as the world's most powerful military, including updating our war plans, improving our acquisition performance both in peacetime and in wartime, building bridges to the high-tech community, and modernizing our talent management systems. But much more remains to be done. Tomorrow's SecDef must resist the tendency to assume that world leadership is America's birthright. It's not—and the unconscious belief that putting the Pentagon on "cruise control," thinking that what worked yesterday will surely be good enough tomorrow, is a danger to be zealously resisted. Communicating this sense of urgency throughout the DOD as well as to the rest of government and to the nation as a whole will test the leadership skills of every future SecDef.

Adjusting to new political and economic realities. Second, even as we redouble our efforts to ensure that America's military is prepared for a new era of difficult global challenges, we need to also adjust to the tough economic and political realities within which the Pentagon must now operate. That's likely to mean becoming even more vigilant about financial matters, with the DOD budget now being held hostage not to competing priorities or to conflicts between hawks and doves in Congress but to pure Washington gridlock—for which there is no end in sight.

Especially under these circumstances, leaders of the DOD must always remember that the money we are spending is not our money—it belongs to the American people, and there's never an excuse for wasting it. Among other things, this means avoiding the tendency to blame ballooning costs and missed deadlines in important programs on "Pentagon bureaucracy," congressional interference, or federal acquisition regulations. All these factors can indeed be heavy-handed, clumsy, and unhelpful. But when the people you must work with and the rules you must follow seem to be thwarting you from doing what is right, the easy, lazy thing to do is to shrug your shoulders and complain. Instead, look again for a work-around that will let you do what you know is right: a clever way to redefine the problem, to create a legitimate exception to the rules, or to connect the dots in an unexpected fashion. As a former acquisition executive, I can tell you that there is always, always a way around the system to get a sensible result. You just have to know enough about the system, and work hard enough to find the solution.

Being politically adroit. Third, every future SecDef must practice leadership by being politically adroit—not in the sense of "playing politics" with departmental priorities, but in finding ways to shield the DOD from the worst effects of partisanship and political gridlock. This requires having a sophisticated awareness and understanding of how power conflicts and ideology complicate your ability to do what's best for the department and for the nation—and then finding creative ways to overcome those political barriers.

In this book, I've offered a number of examples of how I tried to do this on behalf of the DOD, from mastering the art of giving congressional testimony to managing the details of a policy announcement so as to minimize its political vulnerability. Here's another example. I'm a big believer in having a special kind of to-do list in my right-hand desk drawer. It's a list of actions that I know are the right thing to do but for which the right time has not yet emerged. It might include making a change in departmental regulations that is likely to be controversial, or removing from a sensitive position a particular individual who is not quite up to par but who has not committed any offense worthy of firing. Having a list like this is important because it enables me to quickly recognize when circumstances change and the move I need to make becomes possible.

No less a leader than Abraham Lincoln himself made use of this technique. He wrote the Emancipation Proclamation, freeing the slaves held in the Confederate states, and presented it to his cabinet in July 1862. But at the advice of his Secretary of State, William Seward, Lincoln did not issue it publicly at that time. Instead, he held it until after the Union victory at Antietam so that the proclamation would not be seen as an act of desperation but rather as an expression of confidence in the ultimate triumph of American values.

Every leader should have a list of such important but politically risky acts they are determined to take, and should always be on the lookout for opportunities to put them into effect.

As you can see, running a vast, complex, and essential organization like the DOD demands a large measure of creative leadership—because sometimes you simply have to do what hasn't been done before. When necessary, invent! That's the essence of "thinking outside the five-sided box"—an art that every SecDef must strive to master.

The Mission as North Star

Thankfully, there's a north star that can serve as the permanent, reliable reference point for any Pentagon leader. That is the mission the DOD was created to fulfill: to protect the American people and to make a safer world for our children. When others said that the complexities of today's global challenges are overwhelming, I found that reverting to that core mission provided the clarity I needed to make wise, well-balanced decisions.

The mission as north star can help any SecDef recognize times when traditional military commitments and values can best serve to enhance our readiness and ability to protect the American people and their interests abroad—in other words, circumstances when reinforcement is most important. And focusing on the mission can also reveal when changing conditions demand fresh approaches, new skills, and reformed systems— that is, times when leadership is needed. In both cases, the mission shows the way.

If future secretaries of defense keep the mission at the center of their thinking, their decisions will always be fundamentally sound.

ACKNOWLEDGMENTS

I owe a debt to many with whom I worked on events related here, and they and their roles are noted in these pages. A few deserve special thanks for giving me examples and opportunities along the way: Jim Schlesinger, Brent Scowcroft, Bill Perry, and Bob Gates. I regret that Jim didn't live to see me become secretary—I would like to think he would have been pleased. Bill Perry and I in particular have had a close professional and personal relationship for almost four decades.

My agent, Wayne Kabak of WSK Management, adroitly navigated this book through the publishing world. Wayne helped me find my editor and publisher, John Parsley, who is supported by a talented team at Dutton. Editorial consultant Karl Weber's literary acumen and wisdom were indispensable, and he deserves my deepest appreciation.

Thanks also to all those who helped me recollect and reconstruct events described in the book, including Ylber Bajraktari, Gretchen Bartlett, Bogdan Belei, Robert Belfer, Josh Burek, Maeve Campbell, Peter Cook, Andrew DiIorio, Beth Foster, Deborah Gordon, Jonathan Lachman, Joy Li, Kelly Magsamen, Julie Park, Michael Rhodes, Eric Rosenbach, Sam Said, Elissa Slotkin, Eric Smith, and Gordon Trowbridge. Despite my best efforts to check the accuracy of the events recounted here, inevitably much is dependent on my own memory, which is probably not perfect. I take responsibility for any errors.

The reader will see in these pages that my wife, Stephanie, is as dedicated to the troops as I am. But my dedication to her is boundless. So much of the experience upon which the lessons of this book are based would not have been worthwhile or even possible without her love and that of my children, Will and Ava, who are both doing their own important work to make the world a better place.

Ash Carter
January 2019

NOTES

CHAPTER 1: HOW NOT TO WASTE $700 BILLION

3   **This is seven times the size:** City of New York, Adopted Budget Fiscal Year 2018, Summary of the Expense Budget and Revenue Budget, June 8, 2017, http://www1.nyc .gov/assets/omb/downloads/pdf/erc6-17.pdf; Apple Form 10-K (Annual Report), Filed October 26, 2016, for the period ending September 24, 2016, http://files.shareholder .com/downloads/AAPL/4742298381x0xS1628280%2D16%2D20309/320193/filing.pdf; CIA World Factbook (2016), https://www.cia.gov/library/publications/the-world -factbook/fields/2056.html.

3   **Together, DOD and the other federal agencies:** "The Federal Budget in 2017," Congressional Budget Office, March 2018, https://www.cbo.gov/system/files?file=115th -congress-2017-2018/graphic/53624-fy17federalbudget.pdf.

4   **In recent years, its defense budget has exceeded:** "U.S. Defense Spending Compared to Other Countries," Peter G. Peterson Foundation, May 7, 2018, https://www.pgpf .org/chart-archive/0053_defense-comparison.

5   **A congressman from California:** Charles R. Babcock and Jonathan Weisman, "Congressman Admits Taking Bribes, Resigns," *Washington Post*, November 29, 2005, http://www .washingtonpost.com/wp-dyn/content/article/2005/11/28/AR2005112801827.html.

5   **The most recent high point:** "Military Expenditure (% of GDP), 1960–2017," World Bank, https://data.worldbank.org/indicator/MS.MIL.XPND.GD.ZS?locations=US.

6   **And the highest figure in history:** "US Defense Spending History," USGovernmentSpending.com, https://www.usgovernmentspending.com/defense_spending.

8   **In fiscal year 2016:** "Senate Armed Services Committee Completes Markup of National Defense Authorization Act for Fiscal Year 2016," Senate Armed Services Committee, United States Senate, press release, May 14, 2015, https://www.armed-services.senate .gov/press-releases/senate-armed-services-committee-completes-markup-of-national -defense-authorization-act-for-fiscal-year-2016.

22 **The 1986 report issued by the Packard Commission:** *A Quest for Excellence: Final Report to the President by the President's Blue Ribbon Commission on Defense Management,* June 1986, https://www.documentcloud.org/documents/2695411-Packard -Commission.html.

24 **After a summer-long departmentwide effort:** "Guidance Roadmap," Department of Defense, September 14, 2010.

28 **Apparently the then President-elect Trump:** Amanda Macias, "Trump Wants Boeing to Build Stealth F-18s for a 'Good Price'—but They Don't Exist," CNBC, March 14,

2018, https://www.cnbc.com/2018/03/14/trump-wants-boeing-to-build-stealth
-f-18s-for-a-good-price-but-they-dont-exist.html.

30 **Moreover, the cost controls did not occur:** "2017 Global Aerospace and Defense
Sector Financial Performance Study," Deloitte Touche Tohmatsu Ltd., figure 6,
https://www2.deloitte.com/content/dam/Deloitte/global/Documents/consumer-industrial
-products/gx-cip-global-aerospace-defense-financial-performance-study.pdf.

CHAPTER 2: WORKING AT WAR SPEED

31 **Within months of the start of hostilities:** "Recent Trends in Active-Duty Military
Deaths," Congressional Research Service, June 1, 2018, https://fas.org/sgp/crs/natsec
/IF10899.pdf.

34 **The result was a roughly 32 percent drop:** "Evaluation and Treatment of Genital In-
juries in Combat Warriors," Walter Reed National Military Medical Center, Artiss
Symposium 2012, p. 18, https://www.cstsonline.org/assets/media/documents/Artiss
_Symposium_2012.pdf.

38 **Dave was so appreciative of our quick response:** "Adaptive, Responsive, and Speedy
Acquisitions," interview with General David H. Petraeus, *Defense AT&L,* January–
February 2010, https://apps.dtic.mil/dtic/tr/fulltext/u2/1016187.pdf.

39 **As Secretary of Defense Don Rumsfeld famously remarked:** Eric Schmitt, "Iraq-
Bound Troops Confront Rumsfeld Over Lack of Armor," *New York Times,* December
8, 2004, https://www.nytimes.com/2004/12/08/international/middleeast/iraqbound
-troops-confront-rumsfeld-over-lack-of.html.

55 **One of the first JEONs we generated:** John Keller, "Navy and Airforce Choose DRFM
Jammers from Mercury Systems to Help Spoof Enemy Radar," *Military and Aerospace
Electronics,* June 22, 2018, https://www.militaryaerospace.com/articles/2014/06/mer
cury-drfm-jammer.html.

CHAPTER 3: A SCIENTIST IN THE PENTAGON

57 **There was no relationship between them:** Portions of the autobiographical material
on the following pages are adapted from "Ash Carter Autobiography (2006)," which I
wrote for my students at the Harvard Kennedy School. The entire document may be
accessed at https://www.belfercenter.org/sites/default/files/2018-01/Ash%20Carter
%20Autobiography%202006.pdf.

62 **"We'll lose half of Beaver County":** Martha Sonntag Bradley, "The MX Missile Project," *Utah Historical Quarterly,* August 29, 2016, https://heritage.utah.gov/history
/uhg-mx-missile-project.

62 **"Rube Goldberg scheme":** Michael H. Armacost, *Ballots, Bullets, and Bargains:
American Foreign Policy and Presidential Elections* (New York: Columbia University
Press, 2015), page 190.

62 **"Our fathers came to this western area":** "First Presidency Statement on Basing of MX
Missile," Church of Jesus Christ of Latter-Day Saints, June 1981, https://www
.lds.org/ensign/1981/06/news-of-the-church/first-presidency-statement-on-basing-of-mx
-missile?lang=eng&_r=1.

63 **In short, we concluded that there was no perfect solution:** "MX Missile Basing," U.S.
Congress, Office of Technology Assessment, September 1981, https://ota.fas.org
/reports/8116.pdf.

69 **"I call upon the scientific community":** President Ronald Reagan, "Address to the
Nation on Defense and National Security," March 23, 1983, Atomic Archive, http://
www.atomicarchive.com/Docs/Missile/Starwars.shtml.

70 **"so remote that it should not serve":** Ash Carter, "Directed Energy Missile Defense
in Space," U.S. Congress, Office of Technology Assessment, April 1984, https://www
.princeton.edu/~ota/disk3/1984/8410/8410.pdf.

70 **For example, the conservative columnists:** Michael Gordon, "The War Over 'Star Wars,'" *New York Times,* September 16, 1984, https://www.nytimes.com/1984/09/16/books/the-war-over-star-wars.html.

72 **"On the basis of the responses I have received":** John H. Gibbons, letter to William H. Taft IV, July 13, 1984.

76 **In 1950, he was the principal author of NSC-68:** James S. Lay Jr., "A Report to the National Security Council—NSC-68," President's Secretary's File, Truman Papers, April 12, 1950, https://www.trumanlibrary.org/whistlestop/study_collections/cold war/documents/pdf/10-1.pdf.

79 **Solving the Loose-Nukes Dilemma: The Nunn-Lugar Program:** The account of the Nunn-Lugar program on the following pages is adapted, in part, from Chapter 2 of Ashton B. Carter and William J. Perry, *Preventive Defense: A New Security System for America* (Washington, DC: Brookings Institution Press, 1999).

80 **My Harvard colleagues and I wrote a detailed study:** Ash Carter, Steven E. Miller, Charles A. Zraket, and Kurt M. Campbell, *Soviet Nuclear Fission: Control of the Nuclear Arsenal in a Disintegrating Soviet Union* (Cambridge, MA: Belfer Center for Science and International Affairs, Harvard Kennedy School, 1991).

CHAPTER 4: THE WHITE HOUSE IS ON THE LINE

94 **"Today, I'm pleased to announce":** "President Obama Nominates Ashton Carter as the Next Secretary of Defense," White House Archives, December 5, 2014, https://obamawhitehouse.archives.gov/the-press-office/2014/12/05/remarks-president-nominating-ashton-carter-secretary-defense.

94 **In my response, I thanked President Obama:** Cheryl Pellerin, "Obama Nominates Carter to Be Next Defense Secretary," *DoD News,* December 5, 2014, https://dod.defense.gov/News/Article/Article/603757/obama-nominates-carter-to-be-next-defense-secretary/.

105 **But explaining away the downside:** Jeffrey Goldberg, "The Obama Doctrine," *Atlantic,* April 2016, https://www.theatlantic.com/magazine/archive/2016/04/the-obama-doctrine/471525/.

107 **That may be one of the reasons:** See, for example, Richard Sisk, "Gates and Panetta Blast Obama for Micromanaging Military," Military.com, November 17, 2014, https://www.military.com/daily-news/2014/11/17/gates-and-panetta-blast-obama-for-microman aging-military.html; Dan De Luce, "Hagel: The White House Tried to 'Destroy' Me," *Foreign Policy,* December 18, 2015, https://foreignpolicy.com/2015/12/18/hagel-the-white-house-tried-to-destroy-me/.

110 **It was a brilliant model for the kind of operation:** Helene Cooper and Eric Schmitt, "ISIS Official Killed in U.S. Raid in Syria, Pentagon Says," *New York Times,* May 16, 2015, https://www.nytimes.com/2015/05/17/world/middleeast/abu-sayyaf-isis-commander-killed-by-us-forces-pentagon-says.html.

123 **"In my judgment," I retorted:** "Fareed Zakaria GPS: Interview with Defense Secretary Ashton Carter" (transcript), CNN, January 24, 2016, http://transcripts.cnn.com/TRANSCRIPTS/1601/24/fzgps.01.html.

124 **That story—minus the expletive:** Charlie Savage, "Obama's Plan for Guantánamo Is Seen Faltering," *New York Times,* July 21, 2015, https://www.nytimes.com/2015/07/22/us/politics/obamas-plan-for-guantanamo-is-seen-faltering.html; and Connie Bruck, "Why Obama Has Failed to Close Guantánamo," *New Yorker,* August 1, 2016, https://www.newyorker.com/magazine/2016/08/01/why-obama-has-failed-to-close-guantanamo.

127 **I quickly intervened:** "Hearings Before a Subcommittee of the Committee on Appropriations, House of Representatives, 114th Congress, Second Session," February 25, 2016, https://www.gpo.gov/fdsys/pkg/CHRG-114hhrg22432/html/CHRG-114hhrg22432.htm.

CHAPTER 5: A BOARD OF DIRECTORS WITH 535 MEMBERS

133 **Weapons production was severely curtailed:** Amy Belasco and Pat Towell, "Government Shutdown: Operations of the Department of Defense During a Lapse in Appropriations," Congressional Research Service, October 15, 2013, https://fas.org/sgp/crs/natsec/R41745.pdf.

133 **The *New York Times* reported on the deaths:** Jennifer Steinhauer, "Shutdown Denies Death and Burial Benefits to Families of 4 Dead Soldiers," *New York Times*, October 8, 2013, https://www.nytimes.com/2013/10/09/us/politics/shutdown-holds-up-death-benefits-for-military-families.html.

138 **For this reason, Congress has, in fact, exercised:** See L. Elaine Halchin and Frederick M. Kaiser, "Congressional Oversight," Congressional Research Service, October 17, 2012, https://fas.org/sgp/crs/misc/97-936.pdf.

143 **The topic would be China's pursuit:** William Carter, "Statement Before the House Armed Services Committee, Subcommittee on Emerging Threats and Capabilities: Chinese Advances in Emerging Technologies and Their Implications for U.S. National Security," January 9, 2018, https://docs.house.gov/meetings/AS/AS26/20180109/106756/HHRG-115-AS26-Wstate-CarterW-20180109.pdf.

147 **Another was the debt ceiling:** D. Andrew Austin, "The Debt Limit: History and Recent Increases," Congressional Research Service, November 2, 2015, https://www.senate.gov/CRSpubs/d2c8f833-9796-4b3e-9462-6b1755ef463d.pdf.

148 **Originally created to finance the wars:** Lynn M. Williams and Susan B. Epstein, "Overseas Contingency Operations Funding: Background and Status," Congressional Research Service, February 7, 2017, https://fas.org/sgp/crs/natsec/R44519.pdf.

151 **In fact, according to a May 2016 memo:** Matthew Weed, "Presidential References to the 2001 Authorization for Use of Military Force in Publicly Available Executive Actions and Reports to Congress," Congressional Research Service, May 11, 2016, https://fas.org/sgp/crs/natsec/pres-aumf.pdf.

152 **Subject to those stipulations:** Ash Carter, "Statement on the President's Request for Authorization to Use Military Force Against ISIL Before the Senate Foreign Relations Committee," March 11, 2015, http://archive.defense.gov/Speeches/Speech.aspx?SpeechID=1921.

CHAPTER 6: COMMUNICATING WITH THE PRESS AND THE PUBLIC

157 **Lita Baldor had her scoop:** Lolita C. Baldor and Matthew Lee, "Pentagon: 2 US Navy Boats Held by Iran but Will Be Returned," AP, January 12, 2016, https://apnews.com/78c98f06474d4481bcb9c50f43d0cb0a.

166 **He was finally approved on February 26, 2013:** Jeremy W. Peters, "Hagel Approved for Defense in Sharply Split Senate Vote," *New York Times,* February 26, 2013, https://www.nytimes.com/2013/02/27/us/politics/hagel-filibuster-defense-senate-confirmation.html.

168 **The reports about my departure:** See, for example, Craig Whitlock, "Ashton Carter, Deputy Defense Secretary, to Step Down," *Washington Post,* October 10, 2013, https://www.washingtonpost.com/world/national-security/ashton-carter-deputy-defense-secretary-to-step-down/2013/10/10/204ab64a-31e2-11e3-8686-68fca83a474f_story.html?

170 **But by then, the *New York Times*:** Michael S. Schmidt, "Defense Secretary Conducted Some Official Business on a Personal Email Account," *New York Times,* December 16, 2015, https://www.nytimes.com/2015/12/17/us/politics/defense-secretary-ashton-carter-conducted-some-official-business-on-a-personal-email-account.html.

170 **I had carefully planned my response:** "Ash Carter Explains Email Use to CBS News," December 17, 2015, https://www.cbsnews.com/news/secretary-of-defense-ash-carter-iphone-personal-emails-syria-iraq-isis/.

171 **Like many of my DOD colleagues:** Colby Itkowitz, "How Jane Fonda's 1972 Trip to North Vietnam Earned Her the Nickname 'Hanoi Jane,'" *Washington Post*, September 21, 2018, https://www.washingtonpost.com/news/retropolis/wp/2017/09/18/how-jane -fondas-1972-trip-to-north-vietnam-earned-her-the-nickname-hanoi-jane/?

175 **One of the big social media successes:** "Ashton Carter, Worldwide Troop Talk at the Defense Media Activity," American Rhetoric Online Speech Bank, September 1, 2015, https://www.americanrhetoric.com/speeches/ashcarterworldwidetrooptalk .htm.

CHAPTER 7: CHAIN OF COMMAND

183 **These weaknesses were exposed in various ways:** Colonel Stephen E. Anno and Lieutenant Colonel William E. Einspahr, "Command and Control and Communications Lessons Learned: Iranian Rescue, Falklands Conflict, Grenada Invasion, Libya Raid," Air War College Research Report, January 1989, https://apps.dtic.mil/dtic/tr /fulltext/u2/a202091.pdf.

185 **But in practice, matters are often more complicated:** Steven L. Rearden, "The Role and Influence of the Chairman: A Short History," Joint History Office, Joint Chiefs of Staff, September 28, 2011, http://www.jcs.mil/Portals/36/Documents/History/Institutional /The_Role_and_Influence_of_the_Chairman.pdf.

190 **Most important, practically every NATO member:** NATO itself publishes annual updates regarding defense expenditures by member nations, which you can review on the organization's website at https://www.nato.int/cps/ic/natohq/topics_49198 .htm.

191 **In an interesting example of how diplomatic and military interests:** "The 38th Republic of Korea–United States Security Consultative Meeting Joint Communiqué," U.S. Department of Defense, October 20, 2006, http://archive.defense.gov/news /Oct2006/d20061020uskorea.pdf.

192 **The Americans got unified command:** See "Lessons and Conclusions on the Execution of IFOR Operations and Prospects for a Future Combined Security System: The Peace and Stability of Europe After IFOR," Joint U.S./Russian Research Project of the Foreign Military Studies Office, Center for Army Lessons Learned, U.S. Army Combined Arms Center, Fort Leavenworth, Kansas, and the Center for Military-Strategic Studies, General Staff of the Armed Forces, Moscow, 2nd edition, November, 2000, https://apps.dtic.mil/dtic/tr/fulltext/u2/a434985.pdf.

193 **Le Drian had written a hardheaded:** Jean-Yves Le Drian, *Qui est l'ennemi?* (Paris: Les Éditions du Cerf, 2016).

194 **Most war plans unfold like the script:** Lieutenant Colonel (Retired) Jack E. Mundstock, "Operational Phasing: Phase Names Should Be Driven by Activity in Each Phase," U.S. Army Infantry School, August–December 2016, http://www.benning .army.mil/infantry/Magazine/issues/2016/AUG-DEC/pdf/7)Mundstock_Phasing.pdf.

195 **"Plans are worthless":** Dwight D. Eisenhower, Remarks at the National Defense Executive Reserve Conference, Public Papers of the Presidents of the United States, November 14, 1957, https://babel.hathitrust.org/cgi/pt?id=miua.4728417.1957.001; view=1up;seq=857.

196 **In fact, "resourcing the TPFDD":** "Deployment and Redeployment Operations," U.S. Joint Chiefs of Staff, Joint Publication 3-35, January 10, 2018, http://www.jcs.mil /Portals/36/Documents/Doctrine/pubs/jp3_35.pdf.

200 **These are highly classified:** The Continuity of Government Commission, "The Continuity of the Presidency: The Second Report of the Continuity of Government Commission," Brookings Institution, July 2, 2009, https://www.brookings.edu/wp -content/uploads/2016/06/06_continuity_of_government.pdf.

CHAPTER 8: COMBAT READINESS IN A CRISIS-PRONE WORLD

204 **Many Americans don't realize it:** As of 2018, under the Authorization for the Use of Military Force granted in 2002 to fight al-Qaeda–linked militants, the United States is conducting combat operations in Afghanistan, Iraq, Syria, Yemen, Somalia, Libya, and Niger. See "Report on the Legal and Policy Frameworks Guiding the United States' Use of Military Force and Related National Security Operations," U.S. White House, December 2016. https://assets.documentcloud.org/documents/4411804/3-18-War -Powers-Transparency-Report.pdf.

204 **"And when the president makes a decision":** "Hearings Before the Committee on Armed Services, United States Senate, 114th Congress, First Session," February 4, 2015, https://www.congress.gov/114/chrg/shrg24274/CHRG-114shrg24274.pdf.

207 **For example, the Organization for Security and Co-operation in Europe:** "Things to Know About International Military Exercises," Deutsche Welle, September 12, 2017, https://www.dw.com/en/things-to-know-about-international-military-exercises /a-40468012.

210 **In fact, in 2017, for the first time in many years:** Erika I. Ritchie, "Training Kills More Troops Than War. Here's What's Being Done About It," Military.com, May 14, 2018, https://www.military.com/daily-news/2018/05/14/training-kills-more-troops-war-heres -whats-being-done-about-it.html.

211 **There's an elaborate system for ranking this readiness:** Russell Rumbaugh, "Defining Readiness: Background and Issues for Congress," Congressional Research Service, June 14, 2017, https://fas.org/sgp/crs/natsec/R44867.pdf.

219 **It dates back to October 2015:** Alissa J. Rubin, "Airstrike Hits Doctors Without Borders Hospital in Afghanistan," *New York Times*, October 3, 2015, https://www.nytimes .com/2015/10/04/world/asia/afghanistan-bombing-hospital-doctors-without-borders -kunduz.html.

220 **Spokespeople for MSF moved quickly:** See Willa Frej, "Doctors Without Borders Enraged Over 'Deliberate' Kunduz Hospital Bombing," *Huffington Post*, October 6, 2015, https://www.huffingtonpost.com/entry/doctors-without-borders-deliberate -hospital-bombing_us_5613dca5e4b0368a1a6108dd.

221 **The CENTCOM commander, Joe Votel:** Matthew Rosenberg, "Pentagon Details Chain of Errors in Strike on Afghan Hospital," *New York Times,* April 29, 2016, https:// www.nytimes.com/2016/04/30/world/asia/afghanistan-doctors-without-borders-hospital -strike.html.

223 **This is the principal task for which Operation Noble Eagle:** Lawrence Kapp, "Operations Noble Eagle, Enduring Freedom, and Iraqi Freedom: Questions and Answers About U.S. Military Personnel, Compensation, and Force Structure," Congressional Research Service, February 16, 2005, https://fas.org/sgp/crs/natsec/RL31334.pdf.

CHAPTER 9: CLARITY OF PURPOSE

226 **Clarity of Purpose: Defeating ISIS**: The contents of this chapter are adapted from Ash Carter, *A Lasting Defeat: The Campaign to Destroy ISIS* (Cambridge, MA: Belfer Center for Science and International Affairs, Harvard Kennedy School, 2017). I am grateful to many individuals who helped tell this tale. Among them: my former chief of staff, Eric Rosenbach; Peter Cook, my press secretary, who for more than a year was dual-hatted as assistant to the secretary for public affairs; and Elissa Slotkin, the acting assistant secretary for international security affairs. Thanks also to former staffers Jonathan Lachman and Gordon Trowbridge for helping research and organize the story.

226 **"I wanted to come here to Qayyarah West personally":** "Media Availability with Secretary Carter and Lt. Gen. Townsend in Qayyarah West, Iraq," U.S. Department of Defense transcript, December 11, 2016, https://dod.defense.gov/News/Transcripts

/Transcript-View/Article/1026754/media-availability-with-secretary-carter-and-lt-gen
-townsend-in-qayyarah-west-i/.

229 **In public statements at the time:** See, for example, "Department of Defense Press Briefing by Lt. Gen. Terry in the Pentagon Briefing Room," U.S. Department of Defense transcript, December 18, 2014, https://www.defense.gov/News/Transcripts /Transcript-View/Article/606984/department-of-defense-press-briefing-by-lt-gen-terry -in-the-pentagon-briefing-r/; and "Department of Defense Background Briefing via Teleconference by an Official from U.S. Central Command," U.S. Department of Defense transcript, February 19, 2015, https://www.defense.gov/News/Transcripts /Transcript-View/Article/607013/department-of-defense-background-briefing-via-tele conference-by-an-official-fro/.

231 **I answered by describing our goal:** "Hearings Before the Committee on Armed Services, United States Senate, 114th Congress, First Session," February 4, 2015, https:// www.congress.gov/114/chrg/shrg24274/CHRG-114shrg24274.pdf.

235 **In July 2015, I had to acknowledge:** "Hearing to Receive Testimony on Counter-ISIL (Islamic State of Iraq and the Levant) Strategy," Committee on Armed Services, United States Senate, July 7, 2015, https://www.armed-services.senate.gov/imo/media/doc /15-61%20-%207-7-15.pdf.

237 **In May, when ISIS seized Ramadi:** "EXCLUSIVE: Secretary of Defense, Ash Carter: 'Airstrikes Are Effective but Neither They nor Really Anything We Do Can Substitute for the Iraqis' Will to Fight,'" CNN Press Room, May 25, 2015, http://cnnpressroom .blogs.cnn.com/2015/05/24/exclusive-secretary-of-defense-ash-carter-airstrikes-are -effective-but-neither-they-nor-really-anything-we-do-can-substitute-for-the-iraqis-will -to-fight/.

237 **"The ISF was not driven out of Ramadi":** Jim Garamone, "Dempsey: Iraqi Forces Not Driven from Ramadi, They Drove out of Ramadi," *DoD News*, May 20, 2015, https:// www.defense.gov/News/Article/Article/604687/dempsey-iraqi-forces-not-driven-from -ramadi-they-drove-out-of-ramadi/.

238 **It annoyed me when people who didn't understand:** See, for example, James Phillips, "Obama Refuses to Alter ISIS Strategy," Heritage Foundation, December 17, 2015, https://www.heritage.org/middle-east/commentary/obama-refuses-alter-isis-strategy; Stephen Collinson, Kevin Liptak, and Deidre Walsh, "Will Any of Obama's ISIS Proposals Succeed?" CNN, December 7, 2015, https://www.cnn.com/2015/12/07/politics /obama-speech-isis-visas-guns/index.html; Michael Crowley, "Obama Ponders His Options Against ISIL," Politico, November 16, 2015, https://www.politico.com/story /2015/11/barack-obama-isil-rhodes-paris-terror-attacks-215917; and Ian Schwartz, "Krauthammer: Obama's ISIS Strategy Is to Slowly Roll Back in Iraq, Leave Syria for Next President," RealClearPolitics, https://www.realclearpolitics.com/video/2015/02 /02/krauthammer_obamas_isis_strategy_is_to_slowly_roll_back_in_iraq_leave_syria _for_next_president.html.

241 **At the Senate hearing, John McCain:** "Hearing to Receive Testimony on the U.S. Strategy to Counter the Islamic State of Iraq and the Levant and U.S. Policy Toward Iraq and Syria," Committee on Armed Services, United States Senate, December 9, 2015, https:// www.armed-services.senate.gov/imo/media/doc/15-93%20-%2012-9-15.pdf.

245 **I persisted even when a Georgetown oncologist:** Paul McLeary, "What's a 'Parent Tumor'? Ask Ash Carter," *Foreign Policy,* January 26, 2016, http://foreignpolicy.com /2016/01/26/whats-a-parent-tumor-ask-ash-carter/.

245 **I told soldiers of the 101st:** "Remarks to the 101st Airborne Division on the Counter-ISIL Campaign Plan," U.S. Department of Defense, January 13, 2016, https://www .defense.gov/News/Speeches/Speech-View/Article/642995/remarks-to-the-101st-air borne-division-on-the-counter-isil-campaign-plan/.

246 **The letter leaked:** Michael S. Schmidt and Helene Cooper, "More Is Needed to Beat ISIS, Pentagon Officials Conclude," New York Times, January 28, 2016, https://www .nytimes.com/2016/01/29/world/middleeast/more-is-needed-to-beat-isis-us-military -concludes.html.

CHAPTER 10: STRATEGIC TRANSITION

261 **As a typical example, the official *National Security Strategy* document:** National Security Strategy, The White House, May 2010, http://nssarchive.us/NSSR/2010.pdf.

262 **Similarly, the *Quadrennial Defense Review Report*:** *Quadrennial Defense Review Report*, U.S. Department of Defense, September 30, 2001, https://archive.defense.gov /pubs/qdr2001.pdf.

262 **Five years later, in 2006:** *Quadrennial Defense Review Report*, U.S. Department of Defense, February 6, 2006, http://archive.defense.gov/pubs/pdfs/qdr20060203.pdf.

266 **And, ironically enough, despite this, Dick Cheney:** Dinah Walker, "Trends in U.S. Military Spending," Council on Foreign Relations, July 15, 2014, https://www.cfr.org /report/trends-us-military-spending.

268 **Many have said that the closest thing:** See, for example, Jeffrey Goldberg, "The Obama Doctrine," *Atlantic*, April 2016, https://www.theatlantic.com/magazine /archive/2016/04/the-obama-doctrine/471525/.

270 **It grew out of a project known as *preventive defense:*** A reader interested in learning more about the preventive defense project may consult Ashton B. Carter and William J. Perry, *Preventive Defense: A New Security Strategy for America* (Washington, DC: Brookings Institution Press, 1999).

277 **The Chinese Challenge:** The content of this section is based in part on Ash Carter, "Reflections on American Grand Strategy in Asia," Belfer Center for Science and International Affairs, Harvard Kennedy School, October 2018, https://www.belfercenter .org/publication/reflections-american-grand-strategy-asia.

277 **Even before we touched down on the flight deck:** Michael S. Schmidt, "In South China Sea Visit, U.S. Defense Chief Flexes Military Muscle," *New York Times*, April 15, 2016, https://www.nytimes.com/2016/04/16/world/asia/south-china-sea-us-ash -carter.html.

278 **They include my good friend Graham T. Allison:** Graham Allison, *Destined for War: Can America and China Escape Thucydides's Trap?* (New York: Houghton Mifflin Harcourt, 2017).

282 **In a series of speeches:** See, for example, "Remarks on 'Asia-Pacific's Principled Security Network' at 2016 IISS Shangri-La Dialogue," U.S. Department of Defense, June 4, 2016, https://dod.defense.gov/News/Speeches/Speech-View/Article/791213/remarks -on-asia-pacifics-principled-security-network-at-2016-iiss-shangri-la-di/.

287 **This concept became known as the "second offset":** Edward C. Keefer, "Harold Brown—Offsetting the Soviet Military Challenge 1977–1981," Secretaries of Defense Historical Series, volume IX, Office of the Secretary of Defense, 2017, https://history .defense.gov/Portals/70/Documents/secretaryofdefense/OSDSeries_Vol9.pdf.

288 **The administration's 2017 defense budget:** "Department of Defense (DoD) Releases Fiscal Year 2017 President's Budget Proposal," Department of Defense, February 9, 2017, https://dod.defense.gov/News/News-Releases/News-Release-View/Article/652687 /department-of-defense-dod-releases-fiscal-year-2017-presidents-budget-proposal/.

CHAPTER 11: THE WORLD'S HOTTEST HOT SPOTS

292 **"We don't have to make Iraq and Syria perfect":** Katie Worth, "Ash Carter: No Confusion About U.S. Interests in Fight Against ISIS," *Frontline*, October 11, 2016, https:// www.pbs.org/wgbh/frontline/article/ash-carter-no-confusion-about-u-s-interests-in-fight -against-isis/.

294 **For example, he repeatedly disrespected the American forces:** See, for example, Ray
Rivera, "Karzai Gives 'Last' Warning to NATO on Airstrikes," *New York Times,* May
31, 2011, https://www.nytimes.com/2011/06/01/world/asia/01afghanistan.html.

294 **"I just want to say to all the Americans":** Matthew Rosenberg, "Ashraf Ghani Thanks
U.S. for Support in First Visit as Afghan Leader," *New York Times,* March 23, 2015,
https://www.nytimes.com/2015/03/24/world/asia/an-afghans-sentiment-for-an-ally
-gratitude.html.

295 **Finally, after leaders of other Muslim countries:** "Joint Statement on the Formation
of the Islamic Military Alliance," Embassy of the Kingdom of Saudi Arabia in the
United States, December 15, 2015, http://embassies.mofa.gov.sa/sites/usa/EN/Public
Affairs/Statements/Pages/Joint-Statement-on-the-Formation-of-the-Islamic-Military
-Alliance.aspx.

298 **It's a concept embedded in U.S. law:** H.R. 7177—Naval Vessel Transfer Act of 2008,
Congress.gov, https://www.congress.gov/bill/110th-congress/house-bill/7177.

299 **In fact, the day before my arrival:** Maayan Lubell, "Israel's Netanyahu and UK's Ham-
mond Face Off Over Iran Deal," Reuters, July 16, 2015, https://www.reuters.com
/article/us-israel-britain-iran/israels-netanyahu-and-uks-hammond-face-off-over-iran
-deal-idUSKCN0PQ21T20150716.

313 **"Such an act of catastrophic terrorism":** "Catastrophic Terrorism: Tackling the
New Danger," *Foreign Affairs,* November–December 1998, https://www.foreignaffairs
.com/articles/united-states/1998-11-01/catastrophic-terrorism-tackling-new-danger.

313 **I wrote about "the day after":** For example, in Ash Carter, William J. Perry, and Michael M. May, "The Day After: Action Following a Nuclear Blast in a U.S. City," Belfer
Center for Science and International Affairs, Harvard Kennedy School, Autumn 2007,
https://www.belfercenter.org/publication/day-after-action-following-nuclear-blast-us
-city.

CHAPTER 12: MAINTAINING AMERICA'S HIGH-TECH EDGE

319 **David Dworkin doesn't wear a uniform:** The first three paragraphs of this chapter are
adapted from Ash Carter, "The Pentagon Must Think Outside of Its Five-Sided Box,"
National Interest, December 11, 2016, https://nationalinterest.org/feature/ashton
-carter-the-pentagon-must-think-outside-its-five-sided-18697.

324 **So imagine my astonishment:** "Document: Pentagon Plan to Split Research and Development from Acquisition," Department of Defense Study, U.S. Naval Institute News,
August 2, 2017, https://news.usni.org/2017/08/02/document-pentagon-plan-split
-research-development-acquisition.

328 **The DOD issued a statement:** Jack Corrigan, "The Pentagon's Startup Outreach
Office Is No Longer an Experiment," Nextgov, August 9, 2018, https://www.nextgov
.com/cio-briefing/2018/08/pentagons-startup-outreach-office-no-longer-experiment
/150408/.

329 **We talk a lot these days about "disruptive" technologies:** The content of the following seven paragraphs is adapted from Ash Carter, "Shaping Disruptive Technological
Change for Public Good," Ernest May Lecture at the Aspen Strategy Group, August
2018, Belfer Center for Science and International Affairs, Harvard Kennedy School,
https://www.belfercenter.org/publication/shaping-disruptive-technological-change
-public-good.

339 **The strategy document included:** "The DOD Cyber Strategy," Department of Defense, April 2015, http://archive.defense.gov/home/features/2015/0415_cyber-strategy
/final_2015_dod_cyber_strategy_for_web.pdf.

343 **Another of several examples:** Scott Shane, "Ex-N.S.A. Worker Accused of Stealing
Trove of Secrets Offers to Plead Guilty," *New York Times,* January 3, 2018, https://www
.nytimes.com/2018/01/03/us/politics/harold-martin-nsa-guilty-plea-offer.html.

344 **However, the Trump administration:** Lisa Ferdinando, "Cybercom to Elevate to Combatant Command," *DoD News*, May 3, 2018, https://dod.defense.gov/News /Article/Article/1511959/cybercom-to-elevate-to-combatant-command/.

347 **In response, I would inform people:** "Department of Defense Directive: Autonomy in Weapon Systems," Department of Defense, November 21, 2012, https://www.esd.whs .mil/Portals/54/Documents/DD/issuances/dodd/300009p.pdf.

348 **This happened recently at Google:** Daisuke Wakabayashi and Scott Shane, "Google Will Not Renew Pentagon Contract That Upset Employees," *New York Times,* June 1, 2018, https://www.nytimes.com/2018/06/01/technology/google-pentagon-project -maven.html.

CHAPTER 13: CHOOSING LEADERS

358 **However, it just so happened that moment coincided:** Jesse Hyde, "Fat Leonard's Crimes on the High Seas," *Rolling Stone*, March 11, 2018, https://www.rollingstone .com/politics/politics-news/fat-leonards-crimes-on-the-high-seas-197055/.

359 **"In the military, a combatant command":** Tammy Duckworth, "Lori Robinson," *Time*'s 100 Most Influential People, *Time*, April 20, 2016, http://time.com/4301351 /lori-robinson-2016-time-100/.

365 **Due to the public nature of Lewis's role:** Missy Ryan and Craig Whitlock, "Pentagon Chief Ashton Carter Just Fired His Chief Aide Over 'Misconduct,'" *Washington Post,* November 12, 2015, https://www.washingtonpost.com/news/checkpoint/wp/2015/11 /12/pentagon-chief-ashton-carter-just-fired-his-top-military-adviser-over-misconduct/?

365 **Months later, a detailed report was published:** "Report of Investigation: Ronald F. Lewis Major General, U.S. Army," Inspector General, U.S. Department of Defense, October 4, 2016, https://www.oversight.gov/sites/default/files/oig-reports/DODIG -2017-001.pdf.

367 **Thus, after American service members' bodies were dragged:** John Barry, "The Collapse of Les Aspin," *Newsweek*, December 26, 1993, https://www.newsweek.com /collapse-les-aspin-190744.

372 **Henry Kissinger once remarked:** "High office teaches decision making, not substance. It consumes intellectual capital; it does not create it. Most high officials leave office with the perceptions and insights with which they entered; they learn how to make decisions but not what decisions to make." Henry Kissinger, *White House Years* (Boston: Little, Brown, 1979), p. 27.

CHAPTER 14: FORCE OF THE FUTURE

379 **"He will not only feel comfortable":** Vicky Mouze, "Army ROTC Cadet Joseph Riley Earns Rhodes Scholarship," U.S. Army website, December 5, 2012, https://www .army.mil/article/92387/army_rotc_cadet_joseph_riley_earns_rhodes_scholarship.

380 **"You're killing me, Lieutenant!":** David Barno and Nora Bensahel, "First Steps Toward the Force of the Future," War on the Rocks website, Texas National Security Network, University of Texas, December 1, 2015, https://warontherocks.com/2015/12 /first-steps-towards-the-force-of-the-future/.

381 **In fact, only 30 percent of Americans:** Miriam Jordan, "Recruits' Ineligibility Tests the Military," *Wall Street Journal*, June 27, 2018, https://www.wsj.com/articles/re cruits-ineligibility-tests-the-military-1403909945?mod=e2tw.

382 **By contrast, the eight states of the South Atlantic area:** "Population Representation in the Military Services 2016," Appendix B: Active Component Enlisted Accessions, Enlisted Force, Officer Accessions, and Officer Corps Tables, Office of the Under Secretary of Defense, Personnel and Readiness, CNA website, https://www.cna.org/pop -rep/2016/appendixb/appendixb.pdf.

383 **Statistics show that the percentage of married people:** "2016 Demographics: Profile of the Military Community," U.S. Department of Defense, 2016, p. 49, https://download.militaryonesource.mil/12038/MOS/Reports/2016-Demographics-Report.pdf.

386 **To minimize the chance of that happening:** Ash Carter, "Fact Sheet: Building the Second Link to the Force of the Future—Strengthening Comprehensive Family Benefits," U.S. Department of Defense, January 28, 2016, https://dod.defense.gov/Portals/1/Documents/pubs/Fact_Sheet_Tranche_2_FOTF_FINAL.pdf.

387 **The changes make it possible, for example:** Scott Maucione, "What the Senate's Proposed Changes to Military Personnel Mean for You," Federal News Network, June 7, 2018, https://federalnewsnetwork.com/defense-news/2018/06/what-the-senates-proposed-changes-to-military-personnel-mean-for-you/.

387 **In fact, 85 percent of them live and work:** Kore Blalock Keller, "In Defense of Federal Employees," *The Hill*, February 2, 2017, https://thehill.com/blogs/congress-blog/labor/317532-in-defense-of-federal-employees.

390 **To ensure that the health and readiness status of our forces:** "Transgender Service Member Policy Implementation Fact Sheet," Department of Defense, June 16, 2016, https://dod.defense.gov/Portals/1/features/2016/0616_policy/Transgender-Implementation-Fact-Sheet.pdf.

393 **In recent years, the rate of suicide:** Kym Klass, "Number of Military Suicides Still High, but Help Is on the Rise," *Montgomery Advertiser,* March 10, 2017, https://www.montgomeryadvertiser.com/story/news/2017/03/10/suicide-military-numbers-remain-high-help-rise/98195262/.

394 **Women in Service: The Story Behind a Breakthrough:** The following account of the decision to open all military positions to women is adapted in part from Ash Carter, "No Exceptions: The Decision to Open All Military Positions to Women," Belfer Center for Science and International Affairs, Harvard Kennedy School, December 2018, https://www.belfercenter.org/publication/no-exceptions-decision-open-all-military-positions-women.

394 **When I became SecDef in February 2015:** Ash Carter, "Remarks on the Women-in-Service Review," U.S. Department of Defense speech, December 3, 2015, https://dod.defense.gov/News/Speeches/Speech-View/Article/632495/remarks-on-the-women-in-service-review/.

397 **About four thousand officers and enlisted soldiers:** Richard A. Oppel Jr., "Two Female Soldiers Poised to Graduate from Ranger School," *New York Times,* August 17, 2015, https://www.nytimes.com/2015/08/18/us/two-female-soldiers-poised-to-graduate-from-ranger-school.html.

397 **"She basically took it away from me":** Mark Thompson, "America: Meet Your First Female Rangers," *Time*, August 20, 2015, http://time.com/4005578/female-army-rangers/.

398 **By July 2015, the Pentagon had completed forty-one studies:** Kristy N. Karmack, "Women in Combat: Issues for Congress," Congressional Research Service, December 13, 2016, https://fas.org/sgp/crs/natsec/R42075.pdf.

399 **We looked at comparable organizations:** Several countries, including Australia, Canada, Denmark, Germany, New Zealand, and Norway, have opened all military positions to women. Others, like the United Kingdom, are currently in the process of doing so. Many other nations, such as Pakistan, South Korea, and Israel, have opened some, but not all, combat positions to women. See Anna Mulrine, "8 Other Nations That Send Women to Combat," *National Geographic*, January 25, 2013, https://news.nationalgeographic.com/news/2013/13/130125-women-combat-world-australia-israel-canada-norway/; and Max Fisher, "Map: Which Countries Allow Women in Front-Line Combat Roles?" *Washington Post*, January 25, 2013, https://www.washington

post.com/news/worldviews/wp/2013/01/25/map-which-countries-allow-women-in-front
-line-combat-roles/.

399 **The Marine Corps had reservations:** Kristy N. Karmack, "Women in Combat: Issues
for Congress," *Congressional Research Service*, December 13, 2016, https://fas.org
/sgp/crs/natsec/R42075.pdf.

404 **In the Marine Corps, 181 women:** "Women in Ground Combat: Facts and Figures,"
Women in International Security, February 1, 2017, https://www.servicewomen.org
/wp-content/uploads/2017/02/Women-in-Ground-Combat-Arms-Fact-Sheet-2-1-17.pdf.

404 **A 2017 RAND survey:** Douglas Yeung et al., "Recruiting Policies and Practices for
Women in the Military: Views from the Field," RAND Corporation, 2017, https://www
.rand.org/content/dam/rand/pubs/research_reports/RR1500/RR1538/RAND_RR1538
.pdf.

405 **They call their standards system:** Thomas S. Szayna et al., "Considerations for Integrating Women into Closed Occupations in the U.S. Special Operations Forces,"
RAND National Defense Research Institute, 2016, https://www.rand.org/pubs
/research_reports/RR1058.html.

407 **Whenever I met with a group of Vietnam veterans:** "So here today, it must be said—
you have earned your place among the greatest generations. At this time, I would ask all
our Vietnam veterans, those of you who can stand, to please stand, all those already
standing, raise your hands—as we say those simple words which always greet our
troops when they come home from here on out: Welcome home. (Applause.) Welcome
home. Welcome home. Welcome home. Thank you. We appreciate you. Welcome home.
(Applause.)" Barack Obama, "Remarks by the President at the Commemoration Ceremony of the 50th Anniversary of the Vietnam War," The White House, May 28, 2012,
https://obamawhitehouse.archives.gov/the-press-office/2012/05/28/remarks-president
-commemoration-ceremony-50th-anniversary-vietnam-war.

CHAPTER 15: THE TROOPS DESERVE THE TRUTH

415 **But many also contain thoughtful and moving explanations:** See, for example, James
M. McPherson, *For Cause and Comrades: Why Men Fought in the Civil War* (Oxford:
Oxford University Press, 1997).

INDEX

ABOUT THE AUTHOR

ASH CARTER currently serves as the director of the Belfer Center for Science and International Affairs at Harvard University's Kennedy School. He also is an innovation fellow at the Massachusetts Institute of Technology.

Beginning in 1981 with his first Pentagon job, Carter served, directly or indirectly, eleven secretaries of defense in both Democratic and Republican administrations before serving as the twenty-fifth Secretary of Defense from 2015 to 2017. Leading the largest organization in the world, with more than three million civilian and military employees and an annual budget of more than half a trillion dollars, Secretary Carter became known for his savvy leadership and for ensuring that the Pentagon thought "outside its five-sided box." At a time of global change and congressional gridlock, Secretary Carter transformed the way the Defense Department fought adversaries, stood with allies and partners, planned and budgeted, managed its talent, and partnered with the technology sector.

Before becoming Secretary of Defense, Carter served in the department's number two and number three jobs. As deputy secretary and chief operating officer from 2011 to 2013, he oversaw the department's management and personnel and steered strategy and budget through the turmoil of sequester. As undersecretary of defense for acquisition, technology, and logistics (ATL) from 2009 to 2011, Carter led the department's procurement and research programs, the successful completion of key procurements, urgent projects for equipping troops at war, and global logistics for the largest enterprise on earth.

Earlier in his government career, Carter served as assistant secretary of defense for international security policy from 1993 to 1996. He was responsible for the Nunn-Lugar program, which removed and eliminated nuclear weapons in Russia, Ukraine, Kazakhstan, and Belarus; the military planning during the 1994 crisis over North Korea's nuclear weapons program; and the U.S. nuclear arsenal. Over the past three decades, Carter has also served on the Defense Policy Board, the Defense Science Board, and the Secretary of State's International Security Advisory Board.

For his government service, Secretary Carter has been awarded the Department of Defense Distinguished Service Medal, the department's highest civilian honor, on five separate occasions, and he twice received the Joint Distinguished Service Medal from the Chairman and Joint Chiefs of Staff.

In addition to his government and private sector experience, Secretary Carter has also taught at many of the world's outstanding academic institutions. He is the author or coauthor of eleven books and more than one hundred articles on physics, technology, national security, and management.

Secretary Carter earned his bachelor's degrees in physics and in medieval history, summa cum laude, at Yale University, where he was also awarded Phi Beta Kappa, and he received his doctorate in theoretical physics from Oxford University, where he was a Rhodes scholar. A native of Philadelphia, he is married to Stephanie Carter and has two grown children.